T0339787

REPUBLICAN TREASON

REPUBLICAN TREASON

REPUBLICAN FASCISM EXPOSED

Joseph Burrell

Algora Publishing
New York

Library of Congress Cataloging-in-Publication Data —

Burrell, Joseph, 1930-
   Republican treason : Republican fascism exposed / Joseph Burrell.
     p. cm.
   Includes bibliographical references and index.
   ISBN 978-0-87586-666-6 (trade paper: alk. paper) — ISBN 978-0-87586-667-3 (hard
cover: alk. paper) — ISBN 978-0-87586-668-0 (ebook) 1. Republican Party (U.S.: 1854-)
2. Fascism—United States. 3. Treason—United States. 4. Conservatism—United States.
5. United States—Politics and government—1945-1989. 6. United States—Politics and
government—1989- 7. Democratic Party (U.S.) 8. Liberalism—United States. 9. Political
culture—United States. I. Title.

   JK2356.B95 2008
   324.2734—dc22
                        2008023993

Front Cover: A SWAT team drives past flood victims at the Convention Center in New
Orleans. Officers dispatched to cool hostilities outside the building were overwhelmed by
an angry crowd, the police chief said.
   © Eric Gay / Associated Press

Printed in the United States

TABLE OF CONTENTS

PREFACE

This is not a history book. It is an opinion book. The first four chapters outline a number of observations and assessments about US history and the place this country has occupied on the world stage as contrasted to the lofty values it purports to promote. These observations are further developed and abundantly illustrated and documented in the remaining chapters through excerpts from books, newspapers, and magazines, with occasional observations by the author, all arranged under appropriate chapter headings.

Most of these quotations come from conservatives and Republicans but there are quite a few from liberal democrats as well. These quotations are mixed together to show the nature of the conservative and Republican belief system and to expose it as the despotic, absolutist, and anti-democratic force I believe it is.

A GRAMMATICAL NOTE

The capitalization in this book is not standard. This note explains why. The 1952 issue of the McGraw-Hill Handbook of English says on page 127 that you should use capital letters for "words referring to the Deity and sacred books, but not the words god or goddess referring to pagan gods." The christian grammarians also require the capitalization of "pronouns referring to the Deity."

However, christians themselves don't really believe in "the deity," that is, in just one god. To be a proper christian, you must believe in the sacredness of at least two gods, God the Father and Jesus the Son. In fact, most christians also believe in a third god, the Holy Ghost. Thus, most christians are trinitarians. The Catholics also believe in the sacredness of the Virgin Mary who, like the saints, can perform miracles, answer prayers, have virgin births, and ascend into the sky just as well as any of the other gods and goddesses.

The jewish religion isn't nearly as complex in its god-system but the jewish god is so gaseous and vague that jews aren't even allowed to call his name much less define him. Thus, I can't tell whether or not jews are really monotheists though they say they invented monotheism. The muslims appear to be the only true monotheists in this lot but they have many sects each of which ascribes a different character, a different definition, and a different set of biases to their god. In some configurations, the muslims are supposed to kill all of the christians and jews just as many christians and jews believe they are suppose to kill all of their closest competitors.

In any case, it's quite clear that the many sects of these various religions believe in a whole host of different gods and not at all in one or the same god.

The ancient pagans were never this morally confused and few of them felt a need to kill those whose beliefs diverged from theirs. In truth, the pagans were far more decent and tolerant with regard to religious belief than are any of today's self-proclaimed monotheists and christian grammarians. And so, in my view, the christians, the jews, and the muslims don't deserve their own preferential grammar. Accordingly, I choose not to capitalize the word "christian" or the word "god."

There is a legitimate argument for capitalizing the words "Mohammedan," "Christian," and "Marxist." These three are, of course, named after actual people and it is customary to capitalize the names of people and things named after them. Nevertheless, I think it more equitable not to capitalize these words because they are so often used in a polemical way to proselytize against other competing ideologies. Thus, in the interest of fairness, it could only make sense to capitalize all of them or none of them. Anyhow, these isms are not really based on the actual beliefs and examples of the men who are said to have founded them nor is very much at all known about the first two. Thus, I prefer not to capitalize these words or their derivatives.

If the words "christian," "jew," "marxist," and "muslim" are to be capitalized, then so should the words "atheist," "agnostic," "deist," "pagan," etc. But it makes far better sense to capitalize none of them. Why bother? It requires some effort and all of those many capitals create confusion and spoil the appearance of text on the page. The special respect such practices seek to claim is not deserved in my opinion.

There are similar capitalization rules based on political notions that ought also to be dispensed with. The word "Communist," for example, no longer has any specific meaning. The McCarthyites called just about everyone they disliked "Communists." If they arbitrarily selected you as an enemy or if you criticized or disagreed with them in the least, you were a Communist. At first, a Communist was someone who actually was a member of the Communist Party. Then, the massive and indiscriminate use of the word "Communist" emptied it of just about all meaning. Today, it should never be capitalized unless you are purposefully and specifically labeling someone you know to be an actual member of some Communist Party somewhere. In fact, unless you are talking about actual party membership or something as precise, you should not capitalize communist, socialist, capitalist, marxist, nazi, fascist, tory, conservative, liberal, democrat, or republican.

I also think that the word "Darwinism" should not be capitalized when it is used in the construction "social Darwinism." Social Darwinism is not Darwinist at all; rather, the notion that acquired characteristics can be inherited is Lamarckian. It was Herbert Spencer who propagated this idea. He invented the term "survival of the fittest" and applied it to social, economic, and political life. To call Spencer's invention "Darwinism" is a distortion of what Charles Darwin established as a matter of science. Therefore, I prefer to use the term without the capital, social darwinism.

I do think we ought to capitalize Catholic and Protestant, not for religious but for practical reasons. The word "catholic" means "whole, universal, all-inclusive, having broad sympathies or understanding, liberal, etc." Obviously, this definition cannot be used to describe the Catholic Church. The word "protestant" means "a person who protests." These days very few Protestants ever protest about anything in their particular religious sect or in their dogmatic belief system. Thus, a Catholic is a person who belongs in some way to the Catholic Church. A Protestant is someone who belongs to one of the huge number of sects that claim to be christian but not Catholic. In this case, the point of the capitalization is clarity and practical logic.

On the political side, you should capitalize the name of a particular party. Thus, you should capitalize Democratic Party, Republican Party, Nazi Party, Communist Party, Conservative Party, etc. And you should capitalize Democrat, Republican, Nazi, Communist, Conservative, and the like when you are specifically and narrowly labeling someone as a member of an organized political party. On the religious side, you should capitalize Catholic Church, Methodist Church, Unitarian Church, etc. And you should capitalize Catholic, Methodist, Unitarian, and the like when you are specifically and narrowly labeling someone as a member of an organized church or religious group.

As for other deviations from the orthodox, I do not punctuate as profusely as do newspaper and magazine journalists. In particular, I omit the great flood of commas routinely used by journalists; for example, I usually omit the commas wedged in front of the conjunctions "and" and "but" when they are used to connect independent clauses in a compound sentence. I do this because I think that these two words themselves are sufficient to divide the sentence and to signal the need for a pause. Sometimes, I even omit the commas around non-restrictive clauses and phrases if I think they do not cause any confusion about the meaning of the sentence. Nevertheless, I almost always fence off trivial parenthetical information with commas.

On the other hand, I almost always use a comma after an introductory phrase or even after introductory words such as "However," "Therefore," and "Then." I think that a pause is needed in such cases to give such words their full power to differentiate, continue, or qualify carry-over ideas and trains of thought. Such words are connective tissue and need the comma and the pause for emphasis.

You will not find these "rules" — especially the religious ones — in your grammar book or in your spell checker. They are merely my preferences.

Joseph W. Burrell

Introduction

My purpose in this book is to show the un-American and indeed the treasonous nature of the Republican Party. When I say that the Republican Party is treasonous, I mean that it is hostile to the democratic government of the United States and that it has tried to establish a foreign ideology — fascism — in place of the democratic system established by the American Revolution.

The following extracts from the fifth edition of *The Columbia Encyclopedia* describe some of the important elements of fascism:

> *Fascism*, totalitarian philosophy of government that glorifies state and nation and assigns to the state control over every aspect of national life. The name was first used for the party started by Benito Mussolini, who ruled Italy from 1922 until the Italian defeat in World War II....
>
> *Origins of Fascist Philosophy*....[F]ascism introduced no systematic exposition of its ideology or purpose other than a negative reaction against socialist and democratic egalitarianism. The growth of democratic ideology and popular participation in politics in the 19th century was terrifying to some conservative elements in European society, and fascism grew out of the attempt to counter it.... They appealed to nationalist sentiments and prejudices, exploiting anti-Semitism, and portraying themselves as champions of law, order, Christian morality, and the sanctity of private property....a second ruling concept of fascism is embodied in the theory of social Darwinism. The doctrine of survival of the fittest and the necessity of struggle for life is applied by fascists to the life of a nation-state....Imperialism is the logical outcome of this dogma. Another element of fascism is its elitism....
>
> *Emergence after World War I.* The Russian Revolution of 1917, the collapse of the Central Powers in 1918, and the disorders caused by the Communist attempts to seize power in Germany, Italy, Hungary, and other countries greatly strengthened fascism's appeal to many sections of the European populace.... Governmental paralysis enabled Mussolini in 1922 to obtain the premiership by a show of force. As leader of the National Fascist party, he presented himself as the strong-armed savior of Italy from anarchy and Communism....In Germany....

Adolf Hitler won support from a middle class ruined by inflation, from certain elements of the working class, especially the unemployed, and from discontented war veterans; he also gained the backing of powerful financial interests, to whom he symbolized stability and order....

*The Fascist State....*There are particular similarities with the Communist regime in the Soviet Union under Joseph Stalin. However, unlike Communism, fascism abhors the idea of a classless society.... and the corporate state is a part of fascist dogma.... there can be no doubt that despite all restrictions imposed on them, the capitalist and landowning classes were protected by the fascist system, and many favored it as an obstacle to socialization....Fascism has found adherents in all countries. Its essentially vague and emotional nature facilitates the development of unique national varieties, whose leaders often deny indignantly that they are fascists at all.

Thus, fascism is an alliance between commercial and political power, that is, it is corporatist and statist by definition. As shown, the term "fascism" was not coined until the 1920s when Benito Mussolini first formalized such a system in Italy. However, I believe that the much earlier combination of commercial and political power under the divine rule of a king was the first form of fascism. After all, the royal system put all political power and most commercial power in the hands of one man and, through the mandate of religion, made his rule absolute. Then, after many centuries of this kind of aristocratic rule everywhere in the world, the Enlightenment and the American and French revolutions led to the creation of a democratic polity in opposition to the divine right of kings.

In the United States as in France, reactionary forces tried to overthrow or weaken the democratic impulse raised up by the American and French revolutions. Those efforts were not really successful in the United States until after the Civil War when a one-party system dominated by business interests took control. This happened because the Civil War prepared the way for an intense developmentalism in the defeated South and the undeveloped West; and this developmentalism was left in the hands of Northern commercialists and industrialists, the only elite not impoverished by the war.

The Republican Party ruled the nation during this time but, in the South, a collaborating and racist Democratic Party, with the full tolerance of the national government, held all of the local power. Thus, the devastation of the war left the nation in the hands of two conservative political groups that represented the same values and worked together to advance one cause — the reign of a social darwinist and eugenicist oligarchy of disparate parts.

This book does not describe the three-quarters of a century of Republican rule between the Civil War and the Great Conservative Depression of 1929. It also does not describe the corrupt rule of Richard Nixon and Ronald Reagan, who played important roles in the restoration of the US oligarchy and the rollback of most of the democratic advances of the New Deal. No doubt it would be worthwhile to examine the reactionary behavior of those administrations; but I believe it was Dwight Eisenhower's political warfare model that was seminal in the restoration of Republican plutocracy, the reemergence of predatory capitalism, and the growth of christian, muslim, and zionist fundamentalism. Eisenhower's change in political policy led to a newly aggressive and assaultive imperialism that has widened and intensified under Republican administrations and has frequently resulted in disastrous blowback.

The undemocratic and aggressive history of the Republican Party is long and variable in its many forms and guises. At times, its ideology has even dominated the

Democratic Party (under Woodrow Wilson, Grover Cleveland, and, to a lesser extent, under Bill Clinton); and, at times, Republican presidents (Abraham Lincoln, Theodore Roosevelt, and, domestically, Dwight Eisenhower) have been progressive, and even New Dealish, in many of their policies and actions. Still, the main thrust of the Republican ideology has always been anti-liberal and anti-democratic. The Republican Party has always been the party of big commerce and aggressive christian moralism.

The Republican Party was briefly isolationist and anti-interventionist but it suspended those political tendencies in the interest of advancing the hegemony of capitalism. Thus, during the Cold War, the isolationists became especially perturbed about everything they saw as anti-capitalist and they defined all worker, consumer, civil rights, and environmental movements as communistic which is to say anti-capitalist. Indeed, they joined the neo-conservatives in direct attacks against democratic movements around the world.

The ultimate result is George W. Bush's policy of preemptive and precipitate attack against just about everybody; indeed, Bush and Cheney have said that they are going to attack fifty to sixty countries in the name of anti-terrorism. What is especially dangerous about Bush is his indiscriminate, vengeful, irrational, and fanatical behavior. Bush doesn't need any real provocation; he simply makes something up whenever he is in a mood to attack another country and another people.

Worst of all is the reemergence of the conservatives' belief in the divine right of kings. George Bush's justification for his behavior is that his god put him in power just precisely so he could attack and kill others; and he believes it is his patriotic and christian duty to impose his strange idea of "democracy" on everyone else by force of arms. He claims that he is answerable to absolutely no one and that no laws anywhere apply to him. He claims that he can abuse, rape, torture, and kill anyone he alone chooses in the name of anti-terrorism. He even claims that his god told him to attack the innocent people of Iraq. These are the claims of a royal and divine despot. Bush's arrogant aggressions follow from the proselytizing spirit of predatory capitalism and christian salvationism hyped by Eisenhower's policy of political warfare.

More and more, the Republicans have made clear their contempt for the democratic government of the United States; and they hardly ever conduct an election campaign without smearing their opponents as communist agents or terrorist sympathizers and the government itself as an evil socialist contraption that needs to be hugely reduced in size so it can be "drowned in a bathtub" to quote George W. Bush's ideological mentor, Grover Norquist. The intense hostility of Republicans toward democracy, civil rights, human rights, and worker rights is so clear and insistent that only the radically stupid or the cynically hypocritical can possibly deny it.

Part One. The Republican Party

Abraham Lincoln was the first member of the Republican Party to serve as president. He believed in the dominance of national government over state and local government and he came to believe in the abolition of slavery and in full citizenship for all Americans. He revered the Declaration of Independence and believed in Jefferson's "Jacobin" liberalism, including a belief in the superiority of labor over capital. He was not at all a believer in the principles that now dominate the Republican Party. He was, in fact, a liberal democrat as was the Theodore Roosevelt of the 1912 progressive presidential campaign.

Initially, upon its founding shortly before the Civil War, the Republican Party contained within it strong abolitionist elements. After the war and after Lincoln's death, the Republican Party moved steadily to the right and became increasingly racist and far more conservative than it ever had been before. Rutherford B. Hayes was the first Republican to employ a "Southern Strategy." In a deal with Southern politicians, Hayes agreed to end Reconstruction and withdraw the remaining Northern troops in exchange for the Southern votes that made him president in 1876. This put the South entirely in the hands of white racists. Their party, the Southern Democratic Party, was based on white supremacy and a repressive system of Jim Crow segregation.

Segregation was simply a new kind of informal slavery maintained by regional threat and coercion rather than by any constitutional principle or any legitimate national law. In fact, segregation was clearly unconstitutional but the friendly Northern Republican Party and its judicial appointees supported segregation and refused to implement the "freedom amendments" which were passed by the "radical" Republican legislature in Washington and ratified just after the war. Thus, this country was ruled for nearly three-quarters of a century by Republican presidents with the support of Southern congressional Democrats who quickly came to dominate the legislative system through a seniority rule that put Southerners in charge of nearly all congressional committees.

During this period, the Northern Democratic Party had very little national power until Franklin Roosevelt became president in 1932. It did have some regional and urban power heavily based on old Jeffersonian and abolitionist sentiments and on the influx and support of immigrants. A small handful of Republicans in the North continued to believe in the liberal Republican values of Abraham Lincoln and the prewar abolitionists. Two Democrats did rise to the presidency during this period after the war but they were both conservative in most ways. Grover Cleveland was a run-of-the-mill Northern Democrat who was best known for his hostility to working people and their unions during both the Haymarket Square riots of 1886 and the Pullman strike of 1894. Cleveland sent federal troops to break the strike and jailed Eugene V. Debs on trumped-up charges. He also jailed members of Cox's army in Washington for walking on the grass and carrying banners. These demonstrators wanted the government to build roads and improve the infrastructure as a way of providing jobs for the many citizens in the country who were unemployed because of the "panic of 1893."

Woodrow Wilson was a racist Southerner who became president only because Theodore Roosevelt split the Republican Party when he conducted a campaign against the conservative rule of the Taft Republicans. Wilson was less conservative than the Taft Republicans in most respects but he was far less progressive and liberal than Roosevelt. In short, he was a Southern Democrat more than a National Democrat. Just like Cleveland, Wilson jailed Eugene V. Debs on spurious charges. Wilson used his notorious Espionage Act against Debs and against a number of other citizens who dared to criticize his war. Even worse, he passed a Sedition Act and nurtured the disgusting "Palmer raids," named after his Attorney General. Thus, both Wilson and Cleveland raged against the rights of working people and dissidents and used the law against them at every turn.

In 1932, Franklin Roosevelt established a new kind of political rule based on the rights and needs of the people. FDR's New Deal implemented the progressive ideals advanced by his cousin, Theodore Roosevelt, twenty years earlier. Many of the ideas of Eugene V. Debs were incorporated in New Deal legislation as well. The New Deal reforms pretty much continued in force for the next thirty-six years. Though it is not generally recognized, Dwight Eisenhower fully supported the New Deal programs and tried also to establish a system of universal health insurance (defeated by the AMA to Eisenhower's displeasure) as well as a policy of providing better housing for all Americans. Eisenhower implemented Roosevelt's plans for the building of a network of federal interstate highways and also campaigned unsuccessfully for "a vast expansion of unemployment insurance."

Richard Nixon, the next Republican president, began the assault on New Deal programs and policies and did much harm to the welfare of the people. Ronald Reagan, a fanatical hater of the New Deal and of all the elements of democratic government, hugely escalated Nixon's attack and became a great hero to the Republican conservatives who, for generations, had bitterly opposed every one of the New Deal programs. Reagan and the Republicans wanted to do away with democratic government altogether except for its military and police power and its programs to help business and religious interests rule the population without any input from citizens themselves or any public regulation of private power in the interest of the people.

The latest Republican president, George W. Bush, is even more fanatical and more anti-democratic than his political forebears and he is determined to conquer the world for his god and in the interest of the business class. He has also established "faith-based" programs designed to put billions of dollars of tax money in the hands of his evangelical and fundamentalist supporters. He is simply buying their votes, bribing them to support him politically. He has also persuaded many of the preachers to allow him to use their churches as staging grounds in his political campaigns and even traveled to the Vatican to ask church leaders there to help him defeat John Kerry in the 2004 presidential campaign. Thus, Bush is the first out-and-out theocrat to be president of this country.

Bush seeks to meld together his political power and the religious power of christian fundamentalism. This conglomeration of politics, commerce, and religion is an especially potent kind of fascism, one that has a broad appeal to the citizens of a country as intensely christian, capitalist, and conservative as this one is right now. Bush and his followers have put together a system that betrays all of the principles of the American Revolution and attacks democracy in every way imaginable. It seems unlikely that this country will ever again be truly free and democratic, unless it throws off the yoke of Republicanism.

Chapter 1. The Nature of the Republican Party

It's clear that the Republican Party is hostile to the principles of the American Revolution. Just after the Civil War, it began its assault against democratic government in the interests of private commercial power and the christian religion. Since then, it has made repeated attacks against the civil rights of citizens and has also violently opposed workers unions and the rights of working people. The Republican Party is the rich man's party and today it is intensely racist, sexist, imperialist, police statist, and militarist. Frequently, it has also been deeply corrupt and has produced a large number of financial and political scandals, especially in recent decades.

The Republican Party is the conservative party. At one time, it had abolitionist and progressive members but they were always a minority and they were eventually driven out altogether by Joe McCarthy, Richard Nixon, Barry Goldwater, Ronald Reagan, William Buckley, Newt Gingrich, and, lastly, by the members of the Bush family. The Republican Party is now fanatically conservative from end-to-end. It has moved far away from the principles of Abraham Lincoln and Theodore Roosevelt. It is not at all exaggerated or unfair to call it fascist, that is, capitalist totalitarian.

When Franklin Delano Roosevelt came to power in 1932, he ended three-quarters of a century of Republican tyranny and began to restore civil rights and human rights to the people of the United States in accord with his democratic inclinations and beliefs. From the start of the Civil War all the way to the Great Conservative Depression in 1929 and the rise of Franklin Roosevelt in 1932, all of the presidents of the United States except two had been Republicans and those two (Cleveland and Wilson) were ideological conservatives. We had a one-party dictatorship in the United States during this time.

During their long reign, the Republicans and their industrialist clients were great expanders, developers, and exploiters. It is always their way to use things up and squeeze them dry. In the last half of the 1800's, they raped the entire continent and enormously enriched themselves at the expense of the common people and the commonweal. In the process, they destroyed democracy and converted the nation into an imperialist and colonial power. The government became their obedient servant and they used all of its power to oppress the nation's citizenry and to exploit foreign mar-kets at the point of a gun. Their attack philosophy was social darwinism buttressed by the new "science" of eugenics.

After the Civil War, the Republican Party adopted the economic and political philosophy of social darwinism. This was a foreign philosophy imported from Eng-land and its purpose was to put economic control and the whole life of the nation in the hands of the plutocracy. From the Civil War onward, the plutocracy totally controlled the United States. The conservative subversion and betrayal of the United States through the imposition of this foreign ideology on the people was so complete and so overpowering that true democracy all but disappeared and the workers of the country became the mere servants of the plutocrats. Whenever there was any resistance to the plutocrats, the enlarged army and the ever-growing forces of police authority put it down. During this time, the United States became a land of economic totalitarianism and there was great repression and violence against the people, most of all against working people and their unions.

This social darwinist philosophy restored the old hereditarian belief in a ruling nobility but hitched it to the divine right of capitalists rather than the divine right of kings. Of course, social darwinism was a conservative philosophy. Herbert Spencer invented social Darwinism. He was an English philosopher greatly admired by indus-trialists and other such predators throughout the Western world. Herbert Spencer was not a real Darwinist despite the name of his philosophy. He merely used the concept of natural selection and the Darwinist term "evolution" in a distorted way to justify the predatory behavior of the plutocrats and to demonstrate the supposed superiority of their ruling class. Spencer himself invented the phrase "survival of the fittest" and used it to explain away all manner of economic and political tyranny against the weak and downtrodden.

Spencer's philosophy held that the rich and privileged classes deserved every-thing they had no matter how they had acquired it. Spencer believed that the cap-italist system itself was perfect and that success and failure under it were always deserved. Competition was the engine of capitalism and success was all a matter of evolution following its natural course. The superior beings of the plutocracy rise to the top in a natural fashion and the inferior beings of the lower classes sink down and die as they deserve to do. This extinction of the unfit is necessary to human progress and happiness. Governments must do nothing to alleviate the suffering of the poor or slow down their elimination. The physically, intellectually, morally, and economi-cally feeble must be weeded out by nature and it is the job of governments to help them disappear from the face of the earth. "Nature's failures" must not be allowed to propagate and prosper. Naturally, the social darwinists believed that white Euro-peans were superior to everyone else; Aryan males were on top with their wives and daughters only a step behind them in supremacy.

Though it began in England and on the European continent, social darwinism reached its apex in the United States; and, of course, it is still going strong today. It was a godsend to the laissez-faire capitalists and freed them from all restraint and any pangs of conscience about their rapacious, greedy, and murderous behavior toward workers and poor people. However vicious they became, their new philosophy said that there was absolutely nothing they could do to the poor that was not deserved and fully supported by god's great genetic and evolutionary plan in the sky. Predatory capitalism was the path to heaven and only the rich could get through the eye of the needle and past the pearly gates. God's grace was reserved for the successful alone.

Another Englishman, named Sir Francis Galton, the founder of eugenics, conducted studies that "proved" the existence of a superior class based on breeding. Though he was more interested in biology than economics, his studies supported and complemented the social darwinist philosophy of Herbert Spencer. Galton believed in programs of sterilization and genocide and he insisted that the unfit and unsuccessful had to be eliminated as they were a threat to the betterment of mankind. Naturally, it was the Republican conservatives in the United States who embraced his ideas most ardently as they did the companion ideas of Herbert Spencer. They were greatly worried about the menace of the feeble-minded underclass and the threat of the unfit just as they are today.

Early last century, the conservatives decided to purify the race by sterilizing those they considered subnormal or a burden on the state. By 1917, the conservatives had passed sterilization laws in thirty-three of the forty-eight states. These laws were to continue in effect for almost seventy years. Under them, tens of thousands of poor people were sterilized and millions more were intimidated and terrorized. The sterilized included orphans and children from broken homes, lepers, paupers, the homeless, epileptics, the physically handicapped, the mentally retarded, alcoholics, syphilitics, prostitutes, disobedient and unwanted children, "moral degenerates," young girls who had been raped or who had children out of wedlock, and just anyone the conservatives defined as unfit, impure, or shiftless. The conservatives felt it was their patriotic and christian duty to neuter or exterminate everyone who did not meet their criteria or obey their absolutist rules and dogmas.

When Adolph Hitler came to power in Germany in 1933, one of his first acts was to initiate a eugenics program by passing a sterilization law modeled after the one that enabled the Lynchburg Colony, a notorious sterilization camp in Virginia. In short order, Hitler sterilized half a million unfit Germans. The Lynchburg and other conservatives praised him and urged him to apply the "pruning hook" with vigor. They complained about their own nation's comparative caution, saying "The Germans are beating us at our own game."

Hitler was not a socialist as many of today's Republicans claim. In a speech at the Bamberg Nazi Party meeting in February of 1926, he declared his conservative and capitalist sentiments. When one of his assistants, Otto Strasser, later challenged the loyalty of certain of the capitalists, Hitler said, "Do you think I'd be so crazy as to destroy German industry? They are an elite. They have a right to rule."

Hitler was born a conservative christian and remained a devout Catholic throughout his life. He received religious instruction in school and served as a choirboy at the Benedictine monastery of Lambach. In power, he subsidized the christian religion, mandated school prayer and the teaching of religion in the primary grades, elevated priests to official positions, and said that state loyalty derived from the truths of christianity.

Hitler was a mass murderer but his conservative followers still make excuses for him. Even now, long after his defeat, the conservatives still dearly love his ideas and routinely use them as guides for their political ideology. Go to a Republican Party convention if you wish to hear Hitler's philosophy explicated.

Though there have been numerous atrocities and blood-lettings here at home, I am not saying that Republicans or any Americans committed mass murder against our own population as Hitler and Stalin did. However, I am saying that the American slaughter of Indians at home, the killing of many thousands of Filipinos in our colonial war against that country, the killing of between two and four million people in

Indochina during the Vietnam war, and the killing and wounding of millions of Iraqis during its two wars and the sanctions program were all mass attacks. I don't know how any objective person can deny these charges. The people of the United States are no less murderous than are other aggressors but they go to great lengths to sanitize their aggressions. Unfortunately, many of our journalists, historians, and politicians routinely employ distortions and outright lies to conceal these murderous facts.

When Joseph Stalin became the dictator of the Soviet Union, he adopted the theory of Francis Galton but claimed he was applying it in a marxist manner. Therefore, he set out to suppress, imprison, or kill the unfit so that the "new man" of the communist utopia could emerge from the carnage through heroic competitive struggle and right-thinking conformity. Like the nazis in Germany and the conservatives in the United States, Stalin saw history as a fight between the fit and the unfit. Stalin and Hitler are now dead and their empires are gone but the conservatives in the United States still reign.

Like Hitler, Stalin had a strong christian background. He was raised in a "priest-ridden" family in Georgia and became a dedicated seminarian. He received christian instruction and served as a choirboy at the Gori Church School in Georgia. Thus, he began as a religious fanatic as did many of the old Bolsheviks. Anastas Mikoyan and Yenukidze were also seminarians, Kliment Voroshilov was a choirboy, Lazar Kaganovich was a devout jew, and Lavrenty Beria's mother was so intensely worshipful that she went to a church to die near her god. When these men rejected their christian or jewish beliefs, they replaced them with communist beliefs.

When, in the Great Terror of 1937 Stalin was about to kill his close followers and friends, he said to them, "Maybe it can be explained by the fact that you lost faith." Stalin also said, "The Russian people need a Tsar whom they can worship and for whom they can live and work." He later told Beria that the "enemy of the people is not only one who does sabotage but one who doubts the rightness of the Party Line. There are many of them and we must kill them." The communists believed as much in the inerrancy of the word of their saints (Marx and Lenin) as do the fundamentalist christians in the inerrancy of their bible and the words of their priests and preachers.

Communism was a religion and its very close resemblance to fundamentalist christianity and mohammedanism is striking. Its leaders allowed no dissent or doubt and required the abject submission of adherents on the pain of torture and death. It was driven by religious fervor, especially when it was new, and it proselytized very much in the fashion of christian missionaries preaching to the unbelievers. Its afterlife was the magical and distant "workers' paradise" that would be achieved eventually by the sacrifices of true believers waging crusades against sin and heresy. Like the christian and muslim religionists, the communists also hated secularism and sought to destroy liberalism and its "weak-kneed" respect for the rights of the people and for such abominations as tolerance and individual conscience. They too were racist and anti-semitic and they also tried to co-opt and corrupt science in the interest of their dogma.

The Republican conservative philosophy of those times was exactly the same as the conservative philosophy of these times. Nothing has changed. Of course, the conservatives have cleaned up their language and now use more benign-sounding terms to justify their war against the "unfit" and the "unsuccessful." For example, they continue to attack poor people, welfare mothers, children, the old, the sick, the homeless, the jobless, and minorities but now they call them the "special interests" and say that they should be deprived, punished, shamed, and abused for their own good and for the protection and profit of the middle class.

These beliefs and actions must be understood in the historical light of conservative philosophy. Conservatives worship capitalism. It is their religion. They believe it is not only sacred and magical but entirely self-correcting as well. Both god and Mother Nature ordain it as the one and only economic system appropriate for this world. In fact, even heaven is capitalist. The only economic sin is to interfere with the pristine independence of capitalism. Left alone, the system will always work perfectly even if it does take a few decades, even if a few million poor people have to starve, even if it does cause mass unemployment and vast suffering.

Of course, this is the old social darwinist idea once again, always a part of the conservative belief system. Competition will justly wipe out the unfit and the fit will survive and prosper. The suffering of the poor is necessary and desirable. Morality is in the capitalist machine, not in humanity. Everyone must bow down to the god of capitalism and no one must ever question it or interfere with it in any way. Those who do so are the enemies of god and the state and they must be silenced before they arouse the people against their Republican conservative masters.

The bitterness of the Republicans toward Franklin Roosevelt knew no bounds. They called him a "traitor to his class" and referred to him contemptuously as "that man in the White House." Because he dared to reduce their privileges and their power, they said he was a tyrant, a fascist, and a communist. Their understanding of such terms was surely strange if not downright bizarre. To them, democracy was tyranny and tyranny democracy. They had no sympathy for or understanding of such concepts as justice, fair play, and simple decency. They were and are a cruel lot and nothing matters to them except their own narrow interests, their possessions, and their private power.

Franklin Roosevelt responded, "They are unified in their hate for me and I welcome their hate." He called them "economic royalists" and said, "Organized money is dangerous." He referred to big business as "private government" and the "regimenter of the people." He warned the people that "the liberty of a democracy is not safe if the people tolerate the growth of private power to a point where it becomes stronger than the democratic state itself." He warned against "ownership of government by an individual, by a group, or any controlling private power." The conservatives loathed and despised Franklin Roosevelt but the poor everywhere had pictures of him on their walls.

Franklin Roosevelt put an end to the tyranny of the Republican conservatives in his time but unfortunately his reign did not change things permanently. After his death, they emerged from their estates and country clubs once again and began to attack the programs of the New Deal. Many of those programs have been destroyed and many others weakened but the conservatives have not quite consolidated their recovered power. Not yet. Though much weakened in our present age, the liberals and progressives continue to fight for justice and a fair deal for the people.

Beyond any doubt, the Republican Party is the party of unregulated capitalism. If, as the Republicans demand, capitalism is not regulated in any way by a democratic government representing the people of the United States, then this unregulated capitalism can only be described as totalitarian and despotic. Naked uncontrolled economic force cannot possibly be democratic. Democracy means control by the people acting through their own elected instruments — however imperfect they may be — not control by a self-appointed elite of owners and bosses acting in their own interests alone.

Thus, the Republican Party is the enemy of democratic government and the friend of tyrannical private power. Its goal is the destruction of democratic government and the dominance of a narrow commerce and a repressive christian religion. The Republican Party is the subversive party, the party that always attacks the democratic principles established by the American Revolution. It is the party that tries with all of its might to impose its nineteenth-century darwinist and eugenicist ideas on America and indeed on the whole world. In short, the Republican Party is treasonous in its very nature.

Chapter 2. Eisenhower's Political Warfare

Like Theodore Roosevelt, Dwight Eisenhower was a strange mixture of good and evil. On political matters, at least, he was morally confused and hypocritical. At the end of World War II, he called himself a "militant liberal" but, after becoming close friends with a number of rich conservative businessmen, he began to say he was opposed to "welfare liberalism" and the New Deal and called Franklin Roosevelt and Harry Truman "socialistic." Nevertheless, he wrote his rich friends saying, "There is no difference between the two great parties ... I believe in neither." He added, "I do not want a political career." Then, almost immediately, he began maneuvering to become the Republican candidate for president and said he wanted to keep reactionary and isolationist conservatives like Douglas Mc Arthur and Robert Taft from "creating a paralysis of government" and dominating the Republican Party and the country.

When he became the Republican candidate, he campaigned with Joe McCarthy and refused to criticize his accusatory dishonesty and viciousness. In a deeply cowardly act, he even removed praise for his mentor, George Marshall, from his speeches to appease McCarthy. Still pandering to McCarthy, he made attacks against Harry Truman and "the reds" he supposedly hired and nurtured while also claiming that there was vast crime and corruption in the government for which he implied Truman was personally responsible.

Eisenhower's earlier behavior as a general was very different from his behavior as a politician. Back in 1945 during World War II, Eisenhower stood aside (the Americans and their allies stopped at the Elbe River) and allowed the Soviets to conquer Berlin. He said, "They have a shorter race to run, although they are faced by the bulk of the German forces." Eisenhower was quite right not to hastily commit American forces to the conquest of Berlin. There were more than three and a half million Soviet and German troops in that battle and the Soviets lost more of their men in the assault on Berlin (350,000 in three weeks) than the Americans lost in the entire war. The Germans lost over a hundred thousand. In fact, there was a vast difference in the total burden borne by the Soviets in World War II and that of the Americans and the British. The Soviets lost between twenty-five and thirty million in the European war and the Americans less than 300,000. There was also a great difference in the casualties inflicted on the enemy with the Soviets fighting against and killing something close to two-thirds of the Germans who died in the war. Altogether there were 13.6 million German casualties.

Churchill was incensed by Eisenhower's caution as were the fanatical anti-Soviets in the United States such as Navy Secretary James Forestall and Ambassador to the USSR Averill Harriman who was already planning to use nazi industry and personnel to carry out a US economic war against communism. Diplomat Robert Murphy wrote that Eisenhower "gave it all away" and had allowed the Soviets to have "everything they wanted."

In fact, Eisenhower did like and was liked by Stalin and General Zhukov who became close friends. He visited Moscow and was cheered on every side as a great hero. He said, "I have found the individual Russian to be one of the friendliest persons in the world." And "I think the Russians are friendly. I know all the officers I have met are." Like Franklin Roosevelt and George Marshall, Eisenhower wanted a genuine peace at that time but the raging anti-communist conservatives were already on the rampage against any cooperation with Russia. Eisenhower did not want a cold war but the conservatives did; still, when it became expedient, he joined the McCarthyites and became a vicious cold warrior himself.

There can be little doubt that, to a considerable extent, militant Western anti-communism caused the cold war. It is certainly true that Joseph Stalin was a tyrant, who killed millions of his own people, but a cold war was not in his interest and he was not trying to conquer the world or expand his empire as the anti-communists claimed. He wanted to keep what he had and he wanted to protect his borders. After all, more than twenty-five million of his citizens had just been killed in a war against nazism. Just at the end of the war, George Patton, one of Eisenhower's generals, publicly called for the conquest of the USSR and said he could drive all the way to Moscow within six weeks. Many other generals and admirals called for the immediate use of the atom bomb against the people of the USSR. Harriman and other conservatives were constantly threatening and insulting the Soviet Union and they weren't the least bit subtle about it.

Among other commie haters back home, Henry Luce began attacking the Soviet Union directly in print, in 1944, even before the war ended. A William Bullitt editorial in *Life* magazine claimed, without a shred of proof, that all of Western Europe was about to be invaded and conquered by the Soviet army. Then, Luce hired former Communist Party agents Willie Schlamm and Whittaker Chambers to proselytize for the isolation and alienation of the Soviet Union and the cleansing of the United States and the West of all "pro-communist" views and influences. Of course, they defined "pro-communist" to include American liberalism and the policies of the New Deal.

In March of 1946, Winston Churchill delivered his "iron curtain" speech in Fulton, Missouri with Harry Truman at his side. Europeans knew that Joseph Goebbels, Hitler's chief propagandist, had made a closely similar speech in February of 1945 in which he said that an "iron curtain" had "descended" over Europe. He added, "Behind this curtain, there will be a mass slaughter of peoples with acclamation from the Jewish press in New York." Eisenhower deplored Churchill's speech. Stalin said it was not the first time Churchill had been belligerent toward the USSR. He told the US ambassador, "He tried to instigate war against Russia, and persuaded the United States to join him in an armed occupation against part of our territory in 1919." Thus,

the Cold War began. At that point, Eisenhower still believed in peace and cooperation with the Russians but not for long. The muses of politics were calling and he had
to shed his reputation for being "soft on Russia" to please his Republican courtiers.

Eisenhower never thought much of Winston Churchill. During and after the war
when Eisenhower was himself strongly pro-Russian, Churchill was strongly anti-
Russian and Eisenhower thought his opinions were a threat to the war effort and
to prospects for peace after the war. Then, when Eisenhower himself turned against
his Russian friends for reasons of political expediency, Churchill was then urging
détente and an accommodation with the Russians. The worm had turned and now
Eisenhower was incensed by what he considered Churchill's soft attitude toward the
communist menace and his belated desire for détente. Both men had changed sides
moving in opposite directions. Eisenhower certainly had done so and with a murderous, simulated hate that would soon become genuine or at least politically convenient. In short order and under the cover of anti-communism, Eisenhower would
be up to his neck in plots against and subversions of numerous countries that were
trying to throw off the shackles of colonial rule so that they could become democratic
and independent.

Even before the big bomb, Eisenhower thought that large conventional wars had
become unthinkable, even suicidal. He thought that military action was negative in
character and he despised any talk of the "preventive wars" advocated by Republican conservatives such as Senator William Knowland, Henry Luce, and Claire Booth
Luce. During the war, Eisenhower had become deeply depressed when Truman
dropped two atom bombs on the civilian population of Japan. He said, "Japan was
already defeated and that dropping the bomb was completely unnecessary." He said
he "knew from intelligence reports that the Japanese were at that moment trying to
surrender."

By contrast, Harry Truman called the destruction at Hiroshima "the greatest
thing in history." He also said, "The world will note that the first atomic bomb was
dropped on Hiroshima, a military base. That was because we wished in the first attack to avoid, insofar as possible, the killing of civilians." Eisenhower was appalled.
Later, in the presidency, he cut military budgets and when the generals whined and
pleaded for more money, men, and weapons, he called them "sanctimonious hypocritical bastards." The extent to which he distrusted and even disliked the generals
and admirals was remarkable and even commendable. He knew that they put their
promotions, their careers, and their weaponry ahead of everything else, including
peace.

Rand, Mathieson, and some other right-wing business groups issued the shrill
Gaither Report after Sputnik, in 1957, which claimed the US was about to be annihi-
lated because Eisenhower had allowed a "missile gap" to develop and America's military strength to become weak. John Kennedy used the myth of Eisenhower's missile
gap against Nixon in his 1960 political campaign. Thereafter, the neo-conservatives
and conservatives adopted a political tactic of overstating the strength of the Soviet
Union while downgrading the strength of the United States. Henry Kissinger, Jeanne
Kirkpatrick, Norman Podhoretz, Midge Dector, Henry Jackson, Charles Krauthammer, Ronald Reagan, et al used this tactic repeatedly against Jimmy Carter.

Now, some forty-five years after the phony "missile gap" propaganda was first
used, the conservatives are again using its updated version to militarize America to
the last degree possible, this time in a fake pretense that they are fighting "terrorism." Eisenhower was the last president to give the generals less than they demanded.

Now, no president dares to oppose the overwhelming power of the military-industrial complex.

Eisenhower never repealed any part of the New Deal and said, "Should any political party attempt to abolish social security, unemployment insurance and eliminate labor laws and farm programs, you would not hear of that party again in our political history. There is a tiny splinter group, of course, that believes you can do these things. Among them are H. L. Hunt,... a few other Texas oil millionaires, and an occasional politician or businessman from other areas. Their number is limited and they are stupid." The number is not limited anymore. Today, they dominate the Republican Party and the conservative movement. They are still stupid, however, and, strangely, they claim Eisenhower as one of their heroes.

Following his New Deal instincts, Eisenhower also said he wanted legislation "for a vast expansion in unemployment insurance" and "expanded activity in the business of providing housing of decent standards for every American citizen." He said, "America just has to have better health" and he submitted a national health insurance bill to Congress, which voted it down in July of 1954 under pressure from the American Medical Association. He said, "How in the hell is the American Medical Association going to stop socialized medicine if they oppose such a bill as this. I don't believe the people of the United States are going to stand for being deprived of the opportunity to get medical insurance ... I refuse to admit defeat on this one." At that time, there were 25 million Americans who couldn't afford health insurance. Today, there are nearly 50 million but national insurance is further away than ever. The Clintons were hated, slandered, assaulted, and nearly destroyed at least partly because they tried to do what, first, Truman and, then, Eisenhower wanted done half a century ago.

In the early days of the twentieth century, it took sixty-two days by car to go from New York to San Francisco. Eisenhower made the trip and thought the roads were terrible. Before the car, suburban development was concentrated around trolley lines, but by 1929 there were forty million cars in the country and soon the trolley lines closed down. The *Grapes of Wrath* showed desperately poor people fleeing to California — but they had a car. In the thirties, Hitler built the Autobahn in Germany and later Eisenhower traveled on it. The 160-mile-long Pennsylvania Turnpike opened in 1940. The New Deal spent almost two billion dollars on roads and FDR proposed six toll roads to cover the entire country. But, during World War II, no cars and no roads were built, gas was rationed, and there was a national speed limit of thirty-five miles per hour. As president after the war, Eisenhower proposed and signed a law establishing the interstate highway system, the greatest pork barrel legislation in all of our history. This interstate system totally changed America, not all of it for the good. It was Eisenhower's greatest positive contribution.

Eisenhower refused to commute the Rosenbergs' death sentence for stealing atomic secrets because they wouldn't agree to confess and, according to CIA chief Allen Dulles, because they wouldn't agree to encourage others to defect and to allow themselves to be used "as figures in an effective internal psychological warfare campaign against Communism, primarily on the Jewish issue." An American ambassador to a European country wrote to Eisenhower saying "We should not deceive ourselves by thinking that this sentiment (against the execution) is due primarily to communist propaganda. People of all political leanings feel that the death sentence is completely unjustified and is due to the political climate peculiar to the United States." Although Eisenhower didn't much like Israel and he killed the Rosenbergs simply because they wouldn't join his political warfare campaign, he probably wasn't an anti-semite.

Whatever his moral beliefs were, however, they certainly weren't religious. Though he pretended to be pious in public, he rarely ever attended church at any time in his life. He was all gesture and no christian but he used religion against communism and for partisan political purposes at every opportunity. To those ends, he even snuck the words "under God" into the pledge of allegiance thus making it impossible for any honest citizen to pledge allegiance to his country's flag without also pledging allegiance to the monotheist god of the christians. In a bizarre attack against religious freedom, he said, "Our government makes no sense unless it is founded on a deeply felt religious faith — and I don't care what it is."

Anti-semite or not, christian or not, Eisenhower certainly was a racist of some dimension. His political cold warriors tried to foment civil war in the USSR and Eastern Europe but their propaganda was ineffective because of its superior, racist character. A crude, Anglo-Saxon racism led to jokes and sneering put-downs of Slavs as ignorant peasants, gullible half-wits, and immoral barbarians. One of Eisenhower's rich friends wrote him that there were "250 million Western Europeans from an industrial and intelligent atmosphere who can produce an army superior to one created by 190 million heterogeneous and barbaric peoples." Eisenhower's boys pretty much repeated the smears and slanders of Hitler's propagandists. One of the big supporters of Nixon and Eisenhower was the notorious conservative, Gerald L.K. Smith, who urged citizens to "help Richard Nixon get rid of the Jew communists."

Eisenhower always made it clear to the South that he shared their racial feelings but he told his political aides that open white racism was bad politics. Chief Justice Earl Warren said that Eisenhower "always resented our decision in *Brown* v *Board of Education*." Warren said that, after the decision, Eisenhower never spoke to him again. Eisenhower told the media that his worst mistake was the appointment of Earl Warren as Chief Justice. Warren recalled a dinner at the White House before the decision when he was still acceptable. Eisenhower said of visiting Southerners, "These are not bad people. All they are concerned about is to see that their sweet little girls are not required to sit in schools alongside some big overgrown Negroes." In May of 1952, Eisenhower wrote, "Frankly, I do not consider race relations or labor relations to be issues."

Eisenhower felt uncomfortable with the word "capitalism" and often used euphemisms such as "customer economics" and "peoples' capitalism." Then, a rich business friend named William Robinson explained that US capitalism is based on "the concept of the greatest good for the greatest number ... it can be more aptly called the democratic system." Eisenhower replied that he believed in "making a profit." He thought the United States was middle class from end to end. There was no "proletariat" and no "class" of poor people. Those were communistic concepts. Thus, there were no labor-management tensions and government had no business interfering with management. Businessmen were rightly in charge and workers had a patriotic duty to do their work without complaint.

Eisenhower himself liked to complain about the "illusion called security." In a 1949 speech to working people, he said, "We want to wear fine shirts, have caviar and champagne, when we should be eating hot dogs and beer." That speech left a bad taste in a lot of mouths. At the time, Eisenhower was living on a pension of nearly $19,000 a year plus an added personal allowance of $5,000, full medical benefits, commissary privileges, a chauffeur, a generous housing allowance, and even funeral expenses. In

1949, about seventy percent of the country had a family income of less than $4,000 a year. By today's standards, Eisenhower's income would amount to considerably more than a quarter of a million dollars a year.

Eisenhower believed in and did a number of good things but the more power he got and the more he associated with rich conservative businessmen the more antidemocratic he became and the more he blamed "socialists" for every problem and everything bad in the world. The greatest, the most brutal, and the longest-lasting evil that came out of Eisenhower's reign as president was the "political warfare" model that he used to attack democracy all across the world. That model was used, and is now being used again, to suppress or slaughter millions of innocent people on the pretext, in the past, that they were communists and on the pretext, now, that they are terrorists, harbor terrorists, or are terrorist supporters and sympathizers. The Republicans never miss an opportunity to destroy something and to kill someone somewhere and Eisenhower gave them a model they are still using today to guide their bloody hands.

In 1951, Eisenhower hired C. D. Jackson to develop "an integrated United States psychological warfare program" that would replace Truman's containment policy with a policy of active political warfare. Jackson had been the vice president of Time, Inc. (he was one of Henry Luce's boys) and he was a talented propagandist. He wanted business to "take over" the machinery of government. He said, "Enterprise is the most competent administrator of the welfare of the country." He added that the government bureaucracy was greatly understaffed and that new jobs needed to be created and filled exclusively with businessmen.

His plan for this seizure of government by business and the plan for political warfare were based on three operational expedients: 1. Plenty of money, 2. No holds barred, and 3. No questions asked. Jackson's organization was to include a youth movement based on Hitler's "Fuehrer Schule." Like most conservatives, he was impressed by some of the fascist practices in Germany and Italy. He wanted the same "zeal" in his youth movement and indeed throughout the business/government ruling force he wanted to create.

In short, Jackson's and Eisenhower's political warfare plan was for business to seize secret control of the US government and to use it to undermine popular support for economic and political democracy everywhere in the world by any means necessary (no holds barred, no questions asked) including the subversion of elected governments and the slaughter of innocent people in the interests of a dominant worldwide capitalism under the absolute control of the United States.

In 1954, Eisenhower issued NSC 5412 that introduced a policy designed to "develop underground resistance and facilitate covert and guerilla operations." This policy rejected the right of other countries to territorial integrity and national sovereignty and treated international law as inapplicable to the United States. This policy was directed not just against communism but also against declining colonial powers in the West, especially Britain and France. Those countries were not happy to learn that the United States was going to implement policies designed to control their colonial possessions and cancel out their privileges. They rightly understood that the US was initiating an aggressive contest for control of the earth's resources. This plan justified "propaganda, political action, economic warfare ... preventive direct action including sabotage, anti-sabotage, demolition ... bribery and assassination." This plan was immediately used to manipulate and corrupt elections in Italy, West Germany, and France and to subvert the internal politics of Vietnam, Laos, Indonesia, the Congo, Iran, Guatemala, Cuba, etc.

Eisenhower said it was his "personal conviction" that "almost any one of the new-born states of the world would rather embrace Communism or any other form of dictatorship than to acknowledge the political domination of another government even though that brought a higher standard of living." This was Eisenhower's justification for rejecting the democratic right of foreign citizens to choose their own governments in free elections. Of course, it was and still is a justification for subversive attack and tyrannical control by the US over others. Such a policy can only be called immoral and hypocritical.

Eisenhower's contempt for democracy was underlined when his National Security Council met on August 3, 1954 (just after the Geneva conference) and agreed to "prevent a Communist victory through all-Vietnamese elections." It also ordered "an urgent program of economic and military aid — substituting American advisers for French advisers — to the new South Vietnamese government of Ngo Din Diem." In April of 1954, the Geneva conference between the French and the Vietnamese had produced an agreement for nationwide elections in July of 1956. When Eisenhower canceled the elections, he said it was because Ho Chi Minh would get eighty percent of the vote and that he wasn't going to allow any communist to win an election, however democratic.

Eisenhower's first big target was Iran. In 1951, Prime Minister Dr. Mohammed Mossadeq nationalized the oil properties of the Anglo-Iranian oil company. The British threatened to invade. Truman sent Averill Harriman to mediate. Eisenhower watched from SHAPE headquarters but sent his aide, General Vernon A. Walters, to help Harriman. Harriman and Walters tried to persuade Iran to accept the US as a partner in place of the British. Earlier, Mossadeq had opposed and defeated a Soviet concession. He had just evicted the British and now he refused to let the US take over the oil. At this point, Harry Truman rejected a plot for the overthrow of Iran's elected government.

In 1953, with Eisenhower in the White House, Kermit Roosevelt, the CIA chief in Iran, organized a plot to overthrow Mossadeq who had just received overwhelming support from the Iranian people in a referendum. Roosevelt claimed falsely that Iran's Communist Party was his main support and his controller. Eisenhower said later, "Mossadeq got 99.4 percent of the votes. Iran's downhill course toward Communism was picking up momentum." In fact, the election had been free and had not been manipulated by the communists. Eisenhower knew this very well. He was just using the false charge of communism as a cover for his political attack against the representative government of Iran.

The following extract from an article in the May 19, 2003 issue of *Time* magazine describes what happened:

> As the Iranian government withered, the Eisenhower Administration cut foreign aid. Unrest followed, and angry citizens took to the streets. This prompted suggestions that the communists were coming, even though Mossadeq was as anti-Soviet as he was anti-British. On Aug. 19, 1953, after the deaths of about 300 people in street riots, the 71-year-old Premier was overthrown. He was replaced by a retired army general, Fazollah Zahedi. The American-friendly Shah, Mohammed Reza Pahlavi, who had earlier fled the country, returned triumphantly, resumed the throne and reasserted his control.

The *Washington Post* reported that Iran had been saved from falling into communist hands and that the communists were blaming Brigadier General H. Norman Schwarzkopf "for alleged complicity in the coup." *Time* reported: "This was no military coup, but a spontaneous popular uprising."

It was anything but.

The British approached the CIA with a plan to remove the Premier and get Britain's oil back. The British could not do it alone, since they had left Iran. Allen Dulles, the CIA director, and his brother John Foster Dulles...assigned the task of overseeing the clandestine venture to Kermit Roosevelt, a longtime intelligence operative and the grandson of President Theodore Roosevelt.

The CIA's fingerprints were everywhere. Operatives paid off Iranian newspaper editors to print pro-Shah and anti-Mossadeq stories. They produced their own stories and editorial cartoons and published fabricated interviews. They secured the cooperation of the Iranian military. They spread antigovernment rumors. They prepared phony documents to show secret agreements between Mossadeq and the local Communist Party. They masqueraded as communists, threatened conservative Muslim clerics and even staged a sham firebombing of the home of a pro-Mossadeq newspaper. They incited rioters to set fire to a pro-Mossadeq newspaper. They stage-managed the appearance of Mossadeq's successor, General Zahedi, whose personal bank account they fattened.

Mossadeq was tried for treason, spent three years in prison, and was kept under house arrest until he died in 1967. He denounced foreign conspiracies and said, "My only crime is that I nationalized the Iranian oil industry and removed from the land the network of colonialism and the political and economic influence of the greatest empire on earth."

In his book, *All the Shah's Men: An American Coup and the Roots of Middle East Terror,* Stephen Kinzer said, "It is not farfetched to draw a line from Operation Ajax [the CIA's code name for the coup] through the Shah's repressive regime and the Islamic Revolution to the fireballs that engulfed the World Trade Center in New York." He also noted that this was the CIA's first success in causing a change of regime through subversion and that it set the stage for the overthrow of Guatemala's Jacobo Arbenz Guzman and "set off a sequence of events in that country that led to civil war and hundreds of thousands of violent deaths. Later, the CIA set out to kill or depose foreign leaders from Cuba and Chile to the Congo and Vietnam. Each of these operations had profound effects that reverberate to this day. Some produced immense misery and suffering and turned whole regions of the world bitterly against the United States."

Thus, the Iranian dictatorship was reestablished and the British oil monopoly was ended. British Petroleum got to keep 40 percent; US oil companies got 40 percent, and Dutch and French oil companies were allowed to share the other 20 percent. Most of the details of this CIA coup are still classified.

In December of 1954, His Imperial Majesty Mohammed Reza Shah Pahlavi toasted Eisenhower in the White House with these words, "But for the grace of god and the help of your country I would not be here today." The US helped him arm and train SAVAK, his secret police force. It was well known throughout the world that he was hated by nearly the entire population. Finally, in 1979, his own people overthrew the Shah and the religious mullahs seized control. Thus, Eisenhower's chickens came home to roost on the shoulders of Jimmy Carter and the people of the United States. Today Iran is our bitter enemy and will be so for a long time to come.

The New Deal inspired a democratic revolution in Guatemala in 1944. The revolution overthrew hated dictator Jorge Ubico, a patron of the United Fruit Company (UFCO). The people called UFCO "El Pulpo" and thought of it as "the octopus that strangled all it touched." In Central America, UFCO was a government in itself, one that controlled Honduras, Costa Rica, Guatemala, and many others. In 1936, John Foster Dulles had drawn up a contract that gave UFCO control over all electricity and transportation including the only port in Puerto Barrios as well as 42% of all of the country's land. The contract exempted UFCO from all taxes and import duties. Under Franklin Roosevelt, the US government did not object to the revolution against Ubico. Adolf A. Berle, a state department official, said, "I think this is probably all right." However, UFCO bitterly resented the overthrow of its dictator, Jorge Ubico.

Juan Jose Arevalo, the new leader, came from a popular movement of workers, teachers, professionals, small businessmen, army officers, and campesinos (Mayans who worked the fields and earned three cents a day or less). Free democratic elections conducted after the revolution resulted in the presidency of Arevalo and his successor, Jacobo Arbenz Guzman. Arevalo, who was progressive and democratic, gave everyone including women the vote. In 1944, in imitation of the United States, he enacted a work code that gave workers the right to organize and strike, established a minimum wage, and set up requirements for labor-management contracts. UFCO and its electricity and transportation monopolies were outraged and attacked Arevalo as a "communist dictator." In fact, he hated the Soviet Union and refused to legalize the Communist Party. He was a Roosevelt admirer and an idealist committed to liberty, justice, and national dignity."

In response to UFCO's smears, he condemned "Yankee imperialism" and refused to participate in the US war against Korea. There was nothing the least bit communist about him or his government but UFCO believed that anyone who didn't help it make a huge profit and who believed that workers have rights was a communist. They were running a sweet, very profitable dictatorship in Guatemala and they weren't about to give up any of their power or their profits without a fight.

In March of 1951, Jacobo Arbenz, Arevalo's defense minister, was elected as his successor. Arbenz' announced objective was to convert Guatemala from a dependent nation into an independent one, to transform it from a backward past with a feudal economy into a modern capitalist country, and to elevate the standard of living of the people. He announced a program of equitable land reform to eliminate feudalism and establish a system of modern capitalism. He wanted to "eliminate all feudal-type property, abolish work-servitude and slavery, give small tracts of land to the landless, and expand agricultural credits to small owners. Plantations with acreage in use were excluded and expropriations were limited to "idle lands" on "holdings over 223 acres." He advocated land ownership, literacy, and voting for everyone.

An editor in Guatemala wrote an article for The Nation in March of 1953 in which he said, "The big landowners — especially United Fruit — are doing everything to block implementation of the law and to overthrow the regime that sponsored it. Ignoring the situation described in an official UN publication on the urgent need for land reform in Guatemala, they object even to article 2, which says; 'all forms of slavery and serfdom are herewith abolished.'" In the land reform, UFCO lost 178,000 acres. Based on UFCO's own tax return, Guatemala offered $1,185,115 in compensation. UFCO demanded sixteen million dollars for land it never bought in the first place but got as a gift from its own corrupt dictator.

Arbenz also initiated the building of an electrical center and a network of roads leading to a new Atlantic port, all financed by Guatemala itself. His purpose was to provide an alternative to UFCO's total monopoly over electricity and transport. Again, UFCO screamed "communism" and began organizing a coup with help from Nicaragua's dictator, Anastasio Somoza. The plan was submitted to Harry Truman for approval but he turned it down and the plot collapsed.

When Eisenhower was elected, he was immediately informed of the UFCO plot and was told that Guatemala was under the control of "a Russian-controlled dictatorship." Eisenhower put C. D. Jackson, A.A. Berle, former CIA director William Jackson, and Nelson Rockefeller on a task force to plot the overthrow of Arbenz. Edward L. Bernays, the father of public relations, was a consultant. On the basis of no evidence at all, they got the Council on Foreign Relations to agree "generally that the Guatemalan government was communist." Of course, this was an astonishing lie and everyone knew it including Eisenhower. The same lie was used against Mossadeq in Iran and against many other governments throughout Eisenhower's reign. Furthermore, this same lie was being used by the Republican Party — especially by McCarthy and Nixon — to smear Democrats and all critics. You see, Eisenhower internationalized McCarthyism and used it against just about everybody as a cover for his political warfare against democratic government.

E. Howard Hunt, the CIA operative and later Watergate criminal said, "The National Security Council under Eisenhower and Vice President Nixon had ordered the overthrow of Guatemala's regime." He said he was told "no clandestine project had higher priority." Eisenhower himself said that Guatemala was "openly playing the communist game" and said that the expropriation of United Fruit lands was evidence enough of communism. Eisenhower had moved from being "soft on Russia" to being a vicious McCarthyite who was capable of any lie and any rationalization in the interest of a system of totalitarian capitalism that was even more dishonest and more contemptuous of democracy than was Stalin's communism and Hitler's nazism.

Arbenz naively believed that the United States would eventually understand that he was not a communist, that his government was not communist, and that there were very few communists in Guatemala at all. Eisenhower and the corrupt men around him knew full well that Arbenz was telling the truth, but they were determined to use McCarthyite smears to discredit and overthrow him in the interest of the United Fruit Company. Dulles told Latin American ambassadors that the Soviet Union was trying to "establish a puppet state in this hemisphere" but, when he realized they didn't believe him, he admitted it would be "impossible to produce evidence clearly tying the Guatemalan government to Moscow."

On June 14, 1954, US mercenaries, under the direction of the CIA and with US air support, invaded Guatemala. Eisenhower went on television and denied that he knew anything at all about the attack. He claimed, instead, that there was "a wave of arrests of anti-communists, strict censorship, and killings by Arbenz" and he said, "people are fleeing the country in fear." He said it was a "typical pattern of communist takeover and is not in response to any external threat." He didn't explain why the communists would need to take over since, according to him, Arbenz and his government were already communist.

The White House said of bombings by US planes piloted by US officers "There are no such planes in that part of the world." The USIA said it was an "uprising of Guatemalans against terroristic communist-dominated government." Dulles told the United Nations that there was no battle and "no evidence of bombing of capital or strafing of civilian population." He said, "leftist newspapers were slanting reports in favor of communist-oriented groups eager to put the blame on the US." Britain and France were not persuaded nor was Latin America.

Guatemala sent a petition to the UN outlining the events of the attack. They are listed below, in part:

> June 14, 1954. Planes coming from Honduras and Nicaragua parachuted arms and ammunition to a subsidiary of the United Fruit Company for use by invading forces.

> June 17. Invading forces captured El Florido and advanced fifteen kilometers into Guatemalan territory. This morning aircraft attacked the country, dropped explosive bombs on fuel stores at San Jose and in the city of Retalhuleu. P47 planes of American manufacture attacked Guatemala City, strafing government buildings and private dwellings and bombing military bases.

> June 18. During the night, the passenger train from Guatemala to Puerto Barrios was machine-gunned. At 11:50 PM, a P47 plane attacked the Guatemalan capital.

> June 19. At 8:00 AM, a plane attacked the capital and three others dropped bombs over the villages of Los Mixcos and Potrero Grande. In the city of Chiquimula, a plane machine-gunned the Girls Normal School. In an attack on the capital, the plane strafed civilians. At 11:00 AM, another plane dropped bombs on the gasoline tanks at Puerto Barrios. At 12:00 noon, mercenary invasion forces occupied the town of Esquipulas and at 3:00 PM the town of Jocotan.

In conclusion, the Guatemalan report said that "one of the planes fell over Mexico and the two pilots are American. One is wounded." Moreover, the report said, "Contrary to the false reports published abroad, there has been no uprising in any part of Guatemala."

The people continued to support Arbenz. The Army did not mutiny. There was no uprising. The US ambassador to El Salvador told Dulles that the "lack of substantial progress by Carlos Castillo Armas [the American-appointed head of the invading mercenary army] and the absence of any uprising against the government might result in the fall one by one of the other Central American countries through communist penetration." Eisenhower ordered another bombing attack against the people of Guatemala. All communications were cut to Guatemala City and the Arbenz government didn't know what was going on. Then, the victims began to arrive. Trainloads of the dead and wounded were railroaded to the city and, according to CIA cold warrior Richard Bissell, this had a very powerful impact on Arbenz. Arbenz wanted to stop the bombing and killing and feared that, as rumored, the US would use napalm and bacteria against his people. Therefore, he resigned and went into exile.

The defense commander, Colonel Diaz, took over. To satisfy the US, he outlawed the Communist Party, sent the few communists in the country into exile, invoked martial law, and established a "pro-US government." Though ordered to do so by US Ambassador John Peurifoy, he refused to negotiate with Castillo Armas because he had massacred the people. In response, Peurifoy brought Colonel Diaz a long list of "communists to be shot within 24 hours." Diaz refused. The ambassador replaced him with Colonel Monzon, "a real anti-communist." But Dulles and Eisenhower wanted their boy, Castillo Armas, in power and they continued the bombing. Then, Castillo Armas flew into Guatemala City in the US embassy plane escorted by "nine army planes and three C47 transports." Eisenhower's dictator had arrived. Lying through his teeth, Eisenhower said" Castillo Armas enjoyed the devotion of his people." Dulles said, "Now the future of Guatemala lies at the disposal of the Guatemalan people themselves." E. Howard Hunt and Ambassador Peurifoy were rewarded for their part in the coup with assignments to Indochina.

Castillo Armas canceled the agrarian reform law, burned the crops, and killed hundreds and perhaps thousands of campesinos. He outlawed unions. Nine thousand people were arrested and tortured or killed. Armas, Eisenhower, and Dulles attributed the killings to Arbenz although he was not there during the killings having long since gone into exile. As late as 1953, Eisenhower was still calling Castillo Armas "a farseeing and able statesman." Nixon said he was "a good president who said, 'Tell us what you want us to do and that's what we will do.'" A United Fruit publicity agent said the company was "involved at every level" and wrote of "some reasonably believable atrocity pictures — some had been castrated and they were about to be buried in a mass grave." He added, "Arbenz gets all the credit." Thus, thanks to the Eisenhower-Dulles propaganda and although Arbenz and "communism" could not possibly have been responsible, these pictures "were widely accepted as pictures of the victims of communism."

Armas said that in the name of "God, Fatherland, and liberty" he was dedicated to the "total and definitive eradication of Communism and convinced communists, confessed or concealed, as well as those who hide them." He suspended all political parties and disenfranchised three-quarters of the entire population. The US State Department said this was "a move considered necessary by anti-communists who saw Arbenz manipulate this vote." Dulles wanted all the communists killed because he considered them "a class additional to common criminals not entitled to asylum."

Castillo Armas was assassinated in July of 1957. When Armas died, Eisenhower sent his son to grieve for his favorite dictator. Then he retired to his rich farm in Pennsylvania leaving behind a legacy of undemocratic viciousness unsurpassed in United States history.

Armas' successor was General Fuentes. By this time, Guatemala had become thoroughly militarized and the country was full of competing military leaders who all wanted power for themselves. This militarization was accelerated when the US used Guatemala as a training base for the overthrow of Cuba, the assassination of Castro, and as a command post for the Bay of Pigs operation. The majority of these militarists had been trained by the US at the Pentagon's School of the Americas, a fitting practitioner of Eisenhower's political warfare. In Guatemala, rival military groups emerged to form guerilla units. These competing authoritarians slaughtered four thousand civilians in 1966. From Eisenhower's invasion all the way to now, terrorism and torture and murder have dominated political life in Guatemala. In 1967, the US and German ambassadors were assassinated. Amnesty International said that at least twenty thousand were killed between 1966 and 1976. Most agree that about 300,000 have been killed since Eisenhower destabilized the country and established a system of military dictatorship there.

There were killings and riots in 1978 and the government fell. General Lucas' successor government tortured, murdered, and mutilated thousands of people between July of 1978 and June of 1979. Death lists became routine. Student leaders were machine-gunned after public speeches not acceptable to the government. Dissident faculty members disappeared. Liberationist Catholic priests were killed. The victims were called "communists." Eisenhower and Dulles would have been proud of their spawn.

In 1980, the Spanish embassy was attacked to prevent it from giving sanctuary and asylum to dissidents. Chemical incendiaries were used and people inside the embassy were shot down indiscriminately. Thirty-nine people were killed, including seven Spanish embassy employees. Spain broke relations with the government and closed the embassy. The US government under Reagan remained faithful, even cheered the "anti-communists" in charge of the freedom-loving government.

Like Eisenhower, Reagan had a favorite Guatemalan dictator — Rios Montt. Montt seized control of Guatemala in a bloody coup in 1982 and ruled with a brutal hand for 18 months. His forces exterminated indigenous peoples in more than 400 villages. At least 20,000 noncombatants were killed and hundreds of thousands fled to Mexico. Reagan saw Montt as another one of his beloved "freedom fighters." What Reagan loved, of course, was that Montt was a fundamentalist christian who killed men, women, and children because, he said, they were atheistic communists or supporters of communism.

One of the best examples of an Eisenhower subversion that failed to change a hated regime immediately but that resulted in massive "blowback" years later happened in Indonesia. Quoted below is an extract from a November 27, 1995 *In These Times* review of a book titled *Subversion As Foreign Policy: The Secret Eisenhower and Dulles Debacle in Indonesia,* by Audrey and George Kahin:

> The authors argue persuasively that the civil war of 1957-58 [instigated and supported by the Eisenhower administration] permanently altered the Indonesian political landscape by strengthening the military and destroying the country's fragile parliamentary system. By 1965, Indonesian society had become increasingly militarized, and the army, in the wake of an abortive coup attempt, unleashed its fury on the Communist Party's millions of unarmed supporters in the trade unions and peasant organizations. At least 500,000 people were killed in the carnage; 750,000 others were imprisoned. The CIA proclaims its innocence in the events of 1965, but the agency's files on the matter remain sealed.

For the 200 million people in the Archipelago, including the beleaguered East Timorese, the US intervention of 1957–58 is much more than a historical footnote: 1995 marks the 30th anniversary of military rule in Indonesia.

Also quoted below is an extract from an Edward S. Herman article in *Z Magazine* in December of 2002:

> One of the most dramatic and revealing cases of US official support for client state mass murder was the US relationship to the huge Indonesian killings of 1965–1966, which may have claimed over a million victims, many incidentally on the island of Bali. It is on the record that the United States supplied lists of people (communists) to be killed to the coup and genocide managers, and it is also clear that US officials, pundits, and media were ecstatic at what James Reston saw as a "gleam of light" and *Time* magazine called "The West's best news for years in Asia," referring to an Indonesia being subjected to mass slaughter.

> Less well known is the fact that US officials had been regretful that the Indonesian military seemed to lack the gumption to "clean house," and expressed great pleasure when the house cleaning took place. Thus, Rand Corporation and CIA official Guy Pauker had been despondent in 1959 about the possibility of an army takeover.... After the coup, Pauker exulted that "The assassination of the six army generals by the September 30 Movement elicited the ruthlessness that I had not anticipated a year earlier and resulted in the death of large numbers of Communist cadres (actually, mostly peasant farmers and ordinary citizens who might have supported the Communist Party)" (quoted in Peter

Dale Scott's chapter on Malcolm Caldwell, ed., *Ten Years' Military Terror in Indonesia* (Spokesman, 1975)).

The Iran and Guatemala subversions were the clearest models of Eisenhower's political warfare but the same policies were applied everywhere and everywhere, at home and abroad, the same propaganda was used by the Republicans to attack victims and silence critics. Everywhere around the globe, Eisenhower's forces worked to put down revolts against colonialist oppression and to suppress democratic actions and aspirations. Yet, Eisenhower complained that the communists were trying "to get us" to "spend ourselves into bankruptcy." Thirty years later the followers of Ronald Reagan would cynically borrow and reverse this charge claiming that they themselves had destroyed the Soviet Union by forcing it to spend itself into bankruptcy.

During Eisenhower's presidency, his brother, Edgar, was constantly attacking Eisenhower's New Deal, socialist policies." Joe McCarthy called him a "conscious agent of the communist conspiracy." Early on, the conservatives had repeatedly accused him of being "soft on Russia." Even after making himself into a fanatical and brutal anti-communist, he was still accused of socialism and communism and by those on his side and closest to him. The truth, though, is that Dwight Eisenhower was a vicious and murderous killer of vast numbers of mostly innocent people in the name of a twisted, dishonest, misnamed, and misdirected anti-communism. This was certainly a strange, divided, self-deluded man.

In his surprising farewell address on January 17, 1961, Eisenhower said, "In the councils of government, we must guard against the acquisition of unwarranted influence, whether sought or unsought, by the military-industrial complex. The potential for the disastrous rise of misplaced power exists and will persist." Was he warning us against people like himself or was he still under the delusion that killing people in an open, declared war is worse than killing them in secret through a policy of sadistic political warfare accompanied by McCarthyistic propaganda designed to hide the truth from the people of the United States and the whole world?

CHAPTER 3. THE REPUBLICAN PARTY'S FAKE ANTI-COMMUNISM

By now, I suppose almost everyone agrees that, during the twentieth century, there was a "twilight struggle" between capitalism and communism for control of the world and that capitalism won. Gorbachev's reforms convinced conservative US politicians that socialism had been defeated. They saw it all as a victory for US militarism and a vindication of the policies of McCarthyism at home and interventionism abroad. They thought that Gorbachev's reforms were an unconditional surrender to capitalism and that, therefore, history had ended. They thought that communism was socialism, that it was dead, and that it would never be heard from again. I think they were wrong.

Among others, the English historian A.J. P. Taylor noted long ago that Russian communism was really state capitalist, not socialist. In a speech to the National Press Club on March 25, 1991, Lech Walesa said of Poland, "In our communist system, everything resembled one huge enterprise." Similarly, all of Russia was one gigantic business under the rule of a communist chief executive officer with a Board of Directors called the Politburo and a network of party functionaries who acted as company managers. On ABC's Nightline in June of 1991, Boris Yeltsin said of the Russian worker, "He doesn't own land. He doesn't own the factory, the enterprise, the shop or anything." It's absolutely clear that Russia was never socialist in any sense nor were any of the other so-called communist countries.

Historically, what really happened was that, initially, a democratic revolution displaced Czar Nicholas II, a divine king, and replaced him with Alexander Kerensky and a parliamentary government. Then, a small group of counter-revolutionary state capitalists (the Bolsheviks) deposed Kerensky and took over the country completely. Workers had nothing to say about any of this. There was no workers' revolution and workers had absolutely no voice in how the new state was shaped or managed. They never even had the right to strike or express their grievances.

Thus, Russian communism took the means of production from the Czar, who owned everything, and put it in the hands of a narrow new class of privileged bosses, who owned everything. Lenin and Stalin were simply czars without the title or the royal blood. Absurdly, today's conservatives try to identify communism with the

French Revolution and claim that every revolt against aristocracy and the divine rule of kings has been an attack against "freedom" and christianity.

The error of confusing communism with socialism, welfarism, and even liberalism completely warped the US political system until every election became an argument about communism. For more than fifty years, the Republican conservative propaganda was that Democrats and liberals were traitors and pro-communists. According to them, New Deal, Fair Deal, and Great Society programs were all socialist schemes. The civil rights movement was a communist plot; Martin Luther King and Earl Warren were communist agents. Jimmy Carter's human rights policies were an attack against "our friends," that is, anti-communist military dictators everywhere. These Republican conservatives claimed that liberals deliberately weakened US values and subverted US military strength in order to prepare the way for communist victory. The world was so polarized by this anti-communist fanaticism that there weren't even words or concepts in common use to describe a third alternative; and there still aren't.

These distortions led quite naturally to McCarthyism. McCarthyism was not just what Senator Joe McCarthy said and did. It was the attack philosophy of Republican conservatism, the political arm of corporate capitalism. This attack philosophy gained political control of the United States under Dwight Eisenhower and Richard Nixon and greatly multiplied it under Ronald Reagan. It is no accident that Nixon and Reagan became the greatest appeasers of the Russian and Chinese communist states. They had used communism against liberalism and the Democratic Party in order to gain power for themselves. Once they had power, it was no longer useful to carry on a war against communism. In control of the United States, they could diminish their cold war with Russia and China while concentrating their attack on liberalism and the Democratic Party.

State capitalism (that is, Soviet communism) was but one form of a broader system that should be called totalitarian capitalism. In the United States and elsewhere in the West, the most repressive forms of corporate capitalism were also a part of the totalitarian system. Thus, economically, there was little difference between the Western countries and the communist countries. Soviet state capitalism and Western corporate capitalism were brothers. In the Soviet-style system, there was no political democracy and no economic democracy. In the United States, there is a carefully limited political democracy but no economic democracy. Instead of economic democracy there is an antidemocratic system of predatory capitalism.

You really can't discuss communism in the United States without also discussing anti-communism. In the twentieth century, there was very little communism here but there was an enormous amount of anti-communism and the anti-communism was far more fanatical and far more subversive of democracy than was the communism itself. In fact, anti-communism really wasn't an attack against communism at all; rather, it was an attack against domestic foes — liberalism, unionism, civil rights, and the democratic government of the United States. Accusations of communism were simply the dirty brush used by conservatives to attack their own country and those citizens they disagreed with.

The notion that communism was an entirely new kind of "totalitarian" tyranny far worse than the old "authoritarian" tyranny was absurd. Of course, this view was advanced and supported by those sympathetic to the old tyranny and fanatically determined to support it as a legitimate alternative to what they saw as the absolute evil of communism. Communism was an excuse used by the anti-communist authoritarians to establish and maintain tyrannies of their own. In Western countries, anti-communism became a weapon for the authoritarian conservatives to use dishonestly against liberals, socialists, modernists, progressives, humanists, evolutionists, jews, blacks, and any democrats.

Western capitalists were happy to identify communism with socialism. It not only gave them a useful enemy but also gave them an excuse to attack democratic socialism, in fact, all forms of economic democracy. Consequently, the conservatives saw politics in the twentieth century as a struggle between noble conservative capitalism and evil liberal socialism. Not only has this distortion corrupted history, it has also led to the weakening of democracy in the West as well as to vast confusion in Eastern Europe and the republics of the former Soviet Union. Democracy cannot emerge there or anywhere as long as every principle of economic justice continues to be misrepresented.

I don't think the hostility between the United States and the Soviet Union was a result of communism. If there had been no revolution in the Russian Empire and no communism, there would still have been a cold war or perhaps a hot war. Perhaps it would have been a war between Eastern orthodox christianity and some Western version of christianity. Perhaps it would have been a war between some version of czarist capitalism and what Westerners like to call democratic capitalism. Whatever the ideologies, the hostility was certainly inevitable. At the end of World War II, there were just two dominant countries left and they pretty much controlled the world. There had to be a rivalry; in fact, Alexis de Tocqueville foresaw such a rivalry among others. Communism was all but irrelevant.

Communism became *the* great issue because of the Western — especially the US — fear of the working man and the belief that the industrial masses were about to rise up, seize the production machinery, and depose the property owners and bosses. This fear was exacerbated by the unrest and rebelliousness created in the masses by the brutality of the Great Conservative Depression. At that point, it looked to the capitalists as if Karl Marx had been right. Neither they nor anyone else could imagine that the masses would accept their miserable lot without revolt. Then, Franklin Roosevelt and the New Deal saved the capitalists from themselves.

The Western capitalists had always hated every kind of marxism as they had earlier hated anarchism and democracy. After all, that specter threatened to overthrow them and take away their money and power. The Russian Revolution and the depression terrified them and made them into fanatical and indiscriminate anti-communists. They didn't just hate theoretical communism; they hated everything they could associate with it, everything that they thought might threaten their comfortable lives and destabilize the social, political, and economic order. Thus, they hated civil rights, human rights, and all of the rights of working people; they hated liberalism, progressivism, and democratic government; and, although Roosevelt was in the process of saving them, they hated him too. Naturally, this intense feeling translated into a deep and eternal hostility to the Soviet Union, the only communist country in the world at that time.

Communism certainly complicated the rivalry between the US and the USSR but did not cause it. There was increased class warfare during this time. However, it wasn't workers who went to war; their resentment had been dampened down by the New Deal reforms and the prosperity and patriotism of World War II. It was the capitalists and Republicans who went to war against working people and against every molecule of dissent and non-conformity in the country. They saw enemies everywhere and, by their definition, those enemies were all communists. Their definition included all liberals, all government employees, and most members of the Democratic Party.

As soon as the Second World War ended, they launched a massive attack against communism but the Soviet Union wasn't their main concern. They were worried about the loyalty of their fellow citizens. They saw millions and millions of communists and communist sympathizers all around them. This resulted in McCarthyism and the rise of a fanatical Republican Party that would spend the next fifty years raging against the democratic government of the United States. Even while they falsely attacked others for trying to overthrow the government by "force and violence," that is precisely what they were themselves doing. And, to this very day, the Republican Party remains a subversive, anti-democratic force.

The Soviet Union was never much of a threat to the United States. It was a nuisance and irritant, little more. It was never a rich or prosperous society, either under communism or at any other time. It never had a large middle class. It was never an industrial power. It was never able to adequately feed and care for its own people. In fact, it was always primitive and backward. It did have military power but only because it was very large, had numerous resources, and could put together large armies. Even so, the United States, all by itself, was always far more powerful than the Soviet Union and all of its allies.

Politicians in the United States and the West more broadly saw the Soviet Union as a great threat. It served their purposes to have a great and powerful enemy. It put them in power; it kept them in power. That's what McCarthyism, Nixonism, Reaganism, and Bushism were all about. It's why the imperialist neo-conservative movement arose on the fringes of American and Western political life. Fanatical and irrational anti-communism was the force that drove all of these isms. Without them, life in the United States would be entirely different and far better.

Communist China and the Soviet Union weren't expansionist. They did proselytize through their dogma just like other ideologies and religions — islam, christianity, capitalism, etc. But so what? Communism was always a weak religion. Its success came almost entirely from the abuses and stupidities of capitalism, not from any special appeal of its own. The only part of the communist ideology that was useful, true, and accurate was its criticism of capitalism and there was nothing new or special about that either. The victims of capitalism have always known it was abusive and exploitative and have always bitterly resented it. They still do and they always will. Throughout history, every tyrannical system has always been resented and resisted.

Every overseas effort to redistribute even a little of the property and wealth of the rich oligarchies was regularly assaulted by US forces, both overt and covert. In each case, the US pretended that purely local movements were part of an international communist conspiracy. The US charged those countries with subverting themselves even while it organized coups against them, assassinated their leaders, manipulated their internal politics, blocked their trade, subverted their currencies, shipped arms to subversive forces undermining them, and organized and directed terrorist groups in murderous attacks against their people. In these ways, the US eventually drove many small, terrified, weak countries into the arms of communism, then claimed it had been right all along when it had accused them of being communist satellites.

Conservative Republicans originated this fake anti-communism. Liberal Democrats collaborated. One way to look at it is that the Democrats had little choice because the Republican conservatives were calling them traitors and subversives with every breath and were thus driving them headlong into the oppressive embrace of right-wing dictators. Another way to look at it is that the Democrats were gutless and cowardly, a charge that was certainly true then and is still true now.

The rightists could not or would not see that communism was just another rightist oligarchy. What really scared them was the communist propaganda about raising the workingman up from capitalist slavery and putting him in charge of society. The rightist needn't have worried: the communist propaganda was always a fraud. By the time they began to understand this, if they ever did, the communist "threat" had become a useful tool to them in their virulent campaign against every form of economic democracy.

The cold war was a gigantic con game that served the interests of both the communists and the anti-communists. Both blocks gained and maintained power through opposition to one another. Many millions of innocent and foolish people actually believed their cold war propaganda.

The Soviet Union never made any military attacks against any Western nation. Of course, it did send troops into Eastern European countries on its own borders, that is, the so-called satellites. Those interventions were all carried out to defend existing communist regimes. The purpose quite obviously was to assure a protective border around the USSR. The Soviet Union was merely defending the empire it had put together before, during, and just after the Second World War. As many of his own citizens as he slaughtered and as dictatorial as he was toward the countries on his borders, Stalin was not trying to conquer the world. He was just defending his existing lands and his existing power.

Is there a sense in which the US and the USSR were trying to conquer the world? If so, it wasn't a matter of conquering territory. The Soviets made no attacks against anyone for that purpose. After WW II and except for a handful of advisors and technicians here and there, it sent no troops into or against any other country beyond its own array of perimeter satellites. The USSR had no need of additional property or resources and certainly didn't want to supervise any more troublesome ethnic populations. It already owned one-sixth of all the land on earth and that land was rich in resources. It also had a huge ethnic population speaking a greater number of different languages than in any other place.

The US record was much worse in that it sent troops almost everywhere and fought an endless series of wars against others, most notably Korea, Panama, Vietnam, Nicaragua, El Salvador, Guatemala, Grenada, Haiti, The Dominican Republic, Cuba, Iraq, Serbia, Afghanistan, etc. However, the US wasn't interested in acquiring territory any more than was the USSR. Both countries had more than enough territory and also had many intractable problems with their disparate and sometimes hostile ethnic citizens. The conquest of more territory would have meant large occupation armies and the suppression of resistant populations. For the most part, the Soviet Union was merely defending its borders although it did occasionally give supplies and money to so-called socialist countries. The US was more aggressive and its excuse was that it was fighting a defensive war against evil communism, a communism that wasn't attacking.

What the US was really interested in was markets and a world it could dominate commercially. Capitalism is an extremely aggressive, proselytizing force very much like christianity. By contrast, communism was never the militant aggressor the US and other Western nations said it was. Indeed, the West *was* terrified of communism but not because it was a conquering military horde. This fear came from the dread that working people might be inspired by communism and that at-home citizens might revolt against capitalism. It was an idle and false fear. Communism never represented working people, not in any of the so-called communist countries or anywhere else. It was just another kind of capitalism. True enough, it was heretical and it arranged its commercial structures in configurations different from those in the West. However, the communist countries did not put the workingman in charge or enlarge his power and freedom at all. The communists were just capitalist predators pretending to be socialist lambs.

It's certainly true that communist leaders like Stalin, Mao, Pol Pot, and a few others were mass murderers but mostly they killed their own people and most of those victims were communists themselves or, at least, people who accepted communism or lived compliantly under it. The communist dictators did not, in fact, kill outsiders or very often attack them and they certainly did not attack the West, least of all Western anti-communists.

The anti-communist propaganda of that time was very peculiar. It claimed the communist countries were engaged in a furious assault against the West and were trying to conquer the world for communism. Since it was obvious to any sane observer that the Soviet Union was not attacking any American territory on earth or any US citizens, the anti-communists needed a rationale of some kind to support their claim that the United States was under attack. Thus, they made up the ridiculous canard of "internal subversion."

According to this claim, the Soviet Union was trying to conquer America by subverting its population, that is, by stealing away the loyalty of its citizens. In other words, large numbers of People in the United States were becoming traitors and servants of the Soviet Union. Communism was a threat because of its irresistible appeal to people in the United States and other Westerners. The only way the anti-communists could fight back was by attacking disloyal Americans. However, they couldn't find enough communists to support their thesis. Therefore, they broadened their attack against the population of the United States to include fellow travelers, com-symps, anti-anti-communists, fifth-amendment communists, pinkos, members of workers unions, those who supported civil rights, members of the Democratic Party, socialists, liberals, progressives, intellectuals (eggheads), feminists, pacifist christians, peaceniks, hippies, drug users, dentist who supported the use of fluoride, agnostics, atheists, quakers, unitarians, new ageists, witches, rock musicians, folk musicians, abstract artists, employees of the federal government, and indeed every American who was not a dedicated conservative.

In other words, according to the Republicans, the Soviet Union and China had a vast army of agents and spies inside the United States and all other Western nations and those wily traitors were working to overthrow Western governments by "force and violence." In fact, there were very, very few cases in which internal subversives used force and violence against their own countries' governments, any of their citizens, or any property at all. I know of no such violence in the United States ever but I might have missed something. In truth, there were millions of fanatical anti-communists in the United States and no more than a few hundred or perhaps a few thousand communists. (By contrast, in 1925, there were more than a million members of the KKK in the United States and literally tens of millions of sympathizers.) Furthermore, except for a handful of actual spies, most of these communists were passive and theoretical communists, people who never acted on their beliefs at all.

I can't remember any violence even by that handful of actual spies or any subversion either unless the theft of a few government secrets comes under that heading. Except for the Rosenbergs' theft of some minor details about the atom bomb, what they stole was so trivial that no one then and no one now can even remember it or describe it clearly. The triviality of the take doesn't lessen the guilt, of course, but the Soviet Union at that time was a valued ally, not an enemy. Throughout World War II, the US routinely shared information with its allies and, even when such sharing was not authorized, it was considered only an unwise indiscretion, not a crime. Much more unauthorized information was shared with England, with other Western countries, and later with Israel, Iraq, Saudi Arabia, and Pakistan than with the Soviet Union. Later, the Soviet Union became an enemy and many people were then fervently accused and their retroactive offenses were then hugely magnified long after the context had been obscured.

Of course, the McCarthyites and all conservative Republicans actually believed the United States was full of violent communist subversives but they had believed this ever since communism was first invented in the middle of the nineteenth century. It had always been a target of opportunity for them. Still, upon examination, it turned out that most of those they called subversives were Democratic opponents, liberals, those who supported civil rights for blacks and jews, and virtually all government employees. In addition, there were assorted librarians, charwomen, piano tuners, army dentists, movie actors and directors, song and dance men, scientists, abstract artists, and many writers. The list was almost endless. At times, it seemed that all Americans were subversives, including even some of the people who were attacking communism.

Communists in the US and in Western Europe were not uniformly evil and tyrannical. In fact, most of them worked for civil rights and the rights of working people. Perhaps some of them were insincere but it is quite clear that most Americans who associated themselves with the communist movement did so because they believed in civil rights and were appalled by the viciousness and tyranny of the failed capitalism they saw around them. Communism in the West was never a monolith and it was not a subversive force trying to overthrow democracy. The so-called communist dupes, fellow travelers, pinkos, etc. who were so viciously persecuted by the McCarthyites were very largely loyal and decent people out to democratize their country and increase the civil rights and the economic freedom of their fellow citizens. No doubt they were naive but they were also patriotic, idealistic, and innocent of any wrongdoing.

Internal communism was never of any importance in the United States. It never had any power and it did very little harm. It was not violent and it did not try to overthrow the government or subvert the American way of life. It was, in fact, rather pathetic. The only power and influence it ever had came from the vicious abuses of capitalism and the worst of those abuses, in this country, happened between the Civil War and the Great Conservative Depression during which time the owners and bosses took to assaulting and sometimes killing working people because they dared to ask for a tiny amount of decent and fair treatment. When working people tried to organize themselves into unions, the bosses took up arms against them and tried to intimidate, disempower, smear, and even kill them. Quite often, they were successful. They claimed always that they were attacking communists because they thought that anyone who believed that workers had rights was a communist.

The communists were often present in very small numbers during those confrontations but they neither caused the problems nor controlled the organizers and strikers. However cynical some of them may have been, they were mostly on the side of justice. In fact, most of them were sincere, decent people who foolishly signed onto a useless and rather silly ideology but they did not deserve to be insulted, assaulted, or killed. The owners used the presence of these few communists as an excuse for their violence against workers and their unions; and Republican politicians used the very existence of communism as a reason to spread hatred against the rights of working people and against all progressive ideas, including those in the constitution. Thus, the real fathers of violence in the United States were the anti-communists, not the communists.

I don't think that any American communist ever tried to overthrow the government of the United States by force and violence. I don't know of any violent act ever by a communist against the US government or any organized force dedicated to such violence. In fact, there is little evidence that any American communist ever even advocated violent overthrow except perhaps in some rhetorical flourish about a utopian workers' revolution at some vague point in the dim and unplanned future. However, there have been real acts of violence, threats of violence, and subversions against the government and us all by the conservatives.

For a long time, the South has been full of lynchings, bombings, riots, uprisings, and violent plots against government entities and officials. Across the country, the so-called militias have often resorted to gunfire and bombings and have issued loud threats of violence against the government and against specific officials in the government, including lately Bill Clinton and his family. Right-wing radio talkers have all but pleaded for violent acts against officials, some of them going so far as to provide instructions about just where to shoot Clinton and members of his administration and family. The racists wanted to hang Earl Warren and other members of the Supreme Court and regularly urged, and resorted to, violent resistance to integration, busing, voting by blacks, and affirmative action.

The christians have been bombing abortion clinics at the urging and with the support of Henry Hyde and many other Republicans; they have murdered doctors and medical personnel and, on occasion, federal and state officials. William Buckley screamed hysterically for the castration of Bill Clinton and Jesse Helms called for the military in North Carolina to attack and presumably assassinate him.

Ann Coulter, a loony right-wing Republican, also demanded Clinton's assassination and repeatedly called for the killing of American liberals and the slaughter of muslims. Timothy McVeigh, a homegrown terrorist aroused by the Republican and christian fundamentalist hatred of Bill Clinton and the democratic government of the United States, bombed the federal building in Kansas City and murdered 168 government employees and members of their families. Eric Rudolph, inspired by Republican and christian anti-abortion fanatics, bombed numerous public places and murdered innocent citizens in a rage against the reproductive freedom guaranteed by federal law and court rulings.

Watergate as well as the Iran and Contra scandals were, in fact, violent criminal conspiracies against democratic government by conservative government officials in league with subversive elements in the Republican Party and in its many un-American adjuncts. The impeachment of Bill Clinton was just the end piece of a series of lawless conservative plots, plots that included the most incredible personal vilification ever known in this country and also included subversive efforts to remove him from office, in any way and by any means necessary, no matter how violent or criminal.

The impeachment itself involved acts of coercion, blackmail, and bribery by Republican Tom De Lay as well as the dishonest use of false allegations in raw FBI files improperly supplied by Kenneth Starr and Louis J. Freeh as well as by Bear Bryant, Freeh's fanatical, Clinton-hating assistant. Then, in the presidential election of 2000, De Lay sent criminal thugs to Florida to assault poll workers and stop an honest and objective recount ordered by the Florida Supreme Court. This treasonous subversion certainly rescued the Bush family fix, as the ultraconservatives on the US Supreme Court wouldn't have dared to abort the election with Gore ahead in the count. This was an out-and-out coup carried out by the Republican Party.

Only a year or so ago, an apparently-drunk Charlton Heston appeared on television before a mob of gun lovers where he grabbed a rifle and shook it above his head while screaming out his hatred for Democrats in office and while urging the mob on as they shook their fists and raged uncontrollably against democratic government and anyone who dared to think of regulating their guns. Heston has said that the so-called "right to bear arms" is precious because it would allow him and his gun chums to march on and overthrow the government if it dares to do anything that gun owners and other "patriots" don't like.

In just the same way, Attorney General John Ashcroft has also hinted at the overthrow of the government of the United States by force and violence and has promised to personally interpret and apply the second amendment of the Constitution in accord with the wishes of the extremist gun lovers and without any regard for the rule of law or any court decision whatever.

With his racist employment of the repressive "Patriot Act," Ashcroft has also established the elements of a police state in this country and has created a climate of fear and hate that is on display every day against journalists, entertainers, librarians, book readers, legal immigrants, and just anyone who criticizes or disagrees with George Bush in any way. I have never heard of any American communist behaving like this, ever threatening blatantly to overthrow the government, ever subverting the Constitution, ever stealing an election, ever shooting anyone, ever throwing any bomb.

If communism had been a race or a nationality, the conservatives would be guilty of a vast genocide, perhaps the worst in human history. The enormous hatred of communists inspired in the United States by the McCarthyites would be disgusting to everyone if it had been directed against any other group of people. This hatred was required of US citizens as a proof of patriotic loyalty and even religious morality. It was an article of fanatical belief that every communist and everyone who could be associated with communism in any way, however strained and false, was absolutely evil and demonic. Anyone accused of any form of communism was automatically guilty. It was so evil a force in the minds of the anti-communists that just being accused was proof enough; after all, if your anti-communist hatred was intense enough, then no one could accuse *you* of being a communist, a dupe, or a sympathizer.

In short, it was a sin, a crime, and a treason not to hate communism with all of your being, enough to convince everyone of your deep desire to attack, decimate, spit upon, and kill anyone accused or suspected. Active and violent hatred is what the anti-communists warriors demanded of everyone, hatred without reservation or equivocation, hatred without discrimination or proof of guilt, hatred based on the fervor of faith alone, murderous and merciless hatred, genocidal hatred.

And so it went for fifty years. The Republicans fed on communism with great hunger during that time and got tremendously fat politically off of their own propaganda. Millions of people in the United States believed most of what they said and, in addition to voting for their wonderful patriotism, gave them trillions of dollars to fight communism with. Anti-communism was a terrific business and it enriched many and made still more famous and morally upright. Even today, the US military is still hugely bloated at least partly because the conservative politicians and the generals are afraid that communism will resurrect itself, perhaps this time in the guise of world-terrorism or muslim fanaticism.

No, anti-communism isn't dead. In the 1992 presidential election, George H. W. Bush, James Baker, and their operatives called Bill Clinton a communist and tried to fake paperwork to make it seem that, like Oswald, he had traveled to Moscow and Prague to renounce his citizenship and join the Soviets. Then, conservative judges and prosecutors conspired to cover up the facts so as to protect the Bush family from punishment for its own crimes and treasons. As for all of those millions of internal subversives, they seem to have withered away or converted into something else. You can be sure the Republicans will revive them when they need them again in future elections or to justify still greater military spending.

So what if you can prove that, in the distant past, somebody was a communist? It doesn't mean anything. If you want to become an anti-communist hero, you have to prove that such a person was an actual spy and a foreign agent, that he or she actually did something criminal and subversive. In the days of capitalist failure, people often called themselves communists or socialists or even signed up as actual members of the Communist Party for all kinds of reasons, some of them noble and patriotic. The Great Conservative Depression caused enormous suffering throughout the world. The capitalists were responsible for this suffering and deprivation and, when the economic catastrophe arrived, they hunkered down and intensified their abuse of the poor, the hungry, the homeless, and the jobless. As a direct result, many suffered great agony and some died. That is why large numbers of people became disgusted with capitalism and became socialists or even communists. It was not only understandable, it was inevitable and, under the circumstances, maybe even moral. It was not evil and it did not make those who joined up into traitors and enemies of the state.

All of this rebellion against capitalism frightened and outraged the owners and bosses and they swore they would hunt down and destroy every last communist on earth. Sad to say, they defined communism so as to include progressives, socialists, liberals, moderates, secularists, relativists, trade unionists, humanists, evolutionists, anarchists, democrats, ad infinitum. From that day to this one, the conservatives, especially those in the Republican Party, have been engaged in a vast campaign of accusation and retribution. Everyone who flirted with communism for even a second, everyone who spoke a single word in favor of working people or the poor, everyone who believed in and worked for civil rights, everyone who joined a union or opposed a war, everyone who believed in actual democracy was the enemy and had to be punished. The hate campaign continues even now, after the demise of actually existing Communism. The fanaticism and viciousness of the Republicans is unequaled in US history and there is no question that anti-communism was, in fact, a fascist attack against democracy in the guise of patriotism and state security.

Now, these exact same things are happening all over again. George W. Bush is the new McCarthy and anti-terrorism is the new anti-communism; and, unfortunately for us all, the people of the United States are once again supporting the demagoguery, hatred, and violence of the Republicans including brutal wars against innocent and defenseless civilians who have never threatened or attacked the United States in any way at all.

CHAPTER 4. THE FASCIST ORIENTATION OF THE REPUBLICAN PARTY

To Republicans, the communists were leftist totalitarians but the fascists were noble authoritarians marching steadfastly toward democracy. My view is different. I think that communism and fascism were nearly identical, that they were both rightist and narrowly conservative. Stalin and Hitler were almost the same man. They had personalities and styles that were somewhat different but both lusted after absolute personal power; and they both imposed their murderous programs on others with no care for the welfare of their citizens. Each wanted the exact same thing: an empire in which the people had to be subservient and utterly loyal to the reigning party and its leaders.

Each believed in a kind of darwinian eugenics that they thought would finally result in the emergence of an aryan "superman" in the one case and a marxist "new man" in the other. Copying the American eugenics model, Hitler sterilized hundreds of thousands and killed millions more all in the name of "purifying" the race. Stalin tried to shape his formless mass through a policy of repression and intimidation, and he killed those who resisted or were not compliant enough. Neither was socialist, liberal, egalitarian, or relativist in any sense whatever. In fact, they were both state capitalists and they were both moral conservatives who believed in a severe puritanical obedience to their political order.

Even those Republicans who say that they reject the racism and elitism of their party nevertheless embrace the social darwinist and eugenicist dogma that has always been at the heart of the conservative philosophy that dominates the Republican Party from end to end. In particular, the beloved "free enterprise" economic model that props up the conservative movement is social darwinist and eugenicist. This model is based on the idea that competitive success is proof of superiority and that those who fail to make money under its rules are unfit and deserve their poverty and misery. A corollary is that government mustn't be allowed to help the unfit because such interference retards the system and rewards the undeserving. Their failures purify the system and make it work properly. The unfit must be sacrificed to the god of free enterprise. Anything else is immoral.

Despite their apparent differences, capitalism, communism, and conservatism are all fascist systems and they are all based on the social darwinist ideas of Herbert Spencer complemented by the eugenicist ideas of Francis Galton. Each of these isms comes from a belief in the triumph of a superior class raised up either by capitalist competition or by the rise of the proletariat. Race and economic status have always played a role in this mix, always to the detriment of people of color and poor people.

Make no mistake about it, the conservative ideology is very much the same as the ideology of Adolph Hitler and, though it is not as obvious, also the ideology of Joseph Stalin. Both dictators believed in the rule of a particular segment of the population, that is, a superior class. For Hitler, it was mostly racial, that is, the Aryans were superior to everybody else. For Stalin, it was "the new man" of communism, the superior creature who was supposed to rise up out of the "dictatorship of the proletariat" and establish a new nirvana of economic equality. Stalin saw himself and his closest followers as forerunners of the superior "new man" and all others as formless clay to be molded by "socialist" competition into proper forms and classes.

Stalin too was a kind of Lamarckian eugenicist. He believed that a weird kind of darwinism (Lysenkoism) would transform workers into an entirely different and better kind of race or class. Instead of thinking that individual human nature was genetically determined, Stalin and his communists thought that whole classes were determined, and fixed, by something like a genetic force. In other words, since the owning class could not be changed, it had to be eliminated. Thus, Stalin's case for fascist tyranny, based on the fixity of classes, was little different, in consequence, from Hitler's case based on Aryan genetic superiority. Both Hitler's superman and Stalin's new man were elite overmen destined, by historical necessity, to stand above others and to rule over them.

Stalin's system was an upside down version of Hitler's eugenics. It was the upper classes that were rigidly inferior and they could not be changed. Their inferiority was not so much in the blood as in the air and in their irreversible conditioning by their privilege and wealth. Lysenko, Stalin's nutty chief biologist, babbled on and on about changing potatoes into watermelons through natural selection and the Stalinists saw this process as a way for them to produce the new man of communism by a severe conditioning imposed from above and based on "science" and the magic of Stalin's tyrannical intuition.

Hitler and Stalin both hated jews and blacks and their bigotry came from the fascist model and its system of competitive struggle based on the superiority of the few and the servility of the many. The connection between all of these pieces of capitalism (including communism or state capitalism to call it what it really was) and racial and class hatred is clear. Competitive struggle and the rise of the fit to power are at the heart of all of these fascist ideologies. All three of them put some above others and they all persecute the excluded.

The extreme values of the European and American conservatives of today fit like gloves onto the tyrannical hands of these two maniacal oppressors. Of course, Western conservatism has always been connected closely — very closely — to the nazi movement being almost identical to it in its hatred of what it calls permissiveness, moral weakness, relativism, tolerance, civil rights, gender equality, indeed all equality, all democratism, and any expression of liberalistic or Enlightenment ideals.

Obviously, there are distinct and substantial differences between the Republican Party and the Nazi Party. However, I think that both of these political forces share a similar belief system and a similar and negative attitude toward democratic liberalism. I think that this common belief system can be fairly described as conservative and fascist. I think as well that the Germans, the Americans, and the Soviets were and are all three totalitarian to differing degrees. And I think that all three are intensely nationalistic, militaristic, and dominionist.

Within the United States, the Republicans have not engaged in the mass killing of its own people, as was the case in Hitler's Germany and Stalin's Soviet Union. Hitler's aggressions against other countries certainly were more extreme than those of the Soviet Union. In fact, Stalin did not try to conquer the world as Hitler plainly did. Indeed, after the Second World War, Stalin did not attack any Western country, certainly not the United States. His aggressions were carefully limited to interventions in the countries on his own border, his so-called satellites. Militarily, Stalin was extremely cautious. His militarism was defensive in nature. However, his at-home aggressions against his own people continued unabated.

Because it is so well disguised by politicians, journalists, and historians, the US record is less obvious than is the record of the Germans and the Soviets. However, that does not mean it is less aggressive or violent. This aggression has been shared by Republicans and Democrats alike but not equally so. The Republicans are forever attacking the Democrats for being weak and timid on security matters and for lacking resolve when it comes to attacking our enemies, that is, communists, terrorists, and other such foreigners and "traitors." Thus, it is not unfair to assign major responsibility to the Republican Party for our many military and economic attacks against other peoples. Overseas adventurism is mostly a Republican disease.

Republicans regularly employ aggressive military and economic power and regard such behavior as patriotic and nobly christian. They want to impose their will on everyone else. They think that they are good and loyal and that those of us who oppose them or fail to support them to the fullest are evil and disloyal. In their political campaigns, they claim that their Democratic opponents are not only weak and cowardly but deliberately on the side of criminals, communists, terrorists, and morally defective citizens on welfare. To Republicans, the failure of others to be just like them is a sin and a crime.

As I noted elsewhere, the Republicans have not engaged in mass killings at home but their punitive moralism and their predatory commercialism have resulted in enormous suffering, misery, deprivation, injury, and sometimes death. They also regularly engage in police state tactics that can only be described as contemptuous of citizen's rights. And they use fear and hate against one or another ism to arouse the public so as to gain their support for their repressions and punishments of dissenters and political opponents. These are fascist tactics.

It was no accident that Hitler and Stalin became allies for a time. They might have melded together permanently and they could also have easily absorbed Western and US conservatism except for Stalin's pretense that he believed in the rights of working people and except for his efforts to substitute communist worship for christian worship. The alliance ended quickly because Hitler wanted it all for himself, because he had always regarded the Slavs as an inferior race, and because he regarded any form of real or claimed socialism as an obstacle to his political dominance of Europe. Though they pretend otherwise today, Western conservative leaders loved Hitler because they agreed with his philosophy; they would have loved Stalin too except for his anti-christian bias. Most certainly, if he had not been anti-christian, they would have seen that Stalin's rhetoric about the rise of the workingman was phony and they would have ignored it. After all, the conservatives themselves — in their political campaigns but not in private — have always pretended to a phony populism that they represent to the people as "democratic" and even "freedom-loving."

Nevertheless, it was a handful of naive marxist utopians, claiming to be leftists, who, at first, identified most closely with Stalin and the Soviet communists. This was because they hated Hitler, his nazism, his racism, and his anti-semitism and because they believed the communists' claim that they supported civil rights and the rights of working people. Most of these fellow-travelers abandoned the Soviet Union after its alliance with Hitler but a tiny number continued to salute Soviet communism without ever seeing that it had no genuine socialist ideals and was, in fact, a carbon copy of the nazi ideology complete with racist and anti-semitic biases and a strong contempt for the rights of working people.

In fact, there were very few of these fellow travelers in the United States and they had no importance whatever except as targets of opportunity for the Republicans who used them as foils in their anti-communist attack against the New Deal, the Democratic Party, and the democratic government of the United States. It was this dishonest targeting of a trivial movement that allowed the Republican Party to regain its political power and to keep it throughout the last half of the twentieth century and into the twenty first century.

In the United States and Western Europe, the anti-communist movement grew out of the pro-nazi movement. In the United States and England, World War II quieted Hitler's supporters and fellow travelers. When England and the United States went to war against Hitler, the large number of nazi sympathizers in those two countries fell silent for fear of being charged with treason. However, they retained their love for Hitler's ideology and continued to feel (and sometimes said in unguarded moments) that the English and the Americans were fighting on the wrong side. After the war, they came out of the closet and resumed their fascist activities but, of course, most of them abandoned the defense of Hitler himself when it was revealed that he had committed vast atrocities in the name of fascism.

Hitler was indefensible for practical political reasons but his philosophy continued to thrive in the conservative movement and had an especially welcome home in the Republican Party. Even now, more than fifty years after the war, there are still plenty of conservatives who lament that the United States fought against Hitler and on the side of the communists. More and more since then, the Republican Party has moved ever rightward until it has now today become fascist from end to end.

The historical parallel between the Nazi Party and the Republican Party is clear. The nazis themselves started the Reichstag fire and then arrested and jailed a mentally retarded communist and made him their scapegoat. They used this incident to enflame the German people against communism and, with popular support, pushed through emergency legislation (Germany's version of the Patriot Act) to empower Hitler and to prosecute their political opponents in Germany on the pretext that they were communist collaborators and subversives. The below quotation is from a review in *The Nation* on February 16, 2004 by Russell Jacoby of *The Red Millionaire* by Sean McMeekin:

> This act of incendiarism is the most monstrous act of terrorism so far carried out,' reported a 1933 Berlin newspaper. Hitler had been chancellor of Germany for less than a month when an arsonist torched the Reichstag, the German parliamentary building. For the nazis, who blamed the communists for the fire, the conflagration proved a godsend, an excuse to accelerate their mastery of Germany. Nazi minister Herman Goring did not waste time. 'The Commu-

nist deputies must be hanged this very night.' The following day civil liberties were suspended. Within the month, Parliament, purged of Communists and surrounded by storm troopers, gathered in an opera house and approved the so-called Enabling Act, the legal legislation that effectively delivered power to Hitler."

This is just what the Republicans did in the United States. Alger Hiss was their carefully chosen scapegoat. Hiss may well have been a communist, or at least a fellow traveler, and he probably did give some trivial papers to Whittaker Chambers for transmission to Soviet agents. However, the Hiss collaboration with Chambers was a long-past and unimportant transgression, one that was out of context and unworthy of the intense public reaction that took place after the war at the instigation of the Republican Party. Hiss had given minor information to an ally in the fight against Hitler because he thought the Soviets were anti-nazi and on the side of the United States in a titanic life-and-death struggle against fascism as indeed they were.

In truth, the Republicans were attacking Hiss and the Democrats *because* they had worked with the Soviets and the communists against Hitler and the nazis during the war. The intensity of their outrage came from their long-suppressed love of Hitler and his program, not because Hiss had damaged the United States in any serious way. Ironically, the only really important and intensely dedicated US communist during this time, and perhaps ever, was Whittaker Chambers. At most, Alger Hiss was a casual, intermittent, and ineffectual collaborator, nothing more.

The Republicans — especially Nixon and McCarthy — hugely exaggerated the Hiss matter and used it to enflame the people of the United States and to attack the Democratic Party as the party of communism and treason. They continued to use communism as an all-purpose accusation against Democrats — liberals especially — in nearly every election for the next fifty years. As late as 1992, George H. W. Bush labeled Clinton as a communist traitor and concocted a corrupt conspiracy, with James Baker and Attorney General Barr, in which they actually filed charges of treason against Clinton just before the election.

Their criminal plot failed only because a Democratic congressman got wind of the conspiracy and exposed it. Even then and throughout his time in office, the Republicans continued to call Clinton a communist traitor, a financial crook, a serial rapist, and a multiple murderer. They continue to employ those fabrications to this very day and the conservative media continues to spread those lies far and wide. This behavior was and is quite clearly fascist and treasonous.

And so, for more than half a century, anti-communism was the Republican Party's dominant ideology but it really wasn't anti-communist at all. Anti-communism was merely the Republican mask. Behind that mask was a virulent hatred of liberalism and democracy, two values that had been embraced by the New Deal and the Democratic Party of Franklin Roosevelt. Because Roosevelt had reshaped the government making it more responsive to the wants and needs of the people than ever before, the Republicans knew they would have to attack the federal government itself in order to discredit and undermine it in the interest of the fascist (corporatist) power they wanted once more to impose on the people. Therefore, they accused the entire democratic government of the United States of being massively communistic and treasonous. This manifested itself as McCarthyism.

McCarthyism was and still is the central political tactic of the Republican Party. It is being used right now in support of George W. Bushes' misdirected and mostly-fake attack against terrorism. Terrorism has now become an all-purpose excuse for attacking the democratic traditions and institutions of the US government and the patriotism of liberals and members of the Democratic Party. We have been here before and the picture is even uglier now than it was in the earlier days of McCarthyism.

The Nixon, Reagan, and Bush administrations always had a two-track policy toward external communism: friendship toward and detente with the two large communist dictatorships and violent assault and perpetual war against small countries that they conveniently called communist. More often than not, those small countries were weakly or democratically socialist and not communist at all. Anti-communism never was the pure "crusade" the Republicans made it out to be. Their charges were driven by partisan political motives, that is, their hidden purpose was to put the Republican Party in power and to keep it there.

It was no accident that Nixon and Reagan were the first two US presidents to visit China and the Soviet Union; and it was no accident that they established close and loving relationships with the communist leaders of those two countries. Communism was simply the external enemy the Republicans needed to arouse the people of the United States, and, to this very day their electoral successes have depended on accusatory attacks against the Democrats and the government.

The September 11th terrorist attack gave the Republicans a new weapon to use against the Democrats and they gleefully and obscenely greeted the attack and turned it into a jingoistic celebration of US military power and their own political ascendancy. And so, anti-terrorism instantly became their welcome substitute for anti-communism and it is being used once again to accuse Democrats and liberals of treason and fellow traveling. The Republicans always need an external enemy and they will say and do anything to identify their domestic political foes as the enemy of the people.

This time oil plays a large part in the Republican attack strategy because of the oil ideology of the Bush and Cheney families and their longtime, profitable, and very close alliance with certain of the oil dictatorships, such as Saudi Arabia, Kuwait, and Pakistan, that were, in fact, largely responsible for the September 11th attack. Even though he is far more extreme and fascistic than his father, the second Bush is not much different from the first one in his quest for a New World Order under the Republican Party's total control.

Ultimately, it has to be said that the right-wing fascist ideology included both Hitler and Stalin, both nazism and communism; and it has to be said that Western and American conservatism — including its self-proclaimed anti-communism — was also a part of the fascist system. Liberalism and democratic progressivism stood and still stand against this axis of right-wing totalitarianism. Today's capitalist rampage is but the latest attack against democratic government and the liberal belief in a modicum of economic equality. Fascism has always included corporatism as a part of its definition and it is totalitarian corporatism (globalism) that rages about the world now trying to grab title to absolutely all of the property in existence including the land, the air, the water, and even the actual bodies, minds, wants, needs, and labor of human beings.

These globalists are determined to commodify and rule everything imaginable through business arrangements that supplant governments of all kinds. The globalists are using their vast treasuries and their trade agreements to this end and lately the US military, in its anti-terrorist guise, has been assigned the duty of subduing the entire world in the name of "democratic capitalism" and state security by which the Bushites mean the absolute dominance of their brands of totalitarian capitalism and repressive christianity through systems of "preemptive" attack abroad and "faith-based" coercions at home.

An essay of November 21, 2002, by Colin McGinn in the *New York Review* described the philosopher Karl Popper's three-step process for carrying out scientific investigation which claims that science (and indeed all learning) proceeds by trial and error: "first there is the problem; then there are the attempted solutions; finally there is the elimination of those solutions" until only the most likely remain. Thus, for Popper, "science consists of conjectures that have not (yet) been rejected, not of accepted facts..." derived from dogma or authority. "Truth" (whether scientific or political) is always tentative and must be forever testable, reproducible, and falsifiable, that is, it must remain open to criticism and the possibility of rejection. In politics, the "open society...invites and encourages critical discussion: there are no inviolable ideologies, like Marxism, only a plurality of perspectives each subject to critical evaluation.... Hitler and Stalin were, among other things, dogmatic ideologues in the grip of theories they made no effort to falsify, and they produced governments in which criticism and peaceful replacement of a government were not tolerated."

Popper's model rejects the communist and nazi projects but it also, just as much, rejects the absolutism of fundamentalist, traditionalist, and orthodoxist religious and political systems such as those that animate the Republican Party. The commonality of the nazi, the communist, and the conservative systems of belief are obvious.

Part Two. Imperialism in the New World

For a long time, the European countries were violent aggressors who fought one another for control of the whole world. Those predators left their teeth marks everywhere. The christian religion was a part of their aggression. It supplied them with what they claimed was a noble purpose: the spread of their god's word and the dominance of their civilization. They thought they were superior to everyone else and that it was their duty to "educate" and convert the primitive savages and the heathen. They thought they were morally justified in killing others and in destroying their despised civilizations. No one had a right to resist them or practice any religion or any politics different from theirs.

The American continents became battlegrounds for the noble endeavors of the Europeans. North America was contested by the English, the French, the Spanish, and, to a lesser extent, the Russians. The English won those wars but the others left their marks behind. Finally, the English colonies in North America fought and won a war of independence against England and its divine king. It was the first great democratic victory against royalism and aristocracy.

Unfortunately, the new "Americans" then continued the predations begun by their European forebears. In short order, they filled up the entire continent and pushed the native Indians nearly to extinction. The Southern colonies continued the racist slavery of their fathers and multiplied its practice into a way of life. Slavery was a means of establishing a rigid two-class system: the white owners and the enslaved blacks. Of course, a third or middle class of white slave drivers was also necessary to square the circle of that tyranny.

The principles of the American Revolution clashed with the aggressions of the old order with regard to Indian extermination and African slavery. It was the liberals who came to oppose racism and national aggression, at home and abroad. The great liberal documents that justified and enabled the American Revolution became a blue print for the whole world's revolt against and disgust with the ancient tyrannies of kings and other despots. I refer to the Declaration of Independence, the Bill of Rights, and, later on, the Emancipation Proclamation and the Thirteenth, Fourteenth, and Fifteenth amendments to the United States constitution. Then, the Nineteenth amendment advanced female citizenship by establishing the right to vote. Clearly, these documents did not go far enough.

Today the conservatives, still representing the principles of the old royal and aristocratic order, are on the march and they are rolling back the democratic advances of this nation's revolt against unjust authority. They cannot reestablish slavery or female subservience (to their regret), but they can advance American hegemony. They believe that they can defeat democracy at home by attacking the "rights" of citizens in the name of patriotic duty, biblical doctrine, and obedience to their authority; and they think they can conquer the world in the name of anti-communism, anti-terrorism, or any other vague enemy they are able to invent as an excuse for their roll back of the sovereignty of others.

And so, the battle between liberal democracy and conservative authority still rages. In America, sadly, the conservatives are winning but, ironically, all of Europe is now more-or-less democratic and anti-conservative. There are democratic and liberal forms elsewhere as well and the rumblings of democratic liberalism can be heard, sometimes in warped forms, in every neighborhood. Even in the muslim despotisms, the people yearn for more representative governance but, unfortunately, George W. Bush is threatening, attacking, torturing, and slaughtering them in the name of his perverted idea of democracy. He thinks that democracy is rule by invading armies and grasping corporations. Under his hand, Republican America has become a great satan to the rest of the world. Bush says that god is directing his hand and telling him to attack and kill. Lately, with just about every breath, he is using the words "freedom" and "democracy" to mask his predations and assaults. In his hands, America has become vastly more anti-democratic, more totalitarian, and more imperialistic than it has ever been.

The observations, assessments and assertions made above are abundantly illustrated and documented in the excerpts from books, newspapers, and magazines provided in the following chapters.

CHAPTER 5. US IMPERIALISM

1. "The annexation of Texas in 1845 and the Mexican War that almost immediately followed marked a sea change in American foreign relations.... In his 1845 message to Congress, Polk said: 'It is well known to the American people and to all nations that this government has never interfered with the relations subsisting between other governments. We have never made ourselves parties to their wars or their alliances; we have not sought their territories by conquest; we have not mingled with parties in their domestic struggles; and believing our own form of government to be the best, we have never attempted to propagate it by intrigues, by diplomacy, or by force.' This was generally true, at least until Polk's own administration. The federal government was committed to expansion through peaceful means.... But until annexation of Texas and the war with Mexico, it had never conquered territory from foreign powers....

"With the Mexican War, the United States moved from individual to national imperialism."

— Benjamin Moser, essay, *Harper's Magazine*, August 2004.

2. "It was not until the Spanish-American War in 1898 that the nation...acquired its first protectorate (Cuba) and its first overseas colonies, most notably the Philippines....The United States also deemed it necessary to intervene in Cuba on several occasions in the succeeding quarter century to restore order and keep friendly regimes in power. With the advent of the so-called Roosevelt Corollary to the Monroe Doctrine in 1905, the United States began to police the entire Caribbean Basin — a rule that led to interventions up until the 1930s in Nicaragua, the Dominican Republic, Haiti, and other nations.

"The Wilson era was a harbinger of the foreign policy that would emerge in the 1940s. Likewise, America's wartime experience suggested the domestic consequences of intervening abroad. Economic planning, military conscription, and strict censorship became normal features of society....Pacifists, draft opponents, and critics of US involvement in the war were assaulted, intimidated, and imprisoned. Sedition legislation made even mild criticism of government policy a risky venture.

"Most recently, the 'Reagan Doctrine' pledges the United States to assist anti-Soviet insurgent forces seeking to overthrow incumbent governments in several Third World countries. The contrast with the refusal to aid liberal republican movements during the 19th century could scarcely be more striking....The United States has tarnished its image as a symbol of liberty by providing political, economic, and military support for an assortment of 'friendly' Third World dictatorships.

"John Quincy Adams, who warned long ago of a corruption of values if we abandoned our commitment to peaceful neutrality (said), 'The fundamental maxims of (America's) policy would insensibly change from liberty to force.... She might become dictatress of the world. She would be no longer the ruler of her own spirit.'"

— Ted Galen Carpenter, article, *Reason*, August/September 1987.

3. "Although the war in Vietnam is the usual metric used to compare what is today occurring in Iraq, the US war in the Philippines at the turn of the twentieth century is a far more appropriate point of comparison. The United States occupied the Philippines on exquisitely false pretexts, as President William KcKinley's lovely, godstruck thoughts to visiting clergymen on why the United States had moved into the archipelago reveal: 'I am not ashamed to tell you, gentlemen, that I went down on my knees and prayed to Almighty god for light and guidance on more than one night.' God told McKinley that 'there was nothing left for us to do but to take them all, and to educate the Filipinos, and uplift and civilize and Christianize them, and by god's grace do the best we could by them...and then I went to bed, and went to sleep, and slept soundly.' The Bush doctrine, a century foretold. (The Philippines, incidentally, had been Christianized already.)...

"The war in the Philippines was won through several tactics. 'In this country,' William Howard Taft, McKinley's appointed head of the Philippine Commission, argued, 'it is politically most important that Filipinos should suppress Filipino disturbances and arrest Filipino outlaws.' Another tactic was brutality. As one US general had it, 'An eight p.m. curfew went into effect. Any Filipino found on the streets after that hour would be shot on sight. Whenever an American soldier was killed, a native prisoner would be chosen by lot and executed. A young lieutenant witness to these atrocities later wrote, 'The American soldier's officially sanctioned wrath is a thing so ugly and dangerous that it would take a Kipling to describe him.' ...More than 4,000 American soldiers had been killed in combat, thousands more perished of disease, and close to 200,000 Filipino civilians were left dead. As a US senator said on the Senate floor, 'What has been the practical statesmanship which comes from your ideals and sentimentality? You have wasted six hundred millions of treasure. You have sacrificed nearly ten thousand American lives....You have slain uncounted thousands of the people you desire to benefit.... Your practical statesmanship has succeeded in converting a people...into sullen and irreconcilable enemies, possessed of a hatred which centuries cannot eradicate.

— Tom Bissell, essay, *Harper's Magazine*, January 2006.

4. "Wrapping themselves in a rhetorical cloak of democracy and freedom, critics of President Jimmy Carter's human rights focus pursue a curious logic that leads them to support governments that deny democracy and abuse freedom. They insist on drawing a distinction for foreign-policy purposes between 'authoritarian' countries that are seen as friendly toward the United States and 'totalitarian' states seen as hostile....Sadly, this specious distinction, rooted in America's former UN representative Jeanne Kirkpatrick's November 1979 Commentary article 'Dictatorships and Double Standards,' became a central element of the new policy set forth at the start

of the Reagan Administration....The implication that such a distinction provides a basis for condoning terror and brutality if committed by authoritarian governments friendly to the United States is mind-boggling."

— From an article by former Secretary of State Cyrus R. Vance in *Foreign Policy*, Summer 1986, cited by *The Washington Post*, July 1, 1986.

5. "President Alberto Fujimori's 'auto-coup' put an end to democracy in Peru.... Fujimori bought the 'end of history' thesis where it concerns liberal democracy coupled with a market economy. His problem was how to privatize the state-owned sector....His policy aims could only be loudly applauded by Americans.

"This predicament is hardly peculiar to Peru. El Salvador, Guatemala, Nicaragua and the Philippines are all struggling with the same problems. So are East Europe and the old Soviet Union. They have highly statist economies that need privatization.

"How should the West react to emerging dictators in these states? If they are committed to privatization and building a strong and honest state administration, they could create favorable grounds for democracy a few years hence. If they fall back to statist solutions instead of continuing with marketization, they will make future transitions more difficult.

"In a word, if the West is faced with a series of emerging dictatorships, it needs to discriminate among them. A few might be the best hope for a future return to democracy."

— William E. Odum, article, *The Washington Post*, April 12, 1992.

6. "In 1983, in the village of Soccos, Peru, people were celebrating a forthcoming marriage when a contingent of police burst upon them. Women were raped, and then killed. The elderly and children were lined up and machine-gunned. 'When I was escaping, I passed a whole lot of bodies lying around. Women had their breasts and tongues cut out. Some had poles stuck in their vaginas...' narrated a survivor, whose son was among the dead. When she and other survivors traveled to Humanga to denounce the killings, one of them was killed.

"Sixty-nine people, including children and elderly, were rounded up on August 14, 1985, in the village of Acomarca, then massacred and burned by soldiers under the command of Sub-Tenant Telmo Huartdo who was promoted to captain during the Fujimori regime (1990–2000).

"These were among seven of the testimonies presented to the Peruvian Commission of Truth and Reconciliation....

"From 1980-2000, as many as 9,000 people were 'disappeared,' close to 30,000 were killed, and over 1,000,000 were displaced from their communities, many of which were completely destroyed....

"Only after Fujimori fled to Japan in November 2000 has information surfaced alleging that State forces, committed a majority of atrocities and human rights violations. In 2001, The Defensoria del Pueblo — an autonomous government institution — studied 5,000 cases of 'disappeared' persons, concluding that State forces or State-supported paramilitary were responsible for almost 98 percent.

— Graham Russell, report, *Z Magazine*, June 2002.

7. "The concept was that the president (Reagan) had the inherent power to suspend any provision of the written constitution when he decided it was in the national interest. They wanted to move in the direction of full-scale oppression. This concept of inherent power was first developed by William Rehnquist."

— Arthur Kinoy, Rutgers professor, interview, *The Progressive*, October 1992.

8. "The Miami Herald ran a front-page story that said Oliver North had been assigned to the White House (under Reagan) to work in FEMA on the development of an executive order that was to say, 'In the event of military activity by the United States in Central America or anywhere in the world, if a significant number of people objected, 1. The Constitution of the United States shall be suspended, 2. A military government shall be established, 3. The courts shall be suspended and military tribunals established, 4. Camps shall be established where any person who disagrees shall be detained.'"

— Arthur Kinoy, Rutgers professor, interview, *The Progressive*, October 1992.

9. "The United States is now a military form of state capitalism in which top managers of the military forces and their economy have dominant power — economic, political, and military. George Bush is now CEO of that system, with the tacit and active agreement of the two main political parties. The US military-economy management system is monopolistic, centralized, and authoritarian."

— *The Progressive*, interview with Seymour Melman, February 1992.

10. "Katha Pollitt says, 'We have ROTC on campus, Junior ROTC in the high schools....' Here in Chicago, at least, at my cousin's public school, one can join ROTC as early as the sixth grade."

— Matthew Dobrovolskis, letter to the editor, *The Nation*, August 2/9, 2004.

11. "Every ten years or so, the United States needs to pick up some crappy little country and throw it against the wall, just to show the world we mean business."

— Michael Ledeen (Iran-Contra operative, consultant to Secretary of State Alexander Haig, and now resident scholar in the Freedom Chair at the American Enterprise Institute) — cited by Lewis H. Lapham, Notebook, *Harper's Magazine*, June 2003.

12. "There is a need for 'breaking the law from time-to-time' and a need to change the law 'that prohibits American officials from working with murderers' and a need to change the 'executive order, dating to 1975, prohibiting any official of the American government to conduct, order, encourage, and facilitate assassination.'"

— Michael Ledeen, one of Ronald Reagan's Iran-Contra schemers, *Partisan Review* article, cited by Sidney Blumenthal in *The Washington Post*, February 16, 1987.

13. "'Afghanistan and other troubled lands today cry out for the sort of enlightened foreign administration once provided by self-confident Englishmen in jodhpurs and pith helmets,' wrote Max Boot in the *Weekly Standard*. Michael Ledeen in the *American Enterprise* urged the United States to 'wage revolutionary war against the terrorist regimes, and gradually replace them.' Such a course, he argued, would win firm support from the oppressed people of these countries."

— Matthew Lyons, *Z Magazine*, article, January 2003.

14. "Unable to let go of the Cold War, Birchers argued that Bush's war fails to challenge the real sponsors of terrorism: the Communist states of China, Cuba, and even Russia."

— Matthew Lyons, *Z Magazine*, article, January 2003.

15. "The military drafted plans to kill innocent people and commit acts of terrorism in US cities as a pretext to create public support for a war against Cuba...Plans... to assassinate Cuban émigrés, sink boats of Cuban refugees on the high seas, hijack planes, blow up a US ship, or even orchestrate violent terrorism in US cities." These plans were to be "developed to trick the American public into supporting a war to oust Cuba's then new leader, communist Fidel Castro." These plans were approved by the Joint Chiefs of Staff but were rejected by civilian leadership.

Other later ideas: "Create a war between Cuba and another Latin American country so the US could intervene...another idea was to pay someone in the Castro government to attack US forces at the Guantanamo naval base, an act which, Bamford noted, would have amounted to treason...another to fly low level U2 flights over Cuba with the intention of having one shot down as a pretext for war."

— *Body of Secrets* by James Bamford, article in the *Progressive Populist*, December 15, 2001.

16. "The CIA under the Reagan administration set up, equipped, and trained a notorious death squad. Here's what *The Baltimore Sun* found: 'Hundreds of Honduran citizens were kidnapped, tortured, and killed in the 1980s by a secret army unit trained and supported by the CIA. The intelligence unit, known as Battalion 316, used shock and suffocation devices in interrogations. Prisoners often were kept naked and, when no longer useful, were killed and buried in unmarked graves. At least one CIA official was frequently present at the torture chambers.'

"This was not the action of some rogue CIA agent. This was US policy. CIA and State Department officials knew all about it, approved it, and then lied to Congress about it.'

"Honduras is no aberration...The US government set up death squads not just in Honduras, but in El Salvador, Guatemala, and Haiti. It has supplied weapons and training to the most brutal militaries around the world, including Turkey and Indonesia. And it has worked right alongside the torturers in Chile and Argentina. Indeed, *The Baltimore Sun* reports that the CIA was so enamored of the Argentine torturers that it paid them to go to Honduras to train the new kids on the torture block."

— Comment, *The Progressive*, August 1995.

17. "Director of Central Intelligence William Webster openly called on Congress to provide the CIA with greater latitude — including the right to assassinate foreign leaders. (An executive order signed by President Ford in 1976 and strengthened by President Carter in 1978 prohibits any US participation in assassination attempts, though the Reagan Administration clearly violated this order when it bombed Muammar Qaddafi's residence in 1986.)...George Bush has endorsed Webster's call."

— Comment, *The Progressive*, December 1989.

18. "'All wars...are based on national myths, most of which are, at their core, racist,' he contends. They are racist in that they assert the inherent goodness of "us" and the evil of "them." This black and white thinking allows us to kill the enemy without conscience, while celebrating our success in slaying without mercy those who oppose us...we have our own terrorists — such as the Nicaraguan *contras* and the late Jonas Savimbi, whom Ronald Reagan referred to as the Abraham Lincoln of Angola... The Reagan years, he contends, helped to resurrect this 'plague of nationalism.'"

— *War is a Force That Gives Us Meaning* by Chris Hedges, review by Joseph Nevins, *The Nation*, November 18, 2002.

19. "One of the most dramatic and revealing cases of US official support for client state mass murder was the US relationship to the huge Indonesian killings of 1965–1966, which may have claimed over a million victims, many incidentally on the island of Bali. It is on the record that the United States supplied lists of people (communists) to be killed to the coup and genocide managers, and it is also clear that US officials, pundits, and media were ecstatic at what James Reston saw as a 'gleam of light' and *Time* magazine called 'The West's best news for years in Asia,' referring to an Indonesia being subjected to mass slaughter.

"Less well known is the fact that US officials had been regretful that the Indonesian military seemed to lack the gumption to 'clean house,' and expressed great pleasure when the house cleaning took place. Thus, Rand Corporation and CIA official Guy Pauker had been despondent in 1959 about the possibility of an army takeover... After the coup, Pauker exulted that 'The assassination of the six army generals by the September 30 Movement elicited the ruthlessness that I had not anticipated a year earlier and resulted in the death of large numbers of Communist cadres (actually, mostly peasant farmers and ordinary citizens who might have supported the Communist Party).'" (Quoted in Peter Dale Scott's chapter on Malcolm Caldwell, ed., *Ten years' Military Terror In Indonesia* (Spokesman, 1975).)

— Edward S. Herman, article, *Z Magazine*, December 2002.

20. "'It is better to have a strong regime in power than a liberal government if it is indulgent and relaxed and penetrated by Communists,' Kennan wrote. He also favored, in his words, 'police repression by the local government (because) the results are on balance favorable to our purposes.'"

— George Kennan, cited in an article in *The Progresssive*, March 2003.

21. [A]arguably that has been the primary role of the United States for decades. It shattered Indochina, and when it exited in 1975 it not only didn't help rebuild but instead imposed a long boycott on its victim. It destroyed the Sandinista revolution in Nicaragua, and reduced Nicaragua to the stone age, but even after it succeeded in getting into power its own neoliberal leadership in 1990, it abandoned its victim and has allowed it to remain a basket case ever since. It helped South Africa and 'Freedom fighter' Savimbi crush Angola, and then left. It smashed Iraq in 1991, and then, as with Vietnam, inflicted further severe damage on its victim via 'sanctions of mass destruction.' Serbia and Kosovo were severely damaged, and then abandoned. Afghanistan has been treated similarly."

— Edward S. Herman, *Z Magazine*, December 2002.

22. "'The United States,' he writes, 'is becoming not just a militarized state but a military society: a country where armed power is the measure of national greatness, and war, or planning for war, is the exemplary (and only) common project.'

"Why does the US Department of Defense currently maintain 725 official military bases outside the country and 969 at home (not to mention numerous secret bases)? Why does the US spend more on 'defense' than all the rest of the world put together? ... this country is obsessed with war: rumors of war, images of war, 'preventive war,' 'surgical' war, 'prophylactic' war, 'permanent' war. As President Bush explained at a news conference on April 13, 2004, 'this country must go on the offense and stay on the offense.'"

— Tony Judt, review, *The New American Militarism: How Americans are Seduced by War* by Andrew J. Bacevich, *The New York Review*, June 14, 2005.

23. this is from a forum in January 2006 in Arlington, Virginia, sponsored by *Harper's Magazine*:

> DUNLAP: People don't fully appreciate what the military is. By design, it is authoritarian, socialistic, undemocratic. Those qualities help the armed forces to serve their very unique purpose in our society: namely, external defense against foreign enemies....

> DUNLAP: Americans today have an incredible trust in the military. In poll after poll they have much more confidence in the armed forces that they do in other institutions. The most recent poll, just this last spring, had trust in the military at 74 percent, while congress was at 22 percent and the presidency was at 44

percent. In other words, the armed forces are much more trusted that the civilian institutions that are supposed to control them.

BACEVICH: The question that arises is whether, in fact, we're not already experiencing what is in essence a creeping coup d'état. But it's not people in uniform who are seizing power. It's militarized civilians, who conceive of the world as such a dangerous place that military power has to predominate, that Constitutional constraints on the military need to be loosened. The ideology of national security has become ever more woven into our politics. It has been especially apparent since 9/11, but more broadly it's been going on since the beginning of the Cold war....

WASIK: I want to address the question of partisanship in the military. Insofar as there is a "culture war" in America, everyone seems to agree that the armed forces fight on the Republican side. And this is borne out in polls: self-described Republicans outnumber Democrats in the military by more than four to one, and only 7 percent of soldiers describe themselves as liberal....

DUNLAP: The military is an inherently conservative organization, and this is true of all militaries around the world....

KOHN: Well, at this point the military has a long tradition of getting what it wants. If we ever attempted to truly demobilize — i.e., if the military were suddenly, radically cut back — it could lead if not to a coup then to very severe civil-military tension.

— *Harper's Magazine*, April 2006.

24. "In 1983, during the formative years of spin, 241 Marines were blown up by one terrorist blast in Beirut. Two days later, on October 25, Reagan landed 1,200 marines in Grenada, which is 3,000 miles away from Beirut. By the time the invasion force grew to 7,000 marines, the campaign was over....After this instant victory over a ragtag foe, Reagan was stimulated enough to accept his supporters' claim that America had now put an end to our shame in Vietnam. Reagan understood what Americans wanted, and that was spin. It was more important to be told you were healthy than to be healthy....

"The sorriest thing to be said about the US, as we sidle up to fascism (which can become our fate if we plunge into a major depression, or suffer a set of dirty-bomb catastrophes), is that we expect disasters. We await them. We have become a guilty nation. Somewhere in the moil of the national conscience is the knowledge that we are caught in the little contradiction of loving Jesus on Sunday, while lusting the rest of the week for mega-money....For Bush and Rove, 9/11 was the jackpot.

— Norman Mailer, letter, *The New York Review*, November 4, 2004.

25. "If [Venezuelan President Hugo Chavez] thinks we're trying to assassinate him, I think that we really ought to go ahead and do it. It's a whole lot cheaper than starting a war.... We have the ability to take him out, and I think the time has come that we exercise that ability."

— Pat Robertson, 700 Club, July 22, 2005.

26. Russell Mokhiber interviews Robert Weissman:

"Hawaii, Cuba, Philippines, Puerto Rico, Nicaragua, Honduras, Iran, Guatemala, South Vietnam, Chile, Grenada, Panama, Afghanistan, Iraq:

"What do these 14 governments have in common?

"You got it. The United States overthrew them.

"And in almost every case, the overthrow can be traced to corporate interests....

"'Actually, the United States has been overthrowing governments for more than a century,' Kinzer said in an interview.

"He documents this in a new book: Overthrow: America's Century of Regime Change from Hawaii to Iraq (Times Books, 2006)....

"During an interview Kinzer gave on NPR's Fresh Air with Terry Gross earlier this month...Gross tried to get Kinzer to concede that if we hadn't overthrown these governments, the Soviets would have taken over, or today, radical Islam will take over.

"Kinzer didn't give an inch.

"For example, Gross said that had we not overthrown these 14 governments, 'the Soviets might have won the Cold War.'

"'I don't think that's true at all,' Kinzer responded. 'In the first place, the countries whose governments we overthrew, all countries that we claimed were pawns of the Kremlin, actually were nothing of the sort. We now know, for example, that the Kremlin had not the slightest interest in Guatemala at all in the early 1950s. They didn't even know Guatemala existed. They didn't even have diplomatic or economic relations.'

"'The leader of Iran who we overthrew was fiercely anti-communist. He came from an aristocratic family. He despised Marxist ideology.'

"'In Chile, we always portrayed President Allende as a cat's paw of the Kremlin. We now know from documents that have come out that the Soviets and the Chinese were constantly fighting with him and urging him to calm down and not be so provocative towards the US. So, in the first place, the Soviets were not behind those regimes.'...

"The United States had a hand in many other overthrows, but Kinzer limited his cases to those where the United States was the primary mover and shaker."
— *Asheville Global Report*, May 3, 2006. Source: Focus of the Corporation.

27. "What sticks in my mind more than any particular accomplishment of the super secret National Security Agency is its mammoth size. Only a few blocks from my home, I now know, exists a secret Orwellian town where tens of thousands of people live and work. Barbed-wire fences, massive boulders and thick cement barriers, all hidden by tall earthen berms and thick forests, surround it. Armed police patrol the boundaries of Crypto City, as this restricted area near the sleepy hamlet of Annapolis Junction, Maryland, is called. Telephoto surveillance cameras peer down. Heavily armed commandos dressed in black and wearing headgear are on standby in case of trouble....

"Created at the height of the Cold War, the NSA was to be the eyes and ears of the Central Intelligence Agency after the Communists drew an impenetrable 'iron curtain' around their borders and effectively put human spies out of action. Its very existence has been so highly classified that few people outside the top echelons of government knew much about it. Until, that is, Bamford's first book, *The Puzzle Palace*, was published in 1982....

"The NSA is only one component of the US intelligence community, and for a good deal of its existence it has been subservient to the CIA and the Defense Intelligence Agency. Its business was to collect raw information that was then analyzed by other agencies. The Director of Central Intelligence — head of the CIA — supervised the whole thing....

"Richard Nixon, under the rubric of 'national security,' tried to use the intelligence community to hide his involvement in the Watergate scandal; he also used the

NSA to secretly target antiwar protesters. In the 1970s Congress outlawed whole-sale, warrantless acquisition of raw telegrams and arbitrary watch lists containing the names of Americans, but the Foreign Intelligence Surveillance Act did not cover Americans living abroad....

"Under Ronald Reagan, arguably the most zealous cold war president, the intelligence community regained its footing to become once again the chief tool of US foreign policy. Its anti-Soviet activism led to the criminal excesses of the Iran/Contra scandal....

"Throughout the 1980s the intelligence community provided Congress and the public with exaggerated accounts of Soviet military and economic prowess....

"Casey and Gates systematically ignored their own specialists and overstated the 'evidence' of the Soviet economy in general, to buttress their argument....

"The problem...was a blatant politicization of intelligence. Hawks were in charge; those who disagreed were singled out for being 'soft' on communism. Robert Blackwell, a high-level CIA official, talked of palpable tension at Langley. 'Whether anything was being twisted or reordered upstairs or not, people felt that they were under extra burdens to somehow be very careful about how things were said. Douglas MacEachen [Director of the CIA's Office of Soviet Analysis from 1984 to 1989] said the Reagan Administration 'thought of us as the enemy.'...

"Something is obviously wrong with what Bamford calls the largest, best-funded, and 'most advanced spy organization on the planet.'"

— Dusko Doder, book review, *Body of secrets: Anatomy of the Ultra-Secret National Security Agency* by James Bamford, *The Nation*, June 18th, 2001.

28. "This is a form of Kafkaesque progress — toward recognition of the rights of those with the biggest teeth and sharpest claws to rule the jungle, sanctioned by the 'international community'....

"A remarkable feature of the 'new crisis' is that Iran is successfully portrayed as a villain and threat based on a distant prospect of its acquiring nuclear weapons, even as the United States and Israel brandish those weapons and threaten Iran with attack. If Iran did acquire nuclear weapons it could never use them against Israel or the United States without committing national suicide, whereas the United States has used them in the past and could do so now without threat of nuclear retaliation. However, if Iran built a small stock of such weapons it could pose a low probability threat of a nuclear response to a direct attack. So Iran's real 'threat' is the threat of being able to defend itself....

"The United States gets away with this despite the fact that it is unique in having used nuclear weapons — and against civilian populations — continues to improve them, and, more recently, has tried to make them smaller and more 'practical,' and openly threatens to use them once again....The United States has also cooperated with its client Israel in allowing and positively supporting Israel's long-standing nuclear weapons program that has made it the only nuclear power in the Middle East."

— Edward S. Herman & David Peterson, Fog Watch, *Z Magazine*, November 2005.

29. "President Bush has made broad use of his executive powers: authorizing warrantless wiretaps, collecting telephone records on millions of Americans, holding suspected terrorists overseas without legal protections. His administration is even considering using the military to patrol the US border.

"Congress is on notice from the president that he will not enforce parts of legislation he believes interfere with his constitutional authority....

"'The president apparently believes, based on a number of recent statements and policy directives, that anything he approves is automatically legal,' said Stephen Cimbala, a Pennsylvania State University professor who studies national security issues....

"'Concentrating that kind of authority in one person is dangerous,' said Steinberg, now dean of the LBJ School of Public Affairs at the University of Texas."

— Tom Raum, Analysis, The AP, *Asheville Citizen-Times*, May 14, 2006.

30. "In 1998 bin Laden asked an American journalist, 'Was it not your country that bombed Nagasaki and Hiroshima? Were there not women and children and civilians and noncombatants there? You were the people who invented this terrible game, and we as Muslims have to use these same tactics against you.'

"'The function of propaganda,' Hitler wrote in *Mein Kampf,* 'is not to make an objective study of the truth,' but to incite. Bin laden regards himself as an instigator."

— Raffi Khatchadourian, essay, *The Nation*, May 15, 2006

31. Lesley Stahl: "We have heard that a half-million children have died (from the sanction against Iraq). I mean, that's more children than died at Hiroshima."

— Madeleine Albright: "We think the price is worth it."

32. "No Flag is Large Enough to Cover the Shame of Killing Innocent People."

— Lead banner in a parade in Taos, New Mexico on February 15, 2003, cited in *Z Magazine* of May 2000 in an interview with Howard Zinn by David Barsamian.

33, "The common view that internal freedom makes for humane and moral international behavior is supported neither by historical evidence nor by reason....

"The value of being allowed to protest relatively unmolested is certainly real, but it should not lead to a disregard of the fact that established institutions, with overwhelmingly dominant power, tend to line up in goose-step fashion in support of any state foreign venture, no matter how immoral (until the cost becomes too high).... In 1975, the Trilateral Commission...published a study entitled *The Crisis of Democracy*, which interprets public participation in decision-making as a threat to democracy, one that must be contained if elite domination is to persist unhindered by popular demands. The population must be reduced to apathy and conformism if 'democracy,' as interpreted by this liberal contingent, is to be kept workable and allowed to survive....

"For over two decades (1949–1975) the United States attempted to subjugate Vietnam by force and subversion, in the process violating the UN Charter, the Geneva Accords of 1954, the Nuremberg Code, the Hague Convention, the Geneva Protocol of 1925, and finally the Paris agreements of 1973....

"Whatever the attitudes of the US leadership toward freedom at home — and, as noted, this is highly ambiguous — systematic policies toward Third World countries make it evident that the alleged commitment to democracy and human rights is mere rhetoric, directly contrary to actual policy. The operative principle has been and remains economic freedom — meaning freedom for US business to invest, sell, and repatriate profits — and its two basic requisites, a favorable investment climate and a specific form of stability.... Economic freedom has often required political servitude.... Since a favorable investment climate and stability quite often require repression, the United States has supplied the tools and training for interrogation and torture and is thoroughly implicated in the vast expansion of torture during the past decade....

"The rationale given for the US buildup of Third World police and military establishments and regular 'tilt' toward repressive regimes is the demands of 'security.'

This is a wonderfully elastic concept with a virtuous ring that can validate open-ended arms expenditures, as well as support for neo-fascism....

"Among the symbols used to frighten and manipulate the populace of the democratic states, few have been more important than 'terror' and 'terrorism.' These terms have generally been confined to the use of violence by individuals and marginal groups. Official violence, which is far more extensive in both scale and destructiveness, is placed in a different category altogether....The numbers tormented and killed by official violence — wholesale as opposed to retail terror — during recent decades have exceeded those of unofficial terrorists by a factor running into the thousands. But this is not 'terror.'

— Noam Chomsky and Edward Herman, 1979, essay reprinted by *Z Magazine*, April 2006.

34. "Chavez's 'Bolivarian Revolution,' a close replica of Franklin Roosevelt's New Deal — a progressive income tax, public works, social security, cheap electricity — makes him wildly popular with the poor. And most Venezuelans are poor. His critics, a four-centuries' old white elite, unused to sharing oil wealth, portray him as a Castro-hugging anti-Christ...."Bush's reaction to Chavez has been a mix of hostility and provocation. Washington supported the coup attempt against Chavez in 2002, and Condoleezza Rice and Donald Rumsfeld have repeatedly denounced him. The revised *National Security Strategy of the United States of America*, released in March, says, 'In Venezuela, a demagogue awash in oil money is undermining democracy and seeking to destabilize the region.'

"So when the Reverend Pat Robertson, a Bush ally, told his faithful in August 2005 that Chavez has to go, it was not unreasonable to assume that he was articulating an Administration wish. 'If he thinks we're trying to assassinate him,' Robertson said, 'I think that we really ought to go ahead and do it. It's a whole lot cheaper than starting a war...and I don't think any oil shipments will stop.'"

— Greg Palast, interview with Hugo Chavez, *The Progressive*, July 2006.

35. "I would like to invite the citizens of great Britain and the citizens of the US and the citizens of the world to come here and walk freely through the streets of Venezuela, to talk to anyone they want, to watch television, to read the papers. We are building a true democracy, with human rights for everyone, social rights, education, health care, pensions, social security, and jobs....

"Mr. Bush is an illegitimate President. In Florida, his brother Jeb deleted many black voters from the electoral registers. So this President is the result of a fraud. Not only that, he is also currently applying a dictatorship in the US. People can be put in jail without being charged. They tap phones without court orders. They check what books people take out of public libraries. They arrested Cindy Sheehan because of a T-shirt she was wearing demanding the return of the troops from Iraq. They abuse blacks and Latinos. And if we are going to talk about meddling in other countries, then the US is the champion of meddling in other people's affairs. They invaded Guatemala; they overthrew Salvador Allende, invaded Panama and the Dominican Republic. They were involved in the coup d'état in Argentina thirty years ago."

— Hugo Chavez, interviewed by Greg Palast, *The Progressive*, July 2006.

36. "On June 1, 2002 in a speech at West Point, President George Bush made an unprecedented assertion that the US has a right to overthrow any government in the world that is seen as a threat to US security. This may have been startling news to the world, but not to Latin Americans. Since 1846 the United States has carried out no fewer than 50 military invasions and destabilizing operations involving 12 different

Latin American countries. Yet, none of these countries has ever had the capacity to threaten US security in any significant way. The US intervened because of perceived threats to its economic control and expansion. For this reason it has also supported some of the region's most vicious dictators, such as Batista, Somoza, Trujillo, and Pinochet....

"Recently, the Bush administration has stepped up its aggressive stance against Venezuelan democracy. US Secretary of Defense Donald Rumsfeld has compared President Chavez with Hitler and US Director for National Intelligence John Negroponte stated that Venezuela is the main security challenge in this hemisphere. US Secretary of State Condoleezza Rice told a Senate committee last February 16 that Venezuela is 'a particular danger to the region' and that she is 'working with others' to try and make certain that there is a united front against Venezuela.

"In Venezuela there are no illegal political prisoners, no secret prisons, no displaced populations, no practice of torture, no illegal detentions, and no invasions of other countries. With the support of the International Development Bank, Venezuela is undergoing a comprehensive judicial reform to modernize and correct a judicial system that had long been disreputable."

— Maria Paez Victor, essay, *Z Magazine*, June 2006.

37. "The reality is that the only alternative to the communist World Empire is an American Empire, which will be, if not literally worldwide in formal boundaries, capable of exercising decisive world control."

— James Burnham, right-wing intellectual and William Buckley confidant.

38. "America is in a position to reshape norms, alter expectations and create new realities.... the challenge to unipolarity is not from the outside but from the inside. The choice is ours. To impiously paraphrase Benjamin Franklin: History has given you an empire, if you will keep it. The remedy? Unapologetic and implacable demonstrations of will."

— Charles Krauthammer.

[In fairness to Benjamin Franklin, taken out of context by Krauthammer in the above passage, note that Franklin was not *calling for* empire; he was calling for the continuance of democracy, the near opposite of empire. It is specious, not just impious, for Krauthammer to distort and twist those words to justify his own dream of an American empire and a Greater Israel within it. — Author.]

Chapter 6. Attacking Iraq

1. "President Nixon and National Security Adviser Henry Kissinger, visiting Tehran on May 31, 1972, on the way home from a Moscow summit, were asked by the Shah to arm and finance an insurrection of the Iraqi Kurds as a favor to the Iranian ruler, who had cooperated with US intelligence agencies and who had come to feel menaced by his neighbor.

"On March 5, 1975...the Shah concluded an agreement with Iraq...and Iran abruptly pulled the plug on the Kurdish insurrection....

"The insurgents were clearly taken by surprise. Their adversaries, knowing of the impending aid cut-off, launched an all-out search-and-destroy campaign....

"Some 200,000 Kurds escaped into Iran, of whom 40,000 were forcibly returned to Iraq. Appeals for humanitarian assistance and for political asylum in the United States were ignored....

"A Congressional report (of the Pike committee) quoted 'a high US official' as having remarked to the committee's staff, 'Covert action should not be confused with missionary work.'

"Kissinger later denounced the Pike (congressional) report as 'a collection of distortions and untruths.'"

— Daniel Shorr, *The Washington Post*, April 7, 1991.

2. "They ignore the evidence, reported over a decade ago by Adel Darwish and Gregory Alexander in their 1991 book, *Unholy Babylon*, that Washington was extremely alarmed by Qassim and the Communists, and therefore wooed the Baath Party as an alternative. When the Baath briefly came to power in 1963, the CIA passed to Saddam Hussein, probably an agency asset, a list of hundreds of Iraqi Communists, whom the new regime liquidated....Again, Darwish and Alexander report assertions of US backing for the 1968 coup, confirmed to me by other journalists who have talked to retired CIA and State Department officials."

— Juan Cole, book review, *The Nation*, March 29, 2004.

3. In 1979, Jimmy Carter initiated a human rights policy and set up a State Department list of countries supporting terrorism and abusing human rights.

4. In 1982, Ronald Reagan removed Iraq from the State Department list and canceled Carter's human rights policy.

5. In November of 1983, Reagan issued Directive 114 which said that he would do "whatever is necessary and legal" to help Iraq win its war with Iran even though he knew from official documents that Iraq was using chemical weapons "almost daily" against Iran and that Saddam Hussein was trying to build a nuclear bomb.

6. On Dec. 20, 1983, "Ronald Reagan was...giving aid and weapons to both Iran (secretly) and Iraq.... In 1982, Ronald Reagan had taken Iraq off the list of nations that sponsored terrorism. That allowed a floodgate of US 'aid' to go into Iraq. The Reagan administration was actively encouraging manufacturers to sell to Iraq and Saddam Hussein was aggressively buying everything he could get his hands on from the United States.

"Ronald Reagan dispatched his special envoy to Iraq with a handwritten letter from Reagan to be given to Saddam Hussein, with a clear message that what Washington wanted was to restore normal relations.... So when the envoy (Donald Rumsfeld) arrived in Baghdad, not only did he have a handwritten letter, but he also gave Saddam Hussein a pair of golden cowboy spurs, as a present from Ronald Reagan. He shook Saddam's hand, called him 'Mr. President,' and had a meeting that the Iraqi foreign minister described at the time as being about 'topics of mutual interest.' (Shortly) 'Allegations started to emerge about Iraq's use and possession of chemical weapons.'"

— Jeremy Scahill, interview by David Ross, *Z Magazine*, November 2002.

7. "When April Glaspie went to Baghdad as US ambassador in early August 1988, Iraq's war with Iran was into its eighth year and had become one of the deadliest of all time. The casualties of this conflict, which had begun when Iraq invaded its neighbor in 1980, were estimated as high as 1 million soldiers and civilians, possibly the highest toll of any war since World War II."

— Don Oberdorfer, *The Washington Post Magazine*, March 17, 1991.

8. "'Imagine if you were Iranian and watched the boys in your neighborhood board a bus for the front, never to return. Imagine staring in mute horror at the television screen as Saddam rained chemical weapons down on your boys, his death planes guided by US satellite photos. Fast-forward about fifteen years. Now you are watching faded video footage of Donald Rumsfeld shaking Hussein's hand, smiling at the butcher who made our capital's cemetery a city. Now you are listening to President George W. Bush.... Do you believe him?'

"When the Iran-Iraq war stuttered to a truce eight years later, more than a million people on both sides had died. An entire generation of Iranian men had been obliterated..."

— *Iran Awakening: A Memoir of Revolution and Hope*, by Shirin Ebadi, Random House (May 2, 2006) reviewed for *The Nation* May 11, 2006 by Reza Aslan.

9. In 1990, President George H. W. Bush overrode a congressional block on trade credits to Iraq that the Democratic Congress had imposed because of Saddam's use of poison gas against Iraqi Kurds.

10. "In the 1950s under President Eisenhower, the Dulles brothers (John Foster in the State Department and Allen at CIA) began locking down US hegemony around the globe and perfected the hate-the-commies rhetoric that justified the US war machine for decades....

"In 1961, Iraq leader Abdel Karin Qassim spoke out very strongly for the return of Kuwait. Miller reports that the Baghdad CIA station chief gave the order to kill

Qassim to an aggressive young hustler named Saddam Hussein. Saddam did the job very well, killed and tortured other radicals and trade unionists and began his rise to power in the Baath Party with our backing.

"By 1975, the Pentagon had refined plans for our military emplacement in Saudi Arabia and our takeover of the Persian Gulf coast. In 1978, Pentagon analyst Lawrence Mosher drafted a plan for the use of 'the US 100,000 Quick Strike Force, which consists of three divisions rapidly deployable anywhere by air....But one needs a real bogeyman to come in and have to be stopped before you can talk of using the Quick Strike Force'

"In mid-1990, we pushed Saddam's trigger. Secretary of State James Baker sent the message to Saddam, 'We have no interest in your border dispute with Kuwait.' Saddam took the bait and moved his forces to the border of Kuwait. Miller reveals that the night before Saddam entered Kuwait both the US and the Soviet ambassadors left Iraq 'for vacation.' Saddam moved into Kuwait, we stomped on him and the rest is history."

— William Jakobi, guest commentary, *Asheville Citizen-Times, July 22, 2005.*

11. "It is becoming increasingly clear that George Bush, operating largely behind the scenes through the 1980s reelection, initiated and supported much of the financing, intelligence, and military help that built Saddam's Iraq into the aggressive power that the United States ultimately had to destroy."

— Ted Koppel, *Nightline,* June 9, 9192.

12. "We do not have any defense treaties with Kuwait and there are no special defense or security commitments to Kuwait."

— Margaret Tutwiler, State Department spokesperson, in reply to a question at a press conference.

13. "David Hoffman reported that the 'Bush administration in the weeks before the Aug. 2 invasion was gripped by inertia and indecision over whether to get tough on Saddam.' Around the same time, we learned of the meeting at which the US ambassador to Iraq, April Glaspie, told Saddam that his dispute with Kuwait was an 'Arab–Arab' matter about which Washington had 'no opinion.'

— Richard Cohen, column, *Washington Post,* April 30, 1992.

14. "Baker denied that there was any US hostility toward Iraq.... Aziz asked Baker ...to approve new US credit guarantees for Iraq food purchases from the United States.... Bush overrode congressional objections to continuing US Export–Import Bank financing for commercial transactions with Iraq....

"On April 12, five US senators — led by Bob Dole — made a now-famous visit to Saddam in Mosul....Dole told Saddam...that Bush had assured him personally only 12 hours earlier that he was pleased with their visit and that 'he wants better relations, and the US government wants better relations with Iraq.'"...

— Don Oberdorfer, *The Washington Post Magazine,* March 17. 1991.

15. "Preparation for the (first) Gulf War was well in hand before Secretary of State James Baker announced that its *principal* rationale was 'jobs, jobs, jobs.'"

— Christopher Hitchens column, *The Nation,* August 19–26, 2002.

16. "I broke with the administration on Nov. 8, when President Bush abruptly doubled American forces in the Persian Gulf and headed toward war with Iraq instead of giving sanctions a chance to work. I still believe it was unnecessary to kill tens of thousands of Iraqis and heavily damage Baghdad. It was an easy victory but an awful price to inflict on the soldiers and the people of Iraq for the sins of their brutal leader....

"It also seems incoherent to me that Mr. Bush authorized the sale of high-tech equipment to Saddam, which he converted to chemical warfare. It seems equally incoherent to me that the Bush administration told Saddam a week before the Iraqi dictator invaded Kuwait that our government would not become involved in an Arab border dispute."

— George McGovern, letter, *Washington Post*, March 8, 1991.

17. "The day before Iraq sent its troops pouring into Kuwait, the Bush administration approved the sale of $695,000 worth of advanced data transmission devices to the Iraqi government, according to US government records.

"The sale was just one item in $1.5 billion in advanced US products that the Reagan and Bush administrations allowed Iraq to buy from 1985 to 1990.

— Stuart Auerbach, report, *Washington Post*, March 11, 1991.

18. "Every Iraqi leader, from the British-imposed king in 1921...regarded Kuwait as an integral part of Iraq. Kuwait had been set up as an imperial outpost by the British on the eve of World War I.... most Iraqis believed that Kuwait was rightly and legally an Iraqi province."

— William K. Polk, essay, *The New York Review*, February 18,1999.

19. "On July 16, Foreign ambassador Aziz sent a letter to the Arab League.... Kuwait was charged with 'twofold aggression' [for manipulating the market] and for 'stealing' $2.4 billion in Iraqi oil from an oil field that straddles the Kuwait-Iraq border."

— Don Oberdorfer, essay, *The Washington Post Magazine*, March 17, 1991.

20. "It hit the news during the presidency of Richard Nixon, when the US was completing its military encirclement of the Soviet Union, ringing the 'enemy' with listening posts, missile silos, and air and naval bases. There was a large gap to the south of the Soviet state, between our bases in Turkey and Saudi Arabia, and to the east, Australia, the Philippines, and Japan. Diego Garcia sits right in the middle of that gap. So the US insisted that Britain evacuate the 2000 residents of that peaceful island and grant us a long-term lease for the erection of what today is one of the largest air bases in the world, plus radar and listening facilities.

"Britain swept up the hapless residents of Diego Garcia and attempted unsuccessfully to settle them on nearby islands. Ultimately many of the victims were repatriated to England, and today many of them live in poverty in London....

"This travesty is especially sick in that it was perpetrated roughly 10 years after the World Bank published a study of the Soviet economy, concluding that it was not self-sustaining and the Soviet Union was imploding. But the Cold War was so profitable and so useful for US power-moguls that they kept up their hate-the-commies actions unabated.

"It was precisely in this benighted era that the Pentagon began planning for our permanent military emplacement in the Middle East....

"National security adviser Zbigniew Brzezinski staged a secret meeting in Kuwait City with Saddam Hussein, the Emir of Kuwait, and an agent of Saudi King Fahd, and proposed that Saddam invade Iran and seize the Khuzestan oil fields (in the Shiite area of southwestern Iran, adjacent to Iraq.) Brzezinski's plan was that Iraq and Iran would fight like scorpions in a bottle, and would bleed themselves white in the Eastern sands. Eight years of bloody mayhem ensued, in which tens of thousands of people died.

"And in this same period the Pentagon refined the plan for US military takeover of Middle East oil fields....

"We cleverly set up this bogeyman: 'State Dept. officials led Saddam to think he could get away with grabbing Kuwait...Small wonder Saddam concluded he could overrun Kuwait. Bush and Co. gave him no reason to think otherwise. Thus, we deliberately triggered the '91 Gulf war, the staging operation for our current disastrous entry into Iraq."

— William Jakobi, Guest Opinion, *Asheville Citizen Times*, June 21, 2006.

21. Aug. 12, 1990 — Iraq invades Kuwait.

22. "Bush began preparing for war shortly after the Iraq invasion of Kuwait and refused to respond to at least five Iraqi offers of negotiation between August and January 15, the deadline for Iraq to leave Kuwait. On that date, *The Washington Post* reported that the Administration feared a 'nightmare scenario' under which 'the beginnings of a credible Iraqi withdrawal could make it impossible for Bush to launch military action.' A 'nightmare scenario' recurred when the Soviet Union attempted to broker a peace settlement in the days before the ground offensive. But though the Soviet plan would have removed Iraq from Kuwait, Bush would have none of it. He... insisted that the killing continue.

— Allen Nairn, Reflections, *The Progressive*, May 1991.

23. "We called the story 'Flacking for the Emir' and published it in *The Progressive* May 1991 issue. One of Arthur E. Rowse's disclosures was the role Hill & Knowlton played in disseminating 'Perhaps the most widely publicized accusation against Iraq' — a charge that Saddam Hussein's soldiers had brutally allowed Kuwaiti babies to die after removing them from their incubators at three hospitals....

"The story about the incubator atrocity had originated with 'eyewitness' testimony before a Congressional committee by a fifteen-year-old Kuwaiti girl, identified only as 'Nayirah,' who wept as she told of seeing fifteen babies dumped to their deaths.

"The horrifying charge...later embellished to a total of 312 babies, was frequently mentioned by President Bush and members of Congress in the debate over whether to start shooting. Rowse reminded Knoll that this charge, as my article for *The Progressive* reported, was firmly disproved by reporters who visited the hospitals after the war....

"Apparently, it wasn't news that a high-priced PR firm had successfully peddled a fabricated story, but it was news that the firm had used an ambassador's daughter to do its dirty work."

— Erwin Knoll, Memo from the Editor, *The Progressive*, April 4, 1992.

24. "January 17, 1991 — US launches war to repel Iraq from Kuwait. Conflict ends Feb. 28."

— *Public Citizen News*, May/June 2003.

25. "The day the Baghdad shelter was bombed, killing hundreds of people, the Pentagon lied and said it was an Iraqi army command center, even though, as the *London Independent* later established, the Pentagon actually believed they were bombing a shelter for the families of the Iraqi elite....Leslie Gelb, the *New York Times* columnist... said viewers should not be 'too quick to believe (their) eyes' because, he explained, the smoking bodies they saw being hauled up from underground (presumably including those of the tiny, charred children) might be those of civilians who had been working for the Iraq military....

"During the war's final days, when the Iraqis were out of Kuwait, militarily crushed, and desperately trying to surrender, Washington kept attacking nonetheless (and not just on the 'Highway of Death' as the road to Basra became known, but also in Baghdad itself.) White House officials lived in 'fear of a peace deal,' wrote columnists Rowland and Robert Novak, who applauded them for their 'eagerness to avoid peace and confront war.'"

— Allen Nairn, Reflections, *The Progressive*, May 1991.

26. "Pentagon smugness, never in short supply, hit a sewer-line low when a smiling Gen. Colin Powell said that his forces have 'lots of tools. And I brought them all to the party.'

"It is a party — a drunken one turning sadistic. Relentless aerial bombardment — lately about as surgical as operating on a cornea with machetes — is a systematic destroying of Iraq's electricity, water and sewage facilities. That, plus blowing up bridges and obliterating neighborhoods, is called 'softening up' the enemy.

"On February 13, back the fearless warriors went, this time to obliterate with smart bombs what the Pentagon called an Iraqi 'command bunker' but which the world now knows was sheltering hundreds of civilians trying to make it through another hellish night. Scores of noncombatants — women and children — were slaughtered.

"Regardless of what Saddam Hussein is doing to Iraqis, the sadistic ritual of daily bombing by the US military is in keeping with its picking fights — in Grenada, Libya and Panama — with enemies expected to be done in quickly.... After a month in the Gulf, the United States is now involved in war for war's sake, war for the fun of it, war as a party that brings smiles to Gen. Powell....

"After a month of obliterating Iraq, and now downtown Baghdad, the US air war has been revealed as a coward's war."

— Colman McCarthy, column, *Washington Post*, January 17, 1991.

27. Throughout the war American news organizations ran tally boxes of the casualties, listing in one column how many American soldiers had perished and in another column how many Iraqi tanks, APCS, and planes had been 'killed.' There was no mention of Iraqi deaths....Powell's famous declaration about the Iraqi army — 'we're going to cut it off, then we're going to kill it'- neatly edited out all consideration of the enemy's humanity.

"There has not been released, about this war fought in the video age, a single foot of film depicting anything resembling combat involving human beings [100,000 plus civilian dead]. Military censors went crazy when one field commander let reporters watch a gun camera video from an Apache gunship that snuck up on an Iraqi squad. In the tape, terror-stricken teenagers rush wildly in all directions as cannon rounds from the helicopter, which they can't see, slices their bodies in half. The video was quickly withdrawn from circulation. When I asked a senior Pentagon official why, he replied, 'If we let people see that kind of thing, there would never again be any war.'"

— Gregg Easterbrook, book review of various books by and about General Norman Schwarzkopf, *The New Republic*, September 30, 1991.

28. "Late last fall, the Census Bureau assigned a 29-year-old demographer to update the government's population estimate for Iraq....

"How many Iraqis died during the war and its aftermath? The answer, officially taboo in the Bush administration, was indispensable to (Beth Osborne) Daponte's calculations. In January, when a reporter asked for her estimates, she told him: 86,194 men, 39,612 women and 32,195 children died at the hands of the American-led coalition forces, during the domestic rebellions that followed, and from postwar deprivation.

"Wednesday evening, after weeks of turmoil during which she was removed from the Iraq project and her files disappeared from her desk, Daponte was told she is to be fired. Barbara Boyle Torrey, her boss at the Bureau's Center for International Research, wrote that Daponte's report included 'false information' and demonstrated 'untrustworthiness or unreliability.' ...

"The White House and Pentagon consistently have sought to suppress discussion of Iraqi casualties, directing analysts and military officers not to provide estimates or professional judgments....

"'I think that Beth is collateral damage in the government's campaign to avoid discussing the question of Iraqi casualties,' said William M. Arkin, a former intelligence officer who now does military analysis for Greenpeace. 'I think this is an ugly case of retribution....

"Her estimates — a total of 158,000 Iraqi dead, including 40,000 direct military deaths, 13,000 immediate civilian deaths, 35,000 postwar deaths in the Shiite and Kurdish rebellions, and 70,000 deaths due to the public health consequences of wartime damage to electricity and sewage treatment plants."

— Barton Gellman, report, *The Washington Post,* March 6, 1992.

29. Of the 296 men and eight women who died since the US mobilization for war began on Aug. 7, an estimated 182 died in "non-hostile" incidents, deaths attributed to equipment failures, accidents and natural causes. Of those, 106 were killed before the war erupted Jan. 17.

30. "The United States and its allies assembled a mighty force — about 700,000 troops — in the Persian Gulf during the fall and winter of 1990 to take on a formidable foe. Saddam Hussein's Iraq, we were told, had more than 500,000 troops poised to engage in combat, and some of them were elite units — remember the superhuman Revolutionary Guards? — endowed with legendary fighting skills....

"Now, slowly, belatedly, some of the facts come seeping through the bottom of the bloody barrel. Turns out, according to a bipartisan report from the House Armed Services Committee, that there weren't 500,000 Iraqi troops after all, but only about 180,000. That means that the United States and its allies had about a four-to-one edge — 'a very significant advantage,' as House Armed Services Chairman Les Aspin put it. It also means that the war turned into a turkey shoot — a random slaughter of a never-to-be determined number of Iraqis. (The House estimates that 120,000 Iraqi soldiers fled or were killed during the ground assault.)

— Comment, *The Progressive,* June 1992.

31. When the war ended on February 28th, Bush refused to remove Saddam, withdrew American troops, and explained why in the following statement:

"To occupy Iraq would instantly shatter our coalition, turning the whole Arab world against us and make a broken tyrant into a latter-day Arab hero...assigning young soldiers to a fruitless hunt for a securely entrenched dictator and condemning them to fight in what would be an un-winnable urban guerilla war. It could only plunge that part of the world into even greater instability."

— George Bush Sr., from his book, A World Transformed (1998), cited in the *Asheville Global Report,* April 10-16, 2003.

32. "The so-called fighting stopped only 25 days ago, but that has been enough time to show that President Bush has not a clue about what to do with his victory. Liberated Kuwait, choking on the fumes of its burning oil wells, is indulging in an orgy of recriminations; Iraq, with 100,000 dead, and according to the United Nations, bombed back to the 'pre-industrial age,' is racked by disease, want and civil

war; Saudi Arabia is gratefully reverting to feudalism, and Israel to intransigence on the Palestinian question. The only thing arguably improved is Bush's standing in the polls....

"Now, in liberated Kuwait, ghastly atrocities are occurring, but a curious detachment has set in at the White House. Palestinians and Iraqis are being subjected to 'routine torture' of 400 to 500 people taken to detention centers and tortured and beaten."

— Mary McGrory, column, *The Washington Post*, March 26, 1991.

33. "An independent human rights organization has accused the Kuwaiti government of repeated, flagrant human rights abuses over the last six months — including rape, torture and extrajudicial killings — and says that the Bush administration bears responsibility because it defended Kuwait's actions....

"'We have to use torture to make them confess,' one military officer was quoted as saying. 'They would not confess without the use of force,'...

"The report noted a July 1 press conference in which President Bush said he understood the Kuwaitis' feelings of rage and added: 'I think we're expecting a little much if we're asking the people in Kuwait to take kindly to those that had spied on their countrymen...that had brutalized families there and things of that nature.'

"'It is difficult to imagine a more forceful apology for abuse,' Middle East Watch said of bush's remarks.'"

— Tod Robertson, report, *The Washington Post*, September 11, 1991.

34. "One of the reasons we went halfway around the world was to kick the Iraqis out of Kuwait. We returned to that small country the most precious gift anyone can give: the gift of liberty."

— General Norman Schwarzkopf, speech at the US Naval academy in May of 1991.

[It is an astonishing claim. In fact, of the 2.1 million people in Kuwait, only 825,000 were accorded citizenship or "liberty" at all. The others were humble servants (called bidoon), born in Kuwait but of the wrong ancestry to be allowed citizenship or other rights. Others were imported from Saudi Arabia, Iraq, Iran, Algeria, Tunisia, Sudan, Somali, and Palestine to be servants.

When Iraq invaded, all of these stateless people became suspects to the Kuwaitis. It made little difference whether or not they had collaborated with the Iraqis. Their ancestry and low class indicted them. Many were imprisoned, abused, and tortured; others were expelled, including even people who had always lived in Kuwait and had no country of their own to go to. Quite a few were killed. Palestinians in particular were suspect. The simple truth is that, despite Saddam's torture and selective brutality, even Iraq treated its ordinary citizens better than Kuwait did its bidoons.

35. "The real problem, of course, is the Palestinians. Of the 450,000 Palestinians of Kuwait, many have been here for decades; they made the country work. 'The people who know how to run things, the people who always did the work here, were almost all Palestinians,' said one US official involved in the reconstruction. 'They were the judges, the doctors, the dentists, practically all the engineers, all the middle managers.' ...[A] Red Cross official marveled at his difficulties in establishing a coherent relief system. 'The people we are dealing with have no concept of the mechanics of actually getting jobs done,' he said. 'They are very good at talking and sitting and drinking tea all day, but they don't have a clue about things like how to get a lorry from point A to point B.'"

— Michael Kelly, *The New Republic*, April 8, 1991.

36. "The FAO (the UN Food and Agriculture Organization) said in Rome that three years of sanctions [against Iraq] have caused food shortages and that 'a grave humanitarian tragedy is unfolding.'

"It said the mission found many signs associated with coming famine: exorbitant prices, collapse of private incomes. Rising unemployment, sharply reduced food intakes, high morbidity levels, increases in crime and poverty.

"The sanctions have 'caused persistent deprivation, severe hunger and malnutrition for a vast majority of the Iraqi population, particularly the vulnerable groups — children under 5, expectant/nursing women, widows, orphans, the sick, the elderly and disabled,' it said."

— Dilip Ganguly, *The Chattanooga Times*, July 15, 1993.

37. "BuzzFlash.com reports that Iran is currently pursuing its lawsuit against the United States for its previous support of Saddam Hussein. 'At the International Court of Justice, Tehran is accusing the United States of delivering chemicals and deadly viruses to Baghdad during the '80s.' Iran filed suit against the United States in the highest court of the United Nations in 1992. "

— No Comment, *The Progressive*, April 2003.

Chapter 7. Attacking Iraq Again

1. "The vision laid out in the Bush document — The National Security Strategy of the United States — is a vision of what used to be called, when we believed it to be the Soviet ambition, world domination. It's a vision of a world in which it is American policy to prevent the emergence of any rival power, whatever it stands for — a world policed and controlled by American military might. This goes much further than the notion of America as the policeman of the world....There's a name for the kind of regime in which the cops rule, answering only to themselves. It's called a police state....(The Bush) idea of world government looks very much like a benevolent American dictatorship — a dictatorship of the entrepreneuriat, you might say."
— Hendrik Hertzberg, *The New Yorker*, October 14 & 21, 2002.

2. "I've heard the call. I believe God wants me to run for president."
— George W. Bush.

3. "I believe today that my conduct is in accordance with the will of the Almighty Creator."
— Adolf Hitler, cited by Patricia Williams in her column in *The Nation*, April 3, 2006.

4. "If this were a dictatorship, it would be a heck of a lot easier, just as long as I'm the dictator."
— George W. Bush.

5. "They're reminders to all Americans that they need to watch what they say. Watch what they do."
— Former White House Press Secretary Ari Fleischer.

6. "I'm the decider and I decide what's best."
— George W. Bush

7. "Why is this man in the White House? The majority of Americans did not vote for him. Why is he there? And I tell you this morning that he's in the White House because God put him there for such a time as this."
— Lt. Gen. William G. Boykin.

8. "Either you are with us, or you are with the terrorists."

— George W. Bush addressing Congress and the people after the September 11th attacks.

9. "That's the interesting thing about being the President. Maybe somebody needs to explain to me why they do something, but I don't feel like I owe anybody an exclamation."

— George W. Bush to the National Security Council, cited by *Harper's Magazine*, April 2002.

10. "'I will seize the opportunity to achieve big goals. There is nothing bigger than to achieve world peace.' And the way to achieve that, he believes, is often through war. 'As we think through Iraq, we may or may not attack.... but it will be for the objective of making the world more peaceful,' he told Woodward."

— Comment, *The Progressive*, February 2003.

11. "If we need to act, we will act, and we really don't need United Nations approval to do so. We really don't need anybody's permission."

— George W. Bush cited in a Matthew Rothschild column, *The Progressive*, April 2003.

12. "At some point, we may be the only ones left. That's OK with me. We are America."

— George W. Bush, Norman Mailer article, *The New York Review*, March 27, 2003.

13. "God told me to strike at al-Qaeda and I struck them, and then he instructed me to strike at Saddam, which I did."

— George W. Bush, to Palestinian Prime Minister Mahmoud Abbas, June 2003.

14. "There won't be any casualties."

— George W. Bush to evangelist Pat Robertson, discussing the attack he was about to launch on the people of Iraq.

15. "Osama bin Laden has declared war on Crusaders and Jews, while the President, according to an unnamed family member quoted in Peter and Rochelle Schweizer's new book, *The Bushes: Portrait of a Dynasty*, believes that 'we the Christians must strike back with more force and more ferocity than they will ever know.'"

— Daniel Lazare, book review, *The Nation*, June 14, 2004.

16. "We went to war because we were attacked, and we are at war today because there are still people out there who want to harm our country and hurt our citizens. Our troops are fighting these terrorists in Iraq so you will not have to face them here at home."

— George W. Bush, June 18, 2005 radio speech.

17. "Francis Brooke, an INC representative in Washington, has arrived. A Virginian and a Christian fundamentalist, he is a fountain of glowing quotes....'As far as I'm concerned, Syria's next. When they say Perle and these guys like Wolfowitz want to get Syria, they're right. These guys are my friends and I know.'

"Francis Brooke says he would support the elimination of Saddam, even if every single Iraqi were killed in the process. He means it. 'I'm coming from a place different from you,' he says in that soft southern drawl one hears from preachers and con men. 'I believe in good and evil. That man is absolute evil and must be destroyed.'"

— Charles Glass, Dispatch, *Harper's Magazine*, July 2003.

18. "'Go find the Al Qaeda and kill them,' (Cofer) Black said. 'We're going to eliminate them. Get bin Laden, find him. I want his head in a box.' 'You're serious?' Gary asked. 'Absolutely,' Black replied, according to Woodward. 'I want to take it down and show the president.'"

— Anthony Lewis, book review of *Bush at War*, by Bob Woodward, *The New York Review*, February 13, 2003.

19. "'They want to turn these guys into assassins,' a former high-level intelligence officer told me. 'They want to go on rumors — not facts — and go for political effect, and that's what the Special Forces Command is really afraid of. Rummy is saying that politics is bigger than war, and we need to take guys out for political effect: You have to kill Goebbels to get to Hitler. The military is saying, Who is this guy? There's a major clash of wills as to what is the future of Special Forces...He's the strangest guy I've ever run into.'"

— Intelligence officer, article by Seymour Hersh, *The New Yorker*, December 23 & 30, 2002.

20. "They hate him. I mean it. They hate him. He's lucky he hasn't gotten fragged."

— A senior deputy to Secretary of State Colin Powell, talking about Donald Rumsfeld.

21. "President George W. Bush has been fond of using the word *evil* to describe countries and actions he disapproves of, but now his own church is saying he's the one who is evil because of his policies, and it wants him to repent. United Methodist officials recently took a full-page ad in *Christian Century* magazine calling on Bush to 'repent from domestic and foreign policies that are incompatible with the teaching and example of Christ.'

"The President has so far rejected the church's call for a meeting."

— Side Lines, *Free Inquiry*, summer 2003.

22. "What I would like to see [in Iraq] is a government where church and state are separated."

— George W. Bush, April 25, 2003, cited by *The Nation*, June 30, 2003.

23. "Unable to persuade Congress to pass legislation making religious groups eligible for federal funding, George W. Bush issued an executive order doing so...It permits religious organizations receiving federal funding for social service programs to discriminate on the basis of religion and religious belief (also sexual orientation) in hiring. 'God loves you, I love you, and you can count on us both!' Bush told a group of clergy after signing the order.

"In January, Bush took up the cross again. He proposed a new regulation that would permit religious organizations to receive HUD grants to construct or remodel churches, synagogues or mosques."

— *The Nation*, June 30, 2003.

24. "We saw another landmark reached in 2005.... The amount of taxpayer dollars diverted to religious groups via the Bush administration's 'faith-based' initiatives topped the $2 billion mark.

"Since his first days in office, President Bush has chipped away at the foundations of religious liberty by establishing a White House Office of Faith-Based and Community Initiatives to oversee government funding of religious organizations, pressing congress to allow taxpayer-funded discrimination against people of minority faiths, and pandering to his religious right base by calling for a nationwide school voucher program to funnel public dollars to private religious schools....

"Whether it is government sanctioning of religious discrimination, federal 'faith-based' funding of groups that proselytize or a science classroom becoming a pulpit for teaching 'intelligent design,' each attack on religious liberty must be recognized as just one thread in a larger, broader assault on everyone's freedom. And each assault must be vigorously opposed if our country is to remain true to its first founding principle."

— ACLU 2006 Work plan.

25. "Since his inauguration in 2001, President George W. Bush has sought to undermine the separation of church and state at every turn, promoting 'faith-based' initiatives, advocating religious school vouchers and lauding the teaching of intelligent design in public schools.

'Despite this ham-fisted religious agenda, however, there is one place where Bush would like to see a stronger separation of church and state: Iraq.

"During a Jan. 11 forum on terrorism in Louisville, Kentucky.... (Bush Said) 'And that is why the constitution written in Iraq is an important constitution, because it separates church for the first time in a modern-day constitution in Iraq. The Iraqi example is going to spread. I believe that....

"Iraq's constitution, however, hardly separates religion and government. It bluntly states, 'Islam is the official religion of the state and is a basic source of legislation' and mandates that 'No law can be passed that contradicts the undisputed rules of Islam.'"

— People and Events, *Church & State*, February 2006.

26. "Why should we let the Arabs have the oil?"

— Henry Kissinger.

27. "Ahmad Chalabi favor(s) privatizing the firm and parceling it out in large pieces to major American and British oil companies. 'American companies will have a big shot at Iraqi oil,' Chalabi declared in September 2002.

— Michael T. Klare, article, *The Nation*, May 12, 2003.

28. "Wolfowitz stressed the need for 'deterring potential competitors from even aspiring to a larger regional or global role'...Wolfowitz said the United States should use military power to protect 'access to vital raw materials, primarily Persian Gulf oil.'"

— Comment, *The Progressive*, May 2003.

29. "Fear of the oil weapon leads commentators to fret over how the Arab states will react to President Bush's ambitious plans for the Middle east, even as it inspires some advocates of those plans to declare that they will bring, as Bush's former speechwriter David Frum put it in his recent memoir, 'new prosperity to us all, by securing the world's largest pool of oil.'"

— James Surowiecki, column, *The New Yorker*, February 10, 2003.

30. "In the fall of '98, Clinton...launched 200 cruise missiles to hit those sites....

"The Washington Times, a conservative paper, ran an article that began: 'The White House orchestrated a plan to provoke Saddam Hussein into defying the United Nations inspectors so President Clinton could justify air strikes, former and current government officials charge....'

"The Conservative Caucus in Vienna, Va., went into high gear with a list of 10 reasons to oppose war with Iraq, not the least of which was 'Clinton has compromised the US defense arsenal by making war against a regime far less threatening than China, Russia, Cuba or North Korea.'

"It said that Clinton was 'squandering' $5.5 billion and imperiling the 24,000 American troops then in the Persian Gulf. It praised Rep. Ron Paul, R-Texas, for saying on the floor of the House that 'Saddam Hussein is not threatening our national security.'

"It trotted out Ann Coulter, the right-wing TV ranter, to say, 'A president who uses his duties as commander in chief to bomb foreign countries every time he wants to change the subject ought to be removed with alacrity.'"

— Norman Lockman, syndicated column, April 19, 2004.

31. "Since the program began, an estimated 500,000 Iraqi children under the age of five have died as a result of the sanctions — almost three times as many as the number of Japanese killed during the US atomic bomb attacks.

"News of such Iraqi fatalities has been well documented (by the United Nations among others) though underreported by the media. What has remained invisible, however, is any documentation of how and by whom such a death toll has been justified for so long...It was easy to discover that for the last ten years a vast number of lengthy holds had been placed on billions of dollars worth of what seemed unobjectionable — and very much needed — imports to Iraq. But I soon learned that all UN records that could answer my questions were kept from public scrutiny...I obtained these documents on the condition that my sources remain anonymous. What they show is that the United States has fought aggressively throughout the last decade to purposefully minimize the humanitarian goods that enter the country. And it has done so in the face of enormous human suffering, including massive increases in child mortality and widespread epidemics.

"According to Pentagon officials, that was the intention. In a June 23, 1991, *Washington Post* article, Pentagon officials stated that Iraq's electrical grid had been targeted by bombing strike in order to undermine the civilian economy. 'People say, You didn't recognize that it was going to have an effect on water or sewage,' said one planning officer at the Pentagon. 'Well, what were we trying to do with sanctions — help out the Iraqi people? No. What we were doing with the attacks on infrastructure was to accelerate the effect of the sanctions.'"

— Joy Gordon, article, *Harpers*, November 2002.

32. According to Dick Cheney, Iraq has been "'very busy enhancing its capabilities in the field of chemical and biological agents...(and) to pursue the nuclear program they began many years ago....We've gotten this from the firsthand testimony of defectors, including Saddam's own son-in-law,' a reference to Lt. Gen. Hussein Kamel, the former Iraqi weapons chief and Iraq's highest ranking defector.

"Ritter pointed out that Cheney was omitting an inconvenient part of Kamel's story," [see below]

— Steve Rendall, *Extra!* March/April 2006.

33. "On Iraq's WMD, Scott Ritter, the former top weapons inspector, claimed that when he left in 1998, 90 to 95 percent of Iraq's chemical and biological weapons (CBW) had been destroyed and any remaining anthrax or sarin would be useless sludge. It was recently disclosed (by Cheney and others) that the number one Iraqi expatriate, Hussein Kamel, whose testimony had been repeatedly cited by US officials, had told his interrogators in 1995 that Saddam Hussein had destroyed his chemical and biological weapons and had none left, a point not made public until March 2003 (John Barry, "The Defector's Secret," *Newsweek*, March 3, 2003).

— Edward S. Herman, article, *Z Magazine*, June 2003.

34. On a trip to Baghdad, Ritter "urged Iraqi officials to allow inspections and warned Americans that attacking Iraq would be a 'historic mistake'.... At CBS Evening News (9/30/02), correspondent Tom Fenton said that Ritter 'is now what some would call a loose cannon.'...

"CNN news executive Eason Jordan told Catherine Calloway: 'well, Scott Ritter's chameleon-like behavior has really bewildered a lot of people.... US officials no longer give Scott Ritter much credibility.' When Paula Zahn interviewed Ritter (CNN American Morning, 8/13/02), she suggested he was in league with Saddam Hussein: 'People out there are accusing you of drinking Saddam's Kool-Aid.'

"Though the absence of WMDs vindicated his views of the Iraqi threat and the value of inspections, it didn't result in his media rehabilitation. Instead of being sought out and consulted for how he got things right, he became largely invisible."

— Steve Rendall, *Extra!*, March/April 2006.

35. "Hans Blix is a seventy-five-year-old Swedish lawyer and public servant... called out of retirement...to lead the United Nations Monitoring, Verification and Inspection Commission (UNMOVIC)...Blix, before he was vindicated by the postwar search for weapons in Iraq, was systematically treated with contempt by leading members of the Bush administration....

"*The Washington Post* reported that Deputy Secretary of Defense Paul Wolfowitz had requested a CIA investigation of Blix's performance at IAEA and had 'hit the ceiling' when nothing could be found to undermine Blix and the inspection program. According to the *Post*, Wolfowitz allegedly feared that the inspection could torpedo plans for military action against Saddam Hussein....

"Of the people Blix talked to, President Jacques Chirac of France was almost alone in believing that the UN inspections had disarmed Iraq long ago....

"France suggested another 120 days for the inspections, a proposal that other European nations and members of the Security Council would have supported; but the US refused...Washington was fed up with Blix for refusing to play the part that was expected of him....

"Hans Blix...was spied on, publicly reviled, and called a liar.... Karl Rove, the highest-ranking Norwegian-American in the White House...was convinced of the historical duplicity of the Swedes.... War was inevitable, the official line ran. Because Saddam Hussein refused to turn over his weapons of mass destruction, an impossible dilemma for the Iraqi despot since he had none to turn over....

"With what seemed great conviction, Powell paraded before the council pictures of alleged installations and sinister vehicles, which we now know to have been a collection of nonexistent smoking guns. He convinced many people, including that most skeptical of journalist, the late Mary McCrory....

"Bush's declaration of war came as an ultimatum to Saddam Hussein to leave Iraq within forty-eight hours. The ultimatum was accompanied by a crescendo of hyperbole about Saddam's WMDs, cooperation with terrorists, and imminent threat to the US and everyone else....

"This is the sense of messianic big ideas not properly thought through, a certainty that sometimes even hints at divine rightness, and an undertone of manifest destiny under the guidance of Almighty God."

— Brian Urquart, book review, *Plan of Attack*, by Bob Woodward, *The New York Review*, June 10, 2004.

36. "Whenever Bush gets criticized, his palace guard descends upon the person who dares to question his Highness.

"That's the way it was when Paul O'Neill, Bush's former Treasury Secretary, said Bush wanted to go to war against Iraq way before 9/11. Within hours, the Bush goons were threatening O'Neill with prosecution for allegedly publicizing classified information.

"That's the way it was when former ambassador Joseph Wilson went public with his account of how the Bush Administration played up the false story of uranium in Niger. Within days, the White House was outing Wilson's wife, Valerie Plame, as a CIA officer, with Karl Rove reportedly saying, 'His wife's now fair game.'"
— Comment, *The Progressive*, May 2004.

> The outing of Valery Plame, Joseph Wilson's wife, by Bush and his staff was really an effort to kill her. Such revelations constituted a crime in the first place because such exposure of agents had resulted in the assassination of American spies. Bush and his closest advisors knew full well that their effort to punish Wilson by endangering his wife's life was both criminal and treasonous; this sort of action is grounds for impeachment and criminal prosecution. The Bush White House and the Republican Party have stonewalled and have delayed the investigation so that it can be brushed aside. There is some renewed interest based on Scott McClellan's book *What Happened*, released just before the end of the Bush presidency. We shall see how far it gets. — Author.]

37. "Paul Wolfowitz: 'Well, I just don't understand why we are beginning by talking about this one man, bin Laden.'

"Clarke:' We are talking about a network of terrorist organizations called Al Qaeda, that happens to be led by bin Laden, and we are talking about that network because it and it alone poses an immediate and serious threat to the United States.'

"Wolfowitz: Well, there are others that do as well, at least as much. Iraqi terrorism, for example.... You give bin Laden too much credit.'" ...

"'At first, I was incredulous that we were talking about something other than getting Al Qaeda. Then I realized with almost a sharp physical pain that Rumsfeld and Wolfowitz were going to try to take advantage of this national tragedy to promote their agenda about Iraq.

"Clarke said he told Powell that this was foolish. 'Having been attacked by Al Qaeda, for us now to go bombing Iraq in response would be like invading Mexico after the Japanese attacked Pearl Harbor....

"'All along, it seemed inevitable that we would invade,' he writes. 'Iraq was portrayed as the most dangerous thing in national security. It was an *idée fixe*, a rigid belief, received wisdom, a decision already made and one that no fact or event could derail.' In the lead up to the war, the Bush Administration repeatedly tried to lump September 11 and Iraq together. Writes Clarke: 'What a horrible thing it was to give such a false impression to our people and our troops.'"
— Comment, *The Progressive*, May 2004.

38. "Simply stated, there is no doubt that Saddam Hussein now has weapons of mass destruction."
— Vice President Dick Cheney, August 26, 2002. Jonathan Schell column, *The Nation*, June 30, 2003.

39. "Right now, Iraq is expanding and improving facilities that were used for the production of biological weapons."
— George Bush, Sept. 12, 2002.

40. "Intelligence gathered by this and other governments leaves no doubt that the Iraq regime continues to possess and conceal some of the most lethal weapons ever devised."
— George W. Bush two days before he attacked Iraq.

41. The Iraq regime possesses and produces chemical and biological weapons. It is seeking nuclear weapons.

— George Bush on Oct. 7, 2002.

42. "Iraq has a growing fleet of manned and unmanned aerial vehicles that would be used to disperse chemical or biological weapons across broad areas. We're concerned that Iraq is exploring ways of using the UAVs for missions targeting the United States.

— George W. Bush on Oct. 7, 2002.

43. "Iraq is reconstituting its nuclear weapons program. Hussein has held numerous meetings with Iraq nuclear scientists, a group he calls his 'nuclear mujahedeen' — his nuclear holy warriors.

— George W. Bush on Oct. 7, 2002.

44. "We have sources that tell us that Saddam Hussein recently authorized Iraq field commanders to use chemical weapons — the very weapons the dictator tells us he does not have.

— George w. Bush on Feb. 8, 2003.

45. "We know that Saddam Hussein is determined to keep his weapons of mass destruction, is determined to make more."

— Colin Powell on Feb. 5, 2003

46. "We know where they are. They are in the area around Tikrit and Baghdad."

— Donald Rumsfeld on March 30, 2003.

47. "Most Americans now believe that Saddam Hussein was behind the September 11 attacks and support the war...in the mistaken belief that it is necessary for self-defense. The 9/11 connection is ceaselessly, demagogically promoted by the administration. In his speech warning of imminent invasion if Saddam failed to leave Iraq in forty-eight hours, George W. Bush alluded to this discredited canard seven times."

— Katha Pollitt, column, *The Nation*, April 7, 2003.

48. "Saddam Hussein's government is well known for its human-rights abuses against the Kurds and Shiites, and for its invasion of Kuwait. What is less well known is that this same government had also invested heavily in health, education, and social programs for two decades prior to the Persian Gulf War. While the treatment of ethnic minorities and political enemies has been abominable under Hussein, it is also the case that the well-being of the society at large improved dramatically... Before the Persian Gulf War, Iraq was a rapidly developing country, with free education, ample electricity, modernized agriculture, and a robust middle class. According to the World Health Organization, 93 percent of the population had access to health care."

— Joy Gordon, article, *Harpers*, November 2002.

49. "Iraq is only the beginning. The *Boston Globe* (9/10/02) reports: 'As the Bush administration debates going to war against Iraq, its most hawkish members are pushing a sweeping vision for the Middle East that sees the overthrow of President Saddam Hussein of Iraq as merely a first step in the region's transformation.... After an ouster of Hussein, they say, the United States will have leverage to act against Syria and Iran, will be in a better position to resolve the Israeli-Palestinian conflict, and will be able to rely less on Saudi oil.

"'There is open discussion within Israel and the US ruling circles of massive "transfer"- the ethnic cleansing of historic Palestine. (Defense Secretary Rumsfeld has called Jewish settlements in the West Bank and Gaza legitimate Israeli spoils of war; Dick Armey, the Republican Majority Leader in the House, has spoken in favor of expelling Palestinians to Jordan.)'

"'The Rand Corporation's Pentagon briefing echoed this theme: It called Iraq the "strategic pivot" and Egypt "the prize." In their view, the entire region should be re-configured to US specifications.'"

— Larry Everest and Leonard Innes, article, *Z Magazine*, December 2002.

50. "The predominant obstacle to peace is Israel's colonization of Palestine. Israel's occupation of Palestine has obstructed a comprehensive peace agreement in the Holy Land..."

— Jimmy Carter, Chris McGreal, *Asheville Global Report*, Mar. 23-29, 2006. Source: *Independent* (UK).

51. "A poll of attitudes among Israel's Jews towards their country's Arab citizens has exposed widespread racism, with large numbers favoring segregation and policies to encourage Arabs to leave the country.

"The poll found that more than two-thirds of Jews would refuse to live in the same building as an Arab. Nearly half would not allow an Arab in their home and 41 percent want segregation of entertainment facilities....

"Some 18 percent said they felt hatred when they heard someone speaking Arabic, and 34 percent agreed with the statement that 'Arab culture is inferior to Israeli culture.'"

— Chris McGreal, *Asheville Global Report*, Mar. 30 — Apr. 5, 2006. Source: *Guardian* (UK).

52. "More than half of US citizens believe there are more violent extremists within Islam than in any other religion and that the faith encourages violence against non-Muslims, according to a Washington Post-ABC News poll released on Mar. 9....

"Nearly half of US citizens, 46 percent, said they held unfavorable attitudes towards Islam — compared with 24 percent in January 2002. The Post quoted analysts as saying that the demonization of Islam by politicians and the media during the past four years had led to an erosion of tolerance."

— Suzanne Goldenberg, *Asheville Global Report*, Mar. 16 — 22, 2006. Source: *Guardian* (UK).

53. "The pro-Israel lobby in the United States has manipulated Washington's policies in the Middle East to the point where it is the US that does most of the fighting, dying and rebuilding while Israel reaps most of the security benefits, argues a new study by two US scholars.

"'This situation has no equal in American political history,' says the 83-page study, 'The Israel Lobby and US Foreign Policy.' [by John Mearsheimer and Stephen Walt]...

"Since World war II, the United States has channeled $140 billion in support to Israel, notes the study, which also challenges the notion that Israel is a 'crucial ally in the war on terror, because its enemies are America's enemies.'

"'Saying that Israel and the United States are united by a shared terrorist threat has the causal relationship backwards; rather the United States has a terrorism problem in good part because it is so closely allied with Israel, not the other way around,' the authors argue....

"At home, the lobby has worked hard to suppress its critics, something the authors say has not been good for democracy, especially one that now claims to be promoting freedom in the Arab world.

"'Silencing skeptics by organizing blacklists and boycotts — or by suggesting that critics are anti-Semites — violates the principle of open debate upon which democracy depends,' they say."

— Emad Mekay, *Asheville Global Report*, Mar. 30 — Apr. 3, 2006.

54. "On June 8, 1967 I was a 20-year-old 3rd class petty officer in damage control at the time of a sneak attack by our so-called ally, Israel, Our ship was identified as 'friendly Americans' only hours before the slaughter began at 2 p.m.

"The Israeli jet aircraft were ruthless and stubborn in their attempt to sink the USS *Liberty* and murder all hands aboard. They hit nearly every antenna on our ship – no accident for sure. The Israeli reconnaissance aircraft took pictures of our ship in the morning hours and nothing was missed. The attacking aircraft dropped napalm on the bridge of our ship to burn us alive.

"Soon after the jets were done with us we saw three motor torpedo boats approaching our ship at a high speed. We then learned who our attackers were. We saw three flags marked with a Star of David. We were in shock because the Israelis were supposed to be our allies. We had no idea who was attacking us until then. The attacking jet airplanes were unmarked. The torpedo boats maneuvered themselves into a torpedo launch attitude, then came the five to six torpedoes.... The torpedoes whizzed by our ship, forward and aft with one hitting its mark, blowing to bits 25 American heroes who stood their ground below the water line and accepted their fate, doing their duty for the United States....

"The captain had given the order to abandon ship, as it appeared we were about to roll over. There were three life rafts left that were floatable. We put them over the side so we could put our most severely wounded in them to try to save their lives. The torpedo gunmen blew two of them out of the water. They took the third raft aboard their boat as a trophy. The torpedo gunmen continued their assault until I guess they ran out of ammunition. They circled the ship and left.

"Old Glory was still on her mast, seven feet by 13 feet. We thought the attack was over. Two Israeli helicopters approached our ship with armed gunmen at the ready to finish us off. They were there a short time and left in the same direction they came....

Terry Halbardier, a radioman got off an SOS from an antenna that was not hit by the Israeli heat-seeking missiles.... The SOS he sent stated we were under attack by unknown jet aircraft. "

— By Phillip F. Tourney, a survivor of the Israeli attack on the USS Liberty, partial quote from the *American Free Press*, December 24, 2007.

55. "It's slightly eerie now to look at what Israel Shahak (professor at Hebrew University) was saying back then and at the accuracy of his predictions: 'The basic trends were established in '74 and '75, including settler organization, mystical ideology, and the great financial support of the United States to Israel.... Between summer '74 and summer '75 the key decisions were taken, and from that time it's a straight line.' Among these decisions, said Shahak, was 'to keep the occupied territories of Palestine,' a detailed development of much older designs consummated in 1967.

"Gradually, through the 1980s...the contours of the Israeli plan emerged, like the keel and ribs and timbers of an old ship: the road system that would bypass Palestinian towns and villages and link the Jewish settlements and military posts; the ever-expanding clusters of illegal settlements; control of the whole region's water.

"It wasn't hard to get vivid descriptions of the increasingly intolerable conditions of life for Palestinians: the torture of prisoners, the barriers to the simplest trip, the harassment of farmers and schoolchildren, the house demolitions. Plenty of people came back from Israel and the territories with harrowing accounts, though few of the accounts made the journey into a major newspaper or onto national television.

"And even in the testimonies that did get published here, there was never recognition of Israel's long-term plan to wipe the record clean of all troublesome UN resolutions, crush Palestinian's national aspirations, steal their land and water, cram them into ever-smaller enclaves, ultimately balkanize them with the wall, which was on the drawing board many years ago. Indeed, to write about any sort of master plan was to incur further torrents of abuse for one's supposedly 'paranoid' fantasies about Israel's bad faith, with much pious invocation of the 'peace process.'"

— Alexander Cockburn, column, *The Nation,* June 19, 2006.

56. "I believed, and to this day still believe, in our people's eternal and historic right to this entire land."

— Israeli Prime Minister Ehud Olmert, Addressing the US Congress in May of 2006.

57. "It is true that a path must be sought to alleviate the suffering of all peoples in the Middle East. Yet, that path lies in acceptance of Torah teachings (Jewish law) and true justice.

"The Jewish people are in a state of divinely ordained exile, since the destruction of the Jewish Temple, some 2,000 years ago. We are expressly forbidden to attempt to leave exile (to have our own state), to go up *en masse* to the Holy Land and to rebel against any nation.

"Exile means that Jews are required to be loyal citizens in every country in which they live. Force of arms and violence against any people, including in the Holy Land, is forbidden....

"Zionism is insensitive to this ancient Jewish belief. It is also oblivious to the suffering that it has created for Palestinian and Jew alike."

— Rabbi Yisroel David Weiss of Neturei Karta International, quoted by the staff of the *American Free Press, December 24. 2007.*

> [The notion that the Israelis are God's chosen people and that he promised them all of the Palestinian lands almost exactly parallels Hitler's claim that the German people were a super Aryan race favored by God, that they had a sacred right to living space in other European countries, and that the Nazis, like the Israelis, had a right approved by God to cleanse away anyone who got in their way. —Author]

58. "In words one would be hard pressed to find in the pages of any major American newspaper, Hedges writes of 'the profound injustice the creation of the state of Israel meant for Palestinians.' And he speaks of 'Palestinian villages in Israel that have been razed in (a) process of state-sponsored forgetting.' Later, he provides an eyewitness account of Israeli troops provoking Palestinian kids in Gaza to throw rocks and then shooting them in cold blood. Never in more than fifteen years of covering wars across the world, he reports, had he 'watched soldiers entice children like mice into a trap and murder them for sport.'"

— *War is a Force That Gives Us Meaning* by Chris Hedges, review by Joseph Nevins, *The Nation,* November 18th, 2002.

59. "As a massive US military buildup intensifies in the Persian Gulf, United Nations (UN) weapons inspectors, in their second month in Iraq, conceded this week that they had found no evidence of the weapons of mass destruction that the White House claims to exist.

"The US has set in motion the final buildup of soldiers and equipment for an invasion of Iraq, which now looks all but certain to happen sometime in February — whatever the UN inspectors inside the country unearth or fail to unearth."

— Eamon Martin, article, *Asheville Global Report,* January 2-8, 2003.

60. "Iraqi armored forces consist mainly of aging Soviet-era armor and are about half the strength of 1991, when Iraq boasted the world's fourth largest army.

"The remnants of Saddam's air force — about 90 French Mirages and Soviet MIGs — remain impounded in Iran, where they fled to escape destruction during the first Gulf War. Other Iraqi planes or helicopters can take off only at peril of being shot down."

— Richard Pyle, AP column, *The Asheville Citizen Times,* March 30, 2003.

61. "The US defense budget approaches $400 billion, larger than the defense budgets of the next 20 countries combined.... Seventy percent of US government-financed research is for new weaponry. The US Navy is larger than all the navies of the world combined."

— Harry J. Petrequin, *Asheville Citizens Times,* March 30, 2003.

62. "Although the assertion that Iraq still had weapons of massive destruction was the official justification for the country's invasion, there has perhaps never been a war in which the inequality of firepower between the combatants has been so great.

"The comparative casualty rates between the Iraqi forces and those of the coalition will be, as in 'Operation Desert Storm,' well over 100 to one."

— John Berger, article, *The Nation,* May 12, 2003.

63. "This will be no war — there will be a fairly brief and ruthless military intervention.... the president will give an order. [The attack] will be rapid, accurate and dazzling.... It will be greeted by the majority of the Iraqi people as emancipation. And I say, bring it on."

— Christopher Hitchens

64. March 19, 2003 — US forces launch missiles and bombs at targets in Iraq, signaling the start of the war.

66. "The scuds he swore he didn't have were fired at Kuwait, and Iraq was launching lame denials while the craters still smoked."

— Peter Bronson, *Cincinnati Enquirer,* March 23, 2003.

67. "In these first 24 hours we had six confirmed scud launches,"

— Karl Zinmeister, *National Review Online,* March 26, 2003.

68. "Jacques Chirac, Gerhard Schroeder, Nelson Mandela, Kofi Anan and other apologists were shown to be feckless fools."

— Karl Zinmeister, *National Review Online,* March 26, 2003.

69. "People in countries with no troops in Iraq have already, as this is written, seen Iraq fighting with weapons Saddam Hussein claimed he did not have."

— Michael Barone, *US News and World Report,* March 31, 2003.

70. "'Swooping silently out of the Persian Gulf night,' exulted James Dao of the *New York Times,* Navy SEALs claimed 'a bloodless victory in the battle for Iraq's vast oil empire.'"

— Michael T. Klare, article, *The Nation,* May 12, 2003.

71. "The first week of invasion proved every assertion false...

No Iraqi shock troops appeared in the field against the American infantry divisions; no Iraqi aircraft presumed to leave the ground; no allied combat unit met with, much less knew where to find, the fabled weapons of mass destruction. The desultory shows of resistance at the river crossings constituted ragged skirmish lines of young men for the most part barefoot and lightly armed, so many of them out of uniform that it wasn't worth the trouble to distinguish between the civilian and the military dead.

"The weakness of the Iraqi target made ridiculous Washington's propaganda poster of Saddam as the second coming of Hitler, and the useful lesson to be learned presented itself on April Fool's Day. Here was the American army in the sinister landscape of Iraq, equipped to fight the Battle of Normandy or El-alamein but conducting a police action in the manner of the Israeli assassination teams hunting down Palestinian terrorists in the rubble of the Gaza Strip. Would it be possible to hide in plain sight the false pretext of Operation Iraqi Freedom?"

— Lewis H. Lapham, Notebook, *Harper's Magazine*, June 2003.

72. "People across the region were reportedly astonished to see Iraqis gleefully dancing on the statue head of Saddam Hussein and gratefully shaking the hands of US Marines...So how to explain the undeniable evidence that many Iraqis regard the US troops as liberators? The Arab press and satellite channels on April 14 were awash with denials, conspiracy theories and tortured reasoning."

— Editorial, *The Washington Post*, April 21-27, 2003.

73. "The pulling down of Saddam's statue on April 9 achieved parity with the crumbling of the Berlin wall, even though the event took place in an all-but-empty plaza cordoned off by a perimeter of US Marines, in the presence of maybe 150 pro-American Iraqis, half of them imported by the Pentagon several days earlier from London. The careful framing of the camera shots sustained the illusion of an immense and wildly cheering crowd."

— Lewis Lapham, Notebook, *Harpers Magazine*, June 2003.

74. "Disingenuous US press coverage of the invasion came with the images of Iraqis cheering US troops in the Baghdad square in front of the Palestine Hotel on April 9 as they hauled down Saddam's statue.

"Remember, the photos of the statue going down, the flag on Saddam's face, the cheering Iraqis, were billed as the images that showed It Was All Worthwhile, up there in the pantheon with Joe Rosenthal's photograph of the raising of the US flag on Iwo Jima and the news film of the Berlin wall going down....

"The clamorous masses in the square never existed. I've yet to see the full image reproduced in any mainstream US newspaper, but I have seen photographs on the web of the entire square when the statue was being pulled down.

"In one small portion of the square, itself sealed off by three US tanks, there's a knot of maybe 150 people. Close-up photographs suggest that the active non-US participants were associates of Ahmad Chalabi, leader of the Iraqi National Congress, the exile group that rode in on the back of those tanks. (Go to www.counterpunch.org/statue.html and see for yourself.)"

— Alexander Cockburn, column, *The Nation*, May 12, 2003.

75. "It won't take weeks. You know that, professor. Our military machine will crush Iraq in a matter of days and there's no question that it will."

— Bill O'Reilly, Fox News, Feb. 10, 2003.

76. "April 9, 2003 — After days of bombing, Baghdad falls into US hands."

— *Public Citizen News*, May/June 2003.

77. "Well, the hot story of the week is victory....The Tommy Franks/Don Rumsfeld battle plan, war plan, worked brilliantly.... all the naysayers have been humiliated so far....The final word is hooray."

— Morton Kendrick, Fox News, April 12, 2003.

78. "The only people who think this wasn't a victory are Upper Westside liberals, and a few people here in Washington."
— Charles Krauthammer, Inside Washington, WUSA-TV, April 19, 2003.

79. "Some journalists, in my judgment, just can't stand success, especially a few liberal columnists and newspapers and a few Arab reporters."
— Lou Dobbs, CNN, April 14, 2003.

80. "More than anything else, real vindication for the administration. One, credible evidence of weapons of mass destruction. Two, you know what? There were a lot of terrorists here, really bad guys. I saw them."
— Bob Arnot, MSNBC, April 9, 2003.

81. "Why don't the damn Democrats give the president his day? He won today. He did well today."
— Chris Matthews, MSNBC, April 9, 2003.

82. "I'm waiting to hear the words, 'I was wrong,' from some of the world's most elite journalists, politicians and Hollywood types.... Maybe disgraced commentators and politicians alike, like Daschle, Jimmy Carter, Dennis Kucinich and all these others...their wartime predictions were arrogant, they were misguided and they were dead wrong.
— Joe Scarborough, MSNBC, April 10, 2003.

83. "Major combat operations in Iraq have ended. In the battle of Iraq, the United States and our allies have prevailed."
— George W. Bush, May 1, 2003.

84. "My friends, here's the news. We are winning in Iraq. We are winning in Iraq. We are winning in Iraq.
— John McCain.

85. "As in recent US military attacks on Third World countries, the media pretended that this was a 'war' as opposed to a straightforward attack by a distant superpower on a virtually defenseless target state – an unlevel playing field par excellence and a massacre of enemy forces that had been disarmed, bombed, spied on under the guise of inspections, and starved for the prior dozen years. These pretenses were essential to allowing the defeat of Iraq to be a military marvel and matter of pride, rather than a source of embarrassment and shame at beating up yet another hapless and deliberately crippled victim."
— Edward S. Herman, *Z Magazine*, June 2003.

Chapter 8. Killing

1. "Sept. 11, 2001 — Al Qaeda terrorists hijack commercial airplanes and crash them into both towers of the World Trade Center and the Pentagon...Shortly after the crash, Bush administration officials speculate that Saddam Hussein...helped plan the attacks and begin calling for regime change."
— *Public Citizen News*, May/June 2003.

2. "There wasn't a single Iraqi among the terrorists who destroyed the World trade Center. Almost all of them were from Saudi Arabia, Washington's best client in the world. Bin Laden is Saudi too...."
— Eduardo Galeano, column, *The Progressive*, May 2003.

3. "They hate America. They align themselves with Saddam Hussein. They align themselves with terrorists all over the world."
— Cliff May on MSNBC's *Hardball* attacking peaceful protesters at the World Bank/IMF meetings, cited in *Extra!*, December 2002.

4. "We should invade their country, kill their leaders and convert them to Christianity."
— Ann Coulter on Islam, *Z Magazine*, May 2002.

5. "We need to execute people like John Walker in order to physically intimidate liberals, by making them realize that they can be killed too! Otherwise, they will turn out to be outright traitors!"
— Ann Coulter, *Extra!* December 2002.

6. "I think the government should be spying on all Arabs, engaging in torture as a televised spectator sport, dropping daisy cutters wantonly throughout the Middle East and sending liberals to Guantanamo."
— Ann Coulter, on her website on Dec. 21 2005.

7. "American pacifist are on the side of future mass murderers of Americans...are objectively pro-terrorist, evil, and liars."
— Michael Kelly column, *Washington Post*: from the *Progressive Populist*, December 15, 2001.

8. "All you have to do is to tell them that they are being attacked, and denounce the pacifists for lack of patriotism and exposing the country to danger. It works the same in every country."

— Hermann Goring

9. Wants to use torture to "jump-start the stalled investigations" and demands that pacifists "shut up" because "it's kill or be killed."

— Jonathan Alter in *Newsweek*: from the *Progressive Populist*, December 15, 2001.

10. "Bomb Afghanistan's infrastructure to rubble — the airport, the power plants, their water facilities, the roads...the Afghans are responsible for the Taliban...if they don't rise up against this criminal government, they starve, period."

— Bill O'Reilly on Fox TV: from the *Progressive Populist*, December 15, 2001.

11. "I'm telling you, I'm telling you that President Bush is doing just what Jesus would have done."

— Bill O'Reilly, *The O'Reilly Factor*, Fox News, cited by *Extra! Update*, April 2003.

12. "As (Colman) McCarthy pointed out, Gandhi was right: 'The only people on earth who do not see Christ's teachings as nonviolent are Christians.'"

— E. J. Lopez, letter to the editor, *The Progressive*, January 2002.

13. In *The Washington Times*, Abe Rosenthal demanded that the US bomb Afghanistan, Iraq, Libya, Sudan, Iran, and Syria.

— *The Progressive Populist*, December 15, 2001.

14. "Kill the bastards...a gunshot between the eyes, blow them to smithereens, poison them...as for countries or cities that host these worms, bomb them into basketball courts.

— Steve Dunleavy, *New York Post*: from the *Progressive Populist*, December 15, 2001.

15. "We have to fight the terrorists as if there were no rules...give war a chance."

— Thomas Friedman, New York Times: from the *Progressive Populist*, December 15, 2001.

16. "Kill them...even if they are not directly involved in this thing."

— Lawrence Eagleburger, the *Progressive Populist*, December 15, 2001.

17. "Let's have rage. Let America explore the rich reciprocal possibilities...a policy of focused brutality...America needs to relearn a lost discipline, self-confident relentlessness — and to relearn why human nature has equipped us with a weapon called hatred."

— Lance Morrow of *Time*: from the *Progressive Populist*, December 15, 2001.

18. Gossip columnist Liz Smith loved Charles Krauthammer's desire for "total war" and said "we will hold them accountable because they have harbored and created these terrorists. We could wipe those countries off the map, and they should be afraid of that."

Someone named Easterbrook said, "A hundred million Muslims would die as US nuclear bombs rained down on every conceivable military target in a dozen Muslim countries." Schell calls this "a crime outside all human experience that would blacken the name of the United States in human memory forever."

— Jonathan Schell column, *The Nation*, November 26, 2001.

19. "The goal is destruction of enemies."

— George Will, from the *Progressive Populist*, December 15, 2001.

20. "We should have given the citizens of Baghdad 48 hours to get out of Dodge by dropping leaflets and going with the AM radios and all that. Forty-eight hours, you've got to get out of there, and flatten the place. Then the war would be over. We could have done that in two days.... You flatten Baghdad, you flatten all the troops,

we know where they go, there's nowhere to hide in the desert. We know where everybody's moving. And you know as well as I do, this war could have been over in two
days.... It's just frustrating for everybody to know that we have been fighting this war
with one hand behind our back.

"'Now after we know that the final battle is going to come in Baghdad, that the
people who remain in Baghdad, the civilians, bear some kind of responsibility for
their own safety. Am I wrong?' O'Reilly's guests that night were in agreement."

— Bill O'Reilly, cited in *Extra*, June 2003.

21. "I pushed my way through the crowd and saw a hand, severed below the
knuckles, sitting grotesquely on a green metal window shutter that had fallen on
some steps. The hand was thick and gray, and its red-and-white guts, at the messily
severed stump, spilled out like electrical circuitry from a cut cable.... Someone told
me that a man's brain was sitting on the floor just inside the nearest workshop door,
but I didn't go to look at it.

"'The dead included an entire family of five,' he said, pointing to the scorched-look-
ing apartment directly above us. The bodies had already been taken to the morgue,
and the many wounded had been taken to hospitals.

"Another man told me his name was Muyad.... I asked him if he knew any of the
victims. He nodded yes, and gestured toward one of the blackened cars. 'His name
was Abu Sayaff. He was my friend.' I nodded in sympathy. 'Bush and Blair...They said
this would be a clean war,' Muyad said. He smiled tentatively. 'This is not clean. This
is dirty — a dirty war'...I told him I was sorry about what had happened. 'Don't be
sorry,' he replied. 'It's not the American people. Most of them are against this war.
We know this.' And then he added, apparently by way of explanation, 'I saw the
director Michael Moore on TV yesterday.'"

— Jon Lee Anderson, article, *The New Yorker*, April 7, 2003.

22. "'I appreciate the attention of those lawyers, but the US administration is
cruel. If they knew anything about human rights it would not have happened.'"...
Outside the office, Kassam is standing alone. I ask him again if he can tell me about
what happened to his family. He stares quietly across a filtration pool. Then, he talks
about 1992 when the war had been over for a year and Iraq's water treatment facilities and its bombed electric grid remained crippled. 'Miriam was my first baby. She
contracted diarrhea.' I ask if it was a water-borne illness, and he nods. 'We couldn't
find medicine. I stayed with her for 42 days. We lost her, and we have lost so many
other children in Iraq.'

"About the prospect for war, he says, 'My anger has no limits. I am angry at those
who carry out war against innocents. I cannot say more.'"

— Terry J. Allen, column, *Amnesty Now*, Spring 2003.

23. "Even more horrifying than the torture of Iraqi prisoners by their American
captors has been the unnecessary suffering and death inflicted on the Iraqi people by
the war itself. One of (the) children on whose unavenged tears the edifice of freedom
has been built in Iraq was 12-year-old Ali Ismael Abbas, who was so badly burned in
a US missile attack on Baghdad that his entire torso was black, his arms so mutilated
that as *New Yorker* correspondent Jon Lee Anderson described the hospital scene, they
'looked like something that might be found in a barbecue pit, his family, which included his pregnant mother, his father and his six brothers and sisters, were all killed
by the blast. Some of their bodies were so unrecognizable that all Anderson could
see in morgue photographs was a collection of charred body parts and some red flesh.
The remains of other family members were mutilated grotesqueries. '[His mother's]

face had been cut in half, as if by a giant cleaver, and her mouth was yawning open.... the body of his brother was all there, it seemed, but from the nose up his head was gone, simply sheared off, like the head of a rubber doll. His mouth, like that of his mother was open, as if he were screaming.' Judging from the poll numbers after the fall of the Iraqi regime, the seven or eight out of ten Americans who backed the war were prepared to build the edifice of freedom and democracy on the broken bodies not of one, but of hundreds, possibly of thousands, of Iraqi children killed or maimed or burned in the conflict."

— Paul Savoy, article, *The Nation,* May 31, 2004.

24. "We're proud of our president. Americans love having a guy as president, a guy who has a little swagger, who's physical, who's not a complicated guy like Clinton or even like Dukakis or Mondale, all those guys, McGovern. They want a guy who is president. Women like a guy who's president. Check it out. The women like this war. I think we like having a hero as our president. It's simple."

— Chris Matthews, MSNBC's Hardball, cited in the *Asheville Global Report,* March 16, 2006. Source: *Counter Punch.*

25. "The public outrage 'suggested' a false moral equivalence between an army that fundamentally fights fair and an enemy that only fights dirty....

"The soldiers who entered Baghdad were heroes to all of us and the gentle treatment they extended to civilian men, women and children in Iraq was touching, reminiscent of the soldiers who liberated Europe a generation ago."

— Suzanne Fields, commentary, *Tribune Media Services,* May 18, 2004.

26. "'You are a democracy,' Watiqa Raheem Faiyad, 25, says from her bed in the front room of her family's house in the southern Iraqi city of Basrah. 'You should do more to stop the war.' The war she was referring to was not the one that ended in 1991, or even the one that may have already begun by the time *Amnesty Now* goes to press, but the one that never stopped: For more than 10 years, the United States has, on a weekly and sometimes daily basis, bombed Iraq — both inside the no-fly zones and outside them. Unlike the sanctions, these sorties, purportedly aimed at protecting Shiite and Kurd minorities, are not endorsed by the UN. Some of the casualties are civilians.

"'I was at South Oil Company...when I heard thunder, a huge sound, and something hit my leg, and I was thrown into the air.' Under her scarf, Faiyad's head is wrapped in bandages; a metal apparatus, like a TV antenna tuned to pain, protrudes through dressings on her leg. According to international news reports, it was a US bomb that fell on her workplace. Faiyad says that the facility was strictly civilian and that the attack killed one and wounded eight.

"'Now when I hear planes I am so afraid,' says Faiyad, adding softly, 'afraid I will never walk again. Who do I blame? I blame the American government, but also the people. It is not too hard for Americans to listen to the news and learn the truth and to educate the ignorant ones who want to make war on us.'"

— Terry J. Allen, column, *Amnesty Now,* Spring 2003.

27. "The number of casualties in Baghdad is so high that hospitals have stopped counting the number of people treated,' the International Committee of the Red Cross (ICRC) said Sunday.

"They lay in lines: the car salesman who'd just lost his eye but whose feet were still dribbling blood, the motorcyclist who was shot by US troops near the Rashid Hotel, the 50-year-old female civil servant, her long dark hair spread over the towel she was lying on, her face, breasts, thighs, arms and feet pock-marked with shrapnel from a cluster bomb.

"Ali Ismael Abbas, 12, was fast asleep when war shattered his life. A missile obliterated his home and most of his family, leaving him orphaned and badly burned and blowing off both his arms.

"'It was midnight when the missile fell on us. My father, my mother, and my brother died. My mother was five months pregnant,' the traumatized boy told Reuters at Baghdad's Kindi hospital.

"'Before the war I did not regard America as my enemy. Now I do,' said Doctor Sadek al-Mukhtar. 'There are the military and there are the civilians. War should be against the military. America is killing civilians.'"

— Compiled by Nicholas Holt, *Asheville Global Report*, Apr. 10–16, 2003.

28. "Slogans and symbols referring to the attacks of Sept. 11, 2001, made clear that a spirit of anti-terrorism vengeance infused the ranks. Soldiers displayed flags from Ground Zero and images of the World Trade Center's twin towers."

— The Asheville Citizen-Times, May 12, 2004.

29. "A Toyota packed with fifteen civilians barreled toward a checkpoint intersection near Karbala, south of Baghdad. US Army guys poured half a dozen rounds into it, killing five children and four or five adults. William Branigh's eyewitness report on the incident in the *Washington Post* on April 1 fingered a captain who had excitedly goaded his men to fire, but who, when he realized what had happened, blamed their platoon leader, roaring at him, 'You just (expletive) killed a family because you didn't fire a warning shot soon enough!'

"According to a story by Dexter Filkins in the *New York Times* of April 6, in another such incident, in which six members of a family in a minibus were killed at a checkpoint, 'one Marine,' according to witnesses there, 'began to cry.'

"A *Times* story on April 14 tells of the killing of six daughters in a single family by an American missile.

"On April 5, sixty tanks and other armored vehicles rolled through Baghdad, a city of five million. While taking light casualties, by US estimates those forces killed between two and three thousand Iraqis, not counting civilians, although civilians were also killed.

"Without UN sanctions, which the Security Council refused to give, the attack on Iraq was a war of aggression, and the killings that we, Britain, and Australia committed are war crimes."

— Ronnie Dugger, article, *Free Inquiry*, summer 2003.

30. "It is hardly possible for them to like America when they consider Washington's record of first supporting Saddam, then punishing his people with sanctions, then bombing the place to get rid of him. Americans are an obvious affront to national pride, and perhaps even more acutely to religious pride.

"The Shiite clergy, despite schisms over their proper role in politics, deliver a surprisingly uniform message. America has served its only purpose by getting rid of Saddam. Its army is here at our sufferance, and sooner or later we will make them leave."

— Max Rodenbeck, article, *The New York Review*, July 3, 2003.

31. "Exactly how many Iraqis American forces have killed is not known. As General Tommy Franks said, 'We don't do body counts.' Everyone agrees that the numbers are substantial. Major Peter Kilner, a former West Point philosophy instructor who went to Iraq last year as part of a team writing the official history of the war,

believes that most infantrymen there have 'looked down the barrel and shot at people, and many have killed.' American firepower is overwhelming, Kilner said. He ran into a former student in Iraq who told him, 'There's just too much killing. They shoot, we return fire, and they're all dead.' ...

"The rate of suicide among soldiers in Iraq is nearly a third higher than the Army's historical average. At least twenty Army men and women have committed suicide in Iraq since the war began, and seven others killed themselves after returning home. 'I haven't killed anybody,' one soldier, a father of two, wrote his mother from Baghdad before killing himself."

— Dan Baum, article, *The New Yorker*, July 12 & 19, 2004.

32. "Begin paying attention to stories from Iraq like the very recent one about US Marines killing a group of civilians near Baghdad. This is the next step in the Iraq war as frustration among our soldiers grows — especially with multiple tours. I served [in Vietnam] with the 11th Light Infantry Brigade, Americal Division, and My Lai was not an isolated incident. We came to be known as the Butcher's Brigade, and we also were the birthplace of the Phoenix Program....

"There's a numbness in my guts as I see the same nightmares becoming reality again in Iraq and I wonder what's happening to America's soul. Is this what we want, another generation suckled on the poison of another renegade leadership? Gooks have become ragheads, every adult male is an insurgent eligible for torture and every Iraqi home filled with men, women and children is a free fire zone."

— Tony Swindell, letter extracted from Alexander Cockburn's column, *The Nation*, April 24, 2006.

33. "The morning I visited the hospital a correspondent from the Arabic satellite channel Al-Jazeera had been killed by an American missile...A few hours later an American tank fired a shell at the Palestine Hotel and killed one journalist from Ukraine and another from Spain.

"I was in my room on the fourth floor...Ten minutes later injured journalists were being carried into cars on stretchers made of blankets. Later that day the American command said their forces had been fired on from the building. It was not a believable statement, since it would seem unlikely that 150-odd journalists would fail to hear or notice this. No one had done so."

— Tim Judah, article, *The New York Review*, May 15, 2003.

34. "No doubt remembering the US attack on its Kabul office in 2002, Al Jazeera notified the US military of the location of its office on the banks of the Tigris. The Pentagon said it had taken due notice and promised it wouldn't be attacked.

"According to Robert Fisk of the *Independent*, the day before the attack, 'the US State Department's spokesman in Doha, an Arab-American called Nabil Khouri, visited Al Jazeera's offices in the city and ... repeated the Pentagon's assurances. Within 24 hours, the Americans had fired their missile into the Baghdad office' scoring a direct hit on the network's Baghdad correspondent, Tariq Ayoub, who was on the roof with his second cameraman filming a battle in the streets nearby. Ayoub died almost instantly.

"About four hours later came the US tank blast at the Palestine Hotel, where some 200 non-Pentagon-sanctioned journalists were located, covering the war from what had been the Iraqi side of the lines. The shell exploded...killing a Ukrainian cameraman, Taras Protsyuk, who was filming the tanks, and seriously wounding three other journalists. On the next floor, Tele 5's cameraman, Jose Couso, was mortally wounded. All eyewitnesses agree, and a French videotape confirms, that contrary to the claims of US Gen. Buford Blount, there had been no fire directed at the tank in the minutes before it fired that shell.'"

— Alexander Cockburn, column, *The Nation*, April 28, 2003.

35. "Two days ago, I went to visit one of my colleagues wounded in the Anglo-American invasion of Iraq. Samia Nakhoul is a Reuters correspondent, a young woman reporter who is married to another colleague, the Financial times correspondent in Beirut. Part of an American tank shell was embedded in her brain — a millimeter difference in entry point and she would have been half paralyzed — after an M1A1 Abrams tank fired a round at the Reuters office in Baghdad in the Palestine Hotel, last week.

"Samia Nakhoul wasn't the only one to be hit. Her Ukrainian cameraman, father of a small child, was killed. So was a Spanish cameraman on the floor above.

"General Buford Blount of the 3rd Infantry Division told a lie: he said that sniper fire had been directed at the tank — on the Joumhouriyah Bridge over the Tigris River — and that the fire had ended 'after the tank had fired' at the Palestine Hotel. I was between the tank and the hotel when the shell was fired. There was no sniper fire — nor any rocket-propelled grenade fire, as the American officer claimed — at the time. French television footage of the tank, running for minutes before the attack, shows the same thing. The soundtrack — until the blinding, repulsive golden flash from the tank barrel — is silent.

"And then yesterday I had to read, in the *New York Times*, that Colin Powell had justified the murder — yes murder — of these two journalists. This former four-star general...actually said, and I quote: 'According to a US military review of the incident, our forces responded to hostile fire appearing to come from a location later identified as the Palestine Hotel...Our review of the April 8th incident indicates that the use of force was justified.'

"The Americans were outraged at al-Jazeera coverage of the civilian victims of US bombing raids. And on April 8, less than three hours before the Reuters office was attacked, an American aircraft fired a single missile at the al-Jazeera office — at those precise map coordinates Mr. al-Ali had sent to Ms. Clarke — and killed the station's reporter Tariq Ayoub."

— Robert Fisk, *Asheville Global Report*, May 1–7, 2003.

36. "Last week, when Tariq Ayoub, an Al Jazeera correspondent, was killed by an American air strike on the Arabic satellite channel's Baghdad offices, military officials...drew up a news release. 'According to commanders on the ground,' the statement read, 'Coalition forces came under significant enemy fire from the building where Al Jazeera journalists were working and, consistent with the inherent right of self-defense, Coalition forces returned fire.'

"Al-Issawi, a producer at the network...was incensed. 'This is not acceptable. I guarantee you there was no fire coming from our building.' Al Jazeera's offices, he noted later, were housed in a clearly marked two-story villa whose precise coordinates had been provided to the Pentagon to avoid just such a tragedy... [H]e did find it curious that American forces had also fired on the offices of Abu Dhabi Television that day, and that they'd bombed an Al Jazeera office in Afghanistan in November, 2001.'"

— Hampton Sides, column, *The New Yorker*, April 21 & 28, 2003.

37. "There has also been a threat that the Arab dissident station Al Jazeera, with an office in Kabul, might continue to show pictures of dead and injured Afghan civilians, and that an independent commercial satellite news service might take pictures

of bombed civilian sites that would best be kept under wraps. The Pentagon handled these problems efficiently. Al Jazeera's office in Kabul was bombed and destroyed. It was not feasible to bomb Al Jazeera's office in Qatar, a friendly state, but State Department head Colin Powell urged the sheik of Qatar to curb Al Jazeera, and National Security Adviser Condoleezza Rice advised US TV stations to avoid transmitting Bin Laden speeches, which allegedly might contain hidden instructions to Al Qaeda forces."

— Edward S. Herman, article, *Z Magazine*, September 2002.

38. "The foreign media treated these incidents very differently than their American colleagues. 'We can only conclude that the US Army deliberately and without warning targeted journalists,' declared the international press watch group Reporters Without Borders. Robert Fisk of the London *Independent* was even more blunt, declaring that the attacks 'look very much like murder.'"

— Amy Goodman, *The Exception to the Rulers.*

39. "Books.... Describe many affecting scenes in which soldiers try to do good, administering first aid, handing out food, arranging for garbage to be picked up. For the most part, the GIs come across as well-meaning Americans who have been set down in an alien environment with inappropriate training, minimal cultural preparation, and no language skills. Surrounded by people who for the most part wish them ill and living with the daily fear of being blown up, they frequently take out their frustrations on the local population. It's in these firsthand accounts that one can find the most searing descriptions of the toll the war has taken on both US troops and the Iraqi people.

— Book review by Michael Massing, *One Bullet Away: The Making of a Marine Officer* by Nathaniel Fick and *Generation Kill: Devil Dogs, Iceman, Captain America. And the New Face of American War* by Evan Wright, *The New York Review*, December 20, 2007.

40. Marines represent what is more or less America's first generation of disposable children.... This sounds idealistic, but, as Wright is quick to note, 'the whole point of their training is to commit the ultimate taboo: to kill. Their culture revels in this.' At the end of team briefings, 'Marines put their hands together and shout, "Kill!"'"

— Michael Massing, ibid.

41. "Civilians bear the brunt, to the consternation of many of the Marines. 'I think it's b*** how these *** civilians are dying!' rages Jeffrey Carazales, a lance corporal from Texas, after he shoots at a building that clearly has civilians in it: 'They're worse off than the guys that are shooting at us. They don't even have a chance. Do you think people at home are going to see this — all these women and children we're killing? F*** no. Back home they're glorifying this mother—. I guarantee you. Saying our president is a *** hero for getting us into this bitch. He ain't even a real Texan.'"

—Michael Massing, ibid.

42. "It's hard to read about Haditha, this place in Iraq where, last November 19, some US Marines went on a rampage, reportedly massacring twenty-four Iraqis, including a man almost eighty years old in a wheelchair and children as young as one, three four, and five.

"'Some victims had single gunshot wounds to the head,' a Defense Department official told *The New York Times.*

"'Most of the shots,' *The Washington Post* reported, 'were fired at such close range that they went through the bodies of the family members and plowed into walls or the floor,' according to doctors who saw the bodies.

"The old man in the wheelchair 'took nine rounds in the chest and abdomen, according to his death certificate,' the *Post* story said."

— Comment, *The Progressive*, July 2006.

43. "I watched them shoot my grandfather, first in the chest and then in the head. Then they killed my granny.

"I hate the Americans. The whole world hates them for what they have done.... They kill people. Then they say 'sorry.' I hate them."

— Eman Waleed to *Time* magazine, cited in *The Progressive*, July 2006.

44. "'The story is unique only in that the evidence that a terrible crime took place appears to be too great for "plausible deniability,' " writes Joshua Holland for Alternet. Among other accounts, Holland cites an AP story quoting Iraq's UN ambassador as saying that the US forces killed his unarmed young cousin in 'cold blood.' Holland also references a March Knight-Ridder story that said Iraq police officials 'accused US soldiers of executing eleven Iraqi civilians, including four children and a six-month-old baby' in the town of Ishaqo. The BBC has since pursued this story, saying it has video 'evidence that US forces may have been responsible for the deliberate killing of eleven innocent Iraqis.' The US military denies the charge.

"Dahr Jamail, writing at truth.org, says 'countless atrocities continue daily, conveniently out of the awareness of the general public.'...

"US attacks on civilians are a regular occurrence, Prime Minister Nuri Kamal al-Maliki said on June 1. US forces 'do not respect the Iraqi people. They crush them with their vehicles and kill them just on suspicion. This is totally unacceptable.'"

— Comment, *The Progressive*, July 2006.

45. "Both Human Rights Watch and Amnesty International USA say there is 'prima facie' evidence against Rumsfeld for war crimes and torture. And Amnesty International USA says there is also 'prima facie' evidence against Bush for war crimes and torture....

"Amnesty International USA has even taken the extraordinary step of calling on officials in other countries, as a last resort, to apprehend Bush and Rumsfeld and other high-ranking members of the Administration who have played a part in the torture scandal...."William Schulz, executive director of Amnesty International USA, added, 'If the United States permits the architects of torture policy to get off scot-free, then other nations will be compelled to take action....

"Acknowledging that the possibility of a foreign government seizing Rumsfeld or Bush might not be 'an immediate reality,' Schulz takes the long view: 'Let's keep in mind, there are no statutes of limitations here.'"

— Matthew Rothschild, article, *The Progressive*, July 2005.

Chapter 9. Torture

1. "Use of force is a poor technique, as it yields unreliable results."
— US Army field Manual on Intelligence Interrogation.

2. "That summer of 2003 they began rounding people up. The insurgency had erupted, and word had come down that insurgents or anyone with information about them had to be found, arrested, and questioned....

"Such detainees wound up at Abu Ghraib. On the ground, this is how the story of torture at the prison began: with house-to-house searches and mass arrests, with ordinary cruelties, routine pranks, and an occupier's insouciance toward international laws....

"At this late date, it is by no means necessary to reprise the volumes of government reports and journalists' accounts outlining the gestation of America's torture policy, from September 11, 2001, to the President's February 7, 2002, directive suspending adherence to the Geneva conventions in what he calls the Global war on terror; from Afghanistan to Guantanamo to Iraq; from the Pentagon's secret 'special access program' of off-the-books abduction and assassination to the White House 'torture memo' to the CIA's 'extraordinary rendition' of terror suspects to the dungeons of foreign lands....

"In the Abu Ghraib trials the fact that, by official policy, America is a torture state and everyone knows was both critical background and inadmissible evidence....

"On October 5, 2005...the White House threatened that the President would veto any military-spending bill that came to him with a provision banning 'cruel, inhuman or degrading treatment' of detainees.'"
— Joann Wypijewski, report, *Harper's Magazine* February 2006.

3. "President George W. Bush has embedded murder, assassination, torture, and mistreatment of prisoners into the structure of the US system of global domination. Many US citizens, rightly outraged, want to know why this sort of barbaric, sadistic violence has become an integral part of US security policy, and what this administration's justification of torture means institutionally for the future governance of this

country. Above all, they want to know how Bush has been able to avoid impeachment for committing high crimes."

— Herbert P. Bix, article, *Z Magazine*, July/August 2005.

4. "The administration's hostility to the UN and to the constraints of international law, reflects a long tradition on the right wing of the Republican Party....

"There are, however, few if any antecedents in American public policy and debate for the American government's present commitment to torture. In recent years there was a hint of a break with accepted norms, in the Pentagon's adamant hostility to proposals for an International Criminal Court.... the government's position (was) an implicit declaration that existing military doctrine included options that could invite condemnation as war crimes.

"The Clinton Administration signed the International Criminal court treaty despite Defense Department opposition, but President George W. Bush formally withdrew the American signature on May 6, 2002....

"Following the terrorist attacks in September 2001, explicit proposals to authorize torture circulated in the administration and in the Pentagon and CIA, even though there was no one yet to torture. Memoranda soon were drafted by the Justice Department on how to protect American military and intelligence officers from eventual prosecution under existing US law for how they treated prisoners....

"On January 9, 2002, a memorandum co-written by John Yoo...provided arguments to support a claim that with respect to prisoners taken in Afghanistan, the United states was not bound by the Geneva Conventions....

"In effect, the question put to government lawyers was how the President and the others could commit war crimes and not be held accountable....

"The resemblance to Nazi practice during the totalitarian decades, particularly in the deliberate denial of any legal recourse to such prisoners, presumably permanently, was obvious and dismaying. In contrast, Russian prisoners were always subjected to a form of trial and condemnation, however spurious and arbitrary. People were discharged from the gulag....

"The Bush Administration simply denies that it authorizes torture, even when issuing the State Department's annual Human rights report criticizing torture in other countries including Egypt, Syria, and others to which the United States has rendered prisoners....

"Confirmation of all these practices has come from dozens of reports, witnesses, participants, and from leaked Red Cross, FBI, US Army, and other official documents. A compilation of documents...assembled by Mark Danner, number more than 600 pages. The reports are so numerous, consistent, and mutually supportive as to put the existence of these practices beyond doubt. The administration's perfunctory denials have sometimes been of such insolent hypocrisy as to suggest that it considers the American reputation for torture an asset in intimidating terrorists, and possibly others as well....

"Many of this war's theorists share a current of political thought ascribed to Leo Strauss, in which the superior person, capable of seeing beyond the parochial concerns of ordinary citizens, is held obliged to impose on a nation actions the citizenry would not understand or approve. Neo-conservatism, represented in the Bush Administration, certainly includes fascism among its influences."

— William Pfaff, article, *Harper's Magazine*, November 2005.

5. "The Federalist Society (is) an organization established by right-wing lawyers in the early 1980s to redress 'liberal bias' in American law schools and the legal pro-

fession. The thinking and influence of Federalist types...are laid bare in the torture memos, which document the triumph of international law-averse officials in the Justice Department, the Pentagon and the White House over dissenting voices in the State Department and sectors of the professional military....

"The earliest memos, dating from late December 2001 and early 2002, introduced the rationale for declaring the Geneva Conventions inapplicable and the advantages of Guantanamo as a prison and interrogation center. The principal intellectual author of these and many subsequent memos is John Yoo...in the Justice Department's Office of Legal Counsel.... Yoo and his OLC colleagues reasoned that the President has the constitutional authority to declare the Geneva Conventions irrelevant to the war in Afghanistan on the grounds that it is a 'failed state,' and to deny prisoner of war status to the Taliban and Al Qaeda as nonstate actors and terrorists who have no rights under international humanitarian law....

"Alberto Gonzales counseled the President that there is no crime if there is no law — one good reason to declare the Geneva Conventions 'obsolete.' To drive home the point, he noted that the War Crimes Act of 1996, which gives domestic courts jurisdiction to prosecute Americans or anyone else for grave breaches of the Geneva Conventions, carries penalties up to the death penalty. He added forebodingly: 'It is difficult to predict the motives of prosecutors and independent counsels who may in the future decide to pursue unwarranted charges based on [the War Crimes Act].'... Secretary of State Colin Powell sent a memo to Gonzales criticizing the faultiness and dangers of this reasoning. Perhaps with the 'Pinochet precedent' (i.e., no sovereign immunity for torture) in mind, he warned that if the United States declined to adhere to the Geneva Conventions, the effect might be to 'provoke some individual foreign prosecutors to investigate and prosecute our officials and troops.'...

"Five days later, in a resounding defeat for the State Department, President Bush endorsed the OLC's analysis in a secret memorandum to his National Security team....

"Public debate heated up with the publication in January 2002 of trophy-shot photos of the first group of hooded, bound and contorted prisoners being transported from Afghanistan and inside the Guantanamo prison."

— Lisa Hajjar, essay, *The Nation*, February 7, 2005.

6. "Amnesty International, a year after the invasion, reported, 'Scores of unarmed people have been killed due to excessive or unnecessary use of lethal force by coalition forces during public demonstrations, at checkpoints and in house raids. Thousands of people have been detained (estimates range from 8,500 to 15,000), often under harsh conditions and subjected to prolonged and often unacknowledged detention. Many have been tortured or ill-treated, and some have died in custody.'

"During the initial offensive in Fallujah, it reported that half of the fatalities 'are said to have been civilians, many of them women and children.'"

— Howard Zinn, op-ed, Hackensack, NJ *Record*, the Fort Wayne, In *News-Sentinel* and the Birmingham, AL *News*.

7. "US armed forces killed scores of patients in an attack on a Fallujah health center and have deprived civilians of medical care, food and water....

"US warplanes dropped three bombs on the clinic, where approximately sixty patients — many of whom had serious injuries from US aerial bombings and attacks — were being treated....

"Thirty-five patients were killed in the air strike, including two girls and three boys under the age of 10. In addition, he said, fifteen medics, four nurses and five health support staff were killed....

"US and allied Iraq military forces stormed the Fallujah General Hospital, which is on the perimeter of the city, at the beginning of the assault, claiming it was under insurgent control and was a center of propaganda about civilian casualties during last April's attack on the city. The soldiers encountered no resistance. Dr. Rafe Chiad, the hospital's director, reached by phone, stated emphatically that it is a neutral institution, providing humanitarian aid....

"US authorities have denied all requests to send doctors, ambulances, medical equipment and supplies from the hospital into the city to tend to the wounded, he said.

"There were severe outbreaks of diarrhea infections among the population, with children and the elderly dying from infectious disease, starvation and dehydration in greater numbers each day. Dr al-Jumaili, Dr. al-Ani and journalist Badrani each stated that the wounded and children are dying because of lack of medical attention and water....Three children died of dehydration when their father was unable to find water for them. The US forces cut off the city's water supply before launching their assault....

"The bombing of hospitalized patients, forced starvation and dehydration, denial of medicines and health services to the sick and wounded must be recognized for what they are: war crimes and crimes against humanity."

— Miles Schuman, article, *The Nation*, December 13, 2004.

8. "'If a soldier is going to war, it's because he raised his right hand and swore to defend the United States against all enemies foreign and domestic. It's not like he's committing murder.' When I mentioned the Ten Commandments, Chaplain (Kenneth) Bush was quick to respond. 'The word in the original Hebrew is *ratzach*, which the King James Bible, written in 1611, translates as "kill" — as in "Thou shalt not kill,"' he said. 'But the later, more accurate translations translate that word as "murder," making the commandment "Thou shalt not commit murder." The Old Testament is full of killing and war.'"

"Dan Knox, the son of a Presbyterian minister (he is my wife's cousin), takes no comfort from the Old Testament...Knox joined the Army in 1966, after seeing a photo essay of the depredations of the Vietcong in *Life*. He felt that it was his duty to defend Southeast Asia from Communism. Knox's infantry suffered huge casualties, but what bothers him most, more than three decades later, is not the fear, the carnage he witnessed, or the loss of friends, but the faces of the people he killed while serving as a helicopter door gunner. 'If they told me to kill a whole village, that's what I'd do,' he said. 'I still see images — a woman and her children rolling in the dust...I'm also watching this funeral party I gunned. In a few minutes, it will be a sampan I gunned on a river, with a woman and her babies falling out of it into the water and kicking around as I shoot them.'"

— Dan Baum, article, *The New Yorker*, July 12 & 19, 2004.

9. "There is no question that hatred of the US government is strong in Iraq, regardless of what people think of Saddam. And few accept that America has any right to overthrow the Iraqi government. Iraqis have seen what occupation looks like, both through British colonization of Iraq and through the lens of Palestinians. 'We don't want Saddam, but that doesn't mean we want America, either,' said Mazen, an unem-

ployed engineer. 'We will not accept a foreign invader or occupier, even if it damns us to more years under an Iraqi dictator. At least he is one of us.'"
— *The Nation*, April 7, 2003.

10. "'You know why we Christians want Saddam to stay in power?' asks a restaurant owner in Baghdad. 'Because he is protecting us from radical Muslims. He always has done this, and if he goes, we are afraid what will happen to us.'"
— *The Nation*, April 7, 2003.

11. "'Today, the situation is the worst we have ever lived in Iraq,' Andy Darmoo, head of the 'Save the Assyrians' campaign, told a recent news conference at United Nations headquarters in New York....

"According to various sources, 8 to 12 percent of the Iraqi population of 26 million belongs to a Christian denomination, mostly Assyrians, Chaldeans, Armenians and Catholics."
— Lisa Soderlindh, *Asheville Global Report*, May 11–17, 2006.

12. "In the Bush war on terrorism, Washington has shown a reckless disregard for basics principles of international human-rights law like the Geneva Conventions, the Convention Against Torture, and the International Covenant on Civil Rights and Political Rights. It has created a climate of lawlessness in which foreign detainees in US custody overseas have been brutally abused, thousands of foreign citizens are held as 'enemy combatants' indefinitely without being accorded the status of prisoners of war, and repressive regimes around the world get a green light to crack down on political dissidents and religious and ethnic minorities in the name of fighting terrorism. The result has been a drastic increase in the number of people convinced that America is their enemy....

"The lawlessness in the administration's foreign policy is also reflected in disdain for civil liberties at home. Thousands of men with foreign backgrounds have been held secretly in US prisons and detention centers without charges for months at a time. The Justice Department has claimed unprecedented authority to arrest US citizens without charges and deny them legal counsel on the mere assertion that they are enemy combatants....

"The lawlessness in American foreign policy today emanates from the top. In a January 2002 memorandum reporting a decision by the president, White House Counsel Alberto Gonzales wrote that the war on 'terrorism renders obsolete [the Geneva Conventions'] strict limitations on the questioning of prisoners.' ...until George W. Bush, no American president had questioned the basic rules of international humanitarian law, including, notably Presidents Lyndon Johnson and Richard Nixon during the Vietnam War and Bush Senior during the Gulf war."
— John Shattuck, essay, *The American Prospect*, October 2004.

13. "The CIA has operated more than 1,000 secret flights over European Union (EU) territory in the past five years, some to transfer terror suspects in a practice known as 'extraordinary Rendition,' an investigation by the European parliament said on Apr. 26....

"They accused the CIA of kidnapping terror suspects and said those responsible for monitoring air safety regulations revealed unusual flight patterns to and from European airports. The report's author, Italian European Parliament minister Claudio Fava, suggested some EU governments knew about the flights....

"Extraordinary renditions would breach European human rights legislation and British domestic law."
— Jim Lobe, *The Asheville Global Report*, May 4-10, 2006. Source: *Guardian* (UK)

14. ACLU Report:

- A father is forced to watch the mock execution of his 14-year-old son.
- Lit cigarettes are placed in the ears of detainees.
- Men's hands are bathed with alcohol and then lit on fire.
- Prisoners are shackled to the floor for 18–24 hours.
- Deaths are deemed 'homicides' by the military, yet autopsies are not performed.

"These and other allegations of torture and abuse are found in government documents secured by the ACLU in our Freedom of Information Act (FOIA) litigation. More than 70,000 pages of government documents show the full nature and extent of the torture and abuse that have occurred on the Bush administration's watch in Iraq, Afghanistan and Guantanamo. To argue that the torture and abuse are merely the actions of a few rogue soldiers is belied by the quantity of documents. Isolated incidents don't produce 70,000 pages of government documents across the FBI, CIA, Departments of State and Defense...

"President Bush, Secretary of Defense Rumsfeld and Vice President Cheney have all asserted at different points over the last several years that the detainees were being treated 'humanely' — even if they were not afforded the legal protections of the Geneva Conventions. The photographs and government memos have proven those statements inaccurate."

— Anthony D. Romero, *Civil Liberties* newsletter, Fall 2005.

15. "The 24-page report by the International committee of the Red Cross says abuse of Iraqi prisoners by American soldiers was broad and 'not individual acts,' contrary to Presidents Bush's contention that the mistreatment 'was the wrongdoing of a few.'

"The report...cites abuses — some tantamount to torture — including brutality, hooding, humiliation and threats of 'imminent execution....Their continued internment several months after their arrest in strict solitary confinement constituted a serious violation of the third and fourth Geneva Conventions.'

"The report said some coalition military intelligence officers estimated 'between 70 percent and 90 percent' of the detainees in Iraq 'had been arrested by mistake.'

"'Arresting authorities entered houses usually after dark, breaking down doors, waking up residents roughly, yelling orders, forcing family members into one room under military guard while searching the rest of the house and further breaking doors, cabinets and other property,' the report said.

"'Sometimes they arrested all adult males present in a house, including elderly, handicapped or sick people,' it said. 'Treatment often included pushing people around, insulting, taking aim with rifles, punching and kicking and striking with rifles,'"

— Asheville Citizen-Times, May 2004.

16. "What horror is this, a secret judgment, and a condemnation without explanations! Is there a more execrable tyranny than that of spilling blood on a whim, without giving the least reason?"

— Voltaire, defending wrongly imprisoned and executed Jean Calas in 1762.

17. "The detainees are being treated humanely.... Remember these are terrorists."

— Scott McClellan, White House press secretary, dismissing a new UN report on Guantanamo Bay prison on Feb. 17.

18. "Despite their confidential nature, Seymour Hersh, Pulitzer Prize-winning reporter, has had access to some of the video footage and other images from Abu Ghraib.

"In a speech on July 8, Hersh revealed what some have suspected:

'And I can tell you it was much worse than they've told you, there are worse videotapes, worse events....

"'Those women who were arrested with young boys, children, in cases that have been recorded, the boys were sodomized, with the camera rolling, and the worst above all of them is the sound track of the boys shrieking....'"

— Bruce Mulley, local column, *Asheville Citizen-Times*, July 22, 2004.

19. "You have to understand the Arab mind.... The only thing they understand is force — force, pride, and saving face."

— Capt. Todd Brown, company commander in Abu Hishma, Michael Schwartz, special report, *Z Magazine*, July/August 2004.

20. "Matthew Schofield, a Knight Ridder reporter in Baghdad, has obtained an Iraqi police report which accuses US troops of executing 11 people, including a 75-year-old woman and a six-month-old infant, in the aftermath of a raid on Mar. 15 on a house about 60 miles north of Baghdad....

"The American forces gathered the family members in one room and executed 11 persons, including five children, four women and two men,' the report said. 'Then they bombed the house, burned three vehicles and killed the animals.'

"The report identified the dead by name, giving their ages."

— Asheville Global Report, Mar. 23 — 29, 2006. Source: Editor and Publisher.

21. "With a heavy dose of fear and violence and a lot of money for projects, I think we can convince these people that we are here to help them."

— Colonel Sassaman in Abu Hashima, Michael Schwartz, special report, *Z Magazine*, July/August 2004.

22. "If the stakes are high enough, torture is permissible. No one who doubts that this is the case should be in a position of responsibility."

— Richard Posner, a right-wing judge on the US Court of Appeals, *The Nation*, March 31, 2003.

> [As of the end of 2007, George W. Bush has abused, raped, tortured, degraded, and murdered uncounted innocent Iraqi civilians (one estimate is more than 125,000, others are far higher) on the false charge that they are terrorists and were responsible for the September 11th attack against the United States. There is no doubt that Bush has committed vast crimes against humanity and against US law as well. — Author.]

25. "[What] prevents people from stating the obvious truth that Bush and his colleagues are exhilarated and thrilled by the thought of war, by the thought of the incredible power they will have over so many other people, by the massiveness of the bombing they're planning, the violence, the killing, the blood, the deaths, the horror?

"From the first days after the World Trade Center fell, you could see in their faces that...they in fact were loving it. Those faces glowed....This, combined with a lust for blood, makes for particularly dangerous leaders, so totally incapable of hearing anyone else's pleas for compromise or for peace.

"It's clear that Bush and his group are in the grip of something. They're very far-gone. Their narcissism and sense of omnipotence goes way beyond self-confidence, reaching the point that they're impervious to the disgust they provoke in others, or even oblivious to it. They've made very clear to the people of the world that they value American interests more than the world's interests and American profits more than the world's physical health.

"They happily summoned the world a year ago to observe what they'd done to the people they'd taken prisoner, proudly exhibiting them -- 31, 2003.

Chapter 10. Dissent

1. "If I had known then what I know now, I would have voted against (the war powers resolution). I have admitted that my vote was wrong."
— Sen. Jay Rockefeller, Senate Intelligence Committee, cited by Clarence Page, *Tribune Media Services,* July 21, 2004.

2. "It's just wrong what we're doing in Iraq. It's morally wrong, it's politically wrong, it's economically wrong."
— Robert S. McNamara, 2004.

3. "The Bush administration secretly authorized the National Security Agency (NSA) nearly four years ago to eavesdrop on US citizens and others inside the United States to search for evidence of terrorist activity without the court-approved warrants ordinarily required for domestic spying. The revelation of the surveillance program, published in the Dec. 16 New York Times, has sparked outrage across the political spectrum and prompted the Bush administration to stridently defend its actions."
— *Asheville Global Report*, Dec.22-28, 2005: Source: ABC News, New York Times, Washington Post.

4. "The revelation that the National Security agency has, since 2001, collected records of billions of phone calls made and received by Americans confirms the worst fears about the lawlessness of the Bush Administration. This President and his aides have displayed disdain for the rule of law and for the truth. Bush initially denied that the spying was taking place. Then when it was exposed, the Administration claimed that the spying was limited in scope."
— Editorial, *The Nation,* June 5, 2006.

5. Senator Byrd said, 'we are a nation of laws and not men.... I defy the Administration to show me where in the Foreign Intelligence Surveillance Act, or the US Constitution, they are allowed to steal into the lives of innocent Americans and spy.... These astounding revelations about the bending and contorting of the constitution to justify a grasping irresponsible administration under the banner of national security are an outrage'.... Representative John Lewis (D., Ga.) told a radio interviewer in Atlanta

that George W. Bush 'is not a king, he is president,' going on to say that if the chance presented itself he would sign a bill of impeachment. John Dean, White House council in the Nixon Administration and a man familiar with the arts of bugging phones and obstructing justice, observed, in conversation with Senator Barbara Boxer (D., Calif.) that 'Bush is the first president to admit to an impeachable offense....

"Norman Ornstein, a scholar at the American Enterprise Institute...sat for an interview on a Washington public radio station....'I think that if we're going to be intellectually honest here,' he said, 'this really is the kind of thing that Alexander Hamilton was referring to when Impeachment was discussed.' The next day, writing in the *Washington Times*, Bruce Fein, former associate deputy attorney general under President Ronald Reagan, said of President Bush that he 'presents a clear and present danger to the rule of law': he later extended the thought by saying that if the President 'maintains this disregard or contempt for the coordinate branches of government, it's that conception of an omnipresent presidency that makes the occupant a dangerous person.'"

— Lewis H. Lapham, essay, *Harper's Magazine*, March 2006.

6. "According to a March study by the Pew Research Center, 93 percent of Jordanians had an unfavorable view of the United states, as did 68 percent of Moroccans, 63 percent of Turks, and 61 percent of Pakistanis. Another poll showed that in Saudi Arabia, 97 percent had an unfavorable view. And in Egypt, a recent poll put the unfavorable rating at 98 percent."

— Comment, *The Progressive*, October 2004.

7. "Suspected foreign fighters account for less than 2% of the 5,700 captives being held as security threats in Iraq, a strong indication that Iraqis are largely responsible for the stubborn resistance.

"The numbers represent one of the most precise measurements to date of the composition of the insurgency and suggest that some Bush administration officials have overstated the role of foreign holy warriors, or jihadists, from other Arab states. The figures also suggest that Iraq isn't as big a magnet for foreign terrorists as some administration critics have asserted.

"In Ramadi, where Marines have fended off coordinated attacks by hundreds of insurgents, the fighters 'are all locals,' says Lt. Col. Paul Kennedy, commander of the 2nd Battalion, 4th Marine Regiment. 'There are very few foreign fighters.'"

— Peter Eisler and Tom Squitieri, *USA Today*, July 6, 2004.

8. "A recent poll commissioned by the CPA itself found that two percent of Iraqis have great confidence in the coalition forces, around eighty percent have none at all, and more than half believe that all Americans behave like the abusive jailers at Abu Ghraib."

— George Packer, Comment, *The New Yorker*, July 5, 2004.

9. "When asked in the *New York Times/CBS* poll if they saw the US military as 'liberators' or 'occupiers,' 71 percent of Iraqis said occupiers."

— Mark Harris, essay, *Z Magazine*, July/August 2004.

10. "'The people who hate George W. Bush hate God,' Doc Burch told the dozen Republicans gathered at an early morning prayer meeting. Burch is the chaplain of the National Federation of Republican Assemblies, which considers itself the 'Republican wing of the Republican Party....We need to understand we're in spiritual warfare,' Burch said.

— Elizabeth Dinovella, essay, *The Progressive*, October 2004.

11. "Bruce Fein is not a fan of George W. Bush.'" He's too stupid to understand the things he's saying,' Fein said the other day on the phone from his law office inside the Beltway....

"Fein is a longtime conservative lawyer and writer. He helped argue the Reagan administration's case in the Iran-Contra controversy of the late 1980s....

"Fein told a Senate committee that Bush should be censured for the secret wiretapping scheme at the center of the National Security Administration controversy.

"'You can lose a republic on the installment plan every bit as efficiently as at one fell swoop with a coup d teat,' Fein told the committee.

"'The problem,' Fein told me, 'is not just the wiretapping scheme but Bush's claim that the president has what amounts to unlimited power everywhere forever.' Fein said Bush is insisting 'that all of the world is a battlefield and that battlefield tactics are as appropriate in the streets of Kandahar as outside the local Domino's Pizza.'

"'And since the so-called war on terror is endless, that power will have no end either,' he said....

"'It's so ridiculous,' Fein said, 'The fact is that not only has he undertaken nation-building, but he has done so with a stupidity and folly that defies imagination.'"

— Paul Mulshine, syndicated column, April 10, 2006.

12. "One, I believe there's an Almighty. And, secondly, I believe one of the great gifts of the Almighty is the desire in everybody's soul, regardless of what you look like or where you live, to be free."

— George w. Bush, quoted in *The New Yorker*, May 8, 2006.

13. "The net result of the so-called liberal media's abdication of its constitutional role — together with an active campaign of deception by the right-wing media, on Fox and elsewhere — is a nation voting in profound ignorance of what its votes will mean. As a recent study by the University of Maryland's Program on International Policy Attitudes demonstrates, even after the final report of Charles Duelfer, demonstrating the complete absence of any WMD program in Iraq, 72 percent of Bush supporters operate in ignorance, and believe Iraq had actual WMD (47 percent) or a major development program (25 percent). No less disturbing, 75 percent of Bush supporters believe Iraq was providing significant support to Al Qaeda, and 63 percent are under the impression that we have discovered evidence to support that contention. A mere 31 percent of Bush supporters are aware that most of the world continues to oppose the US invasion of Iraq, with 42 percent assuming an evenly divided global opinion and more than a quarter believing that the rest of the planet approves.

"It's hard to argue that democracy can be said to be functioning under these circumstances; and it's even harder to defend the role of the American media in upholding a respect for fact over 'faith.' But given this record of almost unprecedented incompetence, ideological fanaticism, mendacity and corruption, faith over reality represents Bush's only chance."

— Eric Alterman, column, *The Nation*, November 15, 2004.

14. "One would have to be close to insane to say that our experience in Iraq has been an unqualified success. If the Iraqis are smart enough to ask us to leave, and if we are smart enough to actually leave, the fact remains that the Iraq operation has gravely undermined American global credibility. It has even more seriously compromised us morally....

"So, in my view, we are not in a phase of a global struggle against terrorism. That formulation, in my view, tends to unite our enemies and divide our friends, instead of uniting our friends and dividing our enemies. It makes it more difficult for us to encourage the moderate Arabs, and it increasingly pits us against all of Islam. And, most importantly of all, it is not responsive to the reality of billions of people for the first time in the history of mankind becoming politically activated."

— Zbigniew Brzezinski, interview by Michael Tomasky, *The American Prospect*, March 2005.

15. "George Bush has made the Christian faith an obscenity. To rationalize what he's doing in Iraq because God told him to do it or to make Jesus some kind of war-monger is another immorality. And for people in America to buy that? I had some-body e-mail me who said, 'You know what, Jesus wants me to slap the c— out of you, because he wants me to slap some sense into you to realize that what we're doing in Iraq is a good thing.' That is just so hypocritical and wrong beyond anything.

"I was a Catholic youth minister for eight years. I am a follower of the teachings of Jesus Christ. And I know that the Jesus that I studied about in the Gospels would not approve of what George Bush is doing. I believe that religious extremism, whether it's Jewish, Muslim, or Christian, has caused a lot of problems in the world for cen-turies. Leaders misuse religion to have the masses follow them. You can't invoke your religion to do things that you know the founder or the prophet of that religion would be against.

"We need to just get our military presence out of Iraq. And I don't think that's going to happen while George Bush is president, so we have to get George Bush out of office. We have to get our troops home. A Mission Accomplished would be for the Iraqi people to rebuild their government and have whatever system of government they want. Because — you know what? — It's their country. It's not the fifty-first state of America....

"We've made a horrible mess of that country. The people there want peace, they want their electricity back, they want their water back, and they want their jobs. They want America out.

"I believe that a lot of our problems with Muslim terrorists center on the conflict between Israel and Palestine....I believe Israel has a right to exist and I believe the Palestinian people have a right to exist. I just believe that killing and occupying an-other country's land is wrong, no matter who does it....I don't like Palestinians killing Israelis, Israelis killing Palestinians. I don't like the insurgents killing Americans. My son was killed by an insurgent. I don't like Americans killing innocent Iraqis either.

"Just because I'm against the policies of the Israeli government toward Palestine does not mean I'm anti-Israeli or anti-Semitic. Just because I'm against George Bush and his policies doesn't mean I'm anti-American. I just believe that we have to force our leaders to work for peace and not for killing....

"You can't be successful in Iraq. The generals on the ground have said that. There is not a military solution. What would happen if we put more troops in? Would that effectively kill more Iraqi people so we could get out of there? It's insane. Are we fighting terrorism or are we creating terrorism? Obviously, we're creating terrorism and an insurgency by our military presence there."

— Cindy Sheehan, interview with David Barsamian, *The Progressive*, March 2006.

16. "We all have lost a loved one in war. I say *lost*, but I don't like that euphemism because Casey wasn't lost; he was killed by George Bush's murderous policies in the Middle East.

— Cindy Sheehan, interview with David Barsamian, *The Progressive*, March 2006.

17. "In Iraq, US forces and their Iraqi surrogates are assaulting civilian targets and openly attacking doctors, clerics and journalists who have dared to count the bodies.

At home, impunity has been made official policy with Bush's nomination of Alberto Gonzales — the man who personally advised the President in his famous 'torture memo' that the Geneva Conventions are 'obsolete' — as Attorney General....

"Fearing he would be seen as soft on terror and disloyal to US troops, Kerry stayed scandalously silent about Abu Ghraib and Guantanamo Bay....

"Even after *The Lancet* published its landmark study estimating that 100,000 Iraqis had died as a result of the invasion and occupation, Kerry repeated his outrageous (and frankly racist) claim that Americans 'have borne 90 percent of the casualties in Iraq.' His unmistakable message: Iraqi deaths don't count....the Kerry campaign and its supporters became complicit in the dehumanization of Iraqis, reinforcing the idea that some lives are insufficiently important to risk losing votes over. And it is this morally bankrupt logic, more than election of any single candidate, that allows these crimes to continue unchecked....

"And this is Kerry's true gift to Bush: not just the presidency, but impunity."
— Naomi Klein, *The Nation*, December 13, 2004.

18. "Over a year ago an international team of epidemiologists, headed by Les Roberts of Johns Hopkins School of Public Health, completed a 'cluster sample survey' of civilian casualties in Iraq. Its findings contradicted central elements of what politicians and journalists had presented to the US public and the world. After excluding any possible statistical anomalies, they estimated that at least 98,000 Iraqi civilians had died in the previous 18 months as a direct result of the invasion and occupation of their country. They also found that violence had become the leading cause of death in Iraq during that period. Their most significant finding was that the vast majority of violent deaths were caused by 'coalition' forces using 'helicopter gunships, rockets or other forms of aerial weaponry,' and that almost half (48 percent) of these were children, with a median age of 8.

"The team's findings were published in the *Lancet*, the official journal of the British Medical association....

"Soon after the study was published, US and British officials launched a concerted campaign to discredit its authors and marginalize their findings without seriously addressing the validity of their methods or presenting any evidence to challenge their conclusions....

"The Iraqi Health Ministry reports, whose accuracy he (Blair) praised, have confirmed the Johns Hopkins team's conclusions that aerial attacks by 'coalition' forces are the leading cause of civilian deaths. One such report was cited by Nancy Youssef in the *Miami Herald* of September 25, 2004 under the headline 'US Attacks, Not Insurgents, Blamed for Most Iraqi Deaths.'...

"Michael O'Toole, the director of the Center for International Health in Australia, says: 'that's a classical sample size. I just don't see any evidence of significant exaggeration.... If anything, the deaths may have been higher because what they are unable to do is survey families where everyone has died....

"By dismissing the study's findings out of hand, US and British officials created the illusion that the authors were suspect or politically motivated and discouraged the media from taking them seriously. This worked disturbingly well. Even opponents of the war continue to cite much lower figures for civilian casualties and innocently attribute the bulk of them to Iraqi resistance forces or 'terrorists.'...

"Roberts wrote, in a letter to the *Independent*, 'Please understand how extremely conservative we were: we did a survey estimating that 285,000 people have died due to the first 18 months of invasion and occupation and we reported it as at least 100,000. '...

"Thanks to Roberts, his international team, Johns Hopkins School of Public Health, and the editorial board of the *Lancet*, we have a clearer picture of the violence taking place in Iraq than presented by 'mainstream' media. Allowing for 16 months of the air war and other deaths since the completion of the survey, we have to estimate that somewhere between 185,000 and 700,000 people have died as a direct result of the war. Coalition forces have killed anywhere from 70,000 to 500,000 of them, including 30,000 to 275,000 children under the age of 15. "

— Nicholas J.S. Davies, investigative report, *Z Magazine*, February 2006.

19. "Now, let me personalize this thing for you.... I have a young fellow in my district who was blinded and he lost his foot. And they did everything they could for him at Walter Reed, then they sent him home. His father was in jail; he had nobody at home. Imagine this: a young kid that age — 22, 23 years old — goes home to nobody. VA did everything they could do to help him. He was reaching out, so they sent him — to make sure that he was blind, they sent him to Johns Hopkins. Johns Hopkins started to send him bills. Then the collection agency started sending bills.... Imagine a young person being blinded, without a foot, and he's getting bills from a collection agency.

"I believe we need to turn Iraq over to the Iraqis. I believe before the Iraqi elections, scheduled for mid-December, the Iraqi people and the emerging government must be put on notice: The United States will immediately redeploy — immediately redeploy.... All of Iraq must know that Iraq is free, free from a United States occupation. And I believe this will send a signal to the Sunnis to join the political process."

— Representative John Murtha, quoted in an Alexander Cockburn column, *The Nation*, December 12 2005.

20. "Since last November when US Rep. John Murtha, D-Pa., began calling for the withdrawal of US troops from Iraq, he has been under fire from hard-core conservatives. Like every combat veteran before him who has come to question the pretext for war or its prosecution, Murtha has been denounced as a traitor, a coward, a defeatist and a liar.

"In mid-May, Murtha put himself in the firestorm again when he revealed details about apparent war crimes committed by US Marines in Haditha, Iraq last fall. 'Our troops over-reacted because of the pressure on them, and they killed innocent civilians in cold blood,' Murtha said....

"However, it's Murtha's outspokenness, not the alleged atrocity, that is roiling the conservative blogosphere, where some correspondents continue to cast him as a cowardly ally of the French, if not a traitorous aide to al-Qaeda....

"[T]he president's henchmen are still sent out to question the patriotism of the war's critics.

"And there remains a reflexive denial of unpleasant truths about the Iraqi enterprise and its effects on the Middle East — and on us.

"It now seems like that a handful of Marines committed atrocities at Haditha; if so, those acts will require the gravest sanctions."

— Cynthia Tucker, syndicated columnist, June 6, 2006.

21. "One of the paintings I selected for the Oval Office portrays a man on horseback, leading a charge up a steep hill."

— George W. Bush, June 16, 2003 fund-raising letter, Paid for by Bush-Cheney '04, Inc.

22. "Either you are with us, or you are with the terrorists."

— George W. Bush addressing Congress and the people after the September 11th attacks.

23. "All you have to do is to tell them that they are being attacked, and denounce the pacifists for lack of patriotism and exposing the country to danger. It works the same in every country."

— Hermann Goring

24. "Classmates threatened 15-year-old Kathy in high school and teachers harassed her. The administration suspended Kathy for wearing tee shirts with messages critical of the US bombing of Afghanistan. Even though Kathy was the one attacked for calling for peace, school officials claimed her actions endangered the safety of her fellow students. Kathy's mother sued, but the judge ruled the school's right to control behavior trumped Kathy's first amendment rights. She had to drop out of school when the administration refused to guarantee her safety. Kathy is being home schooled because her family can't afford private school tuition. Kathy is using an RFC-purchased computer to help further her education."

— Robert Meeropol, fund-raising letter for the *Rosenberg Fund for Children*, November 6, 2002.

25. "Katie Sierra is a fifteen-year-old sophomore at Sissonville High School in West Virginia. On October 22, she notified her principal, Forest Mann, that she wanted to form an anarchist club. He denied her request. It was the only club he'd ever disallowed.

"The next day, Sierra came to school with a T-shirt on that said, 'Racism, Sexism, Homophobia, I'm so proud of people in the land of the so-called free.' The principal suspended her for three days.

"On October 29, the school board president, Bill Ragland, said, 'What in the world is wrong with a kid like that?' Another school board member, John Luoni, accused her of treason, according to her court papers.

"She was told that before she could come back to school, she would have to provide the principal with authorization to obtain her medical records, and would have to meet with a school psychologist, and she couldn't wear T-shirts like the one she wore or organize her anarchist club.

"To make matters worse, says Sierra, Principal Mann mischaracterized her T-shirt in the *Charleston Gazette*, falsely stating it included statements such as 'I hope Afghanistan wins' and 'America should burn.'

"As a result, students at school ganged up on her. 'I got shoved against lockers,' she says. 'People made pictures of me with bullet holes through my head and posted them on, like, the doors in the school. They said some really harsh things. It was scary.'"

"Sierra and her mother sued the school district but lost in the lower courts and in the state supreme court by a 3 to 2 vote."

— Article by Matthew Rothschild, *The Progressive*, January 2002.

26. "Before a concert crowd in London, lead singer Natalie Maines told the audience, 'Just so you know, we're ashamed that the president of the United States is from Texas.' Days later, stateside crowds responded by smashing CDs, pulling the groups music from radio play lists and even passing legislation in South Carolina demanding that the group apologize.

"Beyond the film world, powerful radio station chains with strong ties to the Bush White House have been orchestrating boycotts and hate campaigns against several anti-war performers, most notably the Dixie Chicks, the Texas trio now fearing for their safety.

"The Chicks are expressing concern for their personal safety after the venomous response of right-wing critics. 'We've gotten a lot of hate mail, a lot of threatening mail,' Martie Maguire told reporters in Australia. 'Emily [Robison] had the front gate of her ranch smashed in. We have to have security when we get back to the States. It puts my well-being in jeopardy.'

"In a new statement that voiced support for the Dixie Chicks as 'terrific American artists expressing American values by using their American right to free speech' rocker Bruce Springsteen condemned 'the pressure coming from the government and big business to enforce conformity of thought concerning the war and politics.'"

— Various articles, *Asheville Citizens Times*, May 1, 2003; *The Progressive Populist*, May 1, 2003; *Asheville Global Report*, April 24–30 and May 1–7, 2003.

27. "Welcome to the era of Total Information Awareness...a time of perhaps unprecedented spying and secrecy...the Attorney General has gone to great lengths to rewrite and dismantle civil liberties in this country...his odious record demonstrates that he does not respect the fundamental tenets of our democracy.

"The USA Patriot Act...lets the FBI and other law enforcement agents enter your home when you're not there, ransack your files, use your computer and search your e-mails, and place a 'magic lantern' on your computer to record every keystroke. Then they can leave without telling you they were there.

"In addition, the Patriot Act lets law enforcement find out what books you're buying at stores or checking out at libraries. And it then gags the bookstores and libraries so they can't tell anyone that they've had to fork over your name.

"This is the biggest power grab since Attorney General A. Mitchell Palmer conducted his communist witch hunts under Woodrow Wilson!"

— Comment, *The Progressive*, January 2003.

28. "The Bush administration has already taken advantage of its 'War on Terrorism' to intimidate critics, undermine civil liberties and push through a blatantly pro-corporate agenda on a whole range of issues — from trade union rights to the environment. Now it is moving our country ever closer to an illegitimate and dangerous war on Iraq. The administration must not be allowed to get away with its claim that US military aggression has anything to do with bringing freedom to Iraqis or strengthening global security. Instead, the antiwar movement must come forward as the true champion of democracy and peace in the Middle East, and the advocate of a new foreign policy."

— Joanne Landy, Thomas Harrison and Jennifer Scarlott, Co-Directors, Campaign for Peace and Democracy, paid ad in *The Nation*, January 6, 2003.

29. "Attorney General John Ashcroft is rounding up or interrogating thousands of immigrants in what will go down in history as the Ashcroft Raids. The FBI and the Secret Service are harassing artists and activists. Publishers are firing anti-war columnists and cartoonists. University presidents are scolding faculty members. And rightwing citizen's groups are demanding conformity.

"These threats are real. They are frightening people. They are ruining livelihoods. And they may be just a taste of sour things to come."

— Article by Matthew Rothschild, *The Progressive*, January 2002.

30. "Every purchase you make with a credit card, every magazine subscription you buy and medical prescription you fill, every Web site you visit and e-mail you send or receive, every academic grade you receive, every bank deposit you make, every

trip you book and every event you attend — all these transactions and communications will go into what the Defense department describes as a 'virtual, centralized
grand database.'

"To this computerized dossier on your private life from commercial sources, add
every piece of information that government has about you — passport applications,
driver's license and bridge toll records, judicial and divorce records, complaints from
nosy neighbors to the FBI, your lifetime paper trail plus the latest hidden camera
surveillance — and you have supersnoop's dream: a 'Total Information Awareness'
about every US citizen."

— William Safire, column, the *New York Times*.

31. "The media has continued to largely ignore Patriot Act II, blandly titled Domestic Security Enhancement Act of 2003. Most Americans are still unaware, in Patriot Act II, of the stripping of citizenship, the secret arrests, and the collection of
DNA of 'suspected' terrorists, including American citizens who might have had a
'mere association' with terrorist groups."

— Nat Hentoff, *The Progressive*, May 2003.

32. "They that can give up essential liberty to obtain a little temporary safety
deserve neither liberty nor safety."

— Benjamin Franklin.

33. "Let's talk, then, not about what you're doing to other people but about what
you're doing to yourselves. You're gutting the Constitution. Already your home can
be entered without your knowledge or permission, you can be snatched away and
incarcerated without cause, your mail can be spied on, your records searched. Why
isn't this a recipe for widespread business theft, political intimidation and fraud? I
know you've been told that all this is for your own safety and protection, but think
about it for a minute. Anyway, when did you get so scared? You didn't used to be
easily frightened.

"If you proceed much further down the slippery slope, people around the world
will stop admiring the good things about you. They'll decide that your city on a hill
is a slum and your democracy is a sham, and therefore you have no business trying to
impose your sullied vision on them. They'll think you've abandoned the rule of law.
They'll think you've fouled your own nest."

— Letter to America. By Margaret Atwood, *The Nation*, April 14, 2003.

34. "In the US, signs of a police state are evident everywhere. Thousands of US
citizens of Middle Eastern descent have been arrested without charges...this program
has been encouraged and incited by government officials, especially by the police,
both local and federal, and by assorted veterans' groups and demagogic politicians.
The president has decreed dictatorial powers, setting up anonymous military tribunals to try 'suspicious immigrants and overseas suspects' who can be kidnapped and
tried in the US habeas corpus has been suspended. School children have been forced
to sing quasi-religious anthems and pledge allegiance to the flag. Many employees
who voice criticism of the war or US support of Israeli massacres of Palestinians have
been suspended or fired. All letters, e-mails, and phone calls are subject to control
without any judicial review. The mass media spews government propaganda, churns
out chauvinist stories, and is relatively silent on overseas massacres and domestic
repression.

"The FBI 'exhorted' every US citizen to report any suspicious behavior by friends,
neighbors, relatives, acquaintances, and strangers. Between September and the end
of November almost 700, 000 denunciations were registered. Thousands of Middle

Eastern neighbors, local shop owners, and employees were denounced, as were numerous other US citizens.

"Hundreds and thousands of innocent persons were investigated and harassed by the federal police. Tens of millions of Americans have become paranoid — fearing 'terrorism' in their everyday work, shopping, and leisure activities. People refrain from the mildest criticism of the war or the government for fear they will be labeled terrorist sympathizers, reported to the government, investigated, and lose their job."

— James Petras, article, *Z Magazine*, January 2002.

35. "On March 22, a few hundred peaceful antiwar protesters in Seattle who had gathered around the Federal Building suddenly found themselves being swept down streets by officers in riot gear and then corralled onto the sidewalk. As hundreds of officers encircled and trapped them, snipers were spotted on rooftops and cops formed riot lines, holding rubber bullet guns and M-16s. Injuries inflicted on the demonstrators ranged from head wounds to taser burns. So far, the public defender's office has received 200 complaints about police misconduct, brutality and illegal arrest.

"Seattle attorney Paul Richmond argues that paramilitary police units already appear to have carte blanche to use any and all means to quash dissent. 'As long as weapons and tactics like these are in use,' he adds, 'the civilian population is being viewed as the enemy.'"

— Silja J. A. Talvi, article, *The Nation*, May 12, 2003.

36. "Everywhere, it seems, there are unexplained disappearances and detentions. This week I'm in Indiana, where an item in the Bloomington *Herald-Times* reads, 'One of our students brought us this disturbing news: her father, a naturalized American citizen from India, had disappeared from the New York airport upon his return from a business trip to Germany. It was verified that he was on the flight and his luggage showed up at the family home a few days later.... After frantic calls to hospitals, police, relatives, even the FBI, the family hired a lawyer.' Almost a week later, the FBI admitted that they had him; and after three weeks and the intervention of the Indian Ambassador to the United States, the father, a prominent advertising executive, was ultimately released. There were no charges and, still, no explanation."

— Patricia J. Williams, column, *The Nation*, May 12, 2003.

37. Jackie Anderson was a staff reporter for the *Sun Advocate* in Price, Utah. She wrote a column that said, "War is not the only action available to us. Seeking justice is action. Making peace is action." When she asked why it wasn't running, her editor...told her to talk to the publisher, Kevin Ashby. "This is not the direction I want my newspaper to go in," he told her.

"The next day the publisher asked me to clear my desk." I asked him if I was being fired, and he said, 'No, you quit. I'm accepting your resignation.' And I said, 'I didn't quit.'"

When asked, the editor said, "I'm not going to discuss this. This was a personnel issue. She said she quit her job and then decided she could unquit at her convenience."

— Article by Matthew Rothschild, *The Progressive*, January 2002.

38. Dan Guthrie worked at the Grants Pass *Daily Courier* in Oregon for ten years.... (He) was the columnist who said Bush "skedaddled" on September 11th. "The picture of Bush hiding in a Nebraska hole" was "an embarrassment," he wrote. "The President's men are frantically glossing over his cowardice."

A week later, the publisher fired him, even though the city editor and the editor had signed off on the piece, Guthrie says. "I told them this was going to be hot, and they approved it as it stood.

Dennis Roler issued a front page apology, entitled, "This Is No Time to Criticize the Nation's Leader: Apology for Printing Column."

— Article by Matthew Rothschild, *The Progressive*, January 2002.

39. Tom Gutting worked for the *Texas City Sun*, and on September 22, he, like Guthrie, criticized Bush for not returning to Washington on September 11...."The day the piece ran, says Gutting, "the publisher assured me straightaway that he wouldn't fire me." but a few days later, the publisher, Les Daughtry Jr., changed his mind.

Daughtry, too, issued a front-page apology, saying Gutting's column was "not appropriate to publish during this time."

Gutting is unemployed. "I'm still looking for a job," he says. "I'm hoping it will end soon. I think I've been pretty much blacklisted from the small papers the company owns."

— Article by Matthew Rothschild, *The Progressive*, January 2002.

40. The St. George, Utah, newspaper, *The Spectrum*, apologized on November 13 for a cartoon it ran the previous day from Pulitzer prize-winner Steve Benson. The cartoon depicted President Bush dropping bombs that carried scrawled messages, such as "starving millions of Afghans" and "killing innocent civilians." Many local veterans descended on the paper, threatening to cancel their subscriptions if it didn't issue an apology.

— Article by Matthew Rothschild, *The Progressive*, January 2002.

41. Aaron McGruder, who draws *The Boondocks*, has seen his strip taken out of many papers after September 11 for its anti-war content. And lesser-known cartoonists may be especially vulnerable.

— Article by Matthew Rothschild, *The Progressive*, January 2002.

42. "Todd Persche drew a cartoon for the *Baraboo News Republic* in Wisconsin. Not anymore. After September 11, he drew a couple of cartoons that got him canned. One said, 'When the media keeps pounding on the war drum...it's hard to hear other points of view.' Another was about Big Brother 'turning our civil rights upside down.'

"Persche says, 'In these times, they make you feel like you're not a patriot just because you're dissenting.'"

— Article by Matthew Rothschild, *The Progressive*, January 2002.

43. "Dear Bookseller: Last week, President Bush signed into law an antiterrorism bill that gives the federal government expanded authority to search your business records, including the titles of the books purchased by your customers.... There is no opportunity for you or your lawyer to object in court. You cannot object publicly, either. The new law includes a gag order that prevents you from disclosing 'to any person' the fact that you have received an order to produce documents."

— November 1st letter from the American Booksellers Foundation for Free Expression to its members, cited in an article by Matthew Rothschild, *The Progressive*, January 2002.

44. "Once the government can demand of a publisher the names of the purchasers of his publication, the free press, as we know it disappears. Then the specter of a government agent will look over the shoulder of everyone who reads.... Fear of criticism goes with every person into the bookstall. The subtle, imponderable pressures of the orthodox lay hold. Some will fear to read what is unpopular, what the powers-

that-be dislike.... fear will take the place of freedom in the libraries, book stores, and homes in the land."

— Charles Levendosky, column, *The Progressive Populist*, May 1, 2003.

45. "'I'm terrified,' says Ellen Schrecker, author of *Many Are the Crimes: McCarthyism in America* (Princeton University, 1999). 'What concerns me is we're not seeing an enormous outcry against this whole structure of repression that's being rushed into place by the Bush Administration.'"

— Article by Matthew Rothschild, *The Progressive*, January 2002.

46. "(Ed) Gernon was, until recently, a television producer at CBS responsible for a four-part miniseries on Hitler's rise to power...He thought the timing was apt, and said so in an interview with TV Guide magazine.

"'It basically boils down to an entire nation gripped by fear, who ultimately chose to give up their civil rights and plunged the whole nation into war,' he said. 'I can't think of a better time to examine this history than now.'

"That was too strong for Leslie Moonves, CBS's chief executive, who promptly fired him. No reasons were given although a strong desire not to fall foul of the Bush administration apparently had plenty to do with it.

"Mike Farrell...sees a distinct political strategy at work...' What this is really about is stifling dissent on a national scale. It does not matter a whit whether we are celebrities or not. What galls them so much is that we have access to the media.'

"The Screen Actors Guild has lowered the atmosphere to the McCarthy-era anti-Communist witch hunts of the 1950s. It issued a statement saying that no performer should be denied work on the basis of his or her political beliefs. 'Even a hint of the blacklist must never be tolerated in this nation.'

"Within three hours of that statement being posted, the guild was inundated with the by-now familiar deluge of hate mail."

— Asheville Global Report, April 24-30, 2003.

Chapter 11. Aftermath

1. "On March 19-20, 2003, Bush started his second colonial war (Afghanistan being the first). He attacked without provocation the sovereign state of Iraq, which had already been crucially weakened through a decade of UN economic sanctions and posed no imminent threat to the US or any other state. The war, launched on grounds of fear, was in clear violation of the UN and Nuremberg Charters and the US Constitution, which gives no president the power to wage 'anticipatory' or 'preventive' war absent real, imminent threat...."One year after Bush's victory declaration, the Iraqi nationalist resistance has stretched the US military to its limit and frustrated millennialism expectations. Rather than putting an end to terrorism, Bush and Tony Blair have spread the danger and made their citizens objects of hatred, revulsion, and reprisal throughout the Middle East....

"In this situation, the US state is liable for violations of the 1949 Geneva Accords, the 1984 UN Convention Against Torture, and the charters of the ad hoc UN criminal tribunals for the former Yugoslavia and Rwanda. Individual liability accrues especially to Bush and Rumsfeld, who approved the criminal policies establishing the US global torture system. Bush, whose 'razor-sharp distinction of the "good guys" and the "bad guys"...filtered down through the ranks,' bears primary responsibility for creating the climate which condoned his subordinates torture of detainees."

— Herbert P. Bix, essay, Z Magazine, July/August 2004.

2. "During Congressional debate on a resolution marking the third anniversary of September 11, House Whip Tom DeLay said that the fight against Iraq and the fight against Al Qaeda 'is one and the same conflict.'"

— Comment, The Progressive, October 2004.

3. Senator John McCain "argued that the war in Iraq and the 'war on terrorism' are one....McCain argues that 'only the most deluded of us could doubt the necessity of this war.'"

— Editorial, The Nation, September 20, 2004.

[By now it becomes clear that McCain is the most deluded of all. To believe that the people of Iraq are terrorists is really quite insane. In the entire history of humankind, no Iraqi has ever made an attack of any kind against the United States or ever threatened to do so. Furthermore, since Saddam Hussein destroyed all of his weapons of mass destruction just after the first American attack against Iraq as the United Nations ordered him to do, that country has had absolutely no ability to attack this country. Since 2004 Washington has admitted there were never any dealings between Iraq and bin Laden. These are facts and McCain knows it.

Why does McCain (with Joe Lieberman — the "Democrat" turned "Independent" and now stumping for the Republican candidate) support Bush's lies? Bush has said some highly unflattering and perhaps apocryphal things about McCain, making him out to be a sick, cowardly, unpatriotic, misogynist and alcoholic — and therefore unfit for the presidency. Maybe Bush was right. McCain does not deserve the respect he has gotten from many people. He has tarnished his reputation for "straight talk" in the name of political ambition and warmongering apologetics. *The Author.*]

4. "The American people have got to understand that Iraq is a part of the war on terror."

— George W. Bush, in June of 2006 at a press conference after his return from a trip to Baghdad.

The above endlessly repeated statement is one of Bush's, and the Republican Party's, worst and most murderous lies. When Bush launched his attack against the people of Iraq, there were no terrorists at all in that country, nor had there ever been any attack or any threat of attack against the United States by Iraq. Persuading US citizens to support a war on the basis of this monstrous lie has had brutal and evil consequences for both countries.

Believing this lie, or others like it, American soldiers to abuse, torture, and kill innocent Iraqis, including many women and children. A poll of soldiers in Iraq conducted in June 2007 showed that eighty-nine percent of them believe that the people of Iraq were responsible for the September 11th attack against the United States. In 2004, Bush got reelected largely because people believed this lie; seventy-nine percent of those who voted for Bush believed it. The soldiers who have committed atrocities in Iraq took their orders and their general direction from their officers and the Commander in Chief. The voters in the 2004 election made their choices based on a campaign of misinformation that also came from the top; it was a travesty. *The Author.*]

5. "The invasion of Iraq was a bandit act, an act of blatant state terrorism, demonstrating absolute contempt for the concept of international law...an arbitrary military action inspired by a series of lies upon lies and gross manipulation of the media and therefore of the public."

— Harold Pinter, Nobel Prize speech of December 7, 2005.

8. "When you look at the lead-up to the war in Iraq, I blame President Bush, I blame Congress, I blame the media. But I'm not cutting any slack for the American people. As a nation, we are mute, we are silent."

— Scott Ritter, *Santa Cruz Sentinel*, March 27, 2006.

9. "Bush's abuses of presidential power are the most extensive in American history. He has launched an aggressive war ("war of choice," in today's euphemism) on false grounds. He has presided over a system of torture and sought to legitimize it by specious definitions of the word. He has asserted a wholesale right to lock up American citizens and others indefinitely without any legal showing or the right to see a lawyer or anyone else. He has kidnapped people in foreign countries and sent them to other countries where they were tortured....

"There is a name for a system of government that wages war, deceives its citizens, violates their rights, abuses power and breaks the law, rejects judicial and legislative checks on itself, claims power without limit, tortures prisoners and acts in secret. It is dictatorship."

— Jonathan Schell, column, *The Nation*, January 9/16, 2006

10. "Two million people have been killed in thirteen years of war against Iraq. The war in Palestine is owned and operated by the US, where US-made 'Apache' helicopters and F-16s attack daily. Scores of thousands have died in Afghanistan after 20 years of US war-making there. But in Falmouth, Massachusetts, parents buy children ice cream cones and tell them to watch the wonderful air show."

— Richard Hugus, article, *Z Magazine*, October 2003.

11. "Would you rather fight them over there or over here?"

— Bush statement repeated over and over again all across the United States by Bush supporters.

12. This war is "based on lies and misinterpretations from London and from Washington."

— Former President Jimmy Carter.

14. "The events of the last three years were watched carefully all over the world. As evidence mounted that US actions were indeed comparable to fascism, opposition grew worldwide....

"Existing international and domestic humanitarian law, such as the Geneva Conventions, were declared 'obsolete' by US government lawyers, including current Attorney General Gonzales. They might have been a bit more cautious had they been aware that Field Marshal Wilhelm Keitel, commander of the German armies in World War II, had used almost the exact same wording to declare that the humanitarian law of the time was irrelevant, resulting in actions which earned Keitel the death penalty. (He was executed in 1946.) Keitel said that the humanitarian laws of war of that time were 'a product of a notion...of a bygone era' and were 'obsolete.'...

"Among the techniques the Japanese fascists used on its detainees were various forms of water torture/waterboarding. Following World War I, the International Military Tribunal for the Far East concluded that both the officers who ordered water torture/waterboarding of detainees and those who carried it out were guilty of war crimes. Some were executed....

"Finally, the US military's actions in Fallujah remind one, on a smaller scale, of the Japanese attack on Nanking, China, and the Nazi destruction of Lidice, Czechoslovakia, both infamous examples of the fascist tendency to punish an entire population for refusing to submit to foreign domination. Fallujah was a city resisting the US occupation, where US military contractors had been ambushed, killed, and their bodies hung from a bridge. This marked the entire population of the town for punishment and large sections of the city were leveled with extensive 'collateral damage'-civilian deaths and injuries amounting to US war crimes....

"To uphold the rule of law, foreign governments should investigate top US officials and, if those investigations support prosecution, these governments should arrest any of these officials who enter their territory and begin legal proceedings against them. These and other actions by governments and people who believe in law, peace, and justice are imperative."

— Laurence Shoup, essay, *Z Magazine*, April 2006.

15. "Is President Bush guilty of war crimes? To even ask this question is to go far beyond the boundaries of mainstream US media. A few weeks ago when a class of

seniors at Parsippany High School in New Jersey prepared for a mock trial to assess whether Bush has committed war crimes, a media tempest ensued. Typical was the response of Tucker Carlson, who found the very idea of such accusations against Bush to be unfathomable. The classroom exercise 'implies people are accusing him of a crime against humanity,' Carlson said. 'It's ludicrous.'...

"In a world where might did not make right, (Robert) Parry wrote in a recent piece, 'George W. Bush, Tony Blair, and their key enablers would be in shackles before a war crimes tribunal at the Hague, rather than sitting in the White House, 10 Downing Street, or some other comfortable environs in Washington and London.'

"Over the top? I don't think so. In fact, Parry's evidence and analysis seems much more cogent — and relevant to our true situation — than the prodigious output of countless liberal-minded pundits who won't go beyond complaining about Bush's deceptions, miscalculations, and tactical errors in connection with the Iraq war....

"That article cites key statements by the US representative to the Nuremberg Tribunal immediately after the Second World War. 'Our position,' declared Robert Jackson, a US Supreme Court justice, 'is that whatever grievances a nation may have, however objectionable it finds the status quo, aggressive warfare is an illegal means for settling those grievances or for altering those conditions.'

"During a March 26 appearance on the NBC program 'Meet the Press,' Secretary of state Condoleezza Rice tried to justify the invasion of Iraq this way: 'We faced the outcome of an ideology of hatred throughout the Middle East that had to be dealt with. Saddam Hussein was a part of that old Middle East. The new Iraq will be a part of the new Middle East, and it will be safer.'"

— Norman Soloman, essay, *Z Magazine*, May 2006.

16. "What we have done in Iraq has made neither us nor the world safer. By laying waste to the villages and countryside of Iraq, we have made fertile for fanatics the very land we proclaim to have liberated in the name of democracy. Most Americans see this now as the inevitable truth.

"Should we not have the right but the obligation to defend ourselves when attacked? Of course, and we did. When it was learned that al-Qaeda was behind the attacks on our country in 2001, we quickly took the battle to them in their training camps in Afghanistan.

"As noble as that beginning attempt at retaliation was, it quickly faded into relative obscurity once the administration inexplicably shifted its focus to Iraq. Sometimes I feel as though our entire nation has Attention Deficit Disorder. Why there is not a coast-to-coast outcry is perplexing at best, deeply disturbing at worst.

"There were 19 hijackers on that September day. Of these, 15 were from Saudi Arabia, as was Osama bin Laden. The other hijackers were from Egypt, the United Arab Emirates and Lebanon. Notably, none was from Iraq, their training was not done in Iraq, and Iraq did not fund their attacks. Together, they killed nearly 3,000 innocent people and the 19 hijackers took their own lives in the process.

"In a vainglorious move, the United States launched an unprovoked invasion of Iraq (i.e., we were not attacked by Iraq and were not in imminent danger of being attacked by Iraq). In three years since, we have killed more than 100,000 innocent people and lost nearly 2,500 American lives in the process. Where — where is our moral outrage?"

— Paul Howey, community opinion columnist, *Asheville* Citizen Times, June 11, 2006.

17. From the Doonesbury comic strip of March 27, 2006 by Gary Trudeau:

"Good news, sir — A fantastic poll of the troops in Iraq...

Almost 90% of them believe the war is retaliation for Saddam's role in 9/11!

What? But he had no role, Karl. We already admitted that.

Who cares? As long as it keeps the troops motivated.

But what if they find out?

From who? The media? You worry too much.

18. "In the case of Iraq, it's impossible to be indifferent to the prospect that intelligence has been manipulated, forged, or bullied into shape. Government cynicism — in Vietnam, in the Iran-Contra affair, in the tacit indulgence of Saddam's gassing of the Kurds in 1988 and his slaughter of the Shiites in 1991 — inevitably cripples the country's ability to cope with future crises...The administration is wrong. A serious investigation is urgently needed. The American people cannot be expected, in Ari Fleischer's blithe formulation, to get with the program and 'move on.'"

— David Remnick, item, *The New Yorker*, July 28, 2003.

19. "Where are the weapons? Where's the smoking gun? Where's the mushroom cloud? Where's the imminent threat? Where was ever the threat? Are you kidding?"

— Helen Thomas, interview by Elizabeth DiNovella, *The Progressive*, August 2004.

20. "They knew there weren't any WMDs. There is a famous defector, General Hussein Kamel, that everybody always quotes. In 1995 Kamel was head of the WMD program in Iraq and he defected. He had this massive pile of documents making clear what Saddam Hussein's weapons of mass destruction were. That's what Powell quotes him as saying: Saddam Hussein has this much anthrax now, blah, blah, blah. But what they didn't say is that when Hussein Kamel was interviewed by UNSCOM officials about these documents, he said: Saddam Hussein destroyed these weapons. He said, I ordered the destruction of these weapons before the Gulf War because Saddam Hussein was afraid of what would happen when people realized and it became public knowledge that this is what happened. So he wanted to eliminate them so he didn't get too incriminated. They knew from the start that there was no threat."

— Nafez Mossadeq Ahmed, executive director of the Institute for Policy Research and Development in the United Kingdom, interview by David Barsamian, *Z Magazine*, June 2004.

21. "According to the repeated claims of the Administration, our kids were put at risk in order to disarm Iraq of its chemical and biological weapons, which, intelligence assessments were said to show, posed an urgent threat to our natural security.... So where is Saddam's terrible arsenal? Bush, on his way to Auschwitz, took time out to tell Polish television, 'We found the weapons of mass destruction.' That wasn't true. After more than two months of searching, American forces in Iraq had yet to discover any trace of biological or chemical agents.... As the war drags on, a sense of reality is lacking in the Bush camp's triumphalism; Americans are still killing and dying in almost every news cycle, and Iraqi resentment is mounting against an improvised occupation...the charges now circulating that Bush's war cabinet depended on false information or, worse, falsified it to exaggerate the threat of those weapons in the first place is much more than a technicality."

— Philip Gourevitch, *The New Yorker*, June 16 & 23, 2003.

22. "I don't believe [Saddam Hussein] is a significant military threat today."

— Vice President Dick Cheney, CNN in March 2001, Anthony Arnove, *Asheville Global Report*, March 23–29, 2006 (Source: *In These Times*).

23. "Iraq is probably not a nuclear threat at the present time."

— Secretary of defense Donald Rumsfeld, interview with "Fox News" on February 12, 2001.

24. "Word comes now, via the Washington Post and the New York times, of a small intelligence agency in the State Department — 165 analysts, a tenth of the CIA's complement — that more or less got it right.

"The Bureau of Intelligence and Research at State was critical of the stated reasons for going to war from the very first.

"It challenged as unsubstantiated the views of other intelligence agencies that Saddam was rebuilding his nuclear weapons program.

"Nor would it go along with the theory that Iraq could develop a weapon in the next 10 years, given that it didn't see any movement in that direction at present.

"In addition, it was skeptical of the idea that the conquest of Iraq would help spread democracy across the Arab world.

"The reason this intelligence was given so little weight (none, actually) was that the ruling cabal — Bush, Vice President Cheney, Defense Secretary Rumsfeld, Deputy Defense Secretary Wolfowitz — didn't want to hear it.

"Perhaps the saddest aspect of the farce is that not even Secretary of State Colin Powell paid any attention to the analysis of what were, after all, his own people. Instead, he went before the UN and made a bogus case for the invasion using bogus evidence."

— Donald Kaul, syndicated column, July 31, 2004.

25. "Frankly, they have worked. He (Saddam) has not developed any significant capability with respect to weapons of mass destruction. He is unable to project conventional power against his neighbors."

— Colin Powell speaking to Egypt's foreign minister in Cairo in February 2001 about the UN sanctions in force against Iraq cited by Eric Alterman in his column of August 29, 2004 in *The Nation.*

26. "We have been able to keep weapons from going into Iraq. We have been able to keep the sanctions in place to the extent that items that might support weapons of mass destruction development have had some controls.

"It's been quite a success for ten years."

— Secretary of State Colin Powell, interview with "Face the Nation on February 11, 2001.

27. *The US and the* UN "have succeeded in containing Saddam Hussein and his ambitions. Iraq's forces are about one-third their original size. They don't really possess the capability to attack their neighbors the way they did ten years ago....Iraq is not threatening America.

— Secretary of State Colin Powell, at a meeting with German foreign Minister Joschka Fischer in February of 2001.

28. "Before the war, the Bush administration portrayed Iraq as full of killer poisons with strange names and deadly effects, which terrorists could get hold of and unleash on US cities...

The administration also contended many of the weapons were ready to be used on the battlefield.

"'Our conservative estimate is that Iraq today has a stockpile of between 100 and 500 tons of chemical weapons agent,' Powell said at the United Nations in February.

"In October, US intelligence agencies said that Iraq had begun 'renewed production of chemical warfare agents,' probably including mustard, sarin, cyclosarin and VX.

"Chemical weapons have not been found.

"Powell suggested military units had biological weapons in the field. On May 30, Lt. Gen. James Conway, the top Marine in Iraq, said, speaking about the hunt for chemical and biological weapons: 'We've been to virtually every ammunition supply point between the Kuwaiti border and Baghdad, but they're simply not there.'"

"So far it seems as if all the leads that have been followed up have come to nothing.... so many false claims have been made in the past, it can only be politically driven.

"Powell also had told the United Nations that 'numerous intelligence reports over the past decade from sources inside Iraq' indicated 'a covert force of up to a few dozen scud-variant ballistic missiles.'"

"None has been found.

"US allegations that Iraq was trying to develop a nuclear weapon have also not been verified...No centrifuges have been reported or found.

"In his state of the union address, Bush said that Britain had learned that Saddam 'recently sought significant quantities of uranium from Africa.'"

"The claim rested significantly on a letter or letters between officials in Iraq and Niger...the communications are now accepted as forged."

— John J. Lumpkin, article, *The Associated Press*, June 8, 2003.

29. "The evidence he presented to the United Nations — some of it circumstantial, some of it absolutely bone-chilling in its detail — had to prove to anyone that Iraq not only hasn't accounted for its weapons of mass destruction but without doubt still retains them. Only a fool — or possibly a Frenchman — could conclude otherwise."

— Richard Cohen, *Washington Post*, Feb. 6, 2003, the day after Colin Powell's mendacious speech to the UN Security Council.

30. "Colin Powell did more than present the world with a convincing and detailed x-ray of Iraq's secret weapons and terrorism programs yesterday. He also exposed the enduring bad faith of several key members of the UN Security Council when it comes to Iraq and its 'web of lies,' in Powell's phrase....To continue to say that the Bush administration has not made its case, you must now believe that Colin Powell lied in the most serious statement he will ever make, or was taken in by manufactured evidence. I don't believe that. Today, neither should you."

— Jim Hoagland, *Washington Post*, Feb. 6, 2003.

31. "Colin Powell, the former US Secretary of state, harshly criticized the Bush administration on Sept. 9 for its failures in Iraq, calling the country a mess and voicing concerns that it may slide into civil war.

"Powell who left the administration in January also said that his speech in February 2003 to the UN, making the case for war, was a painful blot on his record....

"Turning to his pre-war address to the UN Security Council, when he forcefully made the case for invasion and offered proof that Iraq had weapons of mass destruction, Powell said that he felt terrible about the claims he made. Asked whether the speech would tarnish his reputation, he replied, 'Of course it will. It's a blot. I'm the one who presented it on behalf of the United States to the world, and [it] will always be part of my record. It was painful. It's painful now....

"Powell, 68, did not blame George Tenet, the CIA's director at the time, for the misleading information.... Instead, he blamed lower-level intelligence analysts for not speaking out during the five days he pored over reports at the CIA as he prepared his speech....

"Powell said that he had "never seen evidence to suggest" a connection between the attacks of Sept. 11, 2001, and the regime of Saddam Hussein, unlike Dick Cheney, the vice-president, who has made such a claim."

— *Asheville Global Report*, Sept 15-21, 2005 (Source: Times (UK))

32. "The only part that kind of annoys me is 'Well, did you lie? Or were you misleading?' No, I didn't lie, and I wasn't misleading. If I was lying and knew what the truth was, which has to be the basis of a lie — you know the truth — we wouldn't have sent 1,400 people wandering around   Iraq looking for the stuff. They didn't find it. So the intelligence was wrong. And that's all you can really say about it."

— Colin Powell, Interview, AARP Magazine, July/August, 2006.

33. "Last week, Murray Waas reported on the *National Journal* Web site that ten days after September 11, 2001, 'Bush was told in a highly classified briefing that the US intelligence community had no evidence linking the Iraqi regime of Saddam Hussein to the attacks and that there was scant credible evidence that Iraq had any significant collaborative ties with Al Qaeda.' This information too, was not shared with Congress before the war, and was likewise kept from the commissions and senatorial committees that have since investigated the run up to it."

— Hendrik Hertzberg, The Talk of the Town column, *The New Yorker*, December 5, 2005.

34. "The independent commission investigating the Sept. 11 attacks said Wednesday that no evidence exists that al-Qaeda had strong ties to Saddam Hussein — a central justification the Bush administration had for toppling the former Iraqi regime. Bush also argued that Saddam had weapons of mass destruction, which have not been found."

— The Associated Press, June 18, 2004.

35. "President Bush on Thursday disputed the Sept. 11 Commission's finding that there was no 'collaborative relationship' between Saddam Hussein and the al-Qaeda terrorist network responsible for the attacks.

"'There was a relationship between Iraq and al-Qaeda,' Bush insisted following a meeting with his Cabinet at the White House."

— Asheville Citizen-Times, June 18, 2004.

36. "As recently as Monday, Cheney said Saddam 'had long-established ties with al-Qaeda,' and Bush defended the vice-president's assertion.

"The commission investigating the Sept. 11 attacks bluntly contradicted the White House. It said there was no evidence Iraq and al-Qaeda had a collaborative relationship.'

— *Asheville Citizen-Times*, June 17, 2004.

37. "After hundreds of American soldiers have died and billions of US dollars have been spent, a Senate panel is saying the justification for the war in Iraq was wrong.

— Ken Guggenheim, report, *The Associated Press*, July 10, 2004.

38. "On October 2, David Kay gave an interim report of his findings before House and Senate intelligence committees. Although he had directed a team of 1,200 people who had searched Iraq for three months, they had not managed to find any biological, chemical, or nuclear weapons. Still, he was hopeful....

"On December 13, Saddam Hussein, despite being considerably smaller than a biological-weapons factory, was found at the bottom of a dirt hole, in a kind of living grave, near his hometown of Tikrit in northern Iraq. Even at that late date, some nine months after the start of the war, neither Iraq's fabled biological-weapons production plants nor the weapons themselves had turned up anywhere. The following January, David Kay, still unable to find the lethal implements, resigned from his post."

— Ed Regis, essay, *Harper's Magazine*, July 2004.

39. "I would say...that would clearly be a more serious issue than even Watergate. It would be a graver charge" and "fit into the definition of high crimes and misdemeanors, which we in Britain used to have as a basis for impeachment, and which, of course, you still have as a basis of impeachment."

— Labor MP Malcolm Savage in a CNBC interview about allegations that legislators and citizens were lied to and led into war by the Bushites, *The Nation*, June 23, 2003.

40. "A key British Foreign Office diplomat responsible for dialoguing with UN inspectors said on June 20 that claims the US and UK governments made about Iraq's alleged weapons of mass destruction (WMD) were 'totally implausible.'

"'I'd read the intelligence on WMD for four and a half years, and there's no way that it could sustain the case that the government was presenting. All of my colleagues knew that, too,' said Carne Ross, a member of the British mission to the UN in New York during the run-up to the invasion."

— *Asheville Global Report*, June 23-29, 2005 (source Guardian (UK))

41. "Four months after Charles A. Duelfer, who led the weapons hunt in 2004, submitted an interim report to Congress that contradicted nearly every prewar assertion about Iraq made by top Bush administration officials, a senior intelligence official says the findings will stand as the ISG's final conclusions and will be published this spring....

"The ISG has interviewed every person it could find connected to programs that ended more than 10 years ago, and every suspected site within Iraq has been fully searched, or stripped bare.

— Dafna Linzer, report, *The Washington Post National Weekly Edition*, January 23, 2005.

42. "Bush, Cheney, Donald Rumsfeld, Condoleezza Rice, and Colin Powell issued 237 statements that were 'misleading at the time they were made,' according to "Iraq on the Record," a report by Representative Henry Waxman of California and the democratic staff of the House Committee on Government Reform."

— Comment, *The Progressive*, April 2006.

43. "My e-mail has included many messages from people who have leaped far ahead of the evidence and concluded that Bush should be impeached and removed from office for actions they deem to be illegal....

"The...weakest instance is the claim that Bush took the nation to war on the basis of false intelligence about Iraq's weapons of mass destruction. But there is no clear evidence as yet that Bush willfully concocted or knowingly distorted the intelligence he received about Saddam Hussein's military programs. Interpretations of that intelligence varied within the government, but the Clinton administration...came to the same conclusions that Bush did — and so did other governments in the Western alliance....

"It is a reach to attempt to make a crime of a policy misjudgment."

— David Broder, syndicated column, January 22, 2006.

[In March 2001 on CNN, Dick Cheney said, "I don't believe (Saddam Hussein) is a significant military threat today." In February 2001 on Fox News, Donald

Rumsfeld said, "Iraq is probably not a nuclear threat at the present time." In February 2001 in Cairo, Colin Powell said, "He (Saddam) has not developed any significant capability with respect to weapons of mass destruction, He is unable to project conventional power against his neighbors." On February 11, 2001 on "Face the Nation," Powell said, "We have been able to keep weapons from going into Iraq. We have been able to keep the sanctions in place....It's been quite a success for two years." In February 2001 at a meeting with German foreign Minister Joschka Fischer, Powell said, "They don't really possess the capability to attack their neighbors the way they did ten years ago....Iraq is not threatening America."

In 1995, Hussein Kamel, the Iraqi defector in charge of Saddam's WMD program, told the CIA that Saddam had destroyed his chemical and biological weapons and had none left. This is a matter of record. Yet, on his way to pay a ceremonial visit to Auschwitz in 2003, George Bush told a Polish television audience, "We found the weapons of mass destruction." Say no more. —Author.]

44. "Colonel Sam Gardner came around to a conclusion that horrified him: The Bush administration had turned psychological operations against Americans. No longer were just foreign enemies being targeted for coercion and deception. Now the target was the US public.

"'It was not bad intelligence. It was much more. It was an organized effort. It began before the war, and continues as post-conflict distortions,' wrote Gardner in a fifty-six-page self-published report....

"What Gardner detailed was blowback on a grand scale. The power of the US military has been deployed to deceive the American public. While the futile search for weapons of mass destruction continued in Iraq, weapons of mass deception were unleashed on an unwitting American population. It was a $200 million PR campaign to deceive the American public.

"In the most basic sense, Washington and London did not trust the peoples of their democracies to come to right decisions, wrote Gardner....

"The American public became the focus of a high-intensity domestic psyops program. The lies coming out of the Bush administration picked up in frequency and audacity. False claims about the presence of nonexistent weapons of mass destruction were but one thread in this elaborate tapestry of deceit. 'Disloyal' allies such as France and Germany were targeted and smeared. The lies took many forms. Sometimes it was an outright official fabrication. At other times, government officials would deliberately not correct a lie gaining currency in the street. There were unofficial leaks and stories planted on background. Finally, there were black operations, where false documents may have been forged in elaborate schemes to smear and deceive. "In total, Gardner asserts, 'There were over fifty stories manufactured or at least engineered, that distorted the picture of Gulf [War] II for the American and British people.' ...

"The themes of the invasion propaganda were twofold. The war on terror is a fight between good and evil (and it didn't hurt to invoke images of a Christian crusade against Islam). And Iraq was responsible for the 9/11 attacks — What propaganda theorists would call the 'big lie,' says Gardner."

— Amy Goodman. *The Exception to the Rulers.*

45. "If you tell a lie big enough and keep repeating it, people will eventually come to believe it."

— Josef Goebbels, Minister of Propaganda under Hitler

46. "It is time the Ted Kennedy-type traitors get a strong message of supporting the administration's effort and not give comfort and aid to the enemy."

— Bob Heltman, letter to the editor, *Asheville Citizen-Times*, March 6, 2004.

47. "In a 2003 interview, Gen. Tommy Franks ran the martial law flag up the pole, stating that a major terrorist attack might mean discarding the Constitution in favor of a military government. You can check out this option in an article called 'When the War Hits Home: US Plans for Martial Law, Tele-Governance and the Suspension of Elections by Wayne Madsen and John Stanton.'

— Bruce Mulkey, local column, *Asheville Citizen-Times*, May 2004.

48. "Sandra Day O'Connor, a Republican-appointed judge who retired last month after 24 years on the Supreme Court, has said the US is in danger of edging towards dictatorship if the party's right wingers continue to attack the judiciary."

— Julian Borger, *Asheville Global Report*, Mar. 16-22, 2006. Source: *Guardian (UK)*.

49. "The Bush administration has been able to convey the impression of having been (along with Congress and the rest of us) the innocent victim of a CIA misinformation campaign — much easier since the committee postponed its examination of the Administrations' pre-war hype until after the election. But this misimpression is also a product of the selective amnesia of much of the media that covered the release of the report.

— Eric Alterman, column, *The Nation*, August 2/9, 2004.

50. Bush and "his henchmen made their case for the invasion of Iraq and sold it to the American people (if not the United Nations), then proceeded to go through with it....

"They're trying to lie their way out of it, of course, but their efforts to show that Saddam Hussein was an imminent threat to us or that he participated in any substantial way in the Sept. 11 attacks are pathetic. Mainly what they and their defenders are arguing is the fallback position: that they were victimized by the 'bad intelligence.'...

— Donald Kaul, syndicated column, July 31, 2004.

51. "The 9/11 Commission reported that Clarke, the CIA, and others had warned the administration as many as forty times of the threat posed by Osama bin Laden, but that is not what the administration wanted to hear, and it did not hear it....

"What brings any student of intelligence to a kind of shocked halt is the fact that CIA analysts did not get anything right — every claim about Saddam's WMD was wrong — completely wrong, flatly wrong, wrong by a country mile....

"But the President did nothing. It would be hard to find words adequate to describe the full range and amplitude of the nothing he did. My own preliminary, working explanation is that for reasons of his own the President *decided* to do nothing. Why? Historians will be occupied for many years before they come to agreement on the answer to that question....

"Much the same is the case with the missing Iraqi weapons of mass destruction. Predicted stockpiles of chemical and biological weapons were not found after the fall of Baghdad because they did not exist....It is unlikely that the United States had ever been more comprehensively and significantly wrong about anything ever, than it was in identifying the reasons for going to war in Iraq....

"Is it possible that in addition to writing a National Intelligence Estimate which was wrong in every particular, and on top of providing the factual basis for about thirty false or distorted claims of Iraqi weapons activity made in a speech before the United Nations Security Council by Secretary of State Colin Powell in February 2003 — is it possible that...the intelligence community really needed a year and a half to conclude that it had been wrong? Think about this for a moment. Before the war, working with the barest smattering of fragmentary information, the CIA could conclude with *high confidence* that these stockpiles existed. But now we are asked to believe that after the war, with unimpeded access to every file, every person, and every street address in Iraq, the CIA could not, over the course of a year, decide whether the stockpiles were there or not? ...

"To accept the Iraqi WMD mistake as honest I would have to believe that CIA analysts steeped in their field of expertise could not tell the difference between a weak case and a strong case. I don't believe that. In my own view they all knew the case was weak but surrendered to pressure from above and hoped to be saved by a miracle — they convinced themselves that *something* would turn up when the troops got to Baghdad and were free to look in all the nooks and crannies. But as Charles Duelfer makes clear in the recently released and exhaustive final report of the CIA's Iraq Survey Group, there was nothing.

"The President insists that the war in Iraq is now the central front of the war on terror.... But defining our opponents as terrorists disguises the more important fact that most of them, probably in excess of 90 percent, are Iraqis angry with Americans. This should not be hard for us to understand. Americans have invaded their country, have killed anywhere between 10,000 and 100,000 civilians, plus an unknown number of combatants in the regular Iraqi army or the resistance, and have vowed to transform their country politically.... It's one of the oldest stories in human history — an invasion followed by military occupation backing a client government has encountered resistance. What else would we expect?

"But if our reason for war was to counter a threat posed by terrorists with weapons of mass destruction, a threat proved since illusory, while the actual resistance we meet in Iraq is angry and nationalist in an uncomplicated way, then it is hard to escape the conclusion that we are fighting an unnecessary war."

— Thomas Powers, essay, *The New York Review*, December 16, 2004.

52. "'Amid such privations,' Banerjee writes, 'one of the few things that thrives now in Baghdad, at least, is a deepening distrust and anger toward the United States.'

"It's tempting to suggest that the Bush Administration is failing to provide Iraq with functioning, efficient, reliable public services because it doesn't *believe* in functioning, efficient, reliable public services — doesn't believe that they should exist, and doesn't really believe that they can exist. The reigning ideologues in Washington — not only in the White House but also in the Republican congressional leadership, in the faction that dominates the Supreme Court, and in the conservative press and think tanks — believe in free markets, individual initiative, and private schools and private charity as substitutes for public provision. They believe that the armed individual citizen is the ultimate guarantor of public safety. They do not, at bottom, believe that society, through the mechanisms of democratic government, has a moral obligation to provide care for the sick, food for the hungry, shelter for the homeless, and education for all; and to the extent that they tolerate such activities they do so grudgingly, out of political necessity. They believe that the private sector is sovereign, and that taxes are a species of theft.

"In a way, Iraq has become a theme park of conservative policy nostrums."

— Hendrik Hertzberg, Comment, *The New Yorker*, June 9, 2003.

53. "President Bush considered provoking a war with Saddam's regime by flying a United States spy plane over Iraq bearing UN colors, enticing the Iraqis to take a shot at it, according to a leaked memo of a meeting between Bush and British Prime Minister Tony Blair.

"The two leaders were worried by the lack of hard evidence that Saddam Hussein had broken UN resolutions. According to the memo, Bush said: 'The US was thinking of flying U2 reconnaissance aircraft with fighter cover over Iraq, painted in UN colors. If Saddam fired on them, he would be in breach."

— Andy McSmith, *Asheville Global Report*, Feb. 9-15, 2006: Source: *Independent* (UK).

54. A "controversy surrounds details of a leaked British government memo recently published by a UK newspaper, the Daily Mirror....

"The Mirror said Bush told UK Prime Minister Tony Blair at a White House summit on Apr. 16, 2004, that he wanted to launch military action on Al Jazeera's headquarters in Doha, Qatar.

— *Asheville Global Report*, Dec.1-7, 2005: Source: Al Jazeera.net

55. "After the fall of Baghdad, three years ago, the United States military began a secret investigation of the decision-making within Saddam Hussein's dictatorship. The study...was completed last year (and) was delivered to President Bush....The extracts describe how the Iraq invasion, more than any other war in American history, was a construct of delusion....

"The study portrays the Iraqi President as a fading adversary who felt boxed in by sanctions and political pressure. Saddam's former generals and civilian aides...describe their old boss as a Lear-like figure, a confused despot in the enervating twilight of a ruthless career: unable to think straight, dependent on his two lunatic and incompetent sons, and increasingly reliant on bluff and bluster to remain in power. Saddam lay awake at night worrying about knotty problems, and later issued memos based on the dreams he had when he drifted into sleep. As the invasion approached, he so feared a coup that he refused to allow his generals to prepare seriously for war....

"Nor did this sham mask any plan to foil the invasion by launching a guerrilla war. There has been long speculation that the insurgency, which has so far taken more than twenty-three hundred American lives, might have been seeded in part by clandestine prewar cell formations or arms distributions. In fact, according to the study, there was no such preparation by Saddam or any of his generals, not even as the regime's 'world crumbled around it'; the insurgency was an unplanned, evolving response to the political failings and humiliations of the occupation."

— Steve Coll, The Talk of the Town, *The New Yorker*, April 3, 2006.

56. "The key revelation here is that Saddam was long convinced that the United States would never launch an all-out assault. He knew that he had no stockpiles of WMD and no working ties with Islamic terrorists targeting America. He was therefore perfectly confident that Bush had no casus belli. As a result, 'He saw no reason why the Americans would want to invade Iraq.'"

— Stephen Holmes, book review, Cobra II: The Inside Story of the Invasion and Occupation of Iraq, by Michael Gordon and Bernard Trainor, The American Prospect, June 2006.

57. "Saddam Hussein knew it made no strategic sense for the US to invade Iraq and therefore assumed it wouldn't happen....

Even after the invasion began. According to Gordon and Trainor, Saddam could not quite believe the United States intended to go all the way to Baghdad....

"Saddam could not imagine that the United States would see an advantage in replacing him with a pro-Iranian, Shiite-dominated regime. Knowing very little about American politics, he could not grasp the ideological fervor of the Pentagon neoconservatives who believed Iraq's democratic transformation would revolutionize the

Middle East. Rumsfeld and the neoconservatives could not imagine that Iraqis would not embrace liberation and pro-Western democracy and they assumed that both the invasion and the occupation to follow would be easy. For the American generals, to challenge the petty tyrant on the Potomac could have ended their careers; for their Iraqi counterparts, taking on the tyrant on the Tigris could have ended their lives."

— Peter W. Galbraith, review of *Cobra II: The Inside Story of the Invasion and Occupation of Iraq* by Michael R. Gordon and Bernard E. Trainor, *The New York Review*, August 10, 2006.

PART THREE. THE CONSERVATIVE BELIEF SYSTEM

The dictionary defines traditional conservatism as opposition to change and defense of the existing order and its institutions. Words used to define it further include prudence, restraint, stability, dependability, safety, efficiency, et cetera. The order and the institutions that these words were first used to define were the rule of divine kings and their aristocratic courts. Two centuries ago, that aristocracy was first threatened by the Enlightenment and then by the American and French revolutions. These uprisings were directed against kings, aristocrats, and priests. The defenders of that old order were such people as Edmund Burke and Joseph de Maistre.

Then, the Industrial Revolution brought wealth to rising numbers of middle class business people. Their power soon began to eclipse the divine order. This new aristocracy of money did not end the old aristocratic order, however. Instead, it melded with the old order and embraced its values. A new conservative order was born. Over time, it began to gobble up the old order without revolting against it. This new order was neither liberal nor populist. The old definitions no longer applied but the love of fixed authority, a stable and rigid order, and a safe haven for money and property still remained.

And so today the Republican Party is the leader of a worldwide conservative movement that began long ago with the rule of divine kings and royal aristocracies. However, the word "conservative" is a misnomer. This movement is not conservative. It is reactionary. It seeks to return us all to the earlier days of fixed authority and dominant aristocracy. To do this, it has had to reshape its belief system.

Thanks to the American and French revolutions, divine kings, royal blood, and formal aristocracies are no longer acceptable. Succession to power can no longer be based on bloodlines and god's holy anointment. All the same, today's conservatives still claim that their god puts them in power and that Jesus is their inspiration and guide. This was in evidence in the administrations of William McKinley, Ronald Reagan, and George W. Bush.

The conservatives are still absolutists. They rage against equality, secularism, relativism (they mean tolerance), civil rights, human rights, democratic government, dissent, and, most of all, liberalism. They fiercely defend the rights of inheritance and attack any taxing of unearned income, that is, the income of those who don't work and live off of their property and wealth. They demand austerity and balanced budgets from government and, at the same time, oppose any government assistance for the poor, the sick, the hungry, the homeless, and the old and worn. No matter what it costs, they seek overseas conquests in the interests of business success and missionary christianity. Accordingly, they fervently support all military and police power and bitterly condemn "peaceniks," pacifists, rehabilitationists, and welfarists as unpatriotic, weak, collaborationist, and subversive of the order and obedience they yearn for. In other words, they retain the beliefs of the old, divine aristocracies and they rage against the very same enemies.

These modern conservatives are social darwinists and eugenicists. With the fall of divine and royal power, they needed a new justification for their system of rule. They now rely on the hegemony of capitalism. The social darwinist and eugenicist movements provided the rationale. This thinking identifies capitalism as god's holy instrument and holds that success under its rules is proof of superiority. In their world, the fit survive and the unfit go under. According to conservatives, the successfully rich and eminent are fit to rule. Workers and the poor are not. The conservatives see biology and the hand of god in their own rise and rule.

They believe that their country and their religion are exceptional and that they themselves are fated to rule the world for god, country, and corporation. Any opposition is sinful and unpatriotic. They think that they have a near divine right to power. This philosophy is embedded in the Republican Party and, though expressed in somewhat different frameworks, it infuses the conservative and the libertarian movements.

In the last few decades, the neoconservatives have joined the conservative meld. That movement began as a kind of confused Trotskyism infused by a corrupted form of dominionist zionism. The operating philosophy of this strange group comes from the writings of Leo Strauss, a former University of Chicago philosophy professor, who said that "the rule of the wise must be absolute rule" and "true democracy is an act against nature and must be prevented at all costs." This describes the true mission of the neoconservative and zionist movements as well as the continuing mission of the old conservative order.

Many conservatives hearken back to the days of English, Roman, and Spartan imperialism and proudly call themselves imperialist and even colonialist. However, journalists and political intellectuals choose to ignore these pronouncements and describe the Iraq war, for example, as an attempt by Republicans, especially neoconservatives, to establish a system of democratic liberalism in Iraq and the Middle East.

Even "liberal hawks" endorse this claim and criticize the Bush war against Iraq only because of its incompetence and its failure to achieve a victory and establish an orderly occupation there. They apparently cannot see that Republicans don't believe in or like democracy and never have. That they see Republicans as somehow liberal is astonishing. The quickest way to insult and anger a Republican or any conservative is to call him or her a liberal. And certainly no one in touch with American reality can believe that Republicans ever miss an opportunity to sneer at and attack the government. This government that they attack so consistently and with such contempt is the democratic government of the United States. Attacking democracy does not amount to supporting it nor does it square with aggressive war and an occupation maintained by armed might and corporate domination.

The conservative movement today is driven by a fear of democracy and a hatred for permissiveness. Permissiveness is the name given to freedom by its enemies. Today, that movement is about opposing, attacking, repressing, and restraining ordinary people; it is about rising above them, holding them down, and knocking them back and away from the table. It is not about the prudence and restraint it claims for itself nor is it about small government or minding your own business or about family values or moral uprightness. At its heart, it is violent and assaultive; it is aggressive toward and distrustful of different others; it is suspicious and stingy; it is greedy and grasping and ungenerous. It is unmerciful and often cruel.

The conservative movement is anti-democratic and anti-humanistic. It opposes every civil right for the dispossessed and embraces every wealthy privilege for the few. It has no active program that does not promote private power, police force, and military conquest over despised enemies. It allies itself and this country with tyrants and death squads across the world just as long as those tyrants are or pretend to be against any ism that threatens oligarchy or promotes the welfare of the people. It isn't about conserving anything. It's about developing everything, using it up – for a profit. It's about establishing wealth and privilege and maintaining them on the backs of working people and consumers. Conservatives even curse the fresh and greening air, the free flowing waters, and the very bosom of the earth.

CHAPTER 12. DEMOCRACY

1. "Fascism should more properly be called corporatism, since it is the merger of state and corporate power."
— Benito Mussolini.

2. "Whoever offends the state's religion, by defaming those who profess it, will be punished with up to two years of imprisonment."
— Mussolini criminal code, written to protect the Catholic Church.

3. "As Primo Levi warned, 'Every age has its Fascism,' not necessarily accompanied by 'terror and police intimidation.' Democracy, Levi pointed out, can be undermined by 'withholding or manipulating information, polluting the judicial system and paralyzing the school system, by encouraging in many subtle ways nostalgia for a world in which order reigns supreme.'"
— Frederika Randall, book review, *The Nation*, June 21, 2004.

4. "If I were Italian, I would don the fascist Black Shirt."
— Winston Churchill.

5. "Mussolini is a genius in the field of government given to Italy by God."
— Cardinal O'Connell of Boston.

6. "Mussolini is a man of Providence."
— Pope Pius XI.

7. "I read with some perplexity Eugene Genovese's apparently favorable reference to 'corporatism' ...Perplexity, because this word, as Genovese has better reason to know than most, was virtually synonymous with fascism in the Italy of the Twenties and Thirties. Palmiro Togliati...offered this summary in his 1935 *Lectures on Fascism*: 'the corporate regime is a regime that is inseparable from total political reaction, from the destruction of every democratic liberty; the state form must be totalitarian so as to force the large working masses under its control; the corporations are an instrument for suppressing any attempt by the working masses to liberate themselves.'"
— John Beverly, letter to *Lingua Franca*, March 1997.

8. On loyalty to the aristocracy: "that generous loyalty to rank and sex, that proud submission, that dignified obedience, that subordination of the heart, which kept

alive, even in servitude itself, the spirit of the exalted freedom," (Edmund Burke expressing his hatred for the French Revolution because it overthrew the divine rights of the king and his aristocracy).

— *English Society* by J.C.D. Clark, review by David A. Bell, *The New Republic*, January 18, 1988.

9. "'The rot began with the Reformation. Protestantism encouraged pride to revolt against authority....There are no longer any moral communities.' The French Revolution was 'an antireligious and antisocial insurrection, a rebellion against God.... There can be no government if those who are ruled consider themselves the equal of those who rule....Man needs authority. A king is the center of society.'

"He was an unwavering anti-liberal. He even defended the Spanish Inquisition. He claimed to despise freedom of speech; and tolerance he considered to be political suicide, a regime's sickly refusal to attack its attackers. Public deliberation is wholly sterile. And the postulate of civic equality is utterly incompatible with any form of state rule.

"Maistre cast himself as an anti-Voltaire....Locke's ideas unleashed the revolutionary monster that had devoured Europe....Natural reverence is effaced by the acids of skepticism.' Equally fallacious, according to Maistre, is the assumption that human freedom consists in being able to do what one wants, unimpeded by authorities or imposed rules.

"'Man was born evil and remains so....Human beings cannot be perfected by enlightenment and secular education.' Secular philosophy is 'the greatest scourge of the universe.' The only reason scientists talk about physical 'laws' is to 'prevent people from praying.' Maistre 'resents liberalism because it mocks authority.'"

— *Joseph de Maistre* by Richard A. Lebraun, review by Stephen Holman, *The New Republic*, October 30, 1989.

10. "So, if you have a corporation, or for that matter, any business with top-down control that's run from the top, it's basically a totalitarian system, as close to totalitarianism as humans have been able to devise. Control is completely in the top. Orders go from top to bottom, down the hierarchy. If you're in the middle somewhere, if you're a manager, you take orders from above and hand them on below. At the very bottom, people are allowed to rent themselves to the system. It's called getting a job.

"And outsiders, their only connection to it is to consume. Hundreds of millions of dollars a year are spent trying to delude and deceive them into consumption. Anybody whose ever looked at a television knows that.

"Well, there's a system of hierarchy and authority. Is it legitimate? Should that totalitarian system be given the rights of a person? In fact, by now, rights far beyond those of a person? Well, those are quite serious questions. It's the responsibility of the system of power to justify itself. Those who challenge it have no responsibility. If it can justify its hierarchy and domination, then it should be tolerated. If it can't, it shouldn't be tolerated. It should be dismantled, just like other totalitarian systems."

— Noam Chomsky, interview by Nicholas Holt, *Asheville Global Report*, Apr. 20–26, 2006.

11. "It was only in societies where liberalism and democracy seemed incapable of dealing with severe social and political crisis...and where the revolutionary left was perceived as a serious threat that the movement could achieve enough momentum to propel its leaders into power. 'An essential step in the fascist march to acceptance and power,' as Paxton writes, 'was to persuade law-and-order conservatives to tolerate fascist violence as a harsh necessity in the face of Left provocation.'

"This enabled the fascists to use their party militias...to challenge the state's monopoly of legitimate violence; by so doing, they made the crisis of the liberal or democratic state seem irreversible, and presented themselves as the only movement capable of resolving it....

"Many Italian conservatives had hoped that fascism might be the instrument for restoring the constitutional independence of the monarchy, which had been eroded by parliamentary democracy....

"In the developed fascist economy, industrialists lost much of their power although...they were not too unhappy about this, since they kept their profits and were assured of a docile labor force whose wages stayed low....

"For fascist leaders this unresolved tension at the heart of the fascist regimes was an added motive for external aggression and war. Not only would war further channel the energies of the true believers, but also the dictators hoped that it would change the balance of domestic forces in their favor.

"Paxton is perhaps limited in his approach by his thesis that fascism can only flourish where it has a democracy to fight. This leads him to the...conclusion that the only two states outside Europe where fascism is to be feared are the United States and Israel.

— Adrian Lyttelton, book review, *The Anatomy of Fascism* by Robert O. Paxton, *The New York Review*, October 21, 2004.

12. "For at least a full century, every industrialized nation has had a strong right-wing base hovering at about 15-20 percent of the population. Energizing that constituency to be a potent force is contingent on many factors, but it is an enduring potential, smoldering, waiting to be stoked by those who would 'go there.' It is a mistake to think of 1930s Germany, Italy and Spain as exceptional and inexplicable political aberrations that could not happen here. We easily forget that those right-wing governments had strong electoral showings and sympathizers in many Western nations."

— Troy Duster, essay, *The Nation*, December 20, 2004.

13. "Like all idolatries, democratism substitutes a false god for the real, a love of process for a love of country" and "if the people are corrupt, the more democracy and the worse the government."

— Pat Buchanan, cited by *Z Magazine*, November 1999.

14. "In his new book, *A Republic, Not An Empire*, Pat Buchanan says that Britain and France were wrong to go to war with Germany in 1939. He also says that Hitler was not a threat to the United States....

"Pat wrote the section of Ronald Reagan's speech at Bitburg, the cemetery in which Nazi SS troops were buried, calling the Nazi soldiers 'victims just as surely as the victims of the concentration camps.'...

"Pat thinks Hitler was 'an individual of great courage' and 'extraordinary gifts,' even 'a soldier's soldier,' in spite of his genocidal habits....

"Among Pat's heroes are the 'soldier-patriots' Francisco Franco and Augusto Pinochet. Both overthrew democracies and suppressed dissent with violence, using anti-communism as a rationale."

— Bob Harris, The Scoop, *Z Magazine*, November 1999.

15. "There is a crisis in this country because of democratic overload and democratic distemper."

— Michael Crozier in a 1970 report for the Trilateral Commission called *The Crisis of Democracy*.

16. "Scalia cites St. Paul to assert that 'the Lord repaid — did justice — through His minister, the state,' a conception he maintains was 'the consensus of Western thought until recent times.' It concerns Scalia that 'that consensus has been upset... by the emergence of democracy,' and he believes that 'the reaction of people of faith to this tendency of democracy to obscure the divine authority behind government should be not resignation to it but resolution to combat it.'"

— Patricia J. Williams, column, *The Nation*, October 7, 2002.

17. "The national government will maintain and defend the foundations on which the power of our nation rests. It will offer strong protection to Christianity as the very basis of our collective morality. Today, Christians stand at the head of our country. We want to fill our culture again with Christian spirit. We want to burn out all the recent immoral developments in literature, in the theatre and in the press; in short, we want to burn out the poison of immorality which has entered into our whole lives and culture as a result of liberal excess during recent years."

— Adolf Hitler, first radio address to the German people, July 22, 1933.

18. "I can't help but recall the words of my ethics professor at Harvard Divinity School, Dr. James Luther Adams, who told us that when we were his age, and he was then close to eighty, we would all be fighting the 'christian fascists.'

"He gave us that warning twenty-five years ago, when Pat Robertson and other prominent evangelists began speaking of a new political religion that would direct its efforts at taking control of all major American institutions, including mainstream denominations and the government, so as to transform the United States into a global Christian empire. At the time, it was hard to take such fantastic rhetoric seriously. But fascism, Adams warned, would not return wearing swastikas and brown shirts. Its ideological inheritors would cloak themselves in the language of the Bible; they would come carrying crosses and chanting the Pledge of Allegiance.

"Adams had watched American intellectuals and industrialists flirt with fascism in the 1930s. Mussolini's "Corporatism," which created an unchecked industrial and business aristocracy, had appealed to many at the time as an effective counterweight to the New Deal. In 1934, *Fortune* magazine lavished praise on the Italian dictator for his de-fanging of labor unions and his empowerment of industrialists at the expense of workers. Then as now, Adams said, too many liberals failed to understand the power and allure of evil, and when the radical Christians came, these people would undoubtedly play by the old, polite rules of democracy long after those in power had begun to dismantle the democratic state. Adams had watched German academics fall silent or conform. He knew how desperately people want to believe the comfortable lies told by totalitarian movements, how easily those lies lull moderates into passivity.

"Adams told us to watch closely the Christian right's persecution of homosexuals and lesbians. Hitler, he reminded us, promised to restore moral values not long after he took power in 1933, then imposed a ban on all homosexual and lesbian organizations and publications. Then came raids on the places where homosexuals gathered, culminating on May 6, 1933, with the ransacking of the Institute for Sexual Science in Berlin. Twelve thousand volumes from the institute's library were tossed into a public bonfire. Homosexuals and lesbians, Adams said, would be the first' deviants' singled out by the Christian right. We would be the next."

— Chris Hedges, essay, *Harper's Magazine*, May 2005.

19. "Even more revolting was Justice Antonin Scalia's speech in Cleveland. He told the City Club there that the government can scale back individual rights during

wartime without violating the Constitution: 'The Constitution just sets minimums. Most of the rights that you enjoy go way beyond what the Constitution requires.' A Supreme Court Justice said that! He is dead wrong. The only right affected by war is the Third Amendment: 'No soldier shall in time of peace be quartered in any house, without the consent of the owner, nor in time of war, but in a manner to be prescribed by law.' The Ninth Amendment specifically says: 'The enumeration in the Constitution of certain rights shall not be construed to deny or disparage others retained by the people.'"

— Molly Ivins, column, *The Progressive*, May 2003.

20. "Some of the problems of governance in the United States today stem from an excess of democracy....Effective operation of a democratic system requires some measure of apathy and noninvolvement by citizens."

— Samuel Huntington in a 1970 report for the Trilateral Commission called *The Crisis of Democracy.*

21. "Walter Lippmann argued that 'the public must be put in its place,' so that the 'responsible men' may rule without interference from 'ignorant and meddlesome outsiders' whose 'function' is to be only 'interested spectators of action,' periodically selecting members of the leadership class in elections, then returning to their private concerns. The statist reactionaries, called 'conservatives,' typically take a harsher line, rejecting even the spectator role. Hence the appeal to the Reaganites of clandestine operations, censorship and other measures to insure that a powerful and interventionist state will not be troubled by the rabble."

— Noam Chomsky, article, *The Nation*, March 29, 1993.

22. "Democracy *can* be exported. Americans have exported democracy to many countries, including Nicaragua, the Philippines, Japan, South Korea, Germany, Italy, Austria, Dominican Republic, Grenada, and Panama....In short, however illogical it sounds, *democracy can be imposed at the point of a bayonet.*"(italics supplied).

— *Exporting Democracy* by Joshua Muravchik, review by Daniel Pipes, *The Washington Post*, June 16, 1991.

23. "Socialism, by its very nature, cannot be dictated, introduced by command. Lenin is completely mistaken in the means he employs: decree, dictatorial power, draconian penalties, rule by terror....Without general elections, without unrestricted freedom of the press and assembly, without a free exchange of openness, life dies out in every public institution.

"Freedom only for the supporters of the government, only for the members of one Party, no matter how numerous, is no freedom. Freedom is always for the one who thinks differently."

— Rosa Luxemburg, quoted in an article by Arthur Weinberg, *The Progressive*, October 1987. [Luxemburg spent the World War I years in a German prison. After the war, the German military arrested her, assassinated her, and dumped her body in the Landwehr Canal.]

24. "Unwanted foreign military occupation, or even the threat of it, is incompatible with democratization."

— Rashid Khalidi, professor of Arab Studies, Columbia University.

25. Integration will result in "perpetual friction, as the incapable are placed consciously side by side with the capable."

— Pat Buchanan to Richard Nixon, cited by *Z Magazine*, November 1999.

26. "Richard Nixon was 'a breath of fresh air.'"

— Arnold Schwarzenegger.

[Many Republicans, such as Richard Nixon's Attorney General, John Mitchell, and his wife, Martha, regularly called members of the Democratic Party 'liberal communists' and 'communist liberals.' —Author.]

27. "I admired Hitler, for instance, because he came from being a little man with almost no formal education up to power. And I admired him for being such a good public speaker and for his way of getting to the people and so on."
— Arnold Schwarzenegger.

28. "If the president does it, that makes it legal."
— Richard Nixon on his Watergate crimes.

29. "If society no longer tolerates elites...then democracy falls apart."
— Michael Ledeen (Iran-Contra operative and consultant to Secretary of State Alexander Haig), from an article by Sidney Blumenthal, *The Washington Post*, February 16, 1987.

30. Civilizations fail because of "resentment against success." People derive their "culture and social ideals from the class above them (but then) lower-class values begin to spread upward.... Causes of resentment are the Soviet Union, environmentalism, rock music....Poverty is not caused or created: it is the default condition of the human race. It is wealth that must be caused. The two main "reflections (of) achievement-resentment today are socialism (obviously) and (less obviously) Christian morality."
— From *Resentment Against Achievement* by Robert Sheaffer, review by Karl Zinmeister, *Reason*, July 1989.

31. "We will have a liberal democracy, or we will return to the Dark Ages."
— Franklin Delano Roosevelt, 1940.

32. "Through their Conservative Party — the party of aristocratic landowners, military officers, high-level bureaucrats, and crucial industrial leaders — they denounced the Jews as a 'degenerate' people determined to support both international financial chicanery and (later) Bolshevik subversion. Their party platform of 1892 called for a war against the Jews, and during Weimar their campaign literature rivaled that of the Nazis in its anti-Semitism. The Conservative Party, like the Nazis, wanted to destroy the Social democrats and liberals of the Progressive Party because both opposed anti-Semitism, threatened the privileges and prerogatives of the elites, and supported the Weimar Republic. In 1932 the conservative nationalists around Hindenburg encouraged him to appoint Hitler chancellor and supported Hitler's successful bid for dictatorial powers in 1933. From then on they cooperated with the terror of the regime."
— John Weiss, letter to the editor, *Harper's Magazine*, April 2006.

33. "In the winter of 1933, before Franklin Roosevelt's first inauguration on March 4, there was a clamor in the US for a military dictatorship. The banks were closing, a quarter of Americans were unemployed, rebellion threatened on the farms. Only drastic reforms, mandated by the president's power as commander in chief, would save the country. Something like the fascism of Mussolini's Italy — viewed benignly by many Americans in those days because it worked (or so everyone said) — would save the country from communist revolution.

"As Jonathan Alter reminds us in *The Defining Moment*, his brilliant book about FDR's first 100 days, men as different as William Randolph Hearst, financier Bernard Baruch, commentator Lowell Thomas and establishment columnist Walter Lippmann argued for the necessity of dictatorship to reorganize the country's economy....

"The US is caught up in a new campaign for a military dictatorship — rule by a military chief with absolute power. The White House, inspired by Vice President Dick Cheney, has argued that in time of great danger, the president has unlimited powers as commander in chief. If he cites 'national security' he can do whatever he wants — ignore Congress, disobey laws, disregard the courts, and override the Constitution's Bill of Rights — without being subject to any review. Separation of powers no longer exists. The president need not consult Congress or the courts. Moreover the rights of the commander in chief to act as a military dictator lasts as long as the national emergency persists, indefinitely and permanently....

"Richard Cheney is a vile, indeed evil, influence in American political life. He is a very dangerous person who would if he could destroy American freedom about which he and his mentor prate hypocritically. His long years in Washington have caused him to lose faith in the legislative and judicial processes of the government. The country, he believes, requires a much stronger executive. Such concentrated power would have been necessary even if the World Trade Center attack had not occurred. He uses the fear of terrorists as a pretext to advance his agenda of an all-powerful president, a military dictator. So long, of course, as he is a Republican."

— Andrew Greeley, essay, *The Progressive Populist*, August 1/15, 2006.

34. In his several books, William Bennett says liberals control our colleges and universities, cause the "utter failure of our institutions of higher learning" and spread the germs of "cultural and moral relativism." They are not just "mistaken," they are "insidious" and are "unpatriotic," resort to "violent misrepresentations...sew widespread and debilitating confusion...weaken the country's resolve...(are guilty of) failures of character...drown out legitimate patriots," are of a "despicable character," and avoid "the honest search for truth."

Bennett goes on to say that Stanley Fish, a professor at Illinois University, and Charles Manson, the killer of Sharon Tate, both believe that "since everything is relative, everything can be justified and all is permitted." He says that his hero, Plato, did not believe in relativism and praises his hostility to democracy. He attacks "tolerance" and says that there is not "enough anger in America."

Bennett says he is a member of the "war party" and his opponents are members of the "peace party." He says he supports military tribunals and the arbitrary and secret detention of "suspects" without formal charges or any due process, says the members of the peace party "have caused damage and they need to be held to account." He attacks their "failure of character" and says, "a vast relearning has to take place." He praises Curtis LeMay for his warrior aggressiveness and eagerness to attack. He says our problems of the last forty years were caused by those "who are unpatriotic" by which he means the liberals who are "the diversity mongers and multiculturalists." He says that "patriotism, honesty, and truth telling" come only from conservatives like him. Among many others, Bennett attacks Jimmy Carter, Lewis Lapham, and Maxine Waters as "internal threats to America."

— See especially *Why We Fight* and *Empower America* by William Bennett.

35. "Resorting to large-scale violence has highly unpredictable consequences, as history reveals and common sense should tell us. That's why sane people avoid it... unless a very powerful argument is offered to overcome 'the sickly inhibitions against the use of military force' (to borrow the phrase of Reaganite intellectual Norman Podhoretz, paraphrasing Goebbels)."

— Noam Chomsky interview, *Z Magazine*, October 2000.

36. "The whole aim of practical politics is to keep the public alarmed (and hence clamorous to be led safely) by menacing it with an endless series of hobgoblins, all of them imaginary."

— H.L. Mencken.

37. In several books and articles, Robert Bork expresses hatred for the sixties, welfare, affirmative action, legalized abortion, popular culture, and judicial tyranny. He attacks the Declaration of Independence because it says men are "created equal" and because it talks of liberty. He wants a radical revision of the Constitution to make it conform to his ideas.

Bork claims witchcraft is "undergoing an enormous revival in feminist circles as the antagonist of Christian faith." He dislikes the transistor radio because it allows children to listen to rebellion-inducing rock and roll and he is disturbed by the sight of "men crying," a sign that "something has gone high and soft in the culture."

He attacks equality, which is against the "natural order, which is hierarchical." He believes in the triumph of the efficient over the inefficient, the rich over the poor, men over women, whites over blacks, the West over the world. His chief enemy is liberalism which means "radical egalitarianism (the equality of outcomes rather than opportunities)" and "radical individualism (the drastic reduction of limits to personal gratification)." These lead to the "suppression of talent" and the "rise of the unworthy" and "denigrate religion and lead to the collapse of morals." He says liberalism "destroys values" and "encourages wicked conduct." He thinks businessmen are always rational and never racist. He claims the Supreme Court has imposed "a liberal social and cultural agenda on the nation."

— See especially *Slouching Toward Gomorra*, by Robert Bork, January 13, 1997.

38. Gertrude Himmelfarb claims that poverty is caused by the poor and that all efforts to end poverty cause poverty — "the self-defeating nature of well-meaning attempts to resolve it." She attacks those in England who tried to help the poor, especially the Fabians, claiming that they were guilty of "class treason" and were responsible for Britain's decline. She attacks Jeremy Bentham, John Stuart Mill, and Charles Darwin for their unconservative ideas.

One of her great heroes is Charles Booth, author of *Life and Labor* (1903). Booth wanted to move the rabble poor (loafers, ruffians, the semi-criminal) to labor colonies as "servants of the state" under a system of "state slavery." Himmelfarb got her idea of the poor and their sympathizers being responsible for poverty, which cannot be a product of capitalism, from Booth. She also likes his idea that the poor are "degenerate stock" and "threaten the nation with imminent racial suicide" and likes his belief "that improvement in working-class wages will sound the death knell of morals and civilization."

— *Pity and Compassion* by Gertrude Himmelfarb, review by Roy Porter, *The New Republic*, November 25, 1991.

39. *On Population* by Thomas Malthus was "published in 1798 to combat the subversive ideas of the Enlightenment, such as the American declaration that all men are created equal....(the ideas of) neo-Malthusians like Himmelfarb, Senator Patrick Moynihan and sundry others — that welfare and lust are to blame for poverty and that Social Security, minimum wages, trade unions and the like are to blame for our loss of economic competitiveness — are lifted straight from that stone hearted preacher of nearly two centuries ago. Nothing new has been added.

"When Dickens created Scrooge, he had the Rev. Thomas Malthus in mind. The portrait was not overdrawn. Like Malthus, Scrooge held that the poor were to blame for their poverty and that charity would only encouraged them to multiply; if they'd rather die than go to the workhouse, 'let them die, then.' But in the end, Scrooge repented. Malthus never did. 'The year of his death — 1834 — was also the year of his greatest triumph,' writes Gertrude Himmelfarb, a modern admirer. That, she explains, was the adoption of the new Poor Law, which ended home relief and replaced it with workhouses 'so appalling as to discourage even the most determined malingerers, and the sexes separated so as to prevent the population increase Malthus warned against.'

"Like the Poor Law of 1834, the election of Reagan in 1980 marked a triumph of Malthusianism. Welfare programs were drastically cut, and taxes too. The Attorney General said that people ate in soup kitchens because the food was free, the President said they slept in the streets as a matter of choice, and the mayor of New York said professionals with attaché cases were using the city's shelters." During the campaign, "Ronald Reagan was stumping the country with anecdotes about welfare queens in Cadillacs and studs buying vodka with food stamps." A governor of Colorado told the terminally ill: "You've got a duty to die and get out of the way. Let the other society, our kids, build a reasonable life."

"Like their prophet, the neo-Malthusians are enthusiastic preachers of moral restraint, chiefly among young blacks....That unemployment is a major cause of crime is denied by conservatives....(they can always find) new biological grounds for inequality. Allen Chase's admirable book *The Legacy of Malthus* recounts the pseudoscientific offensive waged by such influential manipulators of the IQ as the faker Sir Cyril Burt. In this country, tests done at Ellis Island purported to find that 83 percent of Jews, 80 percent of Hungarians, 79 percent of Italians and no fewer than 87 percent of Russians were feeble-minded. That led to a savagely biased immigration law in 1924. Nonetheless, according to Chase, in the next year the eugenicist Charles Davenport complained, 'We have no place to drive the Jews to,' and 'It seems to be against the mores to burn any considerable part of our population.'"

— John L. Hess, article, *The Nation*, April 18, 1987.

40. "He had a genuine sense of the national welfare, a genuine and disinterested devotion to individual liberty, even a genuine sympathy for the unfortunates who were the victims of nature's relentless laws....

"Nor was Malthus the ruthless, mean-spirited, hardhearted man his enemies made him out. His associates all remarked upon his exceptional amiability, good-nature and gentleness."

— Gertrude Himmelfarb, introduction to *On Population* (1960).

41. "Instead of recommending cleanliness to the poor, we should encourage contrary habits. In our towns, we should make the streets narrower, crowd more people into the houses, and court the return of the plague. In the country, we should build our villages near stagnant pools. But above all, we should reprobate specific remedies for ravaging diseases."

— Thomas Malthus, *On Population.*

42. "Dependent poverty ought to be held disgraceful."

— Thomas Malthus, *On Population.*

43. "A man, healthy and in the prime of life, refuses to work. Why should I transfer money to him? Why should I not let him starve, considering it a form of suicide?"

— Charles Murray, *Losing Ground* (1984).

44. "Put shame back in welfare."

— Headline on a column by William Raspberry, *The Washington Post*, August 31, 1982.

45. "We are bound in justice and honor formally to disclaim the right of the poor to support. To this end, I should propose that no child born should ever be entitled to parish assistance....A laborer who marries without being able to support a family may in some respects be considered as an enemy to all his fellow creatures....It is a general complaint among master manufacturers that high wages ruin all their workmen."

— Thomas Malthus, *On Population*.

46. "Welfare...has become a powerful force for destruction of family life."

— White House panel, November 12, 1986.

47. "The right minimum wage: $0. 00. "

— Headline on a *New York Times* editorial.

48. "James Q. Wilson and Richard Hernstein refute the prevailing notion that society somehow makes criminals. Instead, they insist upon the fundamental insight that an individual commits crime because of enduring personal characteristics. These innate factors include level of intelligence, genetic inheritance, anatomical configuration, gender, age, and early developmental pressures rooted in the nature of parental influence....The authors find marginal roles for schools, neighborhoods, peer group values, television violence, and job market conditions as causes of crime. The people who try to blame civilization for criminal behavior look pretty foolish."

— Mayor Edward I. Koch, *Policy Review*, Winter 1986.

49. "A major influence contributing to the achievement of order in the nineteenth-century was the lack of a system of public assistance."

— Roger Starr, *The Rise and Fall of New York City (1985)*.

50. "The right should oppose all civil rights laws and challenge the egalitarian premises of the civil rights movement....Today property rights have been upstaged by civil rights."

— Justin Raimundo at a 1993 John Randolph Club meeting.

51. Since "red staters...believe that evolution is only an opinion, then we are not on the same page as to much of anything else about the planet. We do not share the same constructs of proof, evidence or the scientific method. If every sentence in the Bible is literally true, then what I call fact and what you call truth are separate genres, galaxies apart.... then nothing in the material world remains 'true' — indeed, the entire intellectual grounding of Western thought must be called into question, as must a moral schema grounded in material consequence."

— Patricia J. Williams, column, *The Nation*, November 29, 2004.

52. "There is a growing awareness in a segment of the American population...that we do not have a democracy in this country. Democracy means the people rule. Today unelected, unaccountable CEOs are not just exercising power over us, they are literally ruling us. They are making public policy decisions for us."

— David Cobb, presidential nominee of the Green Party, cited in a William Greider essay in *The Nation*, October 25, 2004.

53. Gertrude Himmelfarb "sets out to seize the Enlightenment from the French and restore it to the British in the interests of changing our ideas about what the Enlightenment involved: To bring the British Enlightenment onto the stage, is to re-define the very idea of Enlightenment. In the usual litany of traits associated with Enlightenment — reason, rights, nature, liberty, equality, tolerance, science, progress — reason invariably heads the list. What is conspicuously absent is virtue...."

"As this suggests, Ms. Himmelfarb imposes a single and rather persuasive theme on her narrative: that the "good" Enlightenment was not a rationalist, secular, radical enterprise at all....

"Like many commentators, she admires the way Burke foresaw as early as 1790 the horrors that were to come — the murder of the royal family, the Terror, and the eventual installation of a military despotism. But more than anything, she shares Burke's fear that an unbridled rationalism will destroy civilization, sweeping away not only traditional authority in the shape of monarchy, landed aristocracy, and established church, but all restraint whatever. This, of course, reflects Ms. Himmelfarb's conviction that something very alarming happened in the 1960's, a process that she described as the "demoralization" of society.

"Rational schemes, she believes, threaten to bring about socialism at best and Stalinism at worst; an appropriate combination of the discipline of the market and the compassion of the better-off does most to relieve the misery of those who fall on hard times through no fault of their own."

— Alan Ryan, book review, *The Roads to Modernity: The British, French, and American Enlightenments* by Gertrude Himmelfarb, *The New York Review*, December 2, 2004.

54. "Ms. Himmelfarb recruits John Wesley to the pantheon of Enlightenment heroes. Wesley was a self-described enemy of democracy and deeply hostile to American independence. The virtues of Methodism are, however, an old theme with Ms. Himmelfarb."

— Alan Ryan, book review, *The Roads to Modernity: The British, French, and, American Enlightenments* by Gertrude Himmelfarb, *The New York Review*, December 2, 2004

55. Mrs. Himmelfarb "is a political conservative because she is first of all a cultural conservative, mistrustful of secularization and deeply frightened by what she thinks of as the twentieth century's abandonment of the moral values that once held civilization together. She shows every sign of becoming more frightened over the past forty years.

"When British Prime Minister Margaret Thatcher argued for a return to 'Victorian values,' she heartily approved of her views....

"This is not an account of the British, French, and American Enlightenments, but a series.... France is only discussed in an essay denouncing the *philosophes* as a gang of elitist, atheist, ultra-rationalist utopians, while America gets one essay praising the Founding Fathers for borrowing their ambitions from the British rather than the French. *The Roads to Modernity* ends with a short epilogue in praise of compassionate conservatism as an embodiment of American Enlightenment ideals: what one might call 'Burkeans for G.W. Bush.'"

— Alan Ryan, book review, *The Roads to Modernity: The British, French, and American Enlightenments* by Gertrude Himmelfarb, *The New York Review*, December 2nd, 2004

56. "They were both rooted in the same Enlightenment ideals of universal human rights, and they both erupted during the waning decades of the 18th century. Why then did the American and French revolutions produce such radically different results: a contentious but stable democracy on one side of the Atlantic, the Terror and the triumph of Napoleon on the other?"

— Paul Gray, book review of *Sister Revolutions: French Lightning, American Light* by Susan Dunn, *Time*, December 6th, 1999.

[It wasn't the French Revolution that caused The Terror or the rise of Napoleon; it was the royalist attack against the revolution. Every country in Europe (all under divine kings and their aristocracies) launched military attacks against France in order to put down the revolution and restore the monarchy. Without those violent attacks and threats of attack, the revolution would have been much milder. The royalists at home in France were killed because they were on the attack against the revolution and democracy principles. Napoleon, a military genius, gained increasing power because by then France needed to defend itself against invasion and occupation by every royal dictatorship in Europe. It's preposterous to claim that the revolution was illegitimate because it replaced a royal dictatorship with a democracy and then that it literally caused another dictator, Napoleon, to rise up and devour the democracy the revolution had struggled to establish.

Make no mistake. The French Revolution was violently and fanatically opposed by the entire aristocracy of Europe, England, and Russia and it was people like Burke and de Maistre who supported the aristocracy and all of the divine kings against democracy. The fight during the French Revolution was a fight between democrats and royalist aristocrats; the fight today sets democrats, rationalists, and secularists against a new royalism embodied in the conservative and neoconservative philosophy that dominates the Republican Party. No wonder Reagan, the Bushes, Himmelfarb, George Will, Leo Strauss, and such other antidemocrats so bitterly hate what the Sixties stood for: fealty to reason, tolerance, democracy, liberty, and equality. —Author]

57. "Modern conservatism was born in reaction to the French Revolution's assault on privacy in the name of civic claims. Conservatism has always been defined by its defense of limits on the claims of the public sector.

"Contemporary American conservatism, born in reaction to the New Deal and subsequent enlargements of the state, has a strong antigovernment cast. The core of this conservatism is objection to conscription of the individual into collective undertakings.

"For 45 years, conservatism has been schizophrenic, favoring strong, power-projecting, ambitious, interventionist, confident government in foreign policy but insisting upon demure, chastened government regarding domestic policy. Conservatives lived with the tension of a divided mind because they correctly understood the radical nature of the totalitarian challenge."

— George F. Will, syndicated column, September 9, 1990.

58. "The Nazis championed traditional family values: their ideology was conservative, bourgeois, patriarchal, and strongly antifeminist. Discipline and conformity were emphasized, marriage promoted, abortion and homosexuality despised.

"Traditionalism also dominated Nazi philosophy, such as it was....the overall thrust opposed the Enlightenment, modernism, intellectualism, and rationality. It is hard to imagine how a movement with that agenda could have been friendly toward atheism, and the Nazis were not. Volkism was inherently hostile toward atheism: freethinkers clashed frequently with Nazis in the late 1920s and early 1930s. On taking power, Hitler banned free thought organizations and launched an 'anti-godless' movement. In a 1933 speech he declared: 'We have...undertaken the fight against the atheistic movement, and that not merely with a few theoretical declarations: we have stamped it out.' ...

"As detailed by historian Ian Kershaw, Hitler made no secret of his intent to destroy democracy. Yet he came to power largely legally; in no sense was he a tyrant imposed upon the German people.

"The Nazi takeover climaxed a lengthy, ironic rejection of democracy *at the hands of a majority of German voters*. By the early 1930s, ordinary Germans had lost patience with democracy; growing numbers hoped an authoritarian strongman would restore order and prosperity and return Germany to great-power status. Roughly two-thirds of German Christians repeatedly voted for candidates who promised to overthrow democracy. Authoritarianism was all but inevitable; at issue was merely who the new strongman would be....

"Industrialists like Henry Ford invested heavily in the new Reich. German Christians also looked to the Nazis for a revival of 'Christian' values to help counter the rise of non-theism. Most welcomed the Nazi's elimination of chronic public strife by terrorizing, imprisoning, and killing the fast-shrinking German left. The leftists had long been despised by traditionalists, who composed four fifths of the population."

— Gregory S. Paul, essay, *Free Inquiry*, October/November 2003.

59. "In 1959, (Leo) Strauss (a University of Chicago philosophy professor) wrote that 'Liberal education can never become universal education. It will always remain the obligation and the privilege of a minority.'

"'It would be absurd to hamper the free flow of wisdom by any regulations; hence the rule of the wise must be absolute rule. It would be equally absurd to hamper the free flow of wisdom by consideration of the unwise wishes of the unwise; hence the wise rulers ought not to be responsible to the unwise subjects.'

"Strauss explains that this would result in the subjection of what is by nature higher to that which is lower. His reading of Plato comes down to this: true democracy is an act against nature and must be prevented at all costs. Seen in this light, the Bush Administration's public claim to be bringing 'democracy' to Iraq, all the while working to ensure that elections do not take place, takes on a new meaning.

"Strauss feared the Marxists would take over the world. He said that Marxists, socialists, and what he now calls liberals aimed toward the same goal."

— Earl Shorris, essay, *Harper's Magazine*, June 2004.

60. When she "received the news of the Declaration (of Independence)...Maria Theresa, dowager queen of Austria, expressed to George III her 'hearty desire to see the restoration of obedience and tranquility in every quarter of your dominions,' and her son, Joseph, told the British ambassador, 'the cause in which England is engaged... is the cause of all sovereigns who have a joint interest in the maintenance of due subordination...in all the surrounding monarchies.'"

— Henry Fairlie, article, *The New Republic*, July 18, 1988.

61. "The American record is filled with declarations in which there is too little that is reasonable and too much that is unbecoming impertinence."

— Catherine the Great of Russia, article, Henry Fairlie, *The New Republic*, July 18, 1988.

62. "The public here is extremely occupied with the rebels (in America), not because they know the cause, but because the mania of independence in reality has infected all the spirits, and the poison has spread imperceptibly from the works of the *philosophes* all the way out to the village schools."

— A.P. Bernstorff, Danish minister of foreign affairs, article, Henry Fairlie, *The New Republic*, July 18, 1988.

63. "George III at once dispatched a personal envoy to Catherine the Great, to request no fewer than 20,000 Russian troops for help in suppressing the American insurrection. But Catherine did not have a high opinion of George, and refused to supply any soldiers or to make the treaty that Britain wanted."

— Henry Fairlie, article, *The New Republic*, July 18, 1988.

64. "The Americans entered the War of Independence with a profound political philosophy that immediately lit fires round the world. They are not yet extinguished."

— Henry Fairlie, article, *The New Republic*, July 18, 1988.

65. "'A strong egalitarian society populated by reasonably normal people is difficult to imagine and psychologically and politically out of reach....Democracy is the enemy of comprehensive equality.' The reviewer adds here, "He means, I think, that political equality is the enemy of economic equality."

— *Equality and Partiality* by Thomas Nagel, review by Michael Walzer, *The New Republic*, February 17, 1992.

66. "Thatcher's goal of killing socialism" led the socialists "to backdoor ways of giving government and other groups (unions, consumer organizations, environmentalists) rights to involvement in business decisions thereby vitiating the rights of the real owners....Socialism is about equality. Since Thatcher came to power in 1979, inequality has increased. This is central to her program. Thatcherism is, aggressively, a meritocratic antidote to decades of egalitarianism."

— George Will column, *The Washington Post*, June 14, 1987.

67. Capitalism is "the creed for the common man....Hayek challenged the whole collectivist philosophy."

— Margaret Thatcher, cited in *Z Magazine*, 1999.

68. Thatcher "had a total blind spot about workers. Workers were bad people to be kept in their place and kept down. Also she was very negative about (ending) apartheid and not very honest about it....She really was the philosopher of the radical right; she cloaked Ronald Reagan in her own intellectual respectability."

— Michael Manley, Prime Minister of Jamaica, interview, *The Progressive*, July 1993.

69. "I'm very much aware that it's you who brought democracy to Chile," Thatcher to Pinochet during his period of house arrest in England.

— cited in *The Nation*, September 30, 2002.

70. "Aspects of Margaret Thatcher's government are described as 'totalitarian', and although her successors are often looked on as being less authoritative, the authors suggest convincingly that, since her departure, British governments of both parties have been increasingly intolerant of the people's freedom. The recent Anti-Terrorism Act, for example, is described as 'brutal.'

— *How We Should Rule Ourselves* by Alasdair Gray and Adam Tomkins, reviewed by Ron Butlin in *Times Literary Supplement*, July 22 2005.

71. "We love you, sir...we love your adherence to democratic rights and processes."

— George H. W. Bush's 1985 toast to Philippines dictator Ferdinand Marcos.

72. "There ought to be limits to freedom."

— Texas Governor George W. Bush, news conference, May 1999.

73. "President Bush has quietly claimed the authority to disobey more than 750 laws enacted since he took office, asserting that he has the power to set aside any statute passed by Congress when it conflicts with his interpretation of the Constitution."

— Nation Briefs, *Asheville Global Report*, May 4-10, 2006.

74. "Freedom is an even fuzzier word than democracy and may include democracy, but also may be referring to the freedom of capital to move around and be free of encumbrances like taxes and restrictions on abuses of the environment and labor.

Neo-liberalism is a 'freedom' movement, but confined to the freedom and rights of capital. The Chicago Boys (i.e., University of Chicago economists, many of whom advised the Pinochet government) were quite enthused with Pinochet's Chile as he was freeing markets from government intervention — at least those forms hurtful to the interests of capital — and making labor markets 'free' of trade unions and thus more 'flexible.' The destruction of democracy in Chile was actually a prerequisite for full-scale neo-liberal freedom, and was completely acceptable to the Boys (including Milton Friedman) and their government and corporate community."

— Edward S. Herman, Fog Watch, *Z Magazine*, March 2005.

75. "Time was when Americans savored freedom's uncertainties and considered security an unworthy goal for a free people....Treating economic security as a right validates the core of contemporary liberalism." He says "statist liberalism" advocates high taxation in the name of "redistributive justice...and favors strict regulation...in the name of a core value of the political left, equality." He goes on to attack the government for "preventing pain" and "for protecting the little people from the interests." He attacks Franklin Roosevelt for saying that 'government by organized money is just as dangerous as government by organized mob' and for saying 'We cannot be content...if some fraction of our people...is ill-fed, ill-clothed, ill-housed, and insecure....true individual freedom requires economic security.' He salutes Goldwater's belief that 'Conservatism holds that man's political freedom is illusory if he is dependent for his economic needs on the state rather than the business interests.' To "liberate" people by making them less secure, Will wants to privatize Social Security and all social programs.

He calls the United States "a crybaby nation'" hung up on "unfairness" and attacks "litigious liberalism which aims to expand government through enforcement of freshly-minted rights."

Will cites a Professor Charles Lawrence of Stanford as saying the 'real purpose' of the Supreme Court's 1954 school-desegregation decision was 'to permit and perhaps require sweeping censorship of speech.' Will goes on to complain about "censorship by liberals on campuses" and says it "has more of a chilling effect than McCarthyism." He asserts that liberals are "First Amendment fanatics (all forms of expression are of equal value)" and that they "have long preached universal disdain for all authority, intellectual as well as political" and that "tolerance is the only obvious value." He then asserts that "the national community" has a right to prevent "flag desecration," "pornography," and other moral deviations from the conservative canon.

— George Will columns, *The Washington Post*, February 2, 1990, April 12, 1992, October 15, 1995, January 20, 1996, February 23, 1996.

76. Charles Krauthammer says that liberalism "means oriented toward socialism, toward more government control" and claims that Stalinism is leftist and implies that liberalism is thus "Stalinist and totalitarian." He says that conservatism is a "belief in individualism and free markets and an aversion to state power."

— Charles Krauthammer column, *The Washington Post*, February 2, 1990

77. "Charles Krauthammer sees no future at all for traditional liberalism: 'It will likely fracture along existing political fault lines and disappear into the landscape.'"

— William Schneider, *Washington Post*, November 24, 1985.

CHAPTER 13. SECULARISM AND RELATIVISM

1. Social decline is caused by "moral relativism" according to Allan Bloom in *The Closing of the American Mind.*
— Cited in *Resentment Against Achievement* by Robert Sheaffer, review by Karl Zin-meister, *Reason,* July 1989.

[But if you don't believe in some degree of relativism, then you must believe in a system of absolutes. Then, as a dedicated absolutist, you must think that you have a duty to push those absolutes on others through the use of coercion and force (the ultimate absolutes). Otherwise, what point is there in believing in absolutes (The Final and Unalterable Truth) and why would you permit the relativism of free and individual choice? —Author]

3. Social decline is caused by "decadent individualism," according to Robert Bellah.
— Cited in *Resentment Against Achievement* by Robert Sheaffer, review by Karl Zin-meister, *Reason,* July 1989.

4. "Francis Fukuyama calls 'relativism the doctrine that maintains that all values are merely relative and attacks all privileged perspectives.' He says he abhors 'liberal democracy's tendency to grant equal recognition to unequal people.' He calls this 'moral relativism.' He says the 'US has every reason to impose its own political norm on Eastern Europe and Russia but not on East Asia or the Muslim world...(because) Japan (for example) is governed by a benevolent one-party dictatorship because the people of Japan choose to be ruled in that fashion.'"
— *The End of History and the Last Man* by Francis Fukuyama, review by George Gilder, *The Washington Post,* January 12, 1992.

5. "It really is wise restraints that make us genuinely free."
— Editorial, *The New Republic,* Feb. 8, 1988.

[In other words, "The only way to make people free is to impose restraints on them."—Author]

6. "On September 11, 2001, Soros...watched the Twin Towers fall on television.... But he soon began to feel that the country was 'heading way off the rails.' The state-

ments of Attorney General John Ashcroft, he said, 'reminded me of Germany, under the Nazis. It was the kind of talk that Goebbels used to line the Germans up. I remember I was thirteen or fourteen. It was the same kind of propaganda about how "We are endangered and we have to be united."...

"'If we always have to rely on troops to protect us from the terrorists, and we can never criticize the Commander-in-Chief without undercutting the troops, then that's the end of our open society.'...

"'The people in the Weimar Republic also thought everything would stay the same,' he said, gazing out the plane's windows. 'They didn't think those things could happen. But I have a particular sensitivity to those matters, because I lived under both Nazi and Communist occupation.'...

"Sir Karl Popper's ideas helped Soros make sense of Fascism and Communism. These two seemingly opposite ideologies, Popper argued, were actually quite alike, for they both falsely claimed absolute truth — which, he held, was unattainable. Popper championed the idea of a society defined by rational debate, where false ideas would lose out to stronger ones."

— Jane Mayer, essay, *The New Yorker*, October 18, 2004.

7. Reagan declared as governor "the state of California has no business subsidizing intellectual curiosity."

— Anthony Lane, essay, *The New Yorker*, October 18, 2004.

8. "Jerry Falwell names those responsible for the September 11th terrorist attack: 'I really believe the pagans, and the abortionists, and the feminists, and the gays and the lesbians who are actively trying to make that an alternative life style...all of them who have tried to secularize America.'

Pat Robertson agreeing with Falwell: 'Well, I totally concur....America had insulted God (through) rampant secularism, pornography, and abortion.'

— Article by Daniel Levitas in *The Nation*, July 22, 2002.

9. "In the nineteen-twenties, Kemal Ataturk, a secular revolutionary, banned the caliphate and established the Republic of Turkey....

"In reaction, in 1928 Hassan al-Banna, a religiously educated teacher living near the Suez Canal, established the Muslim Brotherhood. Banna believed in Islam as a complete system, which provides divine instruction on everything from daily rituals, laws, and politics to matters of the spirit, and to which all other forms of thought and social organization — secularism, nationalism, socialism, liberalism — are alien."

— David Remnick, essay, *The New Yorker*, July 12 & 19, 2004.

10. "Secularism has no future here. Secularism is a product of the West."

— Tariq (name changed for protection from Egyptian police), cited in a David Remnick essay, *The New Yorker*, July 12 & 19, 2004.

11. "The Egyptian government, like all other Arab governments, is a puppet regime, an agent of foreign powers, particularly the United States, which controls the world now. But if democracy were implemented and there were freedom of expression, Islam would rule all aspects of life, including for non-Muslims."

— Sheik Ragab, quoted by David Remnick in an essay in *The New Yorker*, July 12 & 19, 2004.

12. "The need for a strong secularist defense of science is especially urgent, because many of the religious right's policy goals are intimately linked to a profound distrust of science and scientists....

"The (Bush) attack on science is a prime issue for secularists not because religion and science are necessarily incompatible but because particular forms of religious belief — those that claim to have found the one true answer to the origins and ultimate purpose of human life — are incompatible not only with science but with democracy....

"The anti secularists cannot have it both ways. If secularists are in charge of everything, then America is not as religious as the religiously correct claim; if secularists are an insolent minority trying to erode the values of the majority, then they are not in charge of everything."

— Susan Jacob, essay, *The Nation,* April 19, 2004.

[But if you don't believe in secularism, then you don't believe in democracy. Fundamentalist religions — muslim, christian or other — are entirely incompatible with democracy. George W. Bush himself is obviously hostile to democratic government as it impedes the interests of big business and big religion.

One of the reasons promoted for Bush's war on Iraq was the idea that we could impose democracy on the people. Even McClellan's book *What Happened* purports to believe that. But it is a self-evident fact that you can't impose freedom of choice on anyone. What Bush is trying to impose on the people of Iraq is a system of predatory commercialism controlled entirely by American corporations and the military, first and foremost with the —— oil bill that they can't get the Iraqi Parliament to approve, presumably because they don't all agree that their greatest resource should be turned over to their greatest enemy. For Bush, commercial domination is democracy and any resistance to it is terrorism.
—Author]

13. "I did a recent strip about Pat Robertson and Jerry Falwell, who were quick to blame 9/11 on secular humanists — people like you and me. Meanwhile, Robertson was involved in a gold mining investment with Liberia's president, Charles Taylor, who was providing sanctuary to Al Qaeda operatives in return for a million-dollar payoff. I think that's an extraordinary thing to know — that at the same time Robertson was denouncing you and me for our moral laxity, his business partner was literally harboring terrorists! It underlines the sheer hypocrisy of these people.

"Right after 9/11, when Falwell said it was all the fault of people who didn't believe in God, I thought, no, actually it's the fault of people who believe too much in God. Religion is what got us into this mess. More religious zealotry is not going to get us out. But that's not a very popular view in America.

"The wingnuts, the hard right, the Christian conservatives, and the like all seemed to believe that 9/11 was their chance to show that their opponents were not only wrong but actually traitors — people who hate this country and rejoiced to see it attacked. That's beneath contempt, as far as I'm concerned."

— Tom Tomorrow, interview by Robert Elias, *The Progressive,* March 2003.

14. "Facts are stupid things."

— Ronald Reagan, cited in "Talk of the Town," *The New Yorker,* July 28, 2003.

15. "I will never apologize for the United States. I don't care what the facts are."

— George H.W. Bush.

16. "In the summer of 2002, one of President [George W.] Bush's advisers explained to the writer Ron Suskind that guys like me were 'in what we call the reality-based community,' which he defines as people who 'believe that solutions emerge from judicious study of discernible reality.' I nodded and murmured something about enlightenment principles and empiricism. He cut me off. 'That's not the way the world really works anymore,' he continued. 'We're an empire now, and when we act, we create our own reality.'"

— Anthony Grafton, essay, *The New York Review*, December 2, 2004.

17. It's best to "evade reason," follow the "insights of ESP," and look for "religious mysteries."

— *Wealth and Poverty* by George Gilder.

18. Leo "Strauss (a University of Chicago philosopher), buffeted by history in his own life, railed against historicism, which holds that meaning can only arise from within a particular historical context. The Straussians contend that historicism leads to relativism and thus to nihilism, finally to the crisis that could bring about the destruction of the American liberal democracy — a crisis, as Strauss himself said — that comes of the loss of the American sense of superiority.

"Strauss had a great intellectual antagonist, Sir Isaiah Berlin. They represented the polar opposites of political philosophy, the one and the many, the idealist conservative and the pluralist liberal. Berlin...saw political philosophy...as an attempt to negotiate conflicts among the virtues, none more clear than the conflict between liberty and equality. The Oxford don put it with remarkable clarity: 'Liberty for wolves is death to the lambs.' The principle of equality must limit the liberty of the strong if the weak are to be fed and clothed....He carefully drew the distinction between relativism and pluralism: 'I prefer coffee, you prefer champagne. We have different tastes. There is no more to be said. That is relativism."

— Earl Shorris, essay, *Harper's Magazine, June 2004.*

19. Conservatives should be "blaming the liberal culture for the spread of violent crime, pornography, drugs, teen-age pregnancy and AIDS"....and the liberals' "unwillingness to declare that some things are right and some things are wrong has exacted a terrible toll." Conservatives must defeat "the campaign against traditional moral values that has been waged so energetically and for so long by the forces of liberal relativism."

— Norman Podhoretz article, *The Washington Post*, July 2, 1987.

20. "Irving Kristol thinks a 'new class' of professionals wants all power in government hands and is engaged in a 'class struggle' with the business community for status and power. He expresses a bitter hatred for secular humanism, liberalism, and socialism and wants to return to 'traditional moral certainties."'

— *Neo-conservatism* by Irving Kristol, review by Theodore Draper, *Z Magazine*, October 2002.

21. "'Liberals believe in the perfectibility of man....Socialism is totalitarian and liberalism is the ideology of Western suicide.... Western man is both different from and superior in quality to other civilizations and non-civilizations....There has to be a renewed willingness to use superior power and the threat of power to defend the West against challenges and challengers....(there has to be) a regime that will be authoritarian and not liberal."'

"The Soviet Union was 'neither capitalist nor socialist.... their ideologies and myths had a formal meaning different from the real meaning.' He said that socialism wasn't possible and 'There will always be a ruling class.' He thought Stalin a 'great man' and the true heir of Lenin. Burnham's most important doctrine was liberation or rollback rather than containment of communism."

— James Burnham (former Communist, CIA agent, associate editor of National Review — Buckley said he was "the dominant influence."), article by John B. Judis, *The New Republic*, August 31, 1987.

22. "Bloom writes that 'feminists are terrorists...relativism is destroying America's moral fabric...rock and roll is producing cultural rot...relativists believe nothing

is true, everything is permitted, let's all be tolerant.' He goes on to say that, 'Openness is a product of relativism (which) is the belief that one opinion is as good as any other opinion.'" The reviewer says, "No one believes this.... many people do think it is important to show respect for the views of others."

— *The Closing of the American Mind* by Allan Bloom, review by Louis Menand, *The New Republic*, May 25, 1987.

23. "Cardinal Ratzinger had warned that modern society was threatened by a 'dictatorship of relativism.' But it might have been more accurate to say that it is threatened by a dictatorship of absolutism, including his own....

"He battled Hans Kung, the liberal Swiss theologian and his mentor at the University of Tubingen, on questions of doctrinal dissention, and, as Archbishop of Munich, was instrumental in having Kung barred from teaching Catholic theology....During his first years as Prefect, the Jesuits were censured for challenging papal teachings on contraception, parts of their constitution were suspended, and their Vicar General, Vincent O'Keefe, a passionate advocate for social justice, was removed. The reactionary lay order Opus Dei was transformed into a 'personal prelature' accountable to the Pope. The dioceses of progressive Latin-American bishops were gerrymandered out of existence, liberation theologians like Leonardo Boff were called to Rome and silenced as 'Marxists' (they were, more accurately, Christian communitarian evangelists), and the priests they had trained, who were responsible for an ebullient Catholic revival in Latin America, were ordered back into the fold of tradition and obedience."

— Talk of the Town, *The New Yorker*, May 2, 2005.

24. "DeLay wants 'a God-centered America" devoted to "the Constitution and to absolute truth that has been manipulated and destroyed by a liberal world view.... give me one example that proves evolution. One example! You can't.'"

— Tom De Lay, cited in a Patricia Williams column, *The Nation*, June 18, 2001.

25. "Major assaults have been advanced by the Religious Right. Should this powerful force further consolidate its alliance with religious conservatives, we are in for a fundamental challenge to our view that the United States is a secular democracy, that it should be neutral about religion, and that it should not favor religion over non-religion. The First Amendment states that 'Congress shall make no law respecting an establishment of religion, or prohibiting the free exercise thereof.' This is being reinterpreted by Supreme Court Justices William Rehnquist, Antonin Scalia, and Clarence Thomas to mean that Congress shall not favor — or establish — any one sect or denomination of religion over any other; but this does not mean, they say, that government cannot favor religion over non-religion."

— Paul Kurtz, essay, *Free Inquiry*, Dec. 2004/Jan. 2005.

26. "The secular revolution in government, through which the control of the state was necessarily separated from religious power, freed religion from state control and freed the public square from religious influence. Each was allowed to flourish unimpeded by the other. The academy, government, and science could proceed finally without church interference, and religions could go about their business without fear of governmental control or persecution. This worked by and large, for quite some time. Of late, there is a sudden resurgence of theocratic power, in both the Islamic world and here, in our own country, where a certain strain of religious fundamentalism seeks to establish a new theocratic government. In the United States, it is argued falsely that this was the Founders intent, and a baldly religious agenda has been legislated....

"Will the forces of fundamentalism and dogmatism finally undermine the values of the Enlightenment, or will we enjoy a new enlightenment? Can we help to convince the world that the path of reason, humanism, and science is more fruitful than dogma, fear, and mysticism?"

— David Koepsell, essay, *The Secular Humanist Bulletin*, Spring 2005.

27. "There are similarities between absolute power and absolute faith; a demand for absolute obedience, a readiness to attempt the impossible, a bias for simple solutions, the viewing of compromise as surrender, the tendency to manipulate people and experiment with blood. Both absolute power and absolute faith are instruments of dehumanization. Hence, absolute faith corrupts as absolutely as absolute power."

— Dan Stupka, Guest commentary, *Asheville Citizen-Times, May 11, 2005.*

28. "I found that they differed upon matters of detail alone, and that they attributed the peaceful dominion of religion in their country mainly to the separation of church and state. I do not hesitate to affirm that during my stay in America I did not meet a single individual, of the clergy or the laity, who was not of the same opinion on this point....

"American clergy in general...do not support any particular political system. They keep aloof from parties and from public affairs. In the United States, religion exercises but little influence upon the laws and upon the details of public opinion."

— Alexis de Tocqueville, 1831.

29. "George W. Bush has been more determined to merge religion and government than any modern president. Bush, a champion of 'faith-based' initiatives, proudly acknowledges the Religious Right as his base. Yet Bush apparently believes Tocqueville is on his side."

— Essay, *Church & State:* May 2005.

30. "Most of the traditionalists — including M.E. Bradford, University of Michigan historian Stephen Tonsor, and University of South Carolina historian Clyde Wilson — are academics who have always been conservatives and who trace their lineage to Russell Kirk's 1953 book, *The Conservative Mind.* They value order and organic community, class and natural aristocracy. They abhor mass democracy and egalitarianism. They see Christian belief as the foundation of morality and law. Some, like Bradford and Wilson, reflect the legacy of Calhoun and the Confederacy. Others, like Tonsor, appear more influenced by anti-Enlightenment European authoritarianism....

"Tonsor identified conservatism with Christianity. Ignoring the seminal role played in the 1950s by Jewish or agnostic intellectuals such as Henry Hazlitt, Willie Schlamm, James Burnham, Frank Meyer, Max Eastman, Eugene Lyons, Ralph de Toledano, Leo Strauss, and Milton Friedman, Tonsor declared that conservatism's 'world view is Roman or Anglo Catholic.' In contrast, Tonsor, identified neo-conservatism with the 'instantiation of modernity among secularized Jewish intellectuals.'...

"Russell Kirk...said in a telephone interview: 'What really animates the neoconservatives, especially Irving Kristol, is the preservation of Israel. That lies in back of everything.' Paul Gottfried said, 'I don't think one can differentiate the neo-conservatives from the very large Jewish composition of the movement, and the fact that many of the Jewish leaders of the movement broke from the left precisely over the question of Israel and other Jewish issues and therefore are going to take a very strong pro-Israel position.'"

— John B. Judis, essay, *The New Republic*, August 11 & 18, 1986.

31. What Dominionists "share is an obsession with political power.... [They] call for Christian 'dominion' over the nation and, eventually, over the earth itself.... Amer-

ica becomes, in this militant Biblicism, an agent of God, and all political and intellectual opponents of America's Christian leaders are viewed, quite simply, as agents
of Satan. Under Christian dominion, America will no longer be a sinful and fallen
nation but one in which the Ten Commandments form the basis of our legal system,
Creationism and 'Christian values' form the basis of our education system, and the
media and the government proclaim the Good News to one and all. Aside from its
proselytizing mandate, the federal government will be reduced to the protection of
property rights and 'homeland security.' Some...would further require citizens to pay
'tithes' to church organizations empowered by the government to run our social welfare agencies, and a number of influential figures advocate the death penalty for a host
of 'moral crimes,' including apostasy, blasphemy, sodomy, and witchcraft. The only
legitimate voices in this state will be Christian. All others will be silenced."

— Chris Hedges, essay, *Harper's Magazine*, May 2005.

32. "I am appalled at the lack of discernment among Americans about the Christian Nation Movement. For three decades it has swept through America, mocking
the American dream, turning unwary citizens against each other. It is emerging as
one of the horror stories of the century."

Their "idea of family values is to stone a disobedient child to death. Punishable
offenses include homosexual tendencies, drug use, sex before marriage, the tiniest
disrespect or disagreement."

They say "the 8th Commandment, 'Thou Shalt Not Steal,' assured a man that God
said to treat his laborers as property, slaves to do his bidding. No government has
the right to promote such foolish ideas as minimum wage, the 40-hour workweek,
safety regulations, social security, unemployment insurance, or woman's' right to
equal pay.

"They are determined to reclaim the land from the godless rule of the labor unions,
the civil rights and the woman's' movement, homosexuals, and especially Welfare
Queens. No woman is supposed to raise children by herself. Punish her for not following the rules.

"Men and, in particular, white men of property," they claim, "were chosen by god
to rule. The liberals, humanists, or feminists, whether college professors, good teachers, women of character, or politicians who do not cave in to their worldview, have to
be shouted down and destroyed. It does not matter how many lies are told. Pastors
drape themselves in the flag and wrap family values around freedom and democracy,
knowing full well that God law will stamp out any vestige of democratic rule."

"Trace this movement to the Council on National Policy. This ultra-secret organization, founded in 1981, married the Theocratic Right with the Republican Party."

— Gracie Adams (GranGracie@yahoo.com), letter to the *Smoky Mountain News*,
November 9-15, 2005.

33. "Christianity is countercultural. If one embraces Jesus, one has to raise some
serious questions about the American way of life, especially it's consumerism....

"To be a Christian in today's world is to be opposed to America. Why? America
believes in capital punishment, and Jesus says, 'Blessed are the merciful, for they shall
obtain mercy.' America says, 'Blessed are the powerful.' Jesus said, 'Blessed are the
meek, for they shall inherit the earth.'

"We have reached a stage of idolatry when, in any given church in America, you're
going to run into more trouble if you remove the American flag than if you remove
the cross."

— Baptist minister Tony Campolo, quoted in an article by John Oliver Mason in *The Progressive*, August 2005.

34. "Reverends Rod Parsley and Russell Johnson are key players in the effort to wrest control of the GOP from so-called Party moderates....

"Americans must be 'Christocrats' — citizens of both their country and the Kingdom of God — Parsley told his congregation at his World Harvest Church, located just outside Columbus, Ohio. 'And that is not democracy; that is a theocracy,' he said. 'That means God is in control and you are not.'...

"Parsley advocates what some call 'health and wealth' theology," the *Columbus Dispatch* reported. His theology 'emphasizes that the Bible teaches that God wants people to prosper financially and physically. The latter is tied to belief in the power of God's word to heal.'"

— Bill Berkowitz, essay, *Z Magazine*, November 2005.

35. "For all those folks who want to turn this into a Christian nation — it ain't, and it hasn't ever been.... Secular is not a dirty word.... Secular is neutral. The US has always been godless, politically."

— Dr. James M. Dunn, adjunct professor of Christianity and public policy at Wake Forest University in Winston Salem, at a June 9, 2005 forum at UNC Asheville.

CHAPTER 14. CHRISTIAN AND CAPITALIST EXCEPTIONALISM

1. "God and Country are an unbeatable team: they break all records for oppression and bloodshed."
— Luis Buquel

2. "It serves principally to divide us and make us unfriendly to one another."
— Benjamin Franklin on the Christian religion.

3. "The man who builds a factory builds a temple and the man who works there worships there."
— Calvin Coolidge.

4. "The Gospels were pretty unwelcome news to an awful lot of people....Taking seriously the actual message of Jesus, though, should serve at least to moderate the greed and violence that mark this culture. It's hard to imagine a con much more audacious than making Christ the front man for a program of tax cuts for the rich or war in Iraq. If some modest part of the 85 percent of us who are Christians woke up to that fact, then the world might change....

"Since the days of Constantine, emperors and rich men have sought to co-opt the teachings of Jesus. As in so many areas of our increasingly market-tested lives, the co-opters — the TV men, the politicians, the Christian 'interest groups'- have found a way to make each of us complicit in that travesty too. They have invited us to subvert the church of Jesus even as we celebrate it."
— Bill Mckibben, essay, *Harper's Magazine*, August 2005.

5. "According to the sociologist Max Weber...Protestant countries developed a special aptitude for moneymaking. This explained their economic success; the lack of a Protestant ethic explained the failure of others.

Thus "Capital accumulation became an end in itself....Greenfield (thinks) Weber was right to see that the 'spirit of capitalism' required a new morality. But the mechanism that brought this about, she argues, was nationalism, not Protestantism.

"Nationalism can also set up a system of international competition, committing societies 'which define themselves as nations to a race with a relative and therefore forever receding finishing line.'

"Greenfield raises the question of whether an obsession with growth is rational. The problem is not to explain the desire of people to improve their lot, but the organization of modern societies for continuous growth.... It is not clear why the already rich should want to go on getting richer.

"Economists assumed that as people became more efficient at satisfying their wants, they would — and should as rational agents — work less and enjoy life more. This view seems to have been replaced by the view that human wants are insatiable. We are constantly being urged to work harder, and save more, in order to satisfy wants continuously being created by advertising, whose main effect is to enlarge the human capacity for envy. The evidence, moreover, suggests that increasing real income fails to make citizens of rich countries happier. In other words, Western societies remain organized around an objectless disposition to continuous wealth-creation.

"Endogenous growth prepares the intellectual ground for a new form of interventionism, in which Western countries take over...the development of 'human capital' in the poorest countries. The current language of 'failed' states is the embryonic language of the new imperialism."

— Robert Sidelsky, book review, *The Spirit of Capitalism: Nationalism and Economic Growth* by Liah Greenfield and *Lectures on Economic Growth* by Robert E. Lucas, Jr., *The New York Review*, March 13, 2003.

6. "It is the entrepreneurs who know the rules of the world and the laws of God. They are the heroes of economic life."

— *Spirit of Enterprise* by George Gilder.

7. Under capitalism, "the rich won't get richer and the poor poorer. No, there will be more and more rich people."

— *Wealth and Poverty* by George Gilder

8. "Cannibalize yourself."

— *Fortune* magazine, article about investing, *Z Magazine*, April 2001.

9. "God gave me my money."

— John D. Rockefeller.

10. "Blessed are you who are poor, for yours is the kingdom of God. But woe to you who are rich, for you have already received your comfort."

— Jesus Christ, Luke 6:20, 24.

11. "The market is my religion."

— FCC Chair Michael Powell.

12. "The Republican Party is dominated by the evangelical fundamentalists, who have increasingly wedded biblical morality to a free-market ideology, convinced that God and country go hand-in-hand. Those who are wealthy are virtuous in the eyes of God, deserving the bounties bestowed on them. The poor, disadvantaged, and helpless need to fend for themselves, or so evangelical capitalists seem to be saying."

— Paul Kurtz, Center for Inquiry, fund-raising letter of June 5, 2005.

13. "Our goal is a Christian nation. We have a biblical duty; we are called by God to conquer this country. We don't want equal time. We don't want pluralism."

— Randall Terry, *Indiana News Sentinel*.

14. "The Constitution guarantees freedom of religion, not freedom *from* religion."

— Senator Elizabeth Dole, 2004.

15. "Our government makes no sense unless it is founded on a deeply felt religious faith — and I don't care what it is."

— Dwight Eisenhower on Flag Day in 1954

16. "I am now as before a Catholic and will always remain so."

— Adolf Hitler, quoted by Gregory S. Paul, essay, *Free Inquiry*, October/November 2003.

17. "Some higher being...is behind nature.... I insist that members of the SS must believe in God."

— Heinrich Himmler, quoted by Gregory S. Paul, essay, *Free Inquiry*, October/November 2003.

18. "The middle class and the rich reside in well-maintained old and new suburbs and vote Republican, while their impoverished neighbors, who tend to be mostly African-American and who outnumber them in many counties, live in rural slums. While there's no official segregation between the races, there is a cast system with clear distinctions and accompanying inequality that is apparent wherever one goes. There are towns like Jonestown, Mississippi, that in their shocking poverty make one gasp....

"Clarksdale...is the town, they say, where the blues began. One of its legends, Robert Johnson, was reputed to have sold his soul to the devil at a crossroads nearby.... Clarksdale has the despoiled look of a conquered and sacked city. Ranking conditions of poverty is a risky business, but what I encountered in Mississippi surpasses anything I've seen in a long time in this country....

"During my trip, I was asked several times pointblank whether I was a Christian. The first time it happened, I was so surprised I didn't know what to reply....What people were eager to find out was whether I had accepted Jesus as my savior. For these people, Christians are to be distinguished from the rest of Americans, who are something else — liberals, secular humanist, Catholics, atheists, abortionists, etc. They all share one thing in common, however: they are all going to hell....

"Skepticism, empirical evidence, and book learning are in low esteem among the Protestant evangelicals. To ask about the laws of cause and effect would be a sin. They reject modern science and dream of a theocratic state where such blasphemous subject matter would be left out from the school curriculum. Their ideal, as a shrewd young fellow told me in Tuscaloosa, is unquestioned obedience and complete conformity in matters of religion and politics. The complaint about secular humanism is that it permits too much freedom of thought and opinion."

— Charles Simic, essay, *The New York Review*, August 12, 2004.

19. The Empire was "under Providence, the greatest instrument for good the world has ever seen."

— George Nathaniel Curzon, future viceroy of India, 1894.

20. "Our nation is the greatest force for good in history."

— George W. Bush, August 2002.

21. "President Bush's slightly alarming claim to the Amish on July 9 that God speaks through him — that's what he said, God speaks through him — raises some troubling prospects. First of all, I think God has a better grasp of subject-verb agreement than George W. Bush does. Also, when Bush changes his mind, as he frequently does, do we think God has had to rethink things after the polls have come out?"

— Molly Ivins, syndicated column, June, 2004.

22. "God gave the savior to the German people. We have faith, deep and unshakable faith, that (Hitler) was sent by God to save Germany."

— Herman Goering, cited in *Free Inquiry* by Gregory S. Paul, October/November 2003.

23. "A famous study by Samuel Stouffer in the mid-1950s found that a solid majority of US citizens would deny atheists the right to speak in their towns or to teach in a college or university and would have books written by atheists removed from the library. More recently, voters have approved referendums limiting affirmative action, removing rights from gays and lesbians, and attacking immigrants....

"Neither direct nor representative democracy is in and of itself adequate to protect the rights of minorities. Other institutions are necessary to ensure that minorities are not oppressed by the majority."

— Stephen R. Shalom, *Z Papers, Z Magazine*, October 2004.

24. "Evangelical, born-again Christians...are now 40 percent of the electorate, and they support Bush 3–1....Forget about changing their minds. These Christians do not read the same books we do, they do not get their information from anything remotely resembling reasonably balanced sources, and, in fact, consider even CBS and NBC super-liberal networks of porn and the devil's lies. Given how fundamentalists see the modern world, they may as well be living in Iraq or Syria, with which they share approximately the same Bronze Age religious tenets....In other words, just because millions of Christians appear to be dangerously nuts does not mean they are marginal....

"This apocalyptic belief, yearning really, drives an American Christian polity in the service of a grave and unnerving agenda....These Christian conservatives do not believe that peace can lead to the Rapture; indeed, they think it impedes the 1,000-year Reign of Christ. So anyone promoting peace is an enemy, a tool of Satan....

Tens of millions of hardworking, earnest American Christians see it as a war against all that is un-biblical, the goal of which is complete world conquest or, put in Christian terminology, 'dominion.' They will have no less than the 'inevitable victory God has promised his new chosen people. Screw the Jews, they blew their chance. If perpetual war is what it will take, then let it be perpetual. After all, perpetual war is exactly what the Bible promised.... (What will) bring ever-tolerant liberals to openly acknowledge what is truly happening in this country, the thing that has been building for a long, long time — a holy war, a covert Christian jihad for control of America and the entire world. Millions of Americans are under the spell of an extraordinarily dangerous mass psychosis."

— Joe Bageant, essay, *Free Inquiry*, Oct./Nov. 2004.

25. "According to the Harpers magazine story, "The Christian Right's War on America," by Chris Hedges, the dominionists' expressed goals are to replace the Constitution with the Ten Commandments, replace science with creationism and reduce the federal government's role to protecting property rights and providing homeland security. Some seek to replace income taxes with mandatory 'tithes' to church organizations that would operate as agents of the federal government. Others have advocated the death penalty for 'moral crimes' such as apostasy, blasphemy, sodomy and witchcraft.

"Will some enlightened reader please explain where Christ is in this "Christianity" and the difference between such extreme beliefs and those of al-Qaeda and the Taliban?"

— Letter of May 22, 2005 by Jeff Callahan, Flatrock, to the *Asheville Citizen Times*,

26. "In January 2002, Supreme Court Associate Justice Antonin Scalia made a major speech so sweeping and extreme in its contempt for democracy, and so willfully oblivious to the Constitution's grounding in human rather than divine authority, that it might well...have elicited calls for impeachment....Scalia's address opened

with an overview of the death penalty in America but moved quickly to the justice's disdain for secular government....

"He believes that the state derives its power not from the consent of the governed... but from God. God has the power of life and death, and therefore lawful governments also have the right to exact the ultimate penalty. 'Few doubted the morality of the death penalty in the age that believed in the divine right of kings...It is easy to see the hand of the Almighty behind rulers whose forebears, in the dim mists of history, were supposedly anointed by God, who at least obtained their thrones in awful and unpredictable battles whose outcome was determined by the Lord of Hosts, that is, the Lord of Armies.'"

— Susan Jacoby, essay, *Free Inquiry*, Oct./Nov. 2004.

27. "When I do good, I feel good; when I do bad, I feel bad. That's my religion."

— Abraham Lincoln, cited in *Free Inquiry*, Dec. 2004/Jan. 2005.

28. "Finally, they wheeled out God. In at least two states, Arkansas and West Virginia, the Republican Party has been sending out pieces of literature claiming the Democrats are going to take everyone's Bibles away, once again proving that there is no low that the Bush campaign will not stoop to.

"On the front of each package, sent from the Republican National Committee, was a picture of a Bible with the word 'Banned' slapped across it. 'This will be Arkansas... If you don't vote,' it said."

— Matthew Rothschild, Editor's Note, discussing the 2004 presidential campaign, *The Progressive*, November 2004.

29. "Evangelicals might want to take notice of a July 1 article by David Morgan of Reuters reporting that President Bush has asked churchgoing volunteers to turn over church membership directories to his campaign. The goal is to 'identify new churches that can be organized by the Bush campaign and talk to clergy about holding voter registration drives.' ...

"Is the focus of the church Jesus Christ or just a convenient excuse among some 'Christian' groups who have in effect allowed their churches to become PACs (Political Action Committees)?

"Just remember, Jesus Christ is not an American or a Republican."

— David M. Williams, letter to the editor, *Asheville Citizen-Times*, July 11, 2004.

30. "You are striking against God and Nature, whose law it is that man shall earn his bread in the sweat of his brow. You are on strike against God."

— A magistrate to a young seamstress picketing with 20,000 garment workers in New York City in 1909 for recognition of their union, cited in an article by Michael Kazin, *The Nation*, June 16, 2003.

31. "You say you're supposed to be nice to the Episcopalians and the Presbyterians and the Methodists and this, that, and the other thing. Nonsense. I don't have to be nice to the spirit of the Antichrist."

— Pat Robertson, *Washington Post*.

32. "Michael Kazin calls Nazi Germany a godless tyranny, but it was hardly godless under Hitler. Subsidizing religion and mandating school prayer and the teaching of religion in the primary grades, Hitler elevated priests to officialdom and declared that loyalty to the state derives its power from the truths of Christianity. The church never excommunicated Hitler and offered little opposition to the repression, genocide and enslavement of millions."

— Robert W. McCall, letter, *The Nation*, June 16, 2003.

33. "Anti-Semitic practices pioneered by Catholics included the forced wearing of yellow identification, ghettoization, confiscation of Jews' property, and bias on intermarriage with Christians. European Protestantism bore the fierce impress of Martin Luther, whose 1543 tract *On the Jews and Their Lies* was a principal inspiration for [Hitler's book] *Mein Kampf*. In addition to his anti-Semitism, Luther was also a fervent authoritarian.

"When we seek precursors of Nazi anti-Semitism and authoritarianism, it is among European Christians, not among the atheists, that we must search."

— Gregory S. Paul, essay, *Free Inquiry*, October/November 2003.

34. "According to standard biographies, the principal Nazi leaders were all born, baptized, and raised Christian. Most grew up in strict, pious households where tolerance and democratic values were disparaged. Nazi leaders of Catholic background included Hitler, Reinhard Heydrich, and Joseph Goebbels.

"Hitler did well in monastery school. He sang in the choir, found High Mass and other ceremonies intoxicating, and idolized priests. Impressed by their power, he at one time considered entering the priesthood....

"No reliably attributed quote reveals Hitler to be an atheist or in any way sympathetic to atheism. On the contrary, he often condemned atheism, as he did Christians who collaborated with such atheistic forces as Bolshevism. He consistently denied that the state could replace faith and instructed Speer to include churches in his beloved plans for a rebuilt Berlin. The Nazi-era constitution explicitly evoked God....

"Reich-Fuhrer Himmler regularly attended Catholic services until he lurched into an increasingly bizarre Aryanism. He authorized searches for the Holy Grail and other supposedly powerful Christian and Cathar relics. A believer in reincarnation, he sent expeditions to Tibet and the American tropics in search of the original Aryans and even Atlantians. He and Heydrich modeled the S.S. after the disciplined and secretive Jesuits; it would not accept atheists as members."

— Gregory S. Paul, *essay, Free Inquiry*, October/November 2003.

35. "I feel like God wants me to run for president. I can't explain it, but I sense my country is going to need me....I really don't want to run....But I feel God wants me to do this, and I must do it."

— Edmund D. Cohen quoting George W. Bush, *Free Inquiry*, June/July 2004.

36. "In the second year of the US occupation of Iraq many people in the US still tend to think of the United States not as the imperial empire that it is, but as the Promised Land, the embodiment of western virtue, the incarnation of 'freedom and democracy.' ...

"Whether we call this outlook superpower or chosen-ness syndrome, national essentialism or millennialism, at its root lies 'the belief that [US] history, under divine guidance, will bring about the triumph of Christian principles' and eventually the emergence of 'a holy utopia.' Such belief in the unique moral destiny of the US may be held independent of Christian principles. Its historical origins, however, trace back to colonial New England, and even further, to the Bible. It is omnipresent in every part of the country, though its strongest regional base lies in the South and West.

"For the past four years President George W. Bush, his top foreign policy advisers and their aides, have carried religious Manichaeism to new levels. They have trampled on the US constitution, violated international law, and turned nationalism in a more authoritarian, 'potentially fascistic' direction."

— Herbert P. Bix, essay, *Z Magazine*, July/August 2004.

37. "Millions of Americans...have devoured the latest volume in the red-state staple 'Left Behind' series, a fictionalized telling of the end of the world scenario proposed by biblical literalists. In this series' current offering, 'Glorious Awakening,' Jesus returns with shock and awe aplenty for non-Christians.

"'Death is too good for you,' he tells one hapless follower of the antichrist. 'I sentence you to an eternity in the lake of fire.' He then vaporizes his victim, and 'innards and entrails gushed to the desert floor...their blood pooling and rising in the unforgiving brightness of God.'

"This Jesus is...muscle-bound, heavily armed, and mean, more like Arnold Schwarzenegger squinting angrily on the cross in the first 'Conan' movie than poor Graham Chapman looking on the bright side in 'Life of Brian.' I am told that 'Glorious Awakening' is popular reading for our soldiers abroad (in Iraq). It provides a fitting faith for their mission — an absolute belief in the righteousness of their cause and the inhumanity of their enemies.

"It also provides a supernatural and patriotic charter for torturing people who look and think differently — a bully God represented by a bully president serving up good old bully American values to chained, naked men: 'My God is bigger than your God.'"
— Ben Feinberg, guest column, *Asheville Citizen-Times*, June 22, 2004.

38. "President Bush, who is stumbling, does not have a divine right to avoid criticism by wrapping himself in the flag and religion, and implying that critics are unpatriotic or heretical enemies of the state. That would be monarchy. We fought a revolution to kill that rotten idea for good here in America.

"President Bush has taken his aversion to criticism to a higher level. He says that he believes it is his mission to change the world, starting with the Middle East, because freedom comes from God....

"That seems to mean that if you criticize Bush's motives, you are not only unpatriotic but also anti-God.

"I always get worried when I hear politicians start talking about being agents of God's will on earth....

"That's the same approach missionaries once used to save the heathen, even if it meant killing a lot of them to bring the rest around to right thinking. It is the same approach today's radical Islamists espouse to propagate their unpleasant world view."
— Norman Lockman, syndicated column, June 21, 2004.

39. "*The New York Times* reported, 'In his recent trip to Rome, President Bush asked a top Vatican official to push American bishops to speak out more about political issues.' As Josh Marshall brightly observed: 'I guess on one level we can say we've come a long way since 1960, when John F. Kennedy had to forswear that he'd follow the instructions of the pope in his decisions of governance. Today we have a Protestant born-again who tries to enlist the pope to intervene in an American election.'"
— Molly Ivins, syndicated column, June 18, 2004.

40. "The five Americans (who) made their country a world power were in effect a junta that ignored popular will when it suited them and branded as traitors Americans who resisted the imperial lure. (Mark Twain, called treasonous for his anti-imperialism, wrote, 'They are always doing us little complements like that; they are just born flatterers, those boys.') Zimmermann calls them 'the fathers of modern American imperialism and the men who set the United States on the road to becoming a great power.'"

— *First Great Triumph: How Five Americans Made Their Country a World Power* by Warren Zimmerman, review by Charles Glass, *Harpers Magazine,* January 2003.

41. "Symbols often divide people, stifling dissent and Free Inquiry. Some people
use the flag as a gag during wartime — much as religious fanatics beat people over
their heads with the Bible....

"Too much patriotism is like too much religion — or religious fanaticism. It often
leads to xenophobia, intolerance, reactionary forms of nationalism, authoritarianism,
and fascism."

— Norm R. Allen, Jr., article, *Free Inquiry,* June/July 2004.

42. "The author of the letter, 'If US is Christian nation, why doesn't it emulate
Christ?' (AC-T, July12), asserts Christian morality is incompatible with free-market
economics, and that the state should seek guidance from Jesus Christ instead of
'Adam Smith or Friedrich Hayek.' I must disagree. Jesus did everything he did as an
individual, not as an agent of some earthly government. He didn't steal from some
people to give others loaves and fishes. He didn't form his apostles into some bureaucracy in order to cure the sick. Jesus set a great example for us, because he did his
works on his own, without government.

"His actions, his charity, his compassion, were the results of no legislation or regulation. Unlike Jesus, when the government tries charity, it first needs to steal money
from its citizens. I assert that the state cannot emulate Christian principles, because
the modern 'welfare' state is antithetical to those principles. Jesus said, 'Render unto
Caesar what is Caesar's.' Everything the state has, it got through theft and extor-
tion, not through honest trade. Free marketers have no problem with the charity of
individuals, whether mortal or divine. We just have a problem when the government
gets into the act."

— John Robinson, letter to the editor, *Asheville Citizen-Times,* July 25, 2004.

43. "Where does John Calvin fit into all this? We have him to thank for the philosophical foundations of our society. The Pilgrims who settled this country were entrepreneurs who saw America as a hybrid of commerce and religion, based on Calvin's
Geneva model. They were Christian businessmen — an oxymoron, given a rational
interpretation of the New Testament.

"Calvinists believe that being rich is a sign that God favored you. The bottom line
is that, if you're rich, it's because god loves you. This philosophy — if one can call it
that — is the basis for many historical evils, including the belief that white Anglo-
Saxon Protestants (not the Jews) are God's *true* chosen people and that they have the
God-given right to exterminate any and all heathen savages and take their property.

"Calvin's free-market interpretation of Christianity has too often led to racism
and social injustice as well as, ironically, social darwinism. This fact has been apparent since the Puritans began exterminating Indians in 1637, and it's here to haunt us
once again, thanks to Katrina. As a country, we used this philosophy to support the
doctrine of Manifest Destiny, as well as Indian removal, the Spanish-American war,
and probably Vietnam, too. And then there's the sentiment that all those Mid East
desert dwellers and Muslims deserve to die....

"If I were a christian, I would be appalled at this egregious distortion of Jesus'
teaching....

"Jesus was very clear in this: 'It is easier for a camel to pass through the eye of a
needle than for a rich man to enter the gates of heaven" (Matthew 19:24). When a
young man asked Jesus how to become a follower, Jesus replied he should sell all his
possessions and give the money to the poor (Luke 18:22).

"How Calvin and his followers managed to turn Jesus' words on their heads and transform them into the literal opposite of what he intended, a manifesto of unfettered capitalism, is nothing short of psychotic — utterly removed from reality. If I were a Christian, I'd call that other J.C. the antichrist."
— Michael Ray Fitzgerald, essay, *Free Inquiry*, Dec. 2005/ Jan.2006.

44. "A Pentagon task force will investigate the religious climate at the Air Force Academy after allegations of anti-Semitism, favoritism for born-again Christian cadets and conversion attempts by evangelicals on the Colorado Springs campus....

"The Academy's superintendent, Lt. Gen. John Rosa, told the school's civilian oversight board last month that those yielded complaints of 55 instances of religious bias in the past five years, including proselytizing by Christians, use of Bible quotes in official e-mail and an ad promoting Jesus in the base newspaper, signed by 200 academy leaders.

"The Americans United report alleges that non-Christian cadets were harassed by seniors and that Christians were allowed to display crosses in the dorms while cadets were barred from hanging non-religious items.

"The academy is in Colorado Springs, a hub of evangelical Christian groups including the international Bible Society, The Navigators and Youth with a Mission. Across Interstate 25 from the academy is the headquarters of Focus on the Family, which reaches millions on radio and is active on conservative social and political issues."
— *USA Today*, Wednesday, May 4, 2005.

45. "AU's legal team is suing the state of Iowa over a publicly funded program saturated with fundamentalist Christianity. The program, called InnerChange, was started by ex-Watergate felon-turned-religious-Right-activist Charles Colson....

"Officials at Newton Correctional Facility have essentially segregated inmates by religion. Those willing to embrace fundamentalist Christianity get perks and special treatment. Those who aren't, do not....

"InnerChange inmates, for example, get keys to their cells and private bathrooms. They have access to computers and even electronic musical instruments. They have a better chance of being paroled and receive extra visits with their family members....

"InnerChange doesn't try to hide its sectarian character. Program materials state, 'All programming — all day, every day — is Christ-centered." The InnerChange website describes the program as 'a revolutionary, Christ-centered, faith-based program supporting inmates through their spiritual and moral transformation....

"In addition to our case in Iowa, we are pursuing litigation against a county jail in Pennsylvania that offers vocational training to inmates only if they will submit to Christian fundamentalist proselytizing.

"We're also challenging a federal law that actually allocates tax money for the rebuilding of houses of worship in California....

"It's obvious the Bush Administration isn't about to let up. Congress refused to pass the plan, so Bush implemented much of it through executive orders. He set up a slush fund and started handing out taxpayer dollars to houses of worship that will play ball with him....

"Failures like that haven't swayed the ideologues in Congress. Undeterred, congressional faith-based boosters recently announced new plans to force a faith-based component on Head Start, a popular preschool program. They want to make it legal for religious groups running Head start programs to take tax dollars and yet openly discriminate on religious grounds when hiring staff....

"People don't know the whole story. They don't know that Bush, Karl Rove and others have politicized the faith-based initiative and are using it to buy support in religious communities."

— *Americans United for Separation of Church and State*, funding letter of October 2005.

CHAPTER 15. SOCIAL DARWINISM

1. "The notion of manifest destiny was reinforced by 'social Darwinism' (and) was used to justify the superiority of American capitalism by the superiority of the so-called Anglo-Saxon race. The Evangelical preacher Josiah Strong in 1885 wrote a best seller entitled *Our Country*, arguing that 'the wonderful progress of the United States as well as the character of the people are the results of natural selection.' With its biological advantages, Strong predicted, the Anglo-Saxon race 'will spread itself over the earth.'"
— *First Great Triumph: How Five Americans Made Their Country a World Power* by Warren Zimmerman, review by James Chace, *The New York Review*, November 21, 2002.

2. "Only healthy seed must be sown! Check the seeds of hereditary disease and unfitness by Eugenics."
— World War I English eugenics poster.

3. In 1921, the American Eugenics Society called for "the sterilization of 10 percent of the American population in order to prevent the suicide of the white race." Even as late as the year 1972, sixteen thousand men and eight thousand women were forcibly sterilized in the United States.

4. Indiana Senator Albert Beveridge said that God "has marked the American people as His chosen nation to finally lead in the regeneration of the world. This is the divine mission of America.... We are trustees of the world's progress, guardians of it's righteous peace."
— *First Great Triumph: How Five Americans Made Their Country a World Power*, by Warren Zimmerman, review by James Chace, *The New York Review*, November 21, 2002.

5. "Harvard's Nathaniel Southgate Shaler...taught that white supremacy derived from the racial heritage of England. The distinguished Harvard historian Francis Parkman believed that Anglo-Saxon superiority was the key to the British victory over the French in Canada. James K. Hosmer at Johns Hopkins contended that 'English institutions, English speech, English thought, are to become the main feature of the political, social and intellectual life of mankind."

— *First Great Triumph: How Five Americans Made Their Country a World Power* by War-ren Zimmerman, review by James Chace, *The New York Review*, November 21, 2002.

6. "Social Darwinism, meanwhile, is hogwash. Social scientists have long under-stood that one's economic status in society is not a function of one's moral worth. It depends largely on the economic status of one's parents, the models of success avail-able while growing up, and educational opportunities along the way.

"A democracy is imperiled when large numbers of citizens turn their backs on scientific fact. Half of Americans recently polled say they don't believe in evolution. Almost as many say they believe income and wealth depend on moral worthiness."

— Robert B. Reich, *The American Prospect*, December 2005.

7. (In 1690) "Locke published his most important work, *An Essay Concerning Human Understanding*....Until Locke's time, it had generally been believed that there were in-nate differences between the members of the aristocracy and the remainder of the population. Aristotle had maintained that the noble and wise had an inherent right to govern....And then, suddenly, (this view) was upset by...a theory that said that ev-erything we know is the product of experience, that it is learning, not heredity, that makes us what we are.

"Locke's...contemporaries reasoned (that) there was no such thing as hereditary nobility or virtue or wisdom. If environment, not birth, was responsible for the dif-ferences between human beings, then no particular class could claim the right to rule. The members of the aristocracy did not have superior 'blood,' only a better education....

(Nevertheless) "Society was not reconstructed in the years that followed. There were political transformations. The rising middle class was successful in seizing power from the hereditary aristocracy....When the Industrial Revolution arrived, new masters were substituted for the old. Farm laborers left the countryside to find work in the cities, where they were forced to work twelve-and fourteen-hour days in factories. They were not allowed either to form unions or to vote....The most in-fluential proponent of a hereditarian view of human nature [in this period] was Sir Francis Galton."

— *Evolution and Human Nature*, by Richard Morris.

8. "Today (Francis) Galton is best remembered for his studies of heredity and for his founding of the eugenics movement. Eugenics was, as one of Galton's followers put it, 'the science of the improvement of the human race by better breeding.' Believ-ing that heredity was much more important than environment, Galton concluded that efforts should be made to improve humanity's genetic makeup. If this was not done, he thought, then 'racial degeneration' was inevitable....If a study like Galton's were performed today, we would tend to think that it proved very little. We cer-tainly would not believe that it showed that people who are exceptionally successful achieve their positions through superior heredity alone....

"Galton had little patience with the view that all babies were born pretty much alike. Nor did he believe that environment or education could develop qualities that were not already present in an individual. The only thing that mattered was innate ability. Furthermore, eminence was a criterion by which ability could be judged....In Galton's view, the fact that the working classes produced few eminent people was evidence of their inferiority....The inferior...should be discouraged from producing offspring. If they continued to 'procreate children, inferior in moral, intellectual and physical qualities,' then they should be considered to be 'enemies of the state.' Pre-sumably they would be dealt with accordingly....Laws would be passed to prohibit the non gifted from inheriting fortunes, and endowments would be set up to enable the elite to multiply more rapidly. The elite would, of course, continue to treat their inferiors 'with all kindness, so long as they maintained celibacy.' ...Galton admitted... the 'inferior' races would gradually be replaced. He did not think that this would be any great loss.... (He said) 'There exists a sentiment, for the most part quite unreasonable, against the gradual extinction of an inferior race....

"It was in the United States that the eugenics movement was most influential.... American eugenicists...lobbied for the passage of sterilization laws and were influential in persuading Congress to place restrictions on immigration during the 1920s.... The American eugenicists were especially concerned about what they called the 'menace of the feeble-minded.' They believed that such social ills as crime, alcoholism and prostitution were related to subnormal intelligence, and advocated sterilization to prevent the unfit from breeding....By 1958, sterilizations had been ordered for more than sixty thousand people....Many of those subjected to the operation were not even told what was being done....

"It is no accident that Locke's ideas were taken up by the radicals who made the French and American revolutions, or that Galton's theories should have appealed to political conservatives."

— *Evolution and Human Nature*, by Richard Morris.

9. "[John D.] Rockefeller apparently had little difficulty reconciling his unscrupulous business conduct with his image of himself as a God-fearing man. He rarely missed a week teaching his Baptist Sunday-school class. In a much quoted Sunday-school address he stated: 'The growth of a large business is merely a survival of the fittest.... the American beauty Rose can be produced in the splendor and fragrance which bring cheer to its beholder only by sacrificing the early buds which grow up around it. This is not an evil tendency in business. It is merely the working-out of nature and a law of God.' When Rockefeller spoke of 'survival of the fittest,' he was making use of a phrase that had been coined by Herbert Spencer some nine years before *Origin of Species* was published. He was not referring to Darwin's idea that species evolved by natural selection, but rather to Spencer's doctrine that evolutionary ideas could be applied to human societies....

"According to Spencer's neo-Lamarckian theory, human evolution was brought about by human effort. Those individuals who strove to use their minds would pass the resulting increased intellectual capacity along to their offspring. Similarly, acquired moral character was a heritable trait....In particular, Spencer went on, governments must not enact social legislation designed to alleviate the lot of the poor. By doing so, they interfered with the weeding out of the unfit, and increased the burden of misery that future generations would have to bear. The physically and intellectually feeble had to be eliminated if the amount of human happiness was to be increased. It was best that those 'not sufficiently complete to live' should be allowed to die. It made no difference whether the 'incompleteness' consisted of lack of 'strength, or agility, or perception, or foresight, or self-control'; the fundamental law of nature had to be observed....If 'nature's failures' were not helped to propagate their kind, then the survival of the fittest would lead to the betterment of man and society alike. Spencer thought that just such a process was taking place in the United States. The varieties of the Aryan race that formed the population of that country, he said, would eventually produce 'a finer type of man than has hitherto existed.' As a result, America would eventually produce a civilization 'grander than any the world has known.'

"The proponents of laissez-faire capitalism in the United States returned the compliment by popularizing Spencer's theories and applying them to the competitive struggle. The best competitors — the fittest — would win out. This, they claimed, would lead to a continuing improvement of society. If workers were forced to labor long hours for low wages and were subjected to dangerous and unhealthy working conditions, there was nothing wrong with that. After all, Spencer had shown that, if the battle for life was made more fierce, then evolution would progress all the faster. If men like Rockefeller drove their competitors out of business, they were only accelerating the betterment of society."...

"Social Darwinism had an influence upon legislation, executive actions and court decisions alike. Naturally, Spencer's ideas were widely accepted within the Republican Party....The social darwinist philosophy was used to bolster conservative outlooks in a number of different ways. Only the evolutionary process, the conservative advocates of social Darwinism said, could improve society. Therefore one should do nothing to interfere with the competitive struggle. The idea that evolutionary changes must necessarily be slow and gradual also lent support to the conservative outlook by implying that one should do nothing to interfere with the status quo. Although it might take centuries, it was claimed, social evils would eventually disappear of themselves. Any attempt to legislate them out of existence would inevitably backfire, making the process that much slower....

"In fact, many of Spencer's ideas are still part of conservative political doctrine. Spencer was opposed to all forms of government regulation. He believed that governments had only one justifiable purpose: the administration of justice. Everything else, including the delivery of mail and municipal sanitation, should be in the province of private enterprise. In some respects, he was even more conservative than present-day extremists. For example, he was opposed to public education and argued that government-run schools could too easily be used to indoctrinate....Spencer believed that great benefits would accrue to humanity if nothing was done to interfere with this struggle. This implied that the ideal economic system was laissez-faire capitalism, and that conservative political and economic policies were intrinsically the most just."

— *Evolution and Human Nature*, by Richard Morris.

10. "According to the Italian physician Cesare Lombroso, 'born criminals' inevitably exhibited atavistic traits. They were marked with anatomical signs of their apishness and could be identified by certain physical stigmata. Lombroso compared criminals to savages. The lower races, he insisted, also had ape like features. Furthermore, criminality was normal behavior among the less-evolved peoples. Lombroso made much of the flattened nose of blacks, comparing it to the nose of monkeys. (He apparently never noticed that the thin lips of whites are more apelike than the thick ones of blacks.)....

"In England, meanwhile, the physician John Langdon Haydon Down put forward a theory that idiots were atavistic individuals. He found that many congenital idiots exhibited features that were supposedly characteristic of the lower races. Some white idiots were of the 'Ethiopian variety.' He described these as 'white Negroes, although of European descent.' Others resembled Malaysians or American Indians. And there were other types....

"The scientists of the Victorian age were blatant racists. But perhaps it would be naive to expect them to have been anything else. Racist ideas were almost universally held in those days. In this respect, the white Europeans were not very different from the members of the numerous other cultures that have existed on this planet....

"It is somewhat more difficult to forgive the Victorians for distorting scientific fact in order to justify their racial prejudices. Rather than study racial differences in a reasonably objective manner, they propounded outlandish theories that seemed to make the differences seen much greater than they really were."

— *Evolution and Human Nature*, by Richard Morris.

11. "In his influential book, *The Theory of the Leisure Class*, published in 1899, (Thorstein) Veblen launched a wry, often ironic attack upon the capitalist entrepreneurs. Unlike the social Darwinists, he did not consider them to be the 'fittest.' On the contrary, he drew upon the theories of Spencer and Lombroso, and characterized them as throwbacks to an earlier, barbarian, stage of evolution.

"The entrepreneurs, Veblen wrote, exhibited 'predatory aptitudes and propensities carried over by heredity and tradition from the barbarian past of the race.' In this respect, they resembled lower-class criminals. The competitive struggle, in Veblen's eyes, did not lead to human improvement. It did just the opposite; it tended 'to conserve the barbarian temperament, but with substitution of fraud and prudence, or administrative ability, in place of that predilection for physical damage that characterizes the early barbarian.' The capitalist businessmen, in other words, were not the evolutionarily most advanced; they were atavistic throwbacks who retarded social progress."

— *Evolution and Human Nature*, by Richard Morris.

12. "The theory of natural selection, the social-Darwinist concept of the 'survival of the fittest,' Lombroso's criminal anthropology and Galton's ideas about eugenics all found their way into Hitler's thought. Hitler makes so much use of these concepts that *Mein Kampf* can be read as a kind of perverted evolutionary ideology: 'The selection of these minds, as said before, is primarily accomplished by the hard struggle for existence. Many break and perish, thus showing that they are not destined for the ultimate, and in the end only a few appear to be chosen. In the fields of thought, artistic creation, even, in fact, of economic life, this selective process is still going on today, though, especially in the latter field, it faces a great obstacle.'

The 'obstacle,' of course, was 'Jewish-Marxist democracy.'

"Hitler was no more willing to accept the idea that political equality was desirable than he was to believe in the biological equality of the various human 'races.' He used social Darwinist arguments in an attempt to show that democracy would only further the purpose of those who were bent on promoting further racial decline. The parliamentary form of government, Hitler said, had been created by Jews and Marxists, who wanted to 'exclude the preeminence of personality in all fields of human life.' In an ideal state, he claimed, leadership would descend on those 'to whom Nature has given special gifts for this purpose.' ...

"In Hitler's view, it was the Jews who were trying to promote bastardization by spreading the idea of equality. If they were successful, he warned, this would lead to the end of Western civilization; of all the human races, the Aryans were the only ones who were capable of creating culture. If their blood became too diluted, then humanity would fall into a dark age from which it would never recover....

"Although Hitler combined the Aryan myth with a vehement anti-Semitism, he did not consider the Jews the only inferior race — every non-Aryan people, in his view, was less than fully human; blacks were 'half-apes'; Slavs were only fit to be

slaves....Even Germans of partly Aryan ancestry had no right to live if they were insane, mentally deficient, deformed, or sufferers from any hereditary disease."
— *Evolution and Human Nature*, by Richard Morris.

13. "Today the myth of Aryan superiority is so closely identified with Adolf Hitler and his National Socialist (Nazi) party that it is easy to forget that the myth gained currency in many other nations. In the United States, for example, it was transformed into a mystique of AngloSaxon racism and American imperialism. It influenced political theory as well....Near the end of the century, socialDarwinist doctrines were combined with Aryan myth in an attempt to justify militarism and national expansion. It was maintained that the concept of *survival of the fittest* could be applied to 'races' as well as to individuals. It was inevitable, the expansionists thought, that the superior races should govern."
— *Evolution and Human Nature*, by Richard Morris.

14. "'It is remarkable,' Marx said, 'how Darwin recognizes among beasts and plants his English society with its division of labor, competition, opening up of new markets, invention, and the Malthusian struggle for existence.'"
— *Evolution and Human Nature*, by Richard Morris.

15. "At approximately the same time that a racist 'anthropology' was being developed in fascist Germany, an equally absurd kind of biological 'science' was being promulgated within the Soviet Union....Trofim Denisovich Lysenko was a Soviet agronomist who had little scientific training. In the 1930s he achieved fame within the Soviet Union by publicizing the success of agricultural practices that he had developed. In reality, these practices were of little value; in many cases they even proved to be detrimental to Soviet agriculture. Nevertheless, Lysenko's influence increased throughout the decade. As it did, he developed a Lamarckian theory of inheritance of acquired characteristics and engaged in disputes over genetic theory with more orthodox Soviet scientists....In 1948, by order of Stalin, Lysenko's theories were proclaimed official state teachings. Lysenko's critics were purged, scientific journals were subjected to censorship, and textbooks were rewritten to bring them into line with all new official dogma. Lysenko's portrait was hung in all state scientific institutions, and a hymn honoring him was placed in the repertory of the State Chorus....

"Lysenko went on to invent other methods that were presumably based on the alteration of hereditary characteristics. By the 1940s, he would be claiming that one species could be transformed into another by environmental influences, that wheat could be changed into rye, cabbages into rutabagas, pine trees into firs. One of his disciples went so far as to claim to have changed a rabbit into a chicken....

"Obviously, Lysenko's theories were nonsense. However, it is far from obvious why such crackpot ideas should have dominated Soviet biology for two decades."
— *Evolution and Human Nature*, by Richard Morris.

PART FOUR. WHAT REPUBLICANS BELIEVE

Over the last three centuries at least, the conservative movement has defined itself with some precision and it has produced a fairly definite group of spokespersons to spread its propaganda. These spokespersons have variously expressed their contempt for Western liberalism, for the central ideals of the Enlightenment and the American and French revolutions, and for the democratic government of the United States. They are still defending the divine rights of kings although they now attach those divine rights to theocratic and commercial institutions rather than specifically to a divine personage. In other words, they still believe in the same old aristocracy and in all of the values it held dear and forced on the lower orders through the imposition of rigid religious, ideological, and economic dogma. Thus, as of old, the conservative movement is reactionary, elitist, and tyrannical and it is still attacking the democratic revolution that overthrew the kings, the priests, and their followers. It is liberalism that led that democratic revolution and still defends it today against the onslaught of the authoritarian conservatives.

When I speak of the Republican Party, I am not just talking about the official membership of that Party. I am talking about an ancient conservative force led today by the Republican Party. Since the Republican Party's founding a century and a half ago and except for the short period of the New Deal (from 1932 to 1968), this country has been under the control of that Party's ideology. Thus, I finger the Republican Party as the leader and the engine of a worldwide conservative movement of disparate parts. Today it has no effective opposition anywhere on earth.

The struggle now is pretty much the same as it was three centuries ago. It is still a struggle between ordinary people — workers and consumers — and the bosses who rule over the economic, political, and religious spheres. It is still a struggle between democracy and tyranny and the words of the Republicans and the old conservatives make it abundantly clear just how much they despise democratic government and embrace absolutist private power.

CHAPTER 16. CASHOCRACY

1. In the 1964 presidential campaign, H. L. Hunt supported Goldwater with his 300 radio stations which advocated "cashocracy": the more money you had the more votes you should get.
— Robert Sherrill, review of *Before the Storm* by Rick Perlstein, *The Nation*, June 11, 2001.

2. The "understanding of freedom as the unlimited accumulation of wealth was articulated by Ronald Reagan...as 'What I want to see above all else is that this country remain a country where someone can always get rich.'"
— Historian Francis Moore Lappe, interview, *The Progressive*, February 1990.

3. "The poor in this country are the biggest piglets at the mother pig and her nipples. The poor feed off the largess of this government and they give nothing back. Nothing!"
— Rush Limbaugh, radio show.

4. "Can a man possess anything without the help and consent of others? Without this tacit contract, neither profit nor property nor true industry would exist....the superfluity we see all around us is not the sum total of individual effort but the product of general industry, which with a hundred hands working in concert makes more than a hundred men could make separately.

"If I do not respect in others the rights I would have them respect in me, I make myself the common enemy of all and enjoy no more security in the iniquitous possession of my property than did the highwaymen who devoured what spoils they could take from others less fortunate than themselves."
— Jean-Jacques Rousseau, "Letter on Virtue, the Individual, and Society," published with an introduction by Jean Starobinski.

5. Imagine "a whole world turned into a parliamentary system" with people "voting every hour of every day through their mutual funds, their pension funds, their brokers, and more-and-more, from their basements on the Internet." This 'market democracy' thus will substitute "one dollar-one vote in place of the regular democracy's

---

'one person-one vote' system....I don't think there will be an alternative ideology this time around."

— Thomas Friedman, *New York Times* column, cited by *Z Magazine*, April 2001.

6. "Imagine 100 people on a new planet trying to figure out how to do the work. Suppose then one of this group says to the others: 'I have a good idea. Why don't the rest of you all go to work for me producing the means of our existence? I'll take responsibility for organizing the work process and in return take a uniquely large proportion of all the goods we produce for myself and my family and heirs.' Author Philip Green calls this a 'very strange social arrangement" and says "no one should have so much money as to exercise unchecked power over others.'"

— *Equality and Democracy* by Philip Green, review by Matthew Rothschild, *The Progressive*, December 1998

7. "'The rising value of land,' (Henry) George reasoned, is not the result of the owner's efforts but a result of the growth of society. 'If you own land, you need do nothing more. You may sit down and smoke your pipe; you may lie around like the lazzaroni of Naples or the leperos of Mexico; you may go up in a balloon, or down a hole in the ground; and without doing one stroke of work, without adding one iota to the wealth of the community...you will be rich.'"

— Michael Kinsley, article, *The Washington Post*, October 10, 19, 1989.

8. "The richest one per cent of this country owns half our country's wealth, five trillion dollars. One third of that comes from hard work, two thirds comes from inheritance, interest on interest accumulating to widows and idiot sons, and what I do: stock and real estate speculation. It's bullshit. You got ninety percent of the American public out there with little or no net worth. I create nothing. I own."

— Gordon Gekko, *Wall Street* (20th century Fox 1987), item, *Democrat Left*, Fall 2002.

9. "In the real world the American system is not very friendly to shareholders. All the proposals that shareholders 'adopted' this spring, for instance, are non-binding. Companies are free to ignore them.

"American corporations get away with this disregard because of the way corporate governance works. Investors control the corporation not by themselves but through the board of directors, which they elect.... but a healthy republic requires free elections, and corporations don't have those. In most company elections, directors run unopposed. The only way to replace them is to mount a costly proxy fight — at the challenger's expense....The typical American corporation is a shareholders republic in the same way that China is a people's republic."

— James Surowiecki, the Financial Page, *The New Yorker*, June 9, 2003.

10. "The fiscal program he (Alexander Hamilton) proposed at the treasury was based on two controversial and sweeping premises: that the American economy required supervision and strategic management at the national level; and that concentrated wealth was a blessing rather than a curse, because money concentrated became capital."

— Joseph J. Ellis, article, *The New Yorker*, October 29, 2001.

11. "The citizens of the United States must effectively control the mighty commercial forces, which they have themselves called into being. There can be no effective control of corporations while their political activity remains. To put an end to it will be neither a short nor an easy task, but it can be done."

— Theodore Roosevelt, 1910.

12. "Ideally, you'd have every plant you own on a barge."

— Jack Welch, former CEO of GE, *The Nation*, August 19, 2002.

13. When asked to define social responsibility, Welch replied, "Win. By winning, being profitable. Only then can you be a socially responsible company,"

— Jack Welch, former CEO of GE, *The Progressive*, January of 2002.

14. "Microsoft created software for the Chinese government that prevents bloggers from using words like 'freedom' and 'democracy' on the Internet, reports the *Guardian*. The agreement comes only months after Bill Gates praised China's officials, who run a mixed market economy with a Stalinist political system. 'It is a brand new form of capitalism, and as a consumer it's the best thing that ever happened,' Gates said."

— No Comment page, *The Progressive*, August 2005.

15. "A large red banner hung over the middle of each room reading, in Chinese, 'The Customer Is God and the Market Decides everything.'"

— Bill McKibben, essay, *Harper's Magazine*, December 2005.

16. "The bankers of New York City hung his (Hamilton's) portrait in the Chamber of Commerce, a gesture of respect for the one Founding Father who thought and cared a lot about money....Martin Van Buren...depicted Hamilton and the Federalists as covert monarchists who hijacked 'the spirit of 76' and sold the soul of the American Revolution to investment bankers. Jefferson's election became 'the revolution of 1800,' when the money changers were driven from the American temple."

— Joseph J. Ellis, article, *The New Yorker*, October 29, 2001.

17. "We don't pay taxes. Only the little people pay taxes."

— New York hotel queen Leona Helmsley, cited in *The Nation*, June 2, 2003 by Roy Ulrich.

18. Catherine Curtis, host of a radio talk show in 1934 and 1935 said "America owes her supremacy to capitalism....Woman, of course, is the greatest capitalist in the world. We must mobilize to save this capitalism." — *Women of the Far Right* by Glen Jeansome, book review, *The Nation*. July 1, 1996.

19. "I'd do one [a television program] on the close association between big business and big government. They pretend that they're each other's worst enemies, but they're in business together and it's destroying the country. You can't do something like that in three minutes and [CBS] won't give me an hour."

— Andy Rooney, interview, AARP's *Modern Maturity*, May/June 2005.

20. "While the likes of Rush Limbaugh and George Gilder raged against 'elitists,' CEO compensation during the decade went from 85 times more than what average blue-collar employees received in 1990 to 475 times what blue-collar workers received in 1999....

"Just one symptom of how deeply this nonstop propaganda has affected us lies in the fact that President Bush and Congress repealed the estate tax.

"The tax affects the 1.5 percent of Americans with estates of more than $2 million; they can pass along the first $2 million tax-free but have to pay now-lowered taxes on the rest. The people who brought us welfare reform on the grounds that getting $8,000 a year to raise three kids is very bad for a mother's moral fiber now tell us that Junior, who never worked a day in his life, needs to inherit $200 million tax free. And anyone who thinks otherwise is an elitist....

"We all know why such decisions are made: the political process no longer represents the people — it represents money."

— Molly Ivins, syndicated column, August 8, 2005.

21. "*Time* magazine's recent four-part expose on corporate welfare gives us an especially good look at the boundaries of acceptable opinion....The *Time* series is premised, finally, on conservative myths about welfare for the poor (but does point out that) Fortune 500 companies...have erased more jobs than they created this decade.... The officers of America's authoritarian corporations raise the plaintive cry of 'class warfare' at even the slightest mention of social inequality and corporate responsibility. Concerned, no doubt, with the low public esteem in which corporations are held (in a 1996 *Business Week* survey that startled its sponsors, 95 percent of Americans said corporations should cut their profits for the good of workers and communities), corporate America is sure to zero in on the *Times* seemingly anti-capitalist message, leaving discovery of the series deeper conservative essence to hopelessly alienated radicals of the lunatic fringe."

— Paul Street, article, *Z Magazine*, April 1999.

22. "Business enterprises like General Motors are designed to make money. They would be derelict if they didn't seek to avoid taxes and gain special subsidies. Corporate executives, after all, have a fiduciary duty to squeeze every dollar they can from every locality waving blandishments in their face."

— Norman Pearlstone, managing editor, *Wall Street Journal*, cited in a Paul Street article in *Z Magazine*, April 1999.

23. "Most American and foreign corporations operating in the United States paid no income tax between 1996 and 2000, government auditors said Friday....

"The study was done by the General accounting Office, the investigative arm of Congress."

— Associated Press report, April 3, 2004.

24. "'Can capitalism survive capitalists themselves?' asks Kurt Eichenwald in the June 30 *New York Times*....Strange question when you think about it. What is capitalism other than the principle that capitalists are the source of all value and wisdom, and that whatever they do to promote their own material interests is what's good for the rest of us; that the rule of capital is not only inevitable but the best of all possible worlds?"

— *Democratic Left*, item, Fall 2002.

25. "The dominant institution in US society is the corporation, an instrument of aggrandizement for the few that enriches its already wealthy owners through a process of commodification and privatization. This class war has been very successful for the rich. As billionaire Warren Buffet recently exclaimed: 'My class is clearly winning.'"

— Jack Rasmus, essay, *Z Magazine*, October 2005.

26. "This is an industry; it's a business. We exist to make money. We exist to put commercials on the air. The programming that is put on between those commercials is simply the bait we put in the mousetrap."

— Ted Koppel, *Washington Post*, November 8, 2005.

27. "Traditional consumption was regarded as both the privilege and the obligation of the aristocracy and gentry, that is, all those who did not have to work with their hands for a living. Gentlemen saw themselves as patrons of the great working populace and responded to unemployment among the laboring ranks by ordering another pair of boots or a new hat. In the seventeenth century Thomas Mun had argued that 'the purse of the rich' maintained the poor, and in the eighteenth century Montesquieu still agreed: 'If the rich do not spend so lavishly,' he wrote, 'the poor would die.' ...

"In the eighteenth century the rapidly increasing consumption by ordinary people of goods that hitherto had been the preserve of a tiny minority produced a revolution in the English-speaking world. It dramatically confused the social order and in the minds of elites created something of a social crisis, provoking a serious debate over luxury....When common people bought silk shirts and other luxury items, this seemed to be a serious vice and a symptom of social disarray. Although some intellectuals like David Hume defended the spread of luxury, most gentry on both sides of the Atlantic feared and condemned it, and urged common working people to be frugal and industrious and not spend money on goods that were beyond their capacities and social rank."

— Gordon S. Wood, book review, *The Marketplace of Revolution: How Consumer politics Shaped American Independence* by T.H. Breen, *The New York Review*, June 10, 2004.

28. "Karl Rove's cherished period of American history is that of the McKinley Administration (1897–1901). It was, as I read him, the seminal influence of the man who is said to be George W. Bush's brain. Rove has modeled the Bush presidency on that of William McKinley, and modeled himself on Mark Hanna, the man who virtually manufactured McKinley. Hanna had one consummate passion — to serve corporate power....

"Mark Hanna saw to it that first Ohio and then Washington were ruled by business...by bankers, railroads, and public utility corporations. Any who opposed the oligarchy were smeared as disturbers of the peace, socialists, anarchists, or worse....

"This 'degenerate and unlovely age,' as one historian calls it, seemingly inspires Karl rove today.

"The conservatives' stated and open aim is to strip from government all its functions except those that reward their rich and privileged benefactors. They are quite candid about it, even acknowledging their mean spirit in accomplishing it. Their leading strategist in Washington, Grover Norquist, has famously said he wants to shrink the government down to the size that it could be drowned in a bathtub. The White House pursues the same homicidal dream without saying so. Instead of shrinking down the government, they're filling the bathtub with so much debt that it floods the house, waterlogs the economy, and washes away services that for decades have lifted millions of Americans out of destitution and into the middle class. And what happens once the public's property has been flooded? Privatize it. Sell it at a discounted rate to the corporations. It is the most radical assault on the notion of one nation, indivisible, that has occurred in our lifetime."

— Bill Moyers, essay, *The Progressive*, May 2004.

29. "A large fraction of these Bush voters will be victims of the most blatant class warfare since the 1920s as Bush's plans entail the active destruction of a welfare state that had been built during and after the Great Depression, as well as advancing a program of class warfare extending across the globe....

"In his second inaugural speech and follow-up Bush has featured three major programs, two domestic and one global, that he intends to press in his second term: a shift from entitlements to an 'ownership society,' actions to solve the alleged Social Security crisis, and a drive to bring freedom and liberty everywhere in the interest of US security and safety. Each of these is a program for an intensified class war, scantily clothed in Bush rhetoric....

"An 'ownership society' is a code term for a privatized society, where decisions are made by substantial citizens like corporate managers, large stockholders, and banks, alone, outside the orbit of influence of the underlying population. Bush is pushing us toward an exclusively undemocratic world of ownership control while trying to make it sound very populist and democratic. It is part of the propaganda facade covering over his assault on the major entitlements program, Social Security, as part of a larger program of class warfare attacks on all instruments helpful to the underlying population."

— Edward S. Herman, Fog Watch, *Z Magazine*, March 2005.

30. "Under capitalism, no approach to politics is likely to approximate democratic decision-making because the unequal distribution of wealth and income guarantees that political power will also be distributed unequally. Those with money are able to control politicians via campaign contributions and public opinion via their ownership and funding of the media. The wealthy can threaten to, and do, engage in capital strikes — withholding their investment — to punish government policies they oppose."

— Stephen R. Shalom, Z Papers, *Z Magazine*, October 2004.

> [George W. Bush has said he wanted an "ownership" society. He obviously didn't mean that he wants us all to share in the ownership of property now owned by him and the rich class he represents and serves. That would involve the redistribution of property, a reform Republicans call "socialist" or even "communist." What he means, perhaps, is that he wants all of the property and all of the privilege concentrated in even fewer hands than now and he wants the government to represent those owners above all others, that is, above consumers and working people and certainly above the poor and unemployed. Bush doesn't like democracy. He likes oligarchy. And when he says he wants to promote "democracy" worldwide, it's no wonder the "coalition of the willing" is so small. — *Author*]

31. "Our world is one where people exist for the sake of the economy and not, as it should be, the other way around. This insane world is, above all, a *capitalist* world....

"The capitalist class is the *ruling class*, the class with the greatest amount of power, because it's the class that controls employment and monopolizes economic decision-making....

"This structural inequality erodes the promise of political democracy, perhaps nowhere more obviously than in the United States. Voting under capitalism doesn't include the right to decide on what corporations should do, whom they employ or who gets the profits.

"The inherent irrationality of capitalism, of the dictatorship of market forces, is that the object of economic growth is economic growth itself, not the satisfaction of human needs. Capitalism treats human life itself as a 'production cost.' Work, the activity through which humanity appropriates its environment, is a compulsion, opposed to relaxation, to leisure, to 'real' life. Production is ruler of the world....

"Even when the whip of the capitalist market is somewhat softened by state regulation, the system remains ruled by impersonal laws that inevitably impose themselves on the wills of every individual."

— Jason Schulman, essay, *Democratic Left*, Winter 2006.

32. "Since the Reagan years...we have been deluged by the libertarian mantra: that government is evil, that regulations and taxation have stifled the free market, that welfare is abused and needs to be drastically reduced, and that the amassing of wealth is the basic American virtue. A form of Pluto-mania has overcome us....

"Indeed, we are today in danger of developing a *hereditary aristocracy* of absentee landlords and shareholders. This trend will dramatically solidify if the taxation-reduction policies of the George W. Bush administration are not repealed. I am referring here to (a) estate taxes ('death taxes,' as falsely labeled by the Republicans), which are being reduced annually and will disappear entirely in a few years (if this is allowed to stand, huge fortunes will compound untouched), and (b) the rollback of higher tax brackets for the wealthy, including the reduction of capital gains and dividend tax rates (the current rate is 15 percent)."

— Paul Kurtz, essay, *Free Inquiry*, Dec. 2004/Jan. 2005.

33. "The people who call themselves, say, libertarians today, whatever they may have in their minds, they are advocating extreme concentration of power, in fact they're advocating some of the most totalitarian systems that humans have ever suffered under....the classical liberals, the Jeffersons and the Smiths, were opposing the concentrations of power that they saw around them, like the feudal system and the Church and royalty. They thought that ought to be dissolved....Jefferson was a good example. He was strongly opposed to the concentrations of power that he saw developing, and warned that the banking institutions and the industrial corporations which were barely coming into existence in his day would destroy the achievements of the Revolution. As I mentioned earlier, Madison within a few years was already having very strongly stated second thoughts about what he had framed and created."

— Noam Chomsky, *Class Warfare*.

34. "In the 1790s, wealthy merchants leapt to buy and trade public securities, to the delight of Treasury Secretary Alexander Hamilton, who, Fraser notes, 'conceived of the Street as an engine of future national glory....

"Hamilton conceded that stock trading 'fosters a spirit of gambling.' But he resisted market regulation....Thomas Jefferson, appalled that (as he put it) 'the credit and fate of the nation seem to hang on the desperate throws and plunges of gambling scoundrels,' doubted such a line could be drawn. The antidemocratic implications of the links Hamilton was forging between financial elites and the federal government deeply troubled Jefferson, whose critique of moneyed aristocrats as threats to the Republic helped pave the way for his party's political triumph in 1800....

"Pious Protestants considered speculation a form of gambling and thus a sin....'Wall Street is a thousand times deadlier that Monte Carlo,' hissed a character in the 1887 Broadway play *The Henrietta*....At worst, it seemed to be a species of con game....

"From the 1870s on, (J.P.) Morgan and his colleagues struggled to limit self-destructive competition, and by century's end they had engineered the massive consolidations that ushered in corporate capitalism, establishing a privately owned command economy run by financiers like themselves....

"Populists produced ferocious denunciations of the 'Money Kings of Wall Street' that depicted them as fiendish conspirators and sybaritic plutocrats out to overturn the moral foundations of the Republic....

"[Theodore] Roosevelt possessed both a 'highly developed sense of social obligation' and a contempt for financial plutocrats that 'was bred in the bone,' part of an upbringing that dismissed materialistic strivings as unworthy, debilitating, and effeminate."

— *Every Man a Speculator: A History of Wall Street in American Life*, reviewed by Mike Wallace, *The Nation*, April 18, 2005.

35. "In the early US, the corporation played a minor, subordinate role in public and economic affairs. This all changed during the Industrial Revolution as corporate activity and influence grew to the point where, in an 1886 Supreme Court decision, the corporation gained the status of a 'person' under the Fourteenth Amendment. Originally intended to grant newly freed slaves Constitutional protection, that

amendment quickly became a plaything of corporate lawyers....Between 1890 and 1910 there were 307 cases brought by corporations, 19 by African Americans. Thus, the corporation slipped into the Constitution and hijacked the notion of government of, by, and for the 'people.'

"The film...asks, 'What kind of person is the corporation?' the answer is unsettling. A series of legal decisions defined it as an immortal person required to place its owners' short-term financial interests ahead of all competing interests, including the public good. Achbar and Abbot add a unique twist when they diagnose the corporate personality based on typical harms it inflicts on others....The pattern of behavior that emerges includes 'disregard for the safety of others, inability to form lasting relationships, deceitfulness, and failure to conform to social norms.' Dr. Robert Hare, a psychologist and advisor to the FBI, concludes from this evidence that the corporate person 'has all the characteristics ...of the prototypical psychopath.'"

— Daniel McLeod, movie review, *The Corporation*, a documentary by Mark Achbar, Jennifer Abbot, and Joel Bakan, 2004, *Z Magazine*, December 2004.

36. "The Revolutionary War was fought not only for political independence from Great Britain, but also for independence from the British corporations that controlled trade and extracted wealth from the British colonies. Prior to the Civil War and the Fourteenth Amendment to the US Constitution, corporations were prohibited by their charters, issued by the individual states, from lobbying legislatures or participating in elections in any way. Because of their experience with British corporations, US citizens retained a healthy fear of all corporations; hence there were such restrictions as charters of limited duration. The large revenues to US corporations occasioned by the Civil War gave corporate America the resources to break the old mould. They engaged in such practices as hiring private armies to fight union organization and buying newspapers to shape public opinion."

— John A. Frantz, essay, *The Secular Humanist Bulletin*, Summer 2005.

37. "The ex-prime minister [of Singapore] Lee Kuan Yew...once called the citizens of Singapore "digits", as though politics were a mathematical problem. Total control of the digits, of their economic activities, their political choices, but also their private lives, was always Lee's goal. Singapore, once likened to a Disneyland with the death penalty, is truly a place where nothing is left to chance. The languages people speak, the ideal marriage partners for educated women, eating habits in public places, are all subject to elaborate guidelines, more or less forcefully imposed.

"Here, then, in this controlled material paradise, capitalist enterprise and authoritarian politics have found their perfect match. If all physical needs can be catered to — and Singapore comes as close to that blissful state as anywhere in the world — what need is there for dissent, or individual eccentricity? You would have to be mad to rebel. And that is precisely how those few brave or foolhardy men and women who persist in opposition are treated, as dangerous madmen who should be put away for the comfort and safety of all the digits.

"The new Asian model, which also owes something to South Korea when it was still being run by military regimes, and to Pinochet's Chile, is a challenge to those who still take it as a given that capitalism inevitably leads to liberal democracy, or, in other words, that a free market in goods automatically results in a free market in ideas....

"Democratic Japan developed a de facto one-party system, which is not as oppressive as Singapore's, but has made a similar pact with the middle class.... Acquiescence to the political status quo was demanded in return....Governed by bureaucratic mandarins, more or less corrupt Liberal Democratic Party politicians, and the representa-tives of big business, Japan is a paternalistic state that conforms in many respects to the Confucian tradition: obedience in return for order, security and a full bowl of rice.

"The Chinese government has also been quite successful in promoting the idea that to be critical is to be unpatriotic, especially when that system offers so many social and material benefits to the educated urban class.

"Many young, entrepreneurial Chinese have even convinced themselves that capi-talism can be a substitute for cultural and intellectual freedom. A property developer once explained to me that 'commercialization' was the best way to build a free, mod-ern society. She was the perfect example of the post-Maoist yuppie.

"Status, stability, patriotism, and wealth, then, have proved to be sufficient rea-sons for the growing middle class to accept a paternalistic, authoritarian form of capitalism without much protest....Foreign businessmen are happy with this state of affairs...And blessed is the absence of awkward trade unions, opposition parties, political dissent, and other messy manifestations of more democratic societies."

— Ian Buruma, article, *The New York Review*, April 12, 2003.

38. "Chinese people don't learn English because they love it, but because Coca-Cola and Microsoft rule the world."

— Briefly Noted quote, from Li Yang, who claims to have taught English to more than twenty million Chinese, *The New Yorker*, August 11, 2003.

39. "In an August 26 memo, the Republican National Committee declared that the media should no longer use the word 'privatization' to describe Republican pro-posals to put Social Security funds into private investments: 'It is very important that we not allow reporters to shill for Democratic demagoguery by inaccurately char-acterizing "personal accounts" and "privatization" as one and the same,' the memo asserted (*Washington Post*, 9/13/02). Never mind that the Cato Institute's Project on Social Security *Privatization* has long been the Republican Party's leading source of ideas about Social Security; the right has discovered that the word doesn't poll well, and the language has to be revised accordingly. (Cato now has a "Project on Social Security *Choice*.") Some reporters are happy to comply with the new directive; Tim Russert prefaced a question on *Meet the Press* (9/22/02) by noting, 'the Democrats say they're against...private accounts, or "privatizing" is their term.'"

— *Extra! Update*, October 2002.

40. "More than one billion people don't have access to safe drinking water.... The World Bank insists that countries privatize their water."

— Sonia Shah, article, *The Progressive*, August 2001.

41. "Right now in the US, people consume more soft drinks than any other liquid — including ordinary tap water.... Eventually, the number one beverage on earth will be soft drinks — our soft drinks."

— Coca Cola CEO Robert Goizueta, *The Progressive*, August 2001.

42. "Coke will have to seize large amounts of...clean, safe water....It is to the ben-efit of...Coca Cola to allow the quality of water to decline."

— Sonia Shah article, *The Progressive*, August 2001.

43. "'What happens to those who can't afford water once it becomes a commod-ity?' asked Juliette Beck of Public Citizen's California office. 'This whole movement is about taking water away from the public and giving it to the wealthiest developers and corporate farmers in the state.'

"'The water plutocracy keeps holding these exclusive marketing conferences to plot how to break apart the public trust,' said Wenonah Hauter, director of Public Citizen's Water for All campaign. 'They recognize that their vision of turning water into private property will not be popular once the public catches on to what they're up to.'"

— *Public Citizen News*, May/June 2004.

44. "Coca Cola is peddling drugs, albeit mild ones....Fear Coca Cola."

— Sonia Shah article, *The Progressive*, August 2001.

45. "Jackson County commissioners have made it clear what they think of John McGrew's attempts to privatize part of the Tuckasegee River. That should be the end of this bad idea....

"It is an effort toward making private a stretch of navigable waterway that belongs to the people of North Carolina. Previously, McGrew has proposed full privatization, with people paying him to fish in 'his' river....

"Public access to rivers is becoming more difficult as more and more river front property falls into the hands of people who don't want outsiders crossing their land. State and local governments must redouble their efforts to obtain access points.... And the people must be vigilant lest the threat of privatization arises again."

— Editorial, *Asheville Citizen-Times*, July 9, 2004.

46. "Robert F. Kennedy's...bill of particulars against the administration includes: scientists' reports doctored or suppressed, political payoffs to large contributors, $20 billion in federal subsidies to the coal, oil and nuclear industries, and extractive industry lobbyists appointed to oversee former clients....

"One thousand commercial fishermen (Kennedy's clients) are permanently out of work after General Electric (remember them?) dumped PCBs into the Hudson River. And GE may never pay the full cleanup cost. Everyone in the Hudson Valley, he says, has PCBs in their bodies and local towns must now rely on expensive water filtration.

"'Corporate capitalists do not want free markets, they want dependable profits,' Kennedy observes. Polluting (legal or not) is another form of subsidy, one that cheats free-market discipline."

— Thomas M. Sullivan, Guest commentary, *Asheville Citizen-Times*, January 4, 2004.

47. "American civilians own fully one third of the world's 640 million guns, and civilians around the world are increasingly armed. Clearly, some of the 1,500 weapons that the State Department approved for sale to Brazil in 1999 ended up in gang member's hands. Viva Rio has recovered more than 6,500 American made guns used in violence in recent years. In Rio alone some 5,000 to 6,000 children are armed, according to a recent BBC report.

"Small arms manufacturing in the United States is a $2 billion a year industry. The profits are handsome and the exporting companies — as well as the National Rifle Association — have considerable clout. Bob Barr, then a Republican Congressman from Georgia and a board member of the NRA, was part of the official US delegation to the 2001 UN gun conference....

"Meanwhile, the death toll mounts. Globally, an estimated 500,000 people die annually. Closer to home, the September 11 terror attacks that killed 3,000 people provoked worldwide outrage. In the two years since, more than 60,000 Americans have died from firearms; half were homicides."

— Lora Lumpe, essay, *Amnesty Now*, Winter 2003.

48. "As we have written elsewhere, some aspects of life are too precious, intimate or corruptible to entrust to the market....For ordinary citizens, the drive to privatize is most evident in health care.... the for-profit barbarians are at the gates.

"Those who favor for-profit health care argue that the profit motive optimizes care and minimizes costs. In this issue, P. J. Devereaux and colleagues add to the considerable evidence that this dogma has no clothes. Their meticulous meta-analysis demonstrates a pattern of higher payments for care in private, investor-owned hospitals as compared to private not-for-profit hospitals....

"Why does investor ownership increase costs? Investor-owned hospitals are profit maximizers, not cost minimizers. Strategies that bolster profitability often worsen efficiency and drive up costs....

"Privatization results in a large net loss to society in terms of higher costs and lower quality, but some stand to gain.... in government and not-for-profit health institutions, pay differences between the CEO and a housekeeper are perhaps 20:1. In US corporations, a ratio of 180:1 is average. In effect, privatization takes money from the pockets of low wage, mostly female health workers and gives it to investors and highly paid managers."

— *Health Letter*, Public Citizen Health Research Group, July 2004.

49. "After Faxian arrived in India in 401 AD, he...was particularly impressed by the civic facilities for medical care in fifth-century Patna:

All the poor and destitute in the country...and all who are diseased, go to these houses, and are provided with every kind of help, and doctors examine their diseases. They get the food and medicines that their cases require, and are made to feel at ease; and when they are better, they go away of themselves.

"India today has much to learn from China....Shortly after the revolution, Maoist China made an early start in providing widespread health care, and there was nothing comparable in India at the time. By 1979...Chinese on average lived fourteen years longer than Indians.

"Then, after the economic reforms of 1979, the Chinese economy surged ahead, growing much faster than India's. Despite China's much faster economic growth, however, the average rate of increase in life expectancy in India has, since 1979, been about three times as fast as that in China....

"The reforms of 1979 largely eliminated free public health insurance, and most citizens had to buy private health insurance (except when it was provided by the employer, which happens only in a small number of cases)."

— Amartya Sen, essay, *The New York Review*, December 2, 2004.

CHAPTER 17. DEMOCRATIC GOVERNMENT

1. "My goal is to cut government in half in twenty-five years to get it down to the size where we can drown it in a bathtub."
— Grover Norquist, Bush family political advisor, *The Nation*, May 14, 2001.

2. From a short, obscure article hidden on the inside pages of the newspaper and headed *President wants to privatize a high-percentage of federal jobs*: "Up to half of the nation's 1.8 million federal civilian workers eventually could find they have a new boss or, worse, no job....The Bush administration is taking steps to privatize federal jobs at an unprecedented level, and officials proposed rules Thursday to make it easier.... Bush officials said it was just a question of saving money."
— *Asheville Citizen Times*, article, November 15, 2002.

3. "If I could just get a nuclear device inside Foggy Bottom [the State Department], I think that's the answer. I mean, you get through this, and you say, 'We've got to blow that thing up.'"
— Pat Robertson, cited by Patricia Williams in her column in *The Nation*, April 3, 2006.

4. "The Bush administration's grand ambition — one can no longer say grandiose — is to roll back the twentieth century, quite literally. That is, defenestrate the federal government and reduce its scale and powers to a level well below what it was before the New Deal's centralization. With that accomplished, movement conservatives envision a restored society in which the prevailing values and power relationships resemble the America that existed around 1900, when William McKinley was president.

"Grover Norquist...confirms this observation. 'Yes, the McKinley era, absent the protectionism,' he agrees is the goal. 'You're looking at the history of the country for the first 120 years, up until Teddy Roosevelt, when the socialists took over. The income tax, the death tax, regulation, all that.'

"'Leave me alone' is an appealing slogan, but the right regularly violates its own guiding principle. The antiabortion folks intend to use government power to force their own moral values on the private lives of others. Free-market right-wingers fall silent when Bush and Congress intrude to bail out airlines, insurance companies, banks — whatever sector finds itself in desperate need. The hard-right conservatives are downright enthusiastic when the Supreme Court and Bush's Justice Department hack away at our civil liberties. The 'school choice' movement seeks not smaller government but a vast expansion of taxpayer obligations.... What the right is really seeking is not so much to be left alone by government but to use government to reorganize society in its own right-wing image."

— William Greider, article, *The Nation*, May 12, 2003.

5. "I am the federal government."

— House Majority Leader Tom De Lay, Rep. Texas.

6. "Where did the idea come from that everybody deserves free education? Free medical care? It comes from Moscow. From Russia. It comes straight out of the pit of hell."

— State Rep. Debbie Riddle, Republican, Texas.

7. "Put the jam on the lower shelf, where the little man can reach it."

— Senator Ralph Yarborough, a Texas liberal.

8. "The only reason God put Republicans on earth is to cut taxes."

— Stephen Moore, President of Club for Growth, on the Bill Maher show (TV), March 25, 2003.

9. "George Bush is an extraordinarily dangerous president, perhaps the most dangerous one in the history of the Republic, with the exception of Richard Nixon. Bush disdains civil liberties, he countenances torture, he holds himself above the laws of Congress and the treaties the United States is a party to, he has no appreciation for the environment, he fuels bigotry against gays and lesbians, he is hostile to women's reproductive freedom, he is an enemy of organized labor, he is intent on rolling back not just the New Deal but Progressive Era reforms, as well, and he has set this country on a course of war, endless war."

— Comment, *The Progressive*, March 2005.

10. "We need to create a new promise of American life that gets the government in Washington out of the way."

— Lamar Alexander, *Chattanooga Times*, July 28, 1994.

11. "There was a very real revolution in this country.... We are now in charge. Our chairmen are in charge. We can hold hearings, the kind of hearings that we want to see.... The balanced budget amendment to the Constitution, a line item veto, we'll have a crime package, a welfare reform package, a tax cut package...I would like to eliminate the Department of Education, seriously pare down the Environmental Protection Agency, OSHA...the National Endowment for the Arts, we ought to zero them out. The National Endowment for the Humanities, we ought to zero them out. And we will do a lot of that and look forward to it. By the time we finish this poker game, there may not be a federal government left, which would suit me just fine."

— Joel Bleifuss, *Asheville Global Report*, July 13 — 19, 2006. Source: *In these Times* describing a movie called *The Big Buy: Tom Delay's Stolen Congress* by filmmakers Mark Birnbaum and Jim Schermbeck.

12. "The Public be damned."

— Cornelius Vanderbilt.

13. "Public rights come first and private interest second."

— Theodore Roosevelt.

14. "Without censorship, things can get terribly confused in the public mind."

— General William C. Westmoreland, commander of the US war against Vietnam.

15. "This long and very successful effort over many, many years to get people to focus their fears and angers and hatred on the government has had its effect. We all know there's plenty to be upset about there. The primary thing to be upset about is that it is not under popular influence. It is under the influence of the private powers. That's the primary source of things we ought to worry about. But then to deal with that by giving private, unaccountable power even more power is just beyond absurdity. It's a real achievement of doctrinal managers to have been able to carry this off....

"Right now I'd like to strengthen the federal government. The reason is, we live in this world, not some other world. And in this world there happen to be huge concentrations of private power, which are as close to tyranny and as close to totalitarian as anything humans have devised, and they have extraordinary power. They are unaccountable to the public. There's only one way of defending rights that have been attained or extending their scope in the face of these private powers, and that's to maintain the one form of illegitimate power that happens to be somewhat responsive to the public and which the public can indeed influence. So you end up supporting centralized state power even though you oppose it. People who think there is a contradiction in that aren't thinking very clearly."

— Noam Chomsky, *Class Warfare*.

16. "If there is any fixed star in our constitutional constellation, it is that no official, high or petty, can prescribe what shall be orthodox politics, nationalism, religion, or other natters of opinion — or force citizens to confess by word or act their faith therein."

— Supreme Court Justice Robert Jackson, *West Virginia Board of Education* v. *Barnette*, 1943.

17. "Nothing could better illustrate the pending extinction of civil action as a tool for fighting corporate criminality than a measure that will effectively do away with many types of class-action lawsuits.... the Class Action Fairness Act is the first significant Congressional tort 'reform' victory for the radical right and a catastrophe for workers and consumers. The collapse of the Democrats...means improved chances of passing a bill curbing asbestos suits and a reworked malpractice measure that caps damages for pain and suffering and drastically limits suits over dangerous drugs like Vioxx....

"Not satisfied with nibbling away at the welfare state, already the thinnest in the industrialized West, conservatives have spent more than twenty years demonizing lawyers and ridiculing victims in order to eliminate a uniquely American right, rooted in the Seventh Amendment, that allows juries to assess damages in civil courts for corporate misbehavior.

"The right's success with the class-action bill is the story of how a group of legal extremists crafted a message, brought almost every fortune 500 corporation on board and then pumped money into organizing and seeding the culture with that message. If progressives don't match their tenacity, one of the last effective levers for social and economic justice will cease to function."

— Dan Zegart, Comment, *The Nation, March 7, 2005*.

18. "ALEC is the American Legislative Exchange Council, a corporate-funded, extremely right-wing group that sponsors conferences for state legislators and draws

up model bills that are introduced all over the country. ALEC is particularly interested in privatizing government services and deregulating everything.

"People who want to privatize prisons and schools and social services are in it for the money. The real questions of government are always: Who benefits, and who pays? And the answer given this session with jaw-dropping regularity is private corporations profit, while people pay the price in worse services....how does a private corporation do the same job and make a profit? You ask that question and you get a lot of piffle from the right about private industry is more efficient and less bureaucratic than government. Dilbert and I doubt that.

"The right says that in the private sector, pay and performance are related. I look at the CEOs of American corporations, and if there's a connection between pay and performance there, I missed it.

"Man, you stand up in the Texas House today with a bill that really will help the children of Texas and you will not get a single Republican vote.

"They are playing a different game. They are out to take government apart, and then they turn around and say, 'See, I told you government doesn't work,' and they believe in all this with a self-righteous certitude that has to be seen to be believed."
— Molly Ivins, syndicated column, May 31, 2003.

19. "The notion that any private organization is superior to any government agency is more appealing in theory than in practice. The Aug. 2 issue of *Time* quoted a conservative who is already alarmed that compassionate conservatism might benefit left-wing groups. He doesn't want to be that compassionate....

"Watching your tax money being spent on something you disapprove of is a central experience of democracy. But conventional government spending is an expression, however indirectly, of the popular will."
— Michael Kinsley, essay, *Time*, August 16, 1999.

20. "The 2004 budget is toxic. It is an epic of distortion and evasion and contradiction and misleading rhetorical ploys. The object of this malodorous epic is to outline the Bush administration's plan for plunging the nation from surplus into deficit and to cast the blame for the ensuing disaster on the very people — the retired, the sick, the poor — who will feel the brunt of its effects.

"This deficit is designed to enrich those at the very top of the social pyramid while cutting services for those lower down. This is not cyclical Keynesianism. This is not a helpful or even a merely benign program of deficit spending. It is a blueprint for sabotage. It is an instruction manual for how to power up a complicated machine and dash it headlong into a stonewall.

"Today the GOP is not the responsible government party; it is the antigovernment party. 'Government is not the solution to our problem,' Ronald Reagan famously said in his first inaugural address. 'Government is the problem.' Today the phrase reverberates across the years, echoed by a mighty chorus: Limbaugh, Coulter, Liddy, North, O'Reilly, Hannity; Fox News, Conrad Black, FreeRepublic.com; Gingrich, Barr, De Lay; Hayworth, Gramm, Santorum. Yesterday's far right is today's mainstream, and the belief that government is merely misguided has given way to the belief that government is unredeemable; that the liberals who staff it are elitist, un-American, treasonable.

"Conservatives turn a budget debate into a crusade to shut the government down. They paralyze the executive branch with harassing investigations and impeachment proceedings. They joke about assassinating a Democratic president. They fantasize about abolishing entire departments. They cut the wages of federal workers. They dream up ways to make the tax code bear more heavily on the poor, in order to turn the poor against government and 'get their blood boiling with tax rage', as the *Wall Street Journal* recently put it."

— Thomas Frank, Essay, *Harper's Magazine*, June 2003.

21. "Consider Thomas Scully, who was, until recently, the head of Medicare and the point man in the White House's effort to get its drug benefit through Congress. Last spring, Richard Foster, Medicare's chief actuary, analyzed the Bush proposal and estimated that it would cost five hundred and fifty billion dollars over a decade: roughly a hundred and fifty billion more than the President had said it would. Scully, knowing that Congress was already leery about the price tag, and that Foster's estimate might sink the bill, made sure that the numbers never got out. As Foster recalls it, Scully said that he'd fire him if they did. Foster kept his mouth shut, and the bill passed the House by one vote....

"Statistical expediency and fiscal obfuscation have become hallmarks of this White House. In the past three years, the Bush Administration has had the Bureau of Labor statistics stop reporting mass layoffs. It shortened the traditional span of budget projections from ten years to five, which allowed it to hide the long-term costs of its tax cuts. It commissioned a report of the aging of the baby boomers, then quashed it because it projected deficits as far as the eye could see. The Administration declined to offer cost estimates or to budget money for the wars in Afghanistan and Iraq.

"Presidents have tried to put their spin on the data, of course, and there have been notable episodes of deliberate manipulation, as when...David Stockman fabricated numbers in the first Reagan budget. On the whole, though, good economics has trumped politics.

"The people who have made this possible are among the most heavily scorned figures in American life — George Wallace's 'pointy-headed bureaucrats.' Career civil servants are easy targets....

"They're the only professionals in government — the only ones who can say what they think instead of what they believe their bosses or voters want them to. Their long tenures foster expertise and make nonpartisanship possible. Would we trust the unemployment numbers if, every time a new President came along, he replaced the entire Bureau of Labor Statistics with a new crop of cronies and campaign aides?"

— James Surowiecki, essay, *The New Yorker*, April 19 & 26, 2004.

22. "President Bush's administration distorts scientific findings and seeks to manipulate experts' advice to avoid information that runs counter to its political beliefs, a private organization of scientists asserted on Wednesday.

"The Union of Concerned Scientists contended in a report that 'the scope and scale of the manipulation, suppression and misrepresentation of science by the Bush administration is unprecedented."

— *Asheville Citizen-Times*, article, February 21, 2004.

23. "According to the Washington Post, top officials in the Bush administration pressured the Department of Health and Human Services to revise an early draft of a study to play down questions of inequity.

"So out went references to racial disparities, out went talk of bias among health-care providers, out went a passage describing the health gap as a national problem.

"The result: a report that offers little criticism of a health-care establishment that plainly values black and brown lives less than others....

"When the Environmental Protection Agency issued a statement on the quality of asbestos-tainted air at Ground Zero, the site of the Sept. 11, 2001, terrorist attacks in New York, the White House leaned on the agency to remove cautionary language contributed by EPA scientists. The White House also tried to chop up a 2003 EPA study in order to de-emphasize the dangers of global warming.

"There's more. A 2002 report in The New York Times found apparent administration editing of a National Cancer Institute Web site. A statement that originally said science had found no link between abortion and breast cancer had been changed to say that the evidence was inconclusive.

"The Centers for Disease Control and Prevention's Web site once reported that researchers could find no link between education about condom use and increased sexual activity. That line was removed.

"Truth doesn't change its essential character because you tell it to. Facts don't cease being facts because you cut them from a report.

"All that is expressed by those actions is a disregard bordering on contempt for the people and their right to know."

— Leonard Pitts Jr., syndicated column, January 21, 2004.

24. "Unlike his father, George W. Bush is no Republican moderate. Rather, he owes his allegiance to the modern American conservative movement, which over the past fifty years has gone from the political fringe to a position of dominion over the Republican Party, not to mention the entire US government. In the process, the modern Right has adopted a style of politics that puts its adherents in increasingly stark conflict with both scientific information and dispassionate, expert analysis in general. Small wonder, then, that Bush's presidency has been characterized by unprecedented distortions of scientific information....

"At its most basic level, the modern Right's tension with science springs from conservatism, a political philosophy that generally resists change....Consider conservative thinker Edmund Burkes' famous denunciation of the Enlightenment as an age of sophisters, economists, and calculators' in his *Reflections on the Revolution in France*. Perhaps no line better captures the tension between conservatism as a political philosophy and the dynamism of scientific inquiry."

— Chris Mooney, essay, *Free Inquiry*, Dec.2005/Jan.2006.

25. "God said, 'Earth is yours. Take it. Rape it. It's yours.'"

— Ann Coulter.

26. "Today, flat-earthers within the Bush Administration — aided by right-wing allies who have produced assorted hired guns and conservative think tanks to further their goals — are engaged in a campaign to suppress science that is arguably unmatched in the Western world since the Inquisition. Sometimes, rather than support good science, they simply order up their own. Meanwhile, the Bush White House is purging, censoring, and blacklisting scientists and engineers whose work threatens the profits of the Administration's corporate paymasters or challenges the ideological underpinnings of their radical anti-environmentalism agenda. Indeed, so extreme is this campaign that more than sixty scientists, including Nobel laureates and medical experts, released a statement on February 18 that accuses the Bush Administration of deliberately distorting scientific fact 'for partisan political ends."

— Robert F. Kennedy Jr., essay, *The Nation*, March 8, 2004.

27. "'The modern right...has ceded any right to govern a technologically advanced and sophisticated nation.' an unfair assertion? Purely political? How does *The Republican War on Science* author Chris Mooney dare to come to such conclusion? It does so

based on the numerous examples of the pernicious politicization of science by the administration of George W. Bush and the Republican-controlled Congress....

"The conservatives who dominate the Republican party have relied heavily on two key constituencies, both of which have overriding interest in the results of scientific research in certain areas. These constituencies are industry and the religious Right. Companies often invoke 'science' to challenge federal regulations and to protect profits. Religious conservatives attempt to use science to advance their moralistic objectives. And in order to win elections, the Bush White House and members of congress have bent over backwards for both groups.

"Politicians of the Right have also demanded that 'sound science' be the basis for the making of public policy, but as Mooney shows, this 'Orwellian phrase' is rhetorical cover for attempts to ensure outcomes that politicians want by seeking to discredit what they label 'junk science' that stands in the way of their goals."

— Peter Lamal, book review of *The Republican War on Science* by Chris Mooney, *Skeptical Inquirer*, March/April 2006.

28. Novak complained about those who ask, "How can Americans love their nation if they hate its government," and attacked Bill Clinton for saying that it was government-hate that inspired Timothy McVeigh to kill 168 government employees by bombing a government building. Novak then claimed he was being abused for being "politically incorrect" in his opposition to "big government" and said that "Jefferson profoundly distrusted government, even democratic government," apparently even the democratic government that Jefferson himself risked his life to help establish. Novak then concluded his speech by saying, "Never trust the government and always cherish your freedom."

— Robert Novak in a September, 1997 speech in Washington.

29. "The election of 1980 produced a majority Republican electorate that was, in many respects, a top-heavy inversion of the Roosevelt majority. By overwhelming margins, Ronald Reagan's strongest support was among the very rich, steadily declining as one moved down the income ladder. In their book, McClosky and Zaller said: 'The traditional faith in minimal government, originally associated with the desire to prevent the powerful from subjugating the weak, was now invoked to strengthen the economic power of the wealthy few. Thus capitalism and democracy, once allies against inequities of the old European order, increasingly diverged.'

"'In the 1980 campaign, we were able to make the establishment, insofar as it is bad, the government. In other words, big government was the enemy, not big business,' Lee Atwater, deputy campaign manager of the Reagan-Bush '84 Committee, said."

— *The Public Ethos: Public Attitudes Toward Democracy* by Herbert McClosky and John Zaller, review by Thomas B. Edsall, *The New Republic*, March 3, 1986.

30. "In 1798...the Administration of John Adams, faced with the threat of war with France and a growing opposition at home, moved to silence political dissent. The Alien Act allowed the President to deport foreigners he deemed dangerous. The Sedition act essentially made it illegal to criticize the government. Most of the seventeen people indicted under its provisions were Jeffersonian editors....

"Unlike the recent USA Patriot Act, the Sedition act was actually read and debated in Congress. Federalists...insisted that since the act eschewed pre-publication censorship and allowed truth as a defense, it did not violate the First Amendment. Jeffersonians insisted that for government to punish the expression of ideas endangered democracy. Jefferson's election in 1800 put a stop for more than a century to federal legislation against political dissent....

"During World War I Woodrow Wilson...insisted that people he deemed disloyal had 'sacrificed their right to civil liberties.' Stone points out that when Congress passed the Espionage Act of 1917, the first national law to punish political speech since 1798, it rejected some of Wilson's extreme proposals, including a provision authorizing the government to censor the press and punish 'disaffection.' But by 1918, when congress passed the Sedition Act, such caution had evaporated. That law forbade writing or making any statement that brought the government into 'disrepute.'"

— Eric Foner, Book review, *Perilous Times; Free Speech in Wartime From the Sedition Act of 1798 to the War on Terrorism* by Geoffrey R. Stone, *The Nation*, December 6, 2004.

31. Wilson's Sedition Act "made it a crime punishable by 20 years in prison to 'utter, print, write or publish any disloyal, profane, scurrilous or abusive language about the government.' To make certain this law was enforced the FBI created a volunteer organization christened the American Protective League. In just a few short months this watchdog group had nearly 100,000 members."

— John Zavesky, essay, *Z Magazine*, November 2004.

32. "The first time this happened was back in 2002, when my old friend sent an email with a link to a Justice Department website inviting US citizens to sign up as volunteer spies in Attorney General John Ashcroft's 'Operation TIPS.' 'I think you should look into this,' my friend wrote.

"Ashcroft, I learned, hoped these volunteers would become an army of 20 million citizen-spies, keeping track of and reporting on their neighbors. I signed up as a volunteer, and began investigating the program from inside. When I experimentally tried to call in some bogus reports on neighbors, I discovered that the Justice Department was having its TIPS volunteer spies turn their raw reports on suspicious neighbors over, not to the FBI, but to the *Fox* Network's crime-stopper show, *America's Most Wanted.*"

— David Lindorff, article, *Extra*, April 2005.

33. "In obvious panic and disarray, the GOP right wing has turned to a time-honored strategy — kill the messengers. While it slaughters Americans and Iraqis to 'bring democracy' to the Middle East, it has made democracy itself public enemy number one here at home.

"The new totalitarianism has become tangible in particular through a string of prosecutions against non-violent dissenters, an attack on open access to official government papers, and the attempted resurrection by right-wing 'theorists' of America's most repressive legislation, dating back to the 1950s, 1917, and even 1798....

"Evidence of no-warrant spying on thousands of US citizens continues to surface. Like all totalitarian regimes, this one believes its best defense is to terrorize its citizens by intruding, big brother-like, into all facets of personal life. It is moving to prosecute whoever reveals that spying is going on, including a KGB-style search for the hero who leaked Bush's warrantless wire-tap program....

"The repression has reached new theoretical levels. In recent weeks, right-wing journals, such as the *National Review*, have featured articles demanding enforcement of ancient legislation outlawing 'sedition.' With the US now 'at war,' right-wingers say it is fine for Bush to arrest and imprison those who advocate peace. In particular, they cite legislation used in the 1950s to clamp down on 'known Communists.' They also cite acts passed in 1917, during World War I, and the sedition Act, passed under John Adams in 1798. "

— Bob Fitrakis & Harvey Wasserman, Commentary, *Z Magazine*, June 2006.

34. "Every nation has a war party. It is not the party of democracy. It is the party of autocracy. It seeks to dominate absolutely. It is commercial, imperialistic, ruthless. It tolerates no opposition. It is just as arrogant, just as despotic, in London, or in Washington, as in Berlin. The American jingo is twin to the German Junker....If there is no sufficient reason for war, the war party will make war on one pretext, then invent another."

— Robert La Follette, *The Progressive*, June 1917.

35. "They tell us that we live in a great free republic, that our institutions are democratic, that we are a free and self-governing people. That is too much, even for a joke.... Wars throughout history have been waged for conquest and plunder.... and that is war in a nutshell. The master class has always declared the wars; the subject class has always fought the battles."

— Eugene Debs, 1917 speech in Canton, Ohio. For this speech, Debs was sentenced to ten years in prison by the Supreme Court for violating the Espionage Act.

36. "It should have shocked the media, whose job it is to protect our civic institutions, that the Congress of the United States is run today as a rampantly undemocratic fief. Any casual conversation with a Democratic Hill staffer will lead without fail in the inevitable direction: They don't see bills, they don't know when something's coming out, they don't know half the time what they're voting on. From Republicans emanate occasional public grumblings about how things are run — grumblings that tend always to be recanted two days later. [See Robert Kuttner, "America as a One-Party State," February 2004]....

"Isn't the lack of democracy in Congress a bigger problem? Unless I've really missed something important, we have yet to see a major newspaper run an investigative series on the death of democracy inside the very building where our democracy is supposed to be acted out."

— Michael Tomasky, essay, *The American Prospect*, May 2005.

37. "The press is the hired agent of a moneyed system, and set up for no other purpose than to tell lies where their interests are involved."

— Henry Adams, cited by Norman Solomon, Media beat, *Z Magazine*, June 2002.

38. "The most significant factor in John Kerry's defeat was that, according to exit polls, 79 percent of voters who said terrorism or national security determined their vote chose the chicken hawk over the war hero.... Based on the evidence, it is almost a perfectly irrational reaction to reality. Everything the Bush Administration has done in the security realm has proved not merely wasteful and ineffective but counterproductive....

"Almost all reports would appeal to any sane person who believes, for instance, that when a particular group attacks your nation, it is a good idea to fight those people rather than another group of people who may speak a similar language, have a similar skin color, and practice the same religion but had nothing to do with the attack....

"Speak sensibly about foreign policy, and even if they agree with you, they'll go for the guy with the gun."

— Eric Alterman, column, *The Nation*, June 6, 2005.

39. "The founding document of American populism — the People's Party Platform of 1892 — called for a graduated income tax and government ownership of the railroads and the telegraph and telephone systems. 'We believe that the powers of government — in other words, of the people — should be expanded...to the end that

oppression, injustice, and poverty shall eventually cease in the land,' declared the original populists. Talk like that gets you branded a liberal elitist, or worse, these days.

"Yet many of the conservative types who preen as populists — Gingrich and his congressional GOP cohorts, Rush Limbaugh, *The Wall Street Journal* editorial page — not only oppose these Clinton agendas but do so in classically anti-populist terms. They accuse the Clintons of stirring up 'envy,' 'divisiveness,' 'class hatred' and so on."

— TRB column, *The New Republic*, December 20, 1993.

40. "No taxes except excise tax and tariffs....Government doesn't work.... Poverty programs perpetuate poverty....Social Security pensions always disappear when you retire.... Government programs always go astray and government just grows and grows and grows."

— Libertarian Party flyer in 2000.

41. "Government is not the solution to our problem; government is the problem."

— Ronald Reagan over and over again.

42. "The impassioned political argument in American society today should be the one over the sovereignty of corporations and their entrenchment into every institutional system. The giant multinational corporations set the parameters and the paradigms. They get into kid's minds at age two, or three, or four. Every day another frontier falls to commercial intrusion. And when that happens, we begin to lose our sovereignty. We slowly lose the structure we have developed to defend the people, which is our national government. So this is, to me, the dividing line. Either the people are going to recover their country or it's gone forever. There are certain things that shouldn't be for sale."

— Ralph Nader, Forum, *Harper's Magazine*, August 2004.

43. "Americans really feel that they have the best standard of living in the world. They don't, but they don't know they don't. Virtually every nation in Western Europe has universal health care. In Sweden, Norway, and Holland, the social benefits are so generous that poverty has been practically eliminated. Wages in most European countries now outpace wages in the United States."

— Ron D. Daniel's, Forum, *Harper's Magazine*, August 2004.

44. "The living wage: Today we have 47 million full-time workers making less than $10 an hour. Twenty-five percent of all workers make $8.70 an hour or less. And this affects their whole lives. Without a living wage, Americans are forced into frantic, desperate attempts to find additional part-time work, to find day care and all the rest. Wages are the issue that can connect politics to the personal daily experience. It's not a difficult issue; it's not a derivative issue. It's a direct issue."

— Ralph Nader, Forum, *Harper's Magazine*, August 2004.

45. "So along came President Franklin D. Roosevelt with his New Deal. For some reason, FDR thought government could actually make things better for people. He thought, crazily, that government should make sure businesses played fairly. What a concept."

— Joan Claybrook, essay, *Public Citizen*, November/December 2003.

46. "I don't understand how poor people think."

— George W. Bush.

47. "We're the only nation in the world where all our poor people are fat."

— Sen. Phil Gramm, Texas.

48. "Unfortunately, trust in American society is decreasing. Many Americans do not trust their coworkers, friends or family. They do not trust their bosses. Most of all, Americans do not trust the government."

— Chris Cooper, assistant professor of political science, opinion, *Asheville Citizen-Times*, June 13, 2004.

49. "The number of federal workers in relation to the population continues its 20-year decline. Federal employment has for years been rather stable. The big jump in the number of government employees is at the state and local levels. Cities, counties and states now have four to five times more employees than Uncle Sam.

"Since the 1950s, the federal work force has been better trained, educated and paid than the average private sector worker, to handle programs that in size, cost and importance dwarf anything in industry."

— Mike Causey, The Federal Diary, *Washington Post*, August 21, 1988.

50. "Since 1963, the federal work force has held relatively steady at between 2.5 million and 3 million. Real federal spending has risen tenfold. That's because since World War II, Washington has created few agencies like the Forest Service that deliver services directly to citizens. Rather, the big growth has been in 'wholesale' government in which Washington provides funds and legal authority to third parties (private contractors, nonprofits, state and local governments) who in turn deliver the services. This vast and long-standing trend seems to have eluded many conservatives, who keep calling for more privatization and federalism in order to stem the growth of Big Government.

"The greatest recent government catastrophes have all occurred in 'steering' programs, including the S&L debacle, the HUD scandal and the Department of Energy's nuclear weapons plant cleanup mess. If anything, these programs suffered from not having enough federal employees monitoring them."

— Paul Glastris, article, *The New Republic*, October 11, 1993.

51. "The right wing speaks regularly about the menace of 'big government' and the importance of shrinking 'the beast,' but they include in government only its civil functions, not the military establishment or police, which are put in a separate category. This is based on their view that 'government' must be considered bad, whereas the military and police are good. Thus government in its usual meaning didn't shrink under Reagan and isn't being down-sized under Bush-2 because the increase in military and police outlays more than offsets any cutback in civilian expenditures."

— Edward S. Herman, Fog Watch, *Z Magazine*, January 2004.

52. "A small group of businessmen now controls the American machine. The bombers cannot take off, the missiles cannot fly, the warships cannot get underway, and the robots cannot do their deadly duty until these men assent. They are the CEOs of a small cluster of private organizations, and they share the power once vested exclusively in the President and Congress — the power to make war or peace....

"Seven hundred thousand or more employees work in the bowels of the American military machine, and the value of their contracts runs into the hundreds of billions of dollars. Approximately 20,000 soldiers fighting on the American side in Iraq — one out of every ten — are hired gunmen....

"The extent to which war making has been turned over to these organizations is not well known, and this is because those in charge do not want it known."

— Nicholas von Hoffman, essay, *Harper's Magazine* / June 2004.

53. "'The day is at hand,' (Henry) Adams continued, 'when corporations far greater than Erie, swaying power such as has never in the world's history been trusted in the

hands of mere private citizens, ... after having created a system of quiet but irresistible corruption — will ultimately succeed in directing government itself. Under the
American form of society, there is now no authority capable of effective resistance.'"
    — Arthur Schlesinger Jr., cited in an article in *The New York Review*, March 27,
2003.
    54. "We know companies are manipulative but it's the nature of business to go
after every dollar that's legally available. Don't place the blame on the company; place
the blame on government."
    — Ohio state senator Charles Horn, cited by Paul Street, article, *Z Magazine*, April
1999.
    55. "'Reaganites'...bluster about the need to chop government down to size ran
afoul of unpleasant realities....(Then) they convinced themselves that government
spending need not be reduced at all. What made this reversal at least theoretically
possible was, of course, supply-side economics....Conservatives financed their shopping spree by borrowing 'on a scale never before seen in human history.' Reagan's two
administrations 'piled up more debt, in inflation-adjusted dollars, than Roosevelt
and Truman had incurred to win World War II,' Frum reports. 'In just four years,
George Bush accumulated three times more debt (again adjusting for inflation) than
Woodrow Wilson had taken on to fight World War I.'"
    — *Dead Right* by David Frum, review by Alan Pell Crawford, *The Nation*, December
5, 1994.
    56. "The Vehicle and Highway Safety Act of 1966 saved 1.2 million lives over the
next thirty years." [This was the Nader bill.]
    — *The Progressive Populist*, December 15, 2001.
    57. "Its accident rate, for example, is half that of conventional roads."
    — *The Miami Herald* on the interstate highway system, August 1, 1996.
    58. "In 1831 Alexis de Tocqueville asked why the American roads were so bad.
Former South Carolina Congressman Joel Roberts replied, 'In general our roads are
in very bad repair. We haven't the central authority to force the counties to do their
duty. The inspection, being local, is biased and slack.'"
    — *The Miami Herald*, August 1, 1996.
    59. In 1996, the Republicans put forth a federal law to speed up the drug ap-
proval process. It would allow drug companies to choose a third-party review by
private firms friendly to the drug companies. The consumerists said, "There is little
question that unsafe and/or ineffective products which current FDA review keeps off
the market would reach American patients under this dangerously expedited private
pathway, necessarily fraught with conflict of interest."
    — Ralph Nader's *Public Citizen Health Letter*, cited in *The Progressive Populist*, Decem-
ber 15, 2001.
    60. "Today, 135 million workers are paying into the Social Security system, and
records of their earnings and payments are being maintained by the Social Security
Administration (SSA). At the same time, SSA is serving 42 million Social Security
beneficiaries and 5 million individuals who receive Supplemental Security Income
(SSI) benefits. Yet out of each dollar paid in Social Security taxes, *only about one penny*
goes to pay for the administrative expenses necessary to run the largest social insurance system in the world.
    "Every month, 99.8 percent of SSA's beneficiaries receive their checks in the right
amount, at the right address, and on time. This service has continued for more than
half a century.

"Every working day, about 70,000 applications are taken and, for 94 percent of them, a response is in the mail to the customer in fewer than 5 days....Every year, more than 220 million earnings reports are received from thousands of employers across the country; 99.6 percent of those earnings are accurately posted to SSA records.

"Every year, more than 3 million new claims for monthly benefits are filed by retirees and their dependents, as well as by widows, widowers, and children of workers who have died. These claims are processed and the first check is ready to mail in about 14 days — with a 99.8-percent accuracy rate."

— From the *Monday Morning Highlights*, a Federal Bureau of Prisons internal newsletter for its employees (1994).

61. "All developed countries have SS (Social Security) and in some, the tax is far higher. Several countries have tried privatization and it has been a disaster — even in Britain. (Incidentally, the CEO of Britain's National Association of Pensions heaped praise on our SS, '...it delivers efficiencies of scale that most companies would die for,' she said.

"SS pays low-income workers a far higher percentage of earnings than upper income workers. This, and the disability and widow's benefits, would terminate under a privatization plan that was not tax subsidized....

"Taxing any SS benefits is shameful, but privatization would not change this. SS is one of our nation's finest achievements. Any attempt to abolish it is — even by Bush standards — really dumb."

— Carl Davis, letter to the editor, *Asheville Citizen-Times*, June 21, 2006.

62. "Republicans worked hard to keep up a drumbeat of publicity on Medicare's troubles. Rep. Bill Thomas (R-California.), chairman of the House Ways and Means committee on Medicare, has been particularly anxious to ensure that Americans see a crisis in the Medicare program.... Attacks on the Medicare program have become commonplace. Even Bob Dole proudly reminisced about voting against the creation of Medicare. 'We knew it wouldn't work in 1965,' he said.

"Over its thirty year history, Medicare has proved very successful. When it was enacted in 1965 only half the elderly in this country were covered by health insurance. Private insurance had failed to solve this problem, so the government stepped in with the Medicare program and today 98 percent of the elderly have health insurance coverage."

— *Public Citizen Health Research Group*, Health Letter, December 1996.

63. After saying that all the problems in both the United States and the Soviet Union came from the civil servants and not from leaders like him and the communist leaders, Ronald Reagan told students at Moscow State University, "The fact is bureaucracies are a problem around the world.... The sins of governments...and this includes our own government, is that the bureaucracy...has one fundamental rule above all others: preserve the bureaucracy."

64. "Everyone knows it's against the law to steal. That is, unless the government does it....'Thou shalt not steal' is one of the Ten Commandments....What we need is not to reinvent government but to uninvent it."

— *Chattanooga News-Free Press*, editorial, September 5, 1993.

65. "Regulation is the oppressor and corporations are our clients."

— Michael Powell, son of Colin Powell and the FCC Chairman under George W. Bush, *Harpers*, August 2002.

66. "Do away with the IRS as we know it."

— Bob Dole

67. "Kill it! Drive a stake through its heart! Bury it, and hope it never rises again."
— Steve Forbes, *The Washington Post*, Carl Rowan column, August 10, 1996.

68. The old "own more than their share of homes and benefit too much from inflation." There should be severe limits on "immigration, affirmative action, help for the disabled and mentally retarded and on Social Security and Medicare." The elderly have "a duty to die and get out of the way."

— Conservative Richard Lamm, former Democratic governor of Colorado, article by Joan Beck, *Chicago Tribune*.

69. "It wasn't until the sixteenth century on the Continent and 1753 in England that legal formalities to validate marriages were even instituted; prior to that, a declaration that you had already married sufficed. When the church and later the state started sticking their noses into the marriage business, elaborate rules and rituals, licenses and restrictions, began to be imposed....State power consolidated itself...by asserting control over popular and informal local customs such as marriage rites; licensing marriage and regulating divorce were formative elements in the evolution of modern statehood. Obviously, to the extent that the state could intervene in the daily lives of the citizenry, its power grew. Unregulated populations were potentially seditious ones.

"Today, submitting to such regulations seems entirely natural, but let's not forget that licensing our life decisions (not to mention regulating desire) remains a tool of modern population management."

— Laura Kipnis, essay, *Harper's Magazine*, June 2005.

70. "Ban books because they prevent students from being proud to be Americans....Where does it say we have to focus on other cultures? We are a white, Christian, British, Protestant nation....One book that should be banned is the biography of Martin Luther King because it doesn't say he was a leftist hoodlum with significant communist ties."

— Frank Borzellieri, New York City School Board member, 1994.

71. "The book...concluded that 'democratic control of schools is inherently inefficient and promotes bureaucracy.' It says further, 'It is of enormous importance that most people *think* private schools are superior to public schools.' With regret, it goes on to say that 'Americans have a public school ideology,' that 'Many...simply like the idea of a public school system...see it as local democracy' and 'admire the egalitarian principles.'"

— *Schools, Vouchers, and the American Public* by Terry M. Moe, review by Richard Kahlenberg, *The Nation*, November 26, 2001.

72. "Rarely is the question asked: is our children learning?"
— George W. Bush, *cited by Z Magazine*, April 2001.

73. "There were vast fortunes to be made, after all, in an economy based on mass production and organized to favor the large corporation rather than the small business or the family farm. But mass production required mass consumption, and at the turn of the twentieth century, most Americans considered it both unnatural and unwise to buy things they didn't actually need. Mandatory schooling was a godsend on that count.

"In the 1934 edition of his book, *Public School Administration*, Elwood P. Cubberly (said), 'Our schools are...factories in which the raw products (children) are to be shaped and fashioned....And it is the business of the school to build its pupils according to the specifications laid down.'

"School trains children to be employees and consumers.... Well-schooled people are conditioned to dread being alone, and they seek constant companionship through the TV, the computer, the cell phone, and through shallow friendships quickly acquired and quickly abandoned.

"Our schools really are...drill centers for the habits and attitudes that corporate society demands. Mandatory education serves children only incidentally; its real purpose is to turn them into servants."

— John Taylor Gatto, Essay, *Harper's Magazine*, September 2003.

74. "Books with system-supportive themes regularly obtain financial support from right-wing foundations, think tanks, affluent individuals, and publishers....

"This lavish funding reflects the deliberate corporate and right wing effort to alter the intellectual climate by underwriting the production and dissemination of proper thoughts....

"These institutions also push the writings of these proper thinkers with advertising and publicity, sponsored book tours, the distribution of op ed columns, arranging TV and talk show appearances, and by generous donations of their books to libraries and schools."

— Edward S. Herman, article, *Z Magazine*, April 1999.

75. "The aim is...simply to reduce as many individuals as possible to the same safe level, to breed and train a standardized citizenry, to put down dissent and originality. That is its aim in the United States...and that is its aim everywhere else."

— H. L. Mencken, writing about education, *American Mercury*, April 1924.

76. The nation's schools failed to respond to the September 11th terrorist attack with enough "anger, patriotism, and support for military intervention." Professors resorted to 'moral relativism' and some even "pointed accusatory fingers at their fellow Americans." Their message was 'Blame America first."

— From a report called *Defending Civilization* by Lynne Cheney, Martin Peretz, Irving Kristol, and William Bennett.

77. "'What's analogous to McCarthyism is the self-appointed guardians who are engaging in private blacklisting,' says Eric Foner, professor of history at Columbia University. 'That's why the Lynne Cheney thing is so disturbing: Her group is trying to intimidate individuals who hold different points of view. There aren't loyalty oaths being demanded yet, but we seem to be at the beginning of a process that could get a lot worse and is already cause for considerable alarm.'

"We've been here before. From the Alien and Sedition Acts to Lincoln's suspension of habeas corpus and his imprisonment of antiwar editors, from the suppression of speech during World War I and the Palmer Raids to the internment of Japanese Americans during World War II and the repression of the McCarthy days, the government has seized upon times of peril to scapegoat immigrants and to suppress liberties."

— Article by Matthew Rothschild, *The Progressive*, January 2002.

78. The Columbine High School shootings were "the fault of day care and the teaching of evolution in schools."

— Tom De Lay.

79. "After September 11, an essay was published from the National Association of School Psychologists. Its message to educators was: 'Explain that all Arab-Americans are not guilty by association or racial membership.' This entirely reasonable statement aroused the hatred of the Republicans and they went on the attack.

"The smear began on August 19, with a front-page article in the *Washington Times* by that paper's Ellen Sorokin (who said the article advised) 'teachers to take a decidedly blame-America approach.' She singled out a quote advising teachers to avoid 'suggesting that any group was responsible' for the September 11 attacks. She said that the NEA lessons 'can be seen as an affront to Western civilization,' and that they 'defend all other cultures except Western civilization.'

"Then, conservatives began claiming that the NEA was telling teachers not to blame Al Qaeda for last year's attacks. 'The liberal hold on our education system amounts to a kind of moral disarmament of the nation,' asserted Mona Charen (*Baltimore Sun*, 9/2/02.) George Will (*Washington Post*, 8/25/02) declared the NEA and its ilk 'a national menace.' 'The folly of the NEA is staggering,' pronounced *US News & World Report's* John Leno (9/9/02)."

"Most journalists were too cowardly to expose this vile dishonesty but on the evening of her first attack, Robert Kuttner of *American Prospect* guested on Fox's *O'Reilly Factor* (and) laid it right on the line. 'I would say the column in the *Times* is about the most dishonest piece of journalism I've read in years,' he said. 'This is just a completely trumped-up hoax of a charge.'"

— *Extra! Update*, October 2002.

80. "In 1994, Lynne Cheney attacked the *National History Standards* as anti-Western, anti-dead white male, anti free enterprise, and politically correct. She used the Gingrich tactic from his GOPAC handbook: 'Go negative early...never back off...use minor details to demonize the opposition.' Rush Limbaugh, instructed by Cheney via Newt's car phone, tore up history books on national TV in a rage. Charles Krauthammer called the standards an attack on America and 'learning itself.' The *Washington Times* implied they supported communism and attacked America."

— *History on Trial: Cultural Wars* by Gary B. Nash, review by Michael Berube, *The Nation*.

81. "History is for cowards and losers."

— Conservative motivational speaker, *Z Magazine*, April 2001.

82. "One of historian Harold Rugg's conservative critics complained that he was trying 'to give a child an unbiased viewpoint instead of teaching him real Americanism. All the old histories taught "my country right or wrong." That's the point of view we want our children to adopt. We can't afford to teach them to be unbiased and let them make up their own minds.' Rugg's history textbooks were burned in Bradner, Ohio before World War II and the National Association of Manufacturers attacked the books for 'communist overtones and bias against free enterprise.'

— *History on Trial: Cultural Wars* by Gary B. Nash, review by Michael Berube, *The Nation*.

83. "When I lobbied for Planned Parenthood, I learned that many legislators adopted anti choice positions early in their careers for various reasons. Some were influenced by harassment, including their children in Catholic schools receiving failing grades in retaliation for a pro-choice vote, an elderly mother verbally attacked while grocery shopping and phone calls to children saying, 'Your daddy murders babies.'"

— Letter from Liz Hrenda, *The Nation*, December 2, 2002.

Chapter 18. Communists, Democrats, and Liberals

1. "Communists are everywhere...in factories, butcher shops, street corners, in private businesses."
— Howard McGrath, Attorney General, Truman Administration.

2. "The Democrats are on the side of the communists who are about to force the country to take the last step into a thousand years of darkness."
— Ronald Reagan in Goldwater's 1964 campaign, cited in *The Nation*, June 11, 2001.

3. "We have ten years. Not ten years to make up our mind, but ten years to win or lose — by 1970 the world will be all slave or all free."
— Ronald Reagan, Goldwater campaign of 1964, *The Nation*, June 11, 2001.

4. The Democratic Party is "the silent partner — the indispensable ally — of revolutionary communism in the Third World....It wants the other side to win....Liberalism is the dominant wing of the Democratic Party and has passively collaborated with Moscow and Managua....Americans of the left and the right no longer share the same religion, the same values, and the same codes of morality. We only inhabit the same piece of land."
— Pat Buchanan, Norman Ornstein article, *The Washington Post*, July 26, 1987.

5. "Nobody in the military system ever described them as anything other than communism. They didn't give it a race, they didn't give it a sex, they didn't give it an age. They never let me believe it was just a philosophy in a man's mind. That was my enemy out there."
— Lt. William L. Calley, Jr., platoon leader, Charlie Company, Eleventh Brigade, Americal Division, US Army, testifying at his trial for the massacre of 567 old men, women, children, and babies at My Lai in Vietnam.

6. "We believe that men high in this government are concerting to deliver us to disaster. This must be the product of a great conspiracy, a conspiracy on a scale so immense as to dwarf any previous such venture in the history of man. A conspiracy of infamy so black that, when it is finally exposed, its principals shall be forever deserving of the maledictions of all honest men."

— Senator Joseph R. McCarthy.

7. "There are 50,000 professors...who are anti-American, they're radicals, they identify with terrorists, they think of them as freedom fighters. It's a huge danger for the country.'

— David Horowitz, cited by Patricia Williams in her column in *The Nation*, April 3, 2006.

> [Actually, it was Ronald Reagan who called the terrorists "freedom fighters." When the Afghani leaders of the Mujahedeen visited him in the White House, he saluted them as freedom fighters. These people represented the Arab forces in the Afghanistan resistance, including bin Laden, Al Qaeda, and those who became the Taliban after studying in Pakistan in Wahhabist schools funded by the Reagan administration and set up by the Arabists. Thus, it is Horowitz who is anti-America and radical and who identified with Reagan's terrorists and thought them freedom fighters until it became politically convenient for him to change sides. — Author.]

8. "A continuing myth perpetrated by the left wing...is that fascism is a conservative 'philosophy.' National Socialism was liberal to the core in its concept and execution. It is understandable why left-wingers would not want to be associated with Nazis, who were responsible for the extermination of 6 million Jews. The easy way out is to blame it on conservatives. In addition to Hitler, the 20th century was replete with exponents of liberalism. The USSR had Stalin, China had Mao, Vietnam had Ho, Cambodia had Pol Pot, Korea had/has Kim and Cuba has Castro. These liberals were and are unceasingly engaged in abusing, murdering and terrorizing their own peoples. Liberals should take an honest look at history before condemning political conservatives, based on the atrocities committed by Muslim fanatics."

— Joseph H. Moore, letter to the editor, *Asheville Citizen-Times*, June 9, 2004.

9. "Mr. BM, the initials suit you well. You are full of it. And after reading your piece on the Iraqi prison abuse I have come to the conclusion, and am totally convinced you are a communist....I do not consider you an American citizen by conviction, only one fortunate to be born here. I believe if conflict were to rise up here in this nation you would be a turncoat. Just as I feel you are one now."

— Unidentified letter to local columnist Bruce Mulkey from a reader, *Asheville Citizen-Times*, June 12, 2004.

10. "Taking the cold war away from me is like taking horses away from Dick Francis....I think of liberalism as a kind of virus against which there is not a dispositive remedy." He promised to continue the attack against "our enemy, wherever our enemy appears, in whatever form he appears."

— William Buckley, article, *The Washington Post*, October 6, 1990.

11. "Leftist-turned-rightist author David Horowitz urged Republicans to 'stop being so polite.' Call the liberals what they truly are, he advised: 'totalitarians.'"

— David Corn, article, *The Nation*, March 12, 2001.

12. "Long ago, there was a noble word, 'liberal,' which derived from the word free [libre]. Now a strange thing happened to that word. A man named Hitler made it a term of abuse, a matter of suspicion, because those who were not with him were against him, and liberals had no use for Hitler. And then another man named McCarthy cast the same opprobrium on the word. Indeed, there was a time — a short but dismaying time — when many Americans began to distrust the word that derived from free. One thing we must all do. We must cherish and honor the word free or it will cease to apply to us...."

— Eleanor Roosevelt

13. "Anarchism to me means a society in which you have a democratic organization of society.... So I see anarchism as meaning both political and economic democracy, in the best sense of the term.

"I see socialism, which is another term that I would accept comfortably, as meaning not the police state of the Soviet Union. After all, the word 'socialism' has been commandeered by too many people who, in my opinion, are not socialists but totalitarians. To me, socialism means a society in which the economy is geared to human needs instead of business profits."

— Howard Zinn, interview with David Barsamian, *Z Magazine*, May 2006.

14. "Another World is Possible."

— Theme of the World Social Forum.

15. "We are America. Those other people are not."

— Chairman of the Republican National Committee in 1992 to a national TV audience.

16. Democrats are 'the enemy of normal Americans.'

— Newt Gingrich description of Democrats.

19. "More than 30 percent of Americans happily answer to the appellation 'conservative,' while 18 percent call themselves 'liberal.' And yet...a super-majority of more than 60 percent takes positions liberal in everything but name....

"In a May survey published by the Pew Research Center for the People and the Press, 65 percent of respondents said they favor providing health insurance to all Americans, even if it means raising taxes, and 86 percent said they favor raising the minimum wage. Seventy-seven percent said they believe the country 'should do whatever it takes to protect the environment.' A September Gallup Poll finds that 59 percent consider the Iraq War a mistake and 63 percent agree that US forces should be partially or completely withdrawn....

"In fact, all that's necessary to discredit an individual or an idea in the present poisoned atmosphere is to apply the word 'liberal,' which conservatives equate with 'treason,' 'slander' and 'treachery' (Ann Coulter); 'idiocy' (Mona Charen); 'Communism' (David Horowitz); inspiration for child murder (Newt Gingrich); Islamic terrorism (Andrew Sullivan, Christopher Hitchens, Horowitz again); and priestly pedophilia (Rick Santorum)."

— Eric Alterman, column, *The Nation*, November 7, 2005.

20. With eleven rich men (three past presidents of the National Association of Manufacturers), Robert Harold Winborne Welch founded the John Birch Society in Indianapolis in December of 1958. Goldwater said, "I am impressed by the type of people in it. They are the kind we need in politics." Mormon elder Ezra Taft Benson was a member. Dennis Kitchel, Goldwater's campaign manager in 1964, was a member. Cardinal Cushing praised Welch and the JBS as did H L. Hunt.

21. "Hitler believed the two biggest evils in the world were capitalism and communism. Hitler believed if he could defeat communism in the East, he could then concentrate on defeating capitalism in the West, and then socialism could rule the world. 'Nazism' was an American euphemism for 'national socialism.'

"In any area that came under national socialist control, the people were stripped of their guns. The only people allowed to have guns were the military branch and the national socialists.

"Hitler was a strict vegetarian and didn't want anyone to eat meat in his presence.

"So, according to the BBC documentary, Adolf Hitler was a vegetarian socialist who believed in gun control. If Hitler were alive today and living in America, which of the two major political parties would he belong to based on the three facts as presented by the BBC documentary?"

— David Council, letter to the editor, *Asheville Citizen-Times*, November 17, 2003.

22. "I say fear the civilians. They're taking over."

— Goldwater to the Military Order of the World Wars in a speech in 1963, *The Nation*, June 11, 2001.

23. The John Birch Society posted billboards all over the country saying Chief Justice Earl Warren was a communist and should be impeached and hanged. Birch founder Robert Welch said the "State Department deliberately surrendered China to the communists," Ike had "consciously served the communist conspiracy all his life." Civil rights were part of the communist conspiracy; labor unions, churches, schools, and the government were all infiltrated by communists.

24. "Herbert Marcuse's 1934 essay, 'The struggle Against Liberalism in the Totalitarian View of the State'.... described these right-wing intellectuals' frequent inability to pin down the exact source or nature of the supposed liberal threat: 'the concept "liberal" often serves only for purposes of defamation, and political opponents are "liberal" no matter where they stand, and are as such simply "evil." However different the two nations and eras may be, this diffuse resentment is as characteristic of the right in the contemporary United States as it was of Germany in the 1930s.'"

— Casey J. Servais, letter to the editor, *Harper's Magazine*, April 2006.

25. "When [Schlafy] wasn't attacking [Melvin] Price for championing 'big government and big spending' and coddling Communist sympathizers — 'The New Deal party was extremely slow in realizing the dangers of Communism, but my opponent, Melvin Price, was even slower than most of his party' — she was accusing the Truman Administration of treason. The Administration, she declared, handed over atom-bomb ingredients to the 'Reds,' passed around a drawing of the Oak Ridge National Laboratory, and practiced mind-control techniques copied from the Chinese. 'Many government bureaus have developed extensive programs of brainwashing to push through socialized medicine and universal military training,' she announced. Price won, as expected, but by the end of the campaign he was so livid he refused even to shake her hand....

"Starting with Melvin Price, back in 1952, her opponents have invariably been not just wrong or misguided but downright evil. From the Communists and 'perverts' who infiltrated the State Department to the Republican kingmakers, who used 'hidden persuaders and psychological warfare techniques,' and the 'women's libbers,' who placed 'their agents and sympathizers in the media and the educational system,' Schlafy's foes have always aimed at nothing less than the destruction of 'civilization as we know it.'"

— Elizabeth Kolbert, essay, *The New Yorker*, November 7, 2005.

26. The day John F. Kennedy was shot, H.L. Hunt published a full-page newspaper ad warning Dallas and Texans that Kennedy was a communist collaborator and planned to revoke the right to bear arms and thus take away the guns needed to rise up against the oppressors.

— *The Nation*, June 11, 2001.

27. "Containing the Soviet Union was allegedly the heart of US foreign policy during the Cold War from 1945-1991, although an oddity was that except for the Afghanistan invasion — actually deliberately provoked, as Brzezinski has proudly

indicated, to exhaust the Soviet Union — the Soviets never moved beyond their borders and the adjacent Eastern European satellites accepted as part of their sphere of influence at Yalta."

— Edward S. Herman, essay, *Z Magazine*, May 2005.

28. FBI agent Robert Hanssen, who informed for the Soviet Union for money, "was a fervent super patriot who insisted that 'communism was the incarnation of Satan in the world.' He lectured on the evils of communism to civic groups. Moreover, he had embraced Opus Dei, an elitist, conservative order that enjoys greater power in the Catholic Church than its relatively small membership — 80,000 worldwide — would suggest. On Sundays, the Hanssens attended the St. Catherine of Siena Church in Great Falls, Virginia, where Opus Dei members gathered to celebrate Latin mass. Some high-ranking officials, Hanssen's colleagues, also Opus Dei members, attended the church as well, among them FBI Director Louis Freeh and Supreme Court Justice Antonin Scalia."

— Dusko Doder, review, *The Nation*, February 18, 2002.

29. "The person who does not know that Marxism and Jewry are synonyms is uninformed" — 1935 statement by Republican Elizabeth Dilling while she was 'investigating' communism at the University of Chicago under a grant provided by drugstore magnate Charles Walgreen.

— *Women of the Far Right* by Glen Jeansome, book review, *The Nation*, July 1, 1996.

30. *The Red Network*, (1934), *The Roosevelt Red Record and Its Background, (1936), The Plot Against Christianity.* — [These are the] three books written by Elizabeth Dilling and published by her Patriotic Research Bureau, an organization funded by Henry Ford who had just received a medal of honor from Adolf Hitler who kept a picture of Ford on his wall.

— Glen Jeansome, ibid.

31. On September 20, 1939, Hitler-lover Laura Ingalls, an aviatrix, dropped leaflets on the White House written by B. Catherine Curtis which opposed war against Hitler and lend-lease to Great Britain after which she was feted by conservative congressmen in their offices on Capitol Hill.

— Glen Jeansome, ibid.

32. Dilling, Curtis, and Ingalls demanded Roosevelt's impeachment and supported Henry Ford for president with the enthusiastic backing of Hearst and the Chicago Tribune.

— Glen Jeansome, ibid.

33. "Documents declassified in 1940 (showed that Herbert) Hoover acknowledged that food relief would promote US interests in the Russian market and provide an opening for 'active citizens' to wrest control of the Soviet Union.... Some Bolsheviks were bound to be suspicious of the Americans. The Communist Party had been shaped by the Civil War, when sixteen foreign countries, the US among them, had intervened on the side of the Whites. During 1918 and 1919 the ARA (the American Relief Administration) had channeled food to Denikin's army at the request of the US Supreme War Council; at the direction of the State Department it delivered food and guns to General Nikolai Yudenitch's Northwestern Army as it marched through the Baltic region in its offensive against Petrograd.

"Hoover hoped that the ARA would activate the citizenry of Russia, giving them the energy and organization to overthrow the Soviet government."

— Book review by Orlando Figes, *The Big Show in Bololand: The American Relief Expedition to Soviet Russia in the Famine of 1921* by Bertrand M. Patenaude, from the *New York Review*, March 13, 2003.

34. Einstein is "a communist anarchist, an enemy of organized religion, and a German who cannot talk English" — Mrs. Randolph Forthingham of the Woman's Patriot Corporation in a letter asking the FBI to deport Einstein. This is on the first page of the FBI's 1800 page file on Albert Einstein. The file also contains information from Heinrich Himmler requested by J. Edgar Hoover who considered Einstein a Russian spy who was about to give the Russians a blueprint for an atomic bomb.

— Glen Jeansome, ibid.

35. "By the time an animated film (of *Animal Farm*) was made, in 1955, the tale wasn't anti-pinko enough, so a propagandistic anti-swine uprising was added.

"In the post-Soviet-era conclusion, a group of dissident critters escapes the farm and lives to witness its collapse and Napoleon's fall. We flash forward to see order restored — by a handsome blond family of *human* farmers. It's a tiny change, a couple of minutes in all, but a baffling one that squares with neither history nor Orwell's vision. Surely the implication — that the masses self-rule was a foolish aberration — is not one the author, who nearly died fighting for democracy in the Spanish Civil War, would have considered a feel-good send off."

— James Poniewozik, television review of the movie version of *Animal Farm*, George Orwell's satire.

36. "My name is Robert Meeropol, but I was born Robert Rosenberg. When I was three, my parents, Ethel and Julius Rosenberg, were arrested and charged with giving the secret of the Atomic bomb to the Soviet Union. When I was six, the government executed my parents and made me an orphan.

"In the year since the horrific attacks of September 11th, 2001 we have witnessed the most rapid and widespread erosion of our civil liberties since the McCarthy period....Before 9/11 who would have imagined that our government could hold hundreds of people in indefinite detention without charges or that Attorney General Ashcroft could label any organization 'terrorist' and destroy it?

"After my parents' arrest, my relatives were so frightened of being associated with 'communist spies' that they refused to take me into their homes. First I lived in a shelter. Later I lived with friends of my parents in New Jersey, but I was thrown out of that state's public school system after the local school board found out who I was. After my parent's execution, the New York City police seized me from the home of Abel and Anne Meeropol, my future adoptive parents. That time I was placed in an orphanage."

— Robert Meeropol, fundraising letter for the *Rosenberg Fund for Children*, November 6, 2002.

37. Michael Harrington "has faith in the basic decency of American culture. He is totally committed to democracy and to mainstream politics and calls for 'socialists to participate alongside liberals in their common struggle for immediate reform.'... Despite his strong and consistent anti-communism, when he made his first personal contacts with party members during the 1950s, he found himself 'surprised to discover complex and often decent people who had served the wrong cause for right reasons while fighting courageously for social change.'"

— *Taking Sides* by Michael Harrington, review by William Schneider, *The Washington Post*, November 24, 1985.

38. "Joe McCarthy was an unfairly maligned patriot who ultimately became a victim of the immense conspiracy he was attempting to expose."
— Article by Alonzo Hamby.

39. At the end of World War II, the US Army and the CIA recruited "Nazi arms experts and spies, among whom were numerous war criminals....Tens of thousands of Eastern European refugees — often sponsored by religious and ethnic organizations and by the CIA under special immigration programs — came to this country in that period. An estimated 10,000 were Nazi war criminals, but most were simply people who adamantly opposed peace with the Soviet Union or anything that smacked of 'socialism.' Joining with the sizable population of native right-thinkers, they helped create a hate-the-commie-spirit in America which often boiled down to hatred of political liberals, and even moderates."

[Note: Years later, the same policy was followed for thousands of Vietnamese and Cubans. Nearly all of these people became Republicans, quite a few became secret operatives for the CIA, and some were involved in Watergate and the Contra scandals as well as in numerous other conservative schemes and plots.]
— *The Nation*, June 11, 2001.

40. "But Melman argues that communism never really offered anything fundamentally different from our own state capitalism: both systems concentrated power in the hands of military-industrial and political managers and neither system respected workers as persons and potential decision makers. Contrary to capitalist ideology, little has really changed for the better in post-Soviet Russia. One group of party bosses overthrew another group and now owns Russia's economy as their private property, rather than as nominal stewards of the worker's interests....

Meanwhile in the United States, "US corporate elites...view their role in life to be that of giving orders to others....

"The most advanced industrial societies, such as the Western Europeans and Japanese, are moving beyond the mental/manual split that still characterizes US managerial thinking....Far from utopian, these enterprises demonstrate that workplace democracy is a more practical and viable economic system than capitalism."
— Brian D'Agostino, book review, *After Capitalism: From Managerialism to Workplace Democracy* by Seymour Melman, *Z Magazine*, March 2005.

41. "The authors' basic thesis is that the USSR was neither socialist nor Communist since Soviet workers did not control production, nor did they have input in deciding what to do with their enterprises' earnings....

"Soviet farmers were subject to exploitation to a degree incompatible with socialist and communist ideals....State capitalism predominated in Soviet industry as workers were denied the right to participate in decision-making at the factory level, particularly with regard to wages and investments....

"Thus state capitalism, instead of serving as a step in the direction of socialism as Lenin had hoped, was eventually transformed into private capitalism....

"The Soviet fall has also discredited the left in all its variations even though most leftists never defended or identified with the Soviet model....

"If the Soviet Union was capitalist as the authors claim, albeit state capitalist, why was the Cold War so intense and why did it last so long? Was it invented by bureaucrats in the capitals of both nations to justify their abuse of power and irrational expenditures (as New Left writers of the 1960s claimed) or did the Cold War confrontation represent a clash of systems? If the latter was the case, what was the nature of the antagonism between the private capitalism of the US and the state capitalism, which, according to the authors, predominated in the Soviet Union?"

— Steve Ellner, book review, *Class Theory and History: Capitalism and Communism in the USSR*, by Stephen A. Resnick and Richard D. Wolff, *Z Magazine*, October 2005.

42. "Half a century ago, Andrei Sinyavsky, in his seminal essay 'What is Socialist Realism?', suggested that Soviet Communism should be perceived not as a political phenomenon but as a theological system....Soviet Marxism was Hegel and Judeo-Christianity turned upside down."

— Zinovy Zinik, book review, *Comrade Pavlik* by Catriona Kelly, *The Times Literary Supplement*, May 6, 2005.

43. "The Bolshevik Revolution was a leap into the blue, a radical act of will. Its tragedy was not produced by 'History' but by revolutionary zeal that flew in the face of sober Marxist analysis — that of Martov and the Mensheviks, for example. Recasting Marxism into the Bolshevism of 1917, Lenin and Trotsky abandoned Marxism's insistence on democracy and a high level of economic development and implicitly acknowledged this by dropping 'Democratic' from their name and becoming the Communist Party. Martov, who refused to follow suit, was cast into Trotsky's 'dustbin of history.'"

— Ronald Aronson, book review of several books about Trotsky by Isaac Deutscher, *The Nation*, March 14, 2005.

44. "Remember, when the so-called 'real socialism' collapsed without a drop of blood, nobody gave a shit. I knew many leaders of the Communist Parties from the former Eastern block; they converted themselves into businesspeople overnight. These are the countries that were claiming they were governed by the proletariat.

"I don't think there has been anything yet that we could call real socialism....The system was divorced from the people. It was operated in the name of the working people, but it was not the case in reality and the proof was in the incredible simplicity by which it decomposed.

"What an arrogance of that bureaucracy that later recycled itself in just ten minutes into a bourgeois class. They became capitalists. They changed one type of oppression for another, but one way or the other continued to function as an oppressive force. This obviously has nothing to do with the ideals of socialism. But it is also obvious that if capitalism doesn't work for the majority of people, sooner or later we will have to lift up the old banners, which were made dirty and were abused."

— Eduardo Galeano, interview with Andre Vltchek, *Z Magazine*, April 2006.

45. "Porter dismisses the notion that the Soviet-American rivalry was a contest between two superpowers of more or less equal stature. Rather, he asserts that from the early 1950s onward the international order was "effectively unipolar.... The Soviets...lagged at least a generation behind the Americans throughout the 1950s and beyond. Soviet long-range bombers were slow, vulnerable and few in number. Soviet land-based missiles were unprotected and maintained at low levels of readiness. Soviet submarines were noisy and carried short-range missiles tipped with conventional warheads. Launching a missile required the sub to surface. Soviet air defenses were porous.'...

"General Curtis Le May, commander of the Strategic Air Command, believed that SAC could destroy Soviet war-making capabilities 'without losing a man to their defenses.' In 1959 President Dwight Eisenhower assured Senator Lyndon Johnson that 'if we were to release our nuclear stockpile on the Soviet Union, the main danger would arise not from retaliation but from fallout in the earth's atmosphere.'...

"US officials did not share these truths with the American people. For public consumption, the Red Menace remained dire. Portraying the Soviets as ten feet tall served several purposes. It enabled generals like Le May to shake down Congress for better bombers, bigger missiles and an ever-expanding budget....

"Although they continued in public to depict the Communist block as monolithic, Administration officials knew that the reality was quite different. According to Porter, they knew too that 'the USSR neither represented a revolutionary force in world politics nor exercised real control over other Communist movements.'"

— Andrew J. Bacevich, book review of *Perils of Dominance: Imbalance of Power and the Road to Vietnam* by Gareth Porter, *The Nation*, July 4, 2005.

46. Todd Gitlin "replies that ideological brothers often go to war with one another and cites Nazi Germany and the Soviet Union during World War II as an example....Is he saying that the Nazis and Soviets were ideological brothers? If so, he should be aware that the only people who maintained this position at the time were a few isolationists calling for a plague on both their houses and quietly hoping that Hitler would be left alone to finish the job against Stalin."

— Letter from Daniel Lazare about a letter from Todd Gitlin, both letters published in *The New Republic* of April 3, 2006.

47. "The most important event of the late twentieth century began twenty years ago this month. On March 11, 1985, Mikhail Gorbachev became leader of the Soviet Union, and, within a few weeks the full-scale reformation he attempted to carry out both inside his country and in its cold war relations with the West, particularly the United States, began to unfold. *Perestroika*, as Gorbachev called his reforms, officially ended with the Soviet Union and his leadership in December 1991. The historic opportunities for a better future it offered Russia and the world have been steadily undermined ever since....

"Inside the Soviet Union, it meant replacing the Communist Party's repressive political monopoly with multiparty politics based on democratic elections and an end of censorship (*glasnost*) and replacing the state's crushing economic monopoly with market relations based on different forms of ownership, including private property. Both of those reforms, which were directed at czarist and Soviet authoritarian traditions, were well underway by the end of the 1980s, when the Soviet Union had already ceased to be a Communist or, as it was often characterized, 'totalitarian' system....

"Boris Yeltsin, Gorbachev's successor, abruptly jettisoned his predecessor's evolutionary approach for the old Russian tradition of imposing unpopular changes on the nation from above — first the abolition of the Soviet Union itself, then the economic measures know as 'shock therapy.' Not surprisingly, those acts led to more undemocratic ones in the 1990s, enthusiastically supported, it should be recalled, by the Clinton Administration and most media and academic Russia-watchers — Yeltsin's armed dissolution of an elected parliament, oligarchic privatization, the Chechen war, increasingly corrupted mass media and rigged elections. Today's Russian president, Vladimir Putin, may be further undoing Gorbachev's democratization achievements, but the process began when Yeltsin abandoned *perestroika*.

"Twenty years later, then, little, if anything, is left of the historic opportunities Gorbachev opened up for his country and the world. Their loss may be the worst, and most unnecessary, political tragedy of our time"

— Stephen F. Cohen, essay, *The Nation*, March 14, 2005.

48. "Within the American government this collapse (of Communism) was not viewed as a completely happy development. It undercut much of the justification for the global military, bureaucratic and industrial structures that had been put in place during long decades of alarm and confrontation.

"A focus on neglected domestic needs was not to happen, because American foreign policy was not about the Soviet Union. It was, and is, about advancing the economic and political interests of the dominant groups within the United States....This was true throughout the cold war in conflicts like those in Korea, Vietnam and in myriad interventions, coups and proxy wars like those in Guatemala, Iran, Angola, El Salvador, Chile, Brazil, Nicaragua, Afghanistan, Lebanon and Panama, and continuing through the 90s in Somalia, Bosnia, Kosovo and Iraq. It is also why there was no significant reduction of the military budget — or of American military forces in bases around the globe. The disappearance of the long-term serious rival made no significant difference in the American project for a world conducive to US economic and political goals."

— Ronald Steel, discussion of a dozen or so books about American imperialism, *The Nation*, September 20, 2004.

49. "The Cold War was the result of an arrangement, basically, between Britain, the US, and the USSR. I stress the word 'arrangement' because it points to an agreement between the powerful to divide the world into zones and spheres of influence, in order to have an 'arranged peace' among them. This did not mean, however, that the arrangement was written in stone, hence attempts from each side to extend their military and politico-ideological influence into new zones, such as Latin America, Southern Asia, and Iran. Thus, the superpowers fought wars by proxy. In this sense, the war was destined to remain cold because it was designed as such. The world did experience moments during which a 'hot' confrontation between the superpowers was close to becoming reality — the Cuban missile crisis, for instance....

"After the collapse of the USSR, terrorism became the ideological scheme through which NATO, the US, and other Western governments defined their security agendas....

"The US agenda is not that of ethnic reconciliation and healing of wounds. Their agenda, from the beginning, has been that of partition, of divide and rule. This is an ages old imperial tactic. The Romans did it, the British did it, and now the US is doing it in the Balkans, Afghanistan, Iraq, and elsewhere."

— Vassilis Fouskas, interview by Eric Valencic, *Z Magazine*, October of 2004.

50. "The election that was organized in Cuba recently is not what we call a traditional election, but it had extraordinary features. One, the selection of candidates was genuinely democratic. Two, more than 200 foreign observers watched that election and were unanimous in the view that there was a genuine secret-ballot process — no intimidation, no fear, no problem. The campaigning was vigorous and open and not dominated by any security forces; the people were free to vote.

"The result was...88 percent voted, in secret ballot, in support of the government and 12 percent voted no. Not one of that 12 percent has been interfered with. What is more, foreign journalists observed that people like Castro himself, without security, were going to areas that were supposed to be hostile.... This myth that the Cuban people are in general oppression has been exploded by what took place."

— Michael Manley, interview, *The Progressive*, July 1993.

51. "The military drafted plans to kill innocent people and commit acts of terrorism in US cities as a pretext to create public support for a war against Cuba....Plans...

to assassinate Cuban émigrés, sink boats of Cuban refugees on the high seas, hijack planes, blow up a US ship, or even orchestrate violent terrorism in US cities. These plans were to be developed to trick the American public into supporting a war to oust Cuba's then new leader, communist Fidel Castro. These plans were approved by the Joint Chiefs of Staff but were rejected by civilian leadership.

"Other later ideas: 'Create a war between Cuba and another Latin American country so the US could intervene.... Another idea was to pay someone in the Castro government to attack US forces at the Guantanamo naval base, an act that, Bamford noted, would have amounted to treason.... Another to fly low level U2 flights over Cuba with the intention of having one shot down as a pretext for war."

— *Body of Secrets* by James Bamford, article in the *Progressive Populist*, December 15, 2001.

52. "The CIA under the Reagan administration set up, equipped, and trained a notorious death squad." Here's what *The Baltimore Sun* found: 'Hundreds of Honduran citizens were kidnapped, tortured, and killed in the 1980s by a secret army unit trained and supported by the CIA. The intelligence unit, known as Battalion 316, used shock and suffocation devices in interrogations. Prisoners often were kept naked and, when no longer useful, were killed and buried in unmarked graves. At least one CIA official was frequently present at the torture chambers.'

"'This was not the action of some rogue CIA agent. This was US policy. CIA and State Department officials knew all about it, approved it, and then lied to Congress about it.'

"Honduras is no aberration....The US government set up death squads not just in Honduras but also in El Salvador, Guatemala, and Haiti. It has supplied weapons and training to the most brutal militaries around the world, including Turkey and Indonesia. And it has worked right alongside the torturers in Chile and Argentina. Indeed, *The Baltimore Sun* reports that the CIA was so enamored of the Argentine torturers that it paid them to go to Honduras to train the new kids on the torture block."

— Comment, *The Progressive*, August 1995.

53. "Director of Central Intelligence William Webster openly called on Congress to provide the CIA with greater latitude — including the right to assassinate foreign leaders. (An executive order signed by President Ford in 1976 and strengthened by President Carter in 1978 prohibits any US participation in assassination attempts, though the Reagan Administration clearly violated this order when it bombed Muammar Qaddafi's residence in 1986.)....George Bush has endorsed Webster's call."

— Comment, *The Progressive*, December 1989.

54. "'All wars...are based on national myths, most of which are, at their core, racist,' he contends. They are racist in that they assert the inherent goodness of 'us' and the evil of 'them.' This black and white thinking allows us to kill the enemy without conscience, while celebrating our success in slaying without mercy those who oppose us.... We have our own terrorists — such as the Nicaraguan *contras* and the late Jonas Savimbi, whom Ronald Reagan referred to as the Abraham Lincoln of Angola.... The Reagan years, he contends, helped to resurrect this 'plague of nationalism.'"

— *War is a Force That Gives Us Meaning* by Chris Hedges, review by Joseph Nevins, *The Nation*, November 18th, 2002.

55. "One of the most dramatic and revealing cases of US official support for client state mass murder was the US relationship to the huge Indonesian killings of 1965-1966, which may have claimed over a million victims, many incidentally on the island of Bali. It is on the record that the United States supplied lists of people (com-

munists) to be killed to the coup and genocide managers, and it is also clear that US officials, pundits, and media were ecstatic at what James Reston saw as a 'gleam of light' and *Time* magazine called 'The West's best news for years in Asia,' referring to an Indonesia being subjected to mass slaughter.

"Less well known is the fact that US officials had been regretful that the Indonesian military seemed to lack the gumption to 'clean house,' and expressed great pleasure when the house cleaning took place. Thus, Rand Corporation and CIA official Guy Pauker had been despondent in 1959 about the possibility of an army takeover.... After the coup, Pauker exulted that 'The assassination of the six army generals by the September 30 Movement elicited the ruthlessness that I had not anticipated a year earlier and resulted in the death of large numbers of Communist cadres (actually, mostly peasant farmers and ordinary citizens who might have supported the Communist Party).' (Quoted in Peter Dale Scott's chapter on Malcolm Caldwell, *Ten Years' Military Terror In Indonesia* (Spokesman, 1975).)

— Edward S. Herman, article, *Z Magazine*, December 2002.

56. "It is better to have a strong regime in power than a liberal government if it is indulgent and relaxed and penetrated by Communists," Kennan wrote. He also favored, in his words, "police repression by the local government (because) the results are on balance favorable to our purposes."

— George Kennan, cited in an article in *The Progressive*, March 2003.

57. "Arguably that has been the primary role of the United States for decades. It shattered Indochina, and when it exited in 1975 it not only didn't help rebuild but instead imposed a long boycott on its victim. It destroyed the Sandinista revolution in Nicaragua, and reduced Nicaragua to the stone age, but even after it succeeded in getting into power its own neo-liberal leadership in 1990, it abandoned its victim and has allowed it to remain a basket case ever since. It helped South Africa and 'Freedom fighter' Savimbi crush Angola, and then left. It smashed Iraq in 1991, and then, as with Vietnam, inflicted further severe damage on its victim via 'sanctions of mass destruction.' Serbia and Kosovo were severely damaged, and then abandoned. Afghanistan has been treated similarly."

— Edward S. Herman, *Z Magazine*, December 2002.

58. Whittaker Chambers said that, when he aimed at communism, what he hit was "liberalism...which...spasmodically, incompletely, somewhat formlessly, but always in the same direction, has been inching its ice cap over the nation for two decades."

— *Witness* by Whittaker Chambers.

59. "Fairness is a liberal value. Equality is a liberal value. Education is a liberal value. Honesty in government, public service for modest remuneration, safeguarding public resources and the land — these are all values we share. Liberty is a liberal value, trusting people to make their own decisions, letting people speak their minds even if their views are unpopular. So is social solidarity, the belief that we should share the nation's enormous wealth so that everyone can live decently. The truth is, most of the good things about this country have been fought for by liberals (indeed, by leftists and, dare one say it, Communists) — women's rights, civil liberties, the end of segregation, freedom of religion, the social safety net, unions, worker's rights, consumer protection, international cooperation, resistance to corporate domination — and resisted by conservatives. If conservatives had carried the day, blacks would still be in the back of the bus, women would be barefoot and pregnant, medical care

would be on a cash-only basis, there'd be mouse feet in your breakfast cereal and workers would be sleeping next to their machines."
— Katha Pollitt, column, *The Nation*, August 16/23, 2004.

60. The AFL-CIO "has now embraced communist influences."
— Stefan Gleason, *The Nation*, March 12, 2001.

61. "I don't see why we need to stand by and watch a country going Marxist because of the irresponsibility of its own people."
— Henry Kissinger, *The Progressive*, November 2001.

62. "In Chile, the CIA in a cable dated September 17, 1970, set out a plan to 'create the conviction that Allende must be stopped...discredit parliamentary solutions as unworkable...surface ineluctable conclusion that military coup is the only answer. This is to be carried forward until it takes place....The key is psych war within Chile.... Therefore, the station should employ every stratagem, every ploy, however bizarre, to create this internal resistance.'"
— *Fear in Chile* by Patricia Politzer, review by Greg Grandin, *The Nation*, January 21, 2002.

63. "When Michael Manley voted in support of Cuba together with every African state in the Organization of African Unity, he sent a message to Kissinger saying, "I am sorry, we are voting for Cuba, but please, it is not an act of hostility toward America. It is a pursuit of a duty to the antiapartheid struggle." Manley goes on, "Within fourteen days, the number of CIA operatives in Jamaica was doubled....James Reston, who was Kissinger's famous stalking horse in *The New York Times*, had me down as a wild-eyed, dangerous stooge of Castro's."
— Michael Manley, Prime Minister of Jamaica, interview, *The Progressive*, July 1993.

64. "In 1949 the CIA backed a military coup that overthrew the elected government of Syria. It aided the Egyptian government in hunting down pro-Soviet Egyptian communists and in 1963 supplied Iraq's Baath party (soon to be headed by Saddam Hussein) with names of communists, who the Iraqi regime then imprisoned or murdered."
— *Z Magazine*, November 2001.

65. "The CIA, in1968, got frustrated by its inability to break suspected leaders of Vietnam's Liberation Front by its usual methods of interrogation and torture. So the agency began more advanced experiments, in one of which it anesthetized three prisoners, opened their skulls and planted electrodes in their brains. They were revived, put in a room and given knives. The CIA psychologists then activated the electrodes, hoping the prisoners would attack one another. They didn't. The electrodes were removed, the prisoners shot and their bodies burned."
— *Journey into Madness* by Gordon Thomas, from an Alex Cockburn column, *The Nation*, November 26, 2001.

66. "The conservative ideology 'is moving with the speed of a glacier,' explains Martin Anderson, a senior fellow at Stanford's Hoover Institute who served as Reagan's house intellectual, the keeper of the flame, and among the early academics counseling George W. Bush. 'It moves very slowly, stops sometimes, even retreats, but then it moves forward again. Sometimes, it comes up against a tree and seems stuck, then the tree snaps and people say, "My gosh, it's a revolution.""""
— William Greider, article, *The Nation*, May 12, 2003.

67. "Liberals: The common enemy. Conservatives of all denominations want to crush, smash, and vaporize liberals and liberalism in America. They can't even say the word without a snarl....

"Liberals aren't good haters. Whereas the agents and apostles of the right, they really are haters."

— Ralph Nader, Forum, *Harper's Magazine*, August 2004.

68. "I'm dying to find another friend. I am a liberal. I was a liberal the day I was born, and I will be until the day I die. What's a liberal? I care about the poor, the sick, and the maimed. I care whether we go to war for unjust causes. I care whether we shoot people who are innocent. There's no such thing as a liberal media. I think we have a very conservative press. Read the columnists. They are predominantly conservative. I don't relate to them at all. I'm looking for another liberal."

— Helen Thomas, Interviewed by Elizabeth Di Novella, *The Progressive*, August 2004.

69. "Hillary Clinton's secret United Nations agenda — to implement world government...that will destroy American sovereignty and the traditional family."

— Flyer from a group called *America's Survival* at the *Conservative Political Action Conference*.

70. Ann Coulter called Bill Clinton a "pervert, a liar, a felon, and a criminal," called Hillary Clinton "pond scum" and "white trash," and called Pamela Harriman "a whore." She wrote a quick book during the impeachment hearings saying that the only question was 'whether to impeach or assassinate.' She also called for the murder of Vince Mineta, whoever he is.

71. "So all those clowns at the liberal radio network, we could incarcerate them immediately. Send over the FBI and just put them in chains, because they, you know, they're undermining everything and they don't care."

— Bill O'Reilly, Fox News.

72. "'Like the subjects of all former empires, we look at the United States with awe and disgust', Cengiz Candar, the columnist from *Yeni Safak*, said. 'Many people here see George W. Bush as unbearably arrogant. But there is also awe that a country can do virtually anything it wants. Under Clinton, America was seen as more benevolent, and possessing a real freshness and vigor, a force for the good — in Bosnia, for example. But this administration, with all its muscle-flexing and aggressive rhetoric, reminds one of the United States of the nineteen-sixties, of Vietnam, of concocting plots in Chile and Guatemala, a return to all that.'"

— David Remnick, article, *The New Yorker*, November 18, 2002.

73. "Senator James Inhofe said Clinton was a traitor and 'We have had a president who has given or covered up virtually every secret in our nuclear arsenal.'"

— David Corn, article, *The Nation*, March 12, 2001.

74. Theodore Olsen, now the George W. Bush Solicitor General, filed a brief in the Harbury case arguing that the government has a right to lie. Olsen had himself just lied to Congress during his confirmation hearing about his role in the Richard Mellon Scaife-funded "Arkansas Project," a republican plot to smear Bill Clinton in order to subvert the democratic government of the United States by removing him from office on the basis of false allegations and an unjustified impeachment attempt. Olsen's wife had written a book in which she had accused Hillary Clinton of being a communist traitor.

These lies followed the lines of a plot by the first George Bush, along with his aides James Baker and Lee Atwater, between 1990 and the 1992 election, in which they not only called Bill Clinton a communist traitor but also a defector and agent of the Soviet Union. They even filed a criminal referral with their Attorney General, William Barr, and instructed him to initiate prosecution just before the election so the American voters, based on the resulting suspicion, would vote against him and for George Bush. None of these subversions have ever been seriously investigated or prosecuted by the government and the establishment media has never fully reported them or acknowledged their criminal and treasonous character.

— This summary partly based on information in *The Nation*, April 27, 2002.

75. Senator Tom Kuchel said that "10 percent of the letters coming into his office — six thousand a month — were 'fright mail,' mostly centering on two astonishingly widespread rumors: that Chinese commandos were training in Mexico for an invasion of the United States through San Diego, and that 100,000 UN troops — 16,000 of them African Negro troops, who are cannibals — were secretly rehearsing in the Georgia swamps under the command of a Russian colonel for a UN martial-law takeover of the United States." [Inspired by Ronald Reagan, the rightists revived this same charge later claiming that Chinese communist troops were hiding in Central America and were going to invade the United States through Harlingen, Texas.]

— *Before the Storm: Barry Goldwater and the Unmaking of the Modern American Consensus*, by Rick Perlstein, review by Robert Sherrill, *The Nation*, June 11, 2001.

76. A man named David J. Smith, editor of *Newswatch*, said in his magazine that Clinton was going to declare martial law 'when Y2K hits January 1. This is the planned time to transform America permanently to socialism, with communist troops patrolling the streets under the guise of urban pacification.'"

— *The New York Review*, October 23, 1997.

77. "Liberals have a preternatural gift for striking a position on the side of treason. Everyone says liberals love America, too. No they don't. Whenever the nation is under attack, from within or without, liberals side with the enemy."

— *Treason* by Ann Coulter.

78. "I want you to just let a wave of intolerance wash over you. I want you to let a wave of hatred wash over you. Yes, hate is good."

— Randall Terry of the anti-choice *Operation Rescue*, August 1994.

79. "Chelsea is a Clinton. She bears the taint; and though not prosecutable in law, in custom and nature the taint cannot be ignored "

— John Derbyshire, *National Review Online*, February 15, 2001.

80. "And let's not forget that New Yorkers elected — by a landslide — the openly Marxist, treasonous and abortion-mongering, occultic Hillary to a Senate seat."

— Anthony Lo Baido, WorldNetDaily.com, Sept. 2002.

81. "If guns are outlawed, how can we shoot the liberals?"

— State Sen. Mike Gunn, Republican, MS, December of 1996.

82. "Mr. Clinton better watch it if he comes down here. He'd better have a body guard."

— Senator Jesse Helms, Rep., NC.

83. "My only regret with Timothy McVeigh is he did not go to the New York Times Building."

— Ann Coulter, interview by George Gurley, the *New York Observer*, August 26, 2002.

CHAPTER 19. OTHER PREJUDICES

1. "In all of recorded history, blacks have never done anything to suggest that they...are equally intelligent as all other races in the world."
— Jared Taylor at the 1993 John Randolph Club conference.

2. "Kara grew up in the Atlanta area in an African-American activist family. One Martin Luther King day, she went with family and friends to Birmingham to help the black community fight against toxic waste dumping in their neighborhood. The peaceful teenage marchers were maced and brutally beaten by the Birmingham police without provocation. Since then Kara's medical and counseling bills have consumed the family's resources. She lost valuable school time when she relived the trauma while preparing for and testifying at a futile suit against the police in a district with a history of ruling against civil rights plaintiffs. A Rosenberg Fund for Children grant enabled her to obtain intensive tutoring to prepare her to take standardized pre-college exams."

— Robert Meeropol, fund-raising letter for the *Rosenberg Fund for Children*, November 6, 2002.

3. "The Bradens purchased a house in a segregated area of Louisville for an African American family named Wade. Local racists targeted the house and burned a cross in the front yard. Finally, the Wade home was destroyed in a bomb blast. The criminals were never brought to trial; instead, the Bradens and several other anti-racist activists found themselves accused of conspiring in a Communist plot against the state. Carl Braden received a fifteen-year prison sentence for sedition, which the Supreme Court overturned within months. 'The unique thing about the Cold War in the South was that [fighting it] was inextricably tied to the battle against white supremacy,' Anne Braden says. 'That was the reason for all the hysteria against us in Louisville.'"

— *Subversive Southerners* by Catherine Fosl, book review by Darryl Lorenzo Wellington, *The Progressive*, March 2003.

4. "Men on average are a little more intelligent than women....The Supreme Court's 1954 ruling against segregated schools saying there are no differences between the races [caused] the absurd belief in gender equality."

— Michael Levin at the 1993 John Randolph Club conference.

5. "The feminist agenda is not about equal rights for women. It is about socialist, antifamily political movement that encourages women to leave their husbands, kill their children, practice witchcraft, destroy capitalism and become lesbians."

— Pat Robertson, *The Washington Post.*

6. "Women are less equipped physically to 'stay on course' in the brawling areas of business, commerce, industry, and the professions."

— Pat Buchanan, *San Francisco Chronicle.*

7. "We could go back and expound on...the connections with the queers, the labor union connection, the radical feminist connection, the socialist connection."

— George W. Bush's domestic policy adviser Claude Allen, cited by Patricia Williams in her column in *The Nation*, April 3, 2006.

8. "Coontz might have added that the role of stay-at-home mom espoused by conservatives is, ironically, entirely incompatible with the economic policies they also promote, unconstrained market capitalism having been far more radical in destabilizing the middle-class family than anything ever dreamed up by radical feminists. Although feminism often gets the credit (or the blame) for propelling women into the workforce, let's give credit where credit is actually due: the transition from an industrial economy to an information society required new kinds of workers, and women offered an available, cheaper, and typically more acquiescent labor pool.

"Indeed, as women gained economic ground over the last twenty-five years, men have lost it — and in absolute terms, not just relative to women.... Mens' wages have stagnated or dropped in the same period that women were making such gains....In other words, the dirty little economic secret of our time is this: the job market played women against men to depress wages....Women can now be overworked, soulless, corporate drones just like men — what a great accomplishment for us."

— Laura Kipnis, essay, *Harper's Magazine*, June 2005.

9. It would be a mistake "to take Islamic fundamentalism out of the context of other fundamentalisms — Christian and Orthodox Jewish. All three aspire to restore women to the status they occupied in certain ancient nomadic Middle Eastern tribes....

"Religious fundamentalism in general has been explained as a backlash against the modern, capitalist world, and fundamentalism everywhere is no friend to the female sex."

— Barbara Ehrenreich, column, *The Progressive*, December 2001.

10. "Many of those people involved with Adolf Hitler were Satanists, many of them were homosexuals. The two things seem to go together."

— Pat Robertson

11. "'South Africans are bloodthirsty savages.' David Duke represents the 'American ideal.' 'There is no indication that slavery is contrary to Christian ethics.' Lincoln was a 'consummate conniver, manipulator, and a liar' and responsible for 'the sinister Emancipation Proclamation — an invitation to the slaves to rise against their masters.... Negroes, Asians and Orientals have no temperament for democracy.' The Italians and the Irish are the 'losers of political history' and are among "the dull-spirited and pagan, such as the Scandinavians.... the tenets of our republic are altogether alien to the hieratic Jews.' Feminism is 'a revolt against God.'"

— From the *Southern Partisan*, the magazine of a racist organization supported by John Ashcroft and other Republicans, article by Christian Dewar, *Z Magazine*, June 2002.

12. "Twenty-five years ago this December, the General Assembly of the United Nations adopted the Convention on the Elimination of All Forms of Discrimination Against Women (CEDAW)....In the waning days of his presidency, Jimmy Carter hurriedly signed the convention and sent it to the US senate for ratification. But it has languished there ever since, held up by intransigent conservatives opposing both international obligations and women's rights. One hundred seventy seven countries around the world have signed the treaty, leaving the United States among a handful of so-called rogue states — including Iran, Somalia, and Sudan-that have failed to do so.

"For years the famously cantankerous Jesse Helms led the attack against CEDAW, calling it the work of 'radical feminists' with an 'anti-family agenda.' 'I do not intend to be pushed around by discourteous, demanding women,' he said provocatively on the Senate floor in 1999....George W. Bush is now standing in the way, even as he justifies two wars against fundamentalism, at least partly in the name of advancing the status of women abroad....

"Conservative opponents of the treaty in the United States regularly misrepresent and ridicule the work of this committee. Their most common canards repeat the same specious claims that earlier defeated the Equal Rights Amendment to the US constitution: that CEDAW abridges parental rights, threatens single-sex education, mandates combat military service for women, demands legal abortion, sanctions homosexuality and same-sex marriage, prohibits the celebration of Mother's Day, and the like — all not true, of course."

— Ellen Chesler, essay, *The American Prospect*, October 2004.

13. "Your magazine also helps set the record straight. You've got a heritage of doing that, of defending Southern patriots like Lee, Jackson, and Davis. Traditionalists must do more. I've got to do more. We've all got to stand up and speak in this respect or else we'll be taught that these people (confederate soldiers) were giving their lives, subscribing their sacred fortunes and their honor to some perverted agenda."

— John Ashcroft in a 1988 interview with *Southern Partisan* magazine and again in a speech praising The Southern Partisan organization, *Z Magazine*, June 2002.

14. "If you wanted to reduce crime, you could, if that were your sole purpose, you could abort every black baby in this country, and your crime rate would go down."

— William Bennett, quoted by ZZ Packer, essay, *The American Prospect*, December 2005.

15. "How is it that we hear the loudest yelps for liberty among the drivers of negroes?"

— Dr. Johnson.

16. "Provided that he owns them in conformity to Christ's laws for such situations, the Bible is clear that Christians may own slaves.

"Slavery as it existed in the South was a relationship based upon mutual affection and confidence. There has never been a multiracial society that has existed with such mutual intimacy and harmony in the history of the world. The gospel enabled men who were distinct in nearly every way to live and work together, to be friends and often intimates. This happened to such an extent that moderns indoctrinated by 'civil rights' propaganda would be thunderstruck to know the half of it....

"One could argue that the black family has never been stronger than it was under slavery. It was certainly stronger under the southern slave system than it is today under our destructive welfare state....

"Slavery produced in the South a genuine affection between the races that we be-
lieve we can say has never existed in any nation before the Civil War or since."
— From *"Southern Slavery, As It Was,"* a booklet written by Pastor Douglas Wilson
of the Association of Classical and Christian Schools and Pastor Steve Wilkins of the
League of the South. This was required reading for ninth graders at Cary Christian
School in Cary, North Carolina until 2004.

17. "Our country's history is littered with the black bodies of citizens victimized
by institutional racism and broken promises that went by the names 'states rights,'
'Southern custom,' 'separate but equal,' 'selective sterilization,' 'meritocracy,' 'urban
development,' 'war on drugs,' and 'welfare to work.' National surveys show that Katrina tapped into this history and fueled deep racial distrust. In September I conducted a national survey with two colleagues. We found that more than 80 percent
of black Americans believe the federal government's response would have been faster
if most victims had been white; by contrast, only 20 percent of whites believe that.
And nearly 90 percent of African Americans believe the disaster revealed continuing racial inequality, while only 39 percent of whites agree. A wide perceptual gap
separates black and white Americans on each of these issues and leaves many African
Americans feeling that there is no safe place for them in America."
— Melissa Harris Lacewell, Comment, *The American Prospect*, March 2006.

18. "Lemann writes that federal troops were withdrawn from the South in 1877,
at the end of Reconstruction, ostensibly to restore normal governance. But the withdrawal of troops also occurred in the context of a hotly disputed Presidential election,
between the Republican Rutherford B. Hayes and the Democrat Samuel J. Tilden.
Tilden had won the popular vote and led by nineteen votes in the Electoral College,
but fraud and violence in the South had left conflicting returns in South Carolina,
Louisiana, and Florida — a total of nineteen electoral votes, in addition to one contested electoral vote in Oregon. A bicameral congressional commission negotiated a
shabby deal in which Hayes received the contested Electoral College votes — and the
Presidency — effectively in exchange for the withdrawal of federal troops. Everyone
involved knew that this move would undermine whatever advances African-Ameri-
cans had been able to make during Reconstruction."
— Robin Berson, Letter, *The New Yorker*, October 31, 2005.

19. "African American leaders appealed to the newly forming United Nations
for provisions in its charter for universal rights. They joined oppressed and colonial
peoples from around the world in lobbying the 'great powers' to include guarantees
of fundamental human rights in the UN charter....
"But the US government balked at that. The American delegation was wary of the
implications such standards would have for racial equality at home. US delegate Tom
Connolly, a senator from Texas, opposed even language about UN support for education, because, he said, it might read as endorsing 'education irrespective of race....
"Back in Washington, southern Democrats, with their iron grip on the senate, remained alarmed.... The southern senators became increasingly fearful that American
litigants would someday be able to use the UN charter to get segregation laws overturned at home....
"As Cold War hostilities flared...the Soviets made the most of revelations of the
ugliness of Jim Crow and the persistence of de facto racial discrimination throughout
the United States....
"The US strategy was one of half-truths and evasions....American officials maintained that discrimination was already outlawed under the US constitution. But in

1947, this assertion was at odds with Supreme Court rulings, which upheld segregation laws until the *Brown* decision finally found them unconstitutional seven years later....

"Southern senators maintained that ratifying the international Convention for the Prevention and Punishment of the Crime of Genocide, for instance, would be a back-door route to enacting federal anti-lynching legislation, something they had continuously opposed....

"They were not alone. Senator John Bricker of Ohio went so far as to launch an all-out national campaign to convince Congress and the American people that human-rights treaties were designed to erode American liberties. He introduced a constitutional amendment to restrict the president's treaty-making powers....

"In her book, *Eyes Off the Prize*, Carol Anderson says, 'the pervasive notion that there was something un-American and communistic about human rights converged to severely constrict the agenda for real black equality.' ...

"The United States has been particularly hostile to the notion of economic, social, and cultural rights, which for a long time were viewed here as mere Soviet-inspired rhetoric. In the days when any leader who broached such matters was likely to be attacked as a communist, the American movement for racial equality chose to focus largely on the denial of civil and political rights."

— Gay McDougall, essay, *The American Prospect*, October 2004.

20. "'Martin Luther King is a communist.' Whites are superior to blacks in 'intelligence, law abidingness, sexual restraint, and academic performance.' This is propaganda from an organization supported by Senator Trent Lott and Congressman Bob Barr who has been a keynote speaker at its conference and has posed for pictures with members. Jesse Helms has been a featured speaker and the organization is a fervent supporter of George W. Bush. The CCC says its mission is to defend 'the values of the traditional South that have been targeted for destruction.'"

— Council of Conservative Citizens (sometimes called the "Uptown Ku Klux Klan"), article by Christian Dewar, *Z Magazine*, June 2002.

21. "To get into university without achievement or grades, you wanna have a name like Shafiqua, Jeffries, or Leroy."

— Ann Coulter, 2004 interview with *The Independent*.

22. "I think there should be a literacy test and a poll tax for people to vote."

— Ann Coulter, Fox News, August 17, 1999.

23. "Timmerman can't stand anyone who's ever shaken Jackson's hand. He despises the civil rights establishment. He hates Bill Clinton, the Chicago Theological Seminary, African and African-American leaders of every political stripe, hippies, bleeding hearts and the NAACP. Just for extra wallop, every chapter or so he lumps them all together with Lenin, Castro, Hitler, Stalin, socialist plants, radical functionaries, card-carrying members of the Communist Party as well as others 'who are unquestionably enemies of the United States'....He also claims Jackson raised funds for Al Qaeda and claims Clinton arranged it all when he visited Africa ('went on safari')."

— *Shakedown: Exposing the Real Jesse Jackson* by Kenneth R. Timmerman, review by Patricia Williams, *The Nation*, July 15, 2002.

24. Karl Rove — known as "Bush's brain" — "not only goes after Democrats... Rumor and slur campaigns are among his favorite methods. He started using dirty tricks when he was with College Republicans and has since been linked to the rumors that Ann Richards is a lesbian (a perennial for any woman in politics), that

John McCain is crazy as a result of his years in prison camp and several other notable doozies. The campaign against McCain in South Carolina during the primaries was a Rove classic. McCain was simultaneously rumored to be gay and a tomcat who cheats on his wife, who in turn was rumored to be a drug addict. The news that Mc-Cain has a black daughter (adopted from Bangladesh) was spread judiciously under the radar of the national media. Anonymous leaflets put under the windshield wipers of cars parked at white fundamentalist churches on Sunday are good for this purpose, as are certain radio call-in shows."

— Molly Ivins, *The Nation*, June 18, 2001.

25. "Jews are going to hell."

— George W. Bush to a reporter from the *Austin American Statesman* in 1993, cited by *The Nation*, June 3, 2002.

26. "Only Christians have a place in heaven."

— George W. Bush, 1993.

27. Islam is "a very wicked and evil religion. The true God is the God of the Bible, not the Koran."

— Franklin Graham.

28. "Missed you in Bible study."

— George W. Bush to David Frum, a Jew.

29. "The greatest danger to this country lies in the Jews' large ownership and influence." At the time of this speech, Hermann Goring had given Lindbergh a swastika medal for his support and collaboration in praising Germany and promoting its air force.

— Charles Lindbergh in a Des Moines speech in 1941.

30. "Aviation is a tool shaped for Western hands, a scientific art which others only copy in a mediocre fashion, another barrier between the teeming millions of Asia and the Grecian inheritance of Europe — one of those priceless possessions which permit the White race to live at all in a pressing sea of Yellow, Black and Brown....We can have peace and security only so long as we band together to preserve that most priceless possession, our inheritance of European blood, only so long as we guard ourselves against attack by foreign armies and dilution by foreign races."

— Colonel Charles Lindbergh, article in the *Readers Digest*, November of 1939.

31. George W. Bush's "walk with Jesus" began in 1985 when Billy Graham visited him (and saved him?) at his daddy's estate in Kennebunkport. One of his last acts as Governor of Texas was to proclaim June 10 as "Jesus Day." He did not proclaim any day for the Jews of Texas.

32. Following a "prayer breakfast," in February of 1972, Richard Nixon and Billy Graham had a conversation about the "Satanic Jews." Graham said, "This stranglehold has got to be broken or the country's going down the drain.... But I have to lean a little bit, you know. I go and keep friends with Mr. Rosenthal at the *New York Times*, and people of that sort. And all — not all the Jews, but a lot of the Jews are great friends of mine. They swarm around me and are friendly to me. Because they know I am friendly to Israel and so forth. They don't know how I really feel about what they're doing to this country."

Christopher Hitchens wrote, "Graham at first pathetically claimed not to remember. His memory came back in the form of a fawning apology, but he was never subjected to the Farakhan–Jackson treatment. So there you have it: The country's senior Protestant is a gaping and mendacious anti-Jewish peasant; the leaders of official Jewry are cringingly yoked with him for the purpose of a disastrous crusade and meanwhile the cardinals are running a rape fiesta for twitchy 'celibates.'...The strug-gle against theocratic fascism should, therefore, be inseparable from the struggle for a truly secular state."

— The Reverend Billy Graham to Richard Nixon, *The Nation*, August 22, 1994 and again in a Christopher Hitchens column on April 5, 2002.

33. Irving Kristol says Jews should "reward the Moral Majority for supporting Israel by themselves supporting school prayer, antiabortion, and the relations of church and state generally."

— *Neo-conservatism* by Irving Kristol, review by Theodore Draper, *Z Magazine*, Oc-tober 2002.

34. "On Sunday, July 14, televangelist Pat Robertson was presented with the Is-rael Friendship Award at the annual 'Salute to Israel' dinner.... (He has also received) the Millennium Jerusalem 2000 Council Award by the State of Israel, the Defender of Israel Award in 1994 by the Christians' Israel Public Action Campaign, and the Dis-tinguished Merit of Citation Award in 1979 by the National Conference of Christians and Jews." In a June 21 article in the *Forward*, titled 'Born-Again Allies,' Rabbi Lapin argues that it is time for Jews to thank Christian evangelicals for their support of Israel — or risk losing that support....David Klinghoffer, in *National Review* on line said, 'At a minimum, Christians can reasonably ask that groups like the ADL, the Jewish Congress, and Wiesenthal Center lay off....In exchange for their support of Israel, let Foxman et al. declare a moratorium on bashing Christians.'

"Foxman's ADL has been monitoring Robertson's work....in a 1994 ADL report, David Cantor wrote, 'Rbertson's repeated references to America as a Christian order insults not merely Jews but all who value religious freedom.' Evangelicals support Israel because they 'believe it is not possible to reform this world until Jesus returns (the Second Coming)...and because ...Jews must control Israel before Christ will come.' Deanne Stillman of *The Nation* writes that they don't 'mention that once Christ returns, Jews — at least those Jews who have not accepted Jesus as a personal savior — get a one-way ticket to hell.' Gershom Gorenberg, a Jewish expert on the Christian end times (says) 'In my view, any theology that continues to deny the validity of Judaism and to fantasize about looking forward to the conversion or destruction of the Jews is one that should arouse a great deal of caution among Jews.' Harvey Cox, professor of divinity at Harvard University, told *Time*, 'I'd be awfully cautious of this alliance if I were on the Israeli side.'"

— Article, *Z Magazine*, October 2000.

35. George W. "Bush...benefits from the fake 'alliance' of convenience between re-ligious fringe groups: specifically, conservative evangelical Christians who see in the birth and growth of Israel the fulfillment of biblical prophecy leading to the second coming of Christ and Jewish fundamentalists who, equally lunatic, also anticipate the arrival of the 'messiah' once all of biblical Israel has been 'reclaimed' from the Palestinians."

— Herbert P. Bix, essay, *Z Magazine*, July/August 2004.

36. "While most of the suicide bombers on September 11 were Saudis, all of them were members of the Wahhabi Islamic sect...Ever since Wahhab founded this sect (ca. 1800), its modus operandi has been the mass murder of civilians...Recent news stories report that FBI policy suppressed warnings from three different FBI employ-ees which might have averted the September 11 attack. The Bush administration has warned of a new wave of suicide bombers, but their policy still blocks surveillance... The policy of protecting Wahhabi terrorists was set by top Bush administrators who

are oilmen. The purpose: to avoid annoying their good friends, the Wahhabi Saudi princes, who strongly object to surveillance of Saudi citizens. These oilmen are in an extreme conflict of interest. To protect their own wealth and political power that comes from their Saudi connections, they have set policies which may cause thousands of American deaths that could be prevented."

— Paid ad by Biomedical Meta-technology Inc., *The Nation*, July 1, 2002.

37. "The bin Laden/Mullah Omar crime family was trained in Afghanistan by then Pakistani secret police and paid for by Saudi Arabian money. The American "national security" class looked (and looks) upon the Pakistani secret police and the Saudi Arabian royal family as friends and allies. The most glaring example of this collusion was to be seen on September 11 last...when the FBI helped Prince Bandar, the Saudi ambassador, fly several members of the bin Laden clan out of the country with no questions asked.

"If you remember, dear reader, you yourself were unable to fly anywhere that day... without a moment of serious debate, the very institutions that had so signally failed to protect us, and which had been so friendly with the regimes that incubated the assault, were given near-absolute power over American citizens and residents...now look at the vigilance and energy with which law-abiding passengers are treated like criminals as well as fools, and deprived of their in-flight cutlery and their nail scissors...Then they could have earned the sort of unsleeping invigilation that has recently brought Marilyn Meiser, a 75-year-old retired Wisconsin schoolteacher, a fine of $1,000 for taking a bicycling holiday in Cuba."

— Christopher Hitchens, column, *The Nation*, June 10, 2002.

38. "Bin Laden's interest is not Washington and New York, it's the Middle East. He wants Saudi Arabia. He wants to get rid of the House of Saud. There's a great deal of resentment, even inside the royal family, at the continued military presence of the United States there. Saudi Arabia is the most fragile of all Arab States.... the other longstanding injustices in the Arab world: the continued occupation of Palestinian land by the Israelis; the enormous, constant Arab anger with the tens of thousands of Iraqi children who are dying under sanctions; the feelings of humiliation of millions of Arabs living under petty dictators, almost all of whom are propped up by the West."

— Robert Fisk, interview, *The Progressive*, December, 2001.

39. "Crimes (against Muslims) included at least three and as many as seven murders, at least 49 other violent assaults, and dozens of incidents of vandalism and property damage, especially against mosques, most of them within the first week after the attacks.

"Similarly, the 1995 bombing of the federal building in Oklahoma City, which the mainstream press speculated was the work of Muslim terrorists for three days before the FBI identified right-wing individuals as the culprits, gave rise to scores of incidents of harassment, assault, and property damage...As a result, says the report, when last year's attacks took place, Muslims, Arabs, and Sikhs (who have often been mistaken for Muslims) were expecting a major backlash against them...Unlike previous hate crime waves, however, the Sept. 11 backlash distinguished itself by its ferocity and extent," it says. "The full dimensions of the backlash may never be known.

"The potential for backlash persists, the report adds, particularly given continued incitement by Christian Right leaders and politicians associated with them. The just-elected senator from Georgia, C. Saxby Chambliss, for example, called publicly for local sheriffs to 'arrest every Muslim that crosses the state line.'

"But fundamentalist leaders like Pat Robertson and Franklin Graham — both strong supporters of Bush — have refused to apologize for their remarks. Graham last year called Islam 'wicked, violent and not of the same God.' By all accounts, backlash against suspected Arabs and Muslims skyrocketed in the wake of the Sept.11 attacks... The Federal Bureau of Investigation reported a 17-fold increase in anti-Muslim hate crimes, from 28 in 2000 to 481 in 2001, almost all of them after Sept.11...In addition, Muslim and Arab groups around the country received more than 2,000 reports of harassment, violence, and other acts related to Sept. 11. "

— Article, *Asheville Global Report*, November 21-27, 2002.

40. "The incidents are the most deadly series of hate crimes targeting immigrants in recent memory. Although Arabs were the intended targets, the victims were of diverse backgrounds — Guyanese, Indian, Russian, and Yemeni. Larme Price, who confessed to shootings, described the victims as 'Arabs.'

"Other incidents have been reported across the country. In Phoenix, explosives were tossed into the house of an Iraqi-American family. In Chicago, a van parked outside a Palestinian home exploded and a mosque was vandalized. In Indianapolis, an African restaurant owner was severely burned when he was set on fire, while in Los Angeles, Muslim women were threatened with rape.

"'A climate of hostility and suspicion towards Arabs, Muslims, and South Asians has been fostered by federal policies since 9/11,' says Emira Habiby Browne of the Arab-American Family Support Center. 'When government policies single out and target one group of immigrants again and again, that stigmatizes these immigrants and creates fertile ground for bias crimes'.... says Patrick Young, an attorney with the Central American Refugee Center, 'This is about the climate of hatred against Arabs and Muslims, which has left many immigrants around the country dead, beaten, and frightened.'"

— Akhilesh Upadhyay, article, *Asheville Global Report*, Apr. 10-16, 2003.

41. "On May 6, FBI agents arrested (Brandon) Mayfield, a Portland lawyer who happens to be Muslim, and held him on a warrant as 'a material witness' in the terrorist bombings case. Spanish investigators had a fingerprint that reportedly bore a resemblance to Mayfield....

"Unfortunately some officials maligned him anonymously. Newsweek magazine reported that a 'top US counterterrorism official' said Mayfield's fingerprint was an 'absolutely incontrovertible match.' Now, the Spanish say they have matched that print or another one to an Algerian with a police record....

"Mayfield is hardly alone among those of Muslim or Middle Eastern background in finding themselves held for long periods on security matters while authorities leak wild stories. Shortly before his arrest, Mayfield expressed concern to his mother about Army Capt. James Yee; he noted that after a long imprisonment, Yee had been cleared without apology."

— *Seattle Post-Intelligencer*, May 30, 2004.

42. "These people are crazed fanatics and I want to say it now: I believe it's motivated by demonic power, it is satanic and it's time to recognize what we're dealing with.... the goal of Islam, ladies and gentlemen, whether you like it or not, is world domination."

— Pat Robertson, cited under People and Events in *Church and State*, April 2006.

PART FIVE. WHAT LIBERAL DEMOCRATS BELIEVE

Liberal democrats say they believe in civil rights, human rights, and the rights of working people and consumers. They believe as well in the constructive use of government to serve the interests of the people, to advance their welfare, and to protect their rights and their property through the instruments of democracy. They believe that both the predatory greed of uncontrolled capitalism and the proselytizing salvationism of fundamentalist religion are the enemies of democracy and that they must be regulated to prevent them from destroying democratic government and devouring the rights of the people.

The whole history of democracy has been a fight against the power of kings, big men, dictators, priests, preachers, mullahs, and imperial economic exploiters of all kinds. What these tyrants want is money, property, and privilege for themselves and they want it all to flow into their hands in a never-ending stream so that they and their inheritors can always be rich and stay on top. Thus, they know that they must control the work and the consumption of the masses to protect and preserve their greedy system. This struggle between masters and servants is, in large part, about the use and supervision of work.

Religion is also an instrument of conservative control. Its purpose is to keep the people docile and obedient. The religious system parallels and supports the economic system and it seeks, and has, massive amounts of property and privilege. In fact, the religious system is even more rigidly hierarchical and at least as predatory as the money system though it professes to be about morals rather than about material gain. It seeks to supervise the private lives of the people and to tell them what they may and may not believe about the nature of the world and the story of its beginning and its ultimate ending. Thus, religion roots out a wide space for itself in the niches of the economic system and helps that system keep the people under control and servile.

CHAPTER 20. SUPPORTING LIBERAL DEMOCRACY

Upon seeing widespread misery and deprivation in France, Jefferson said, "Legislators cannot invent too many devices to subdivide property. We cannot let this happen in America."

— Historian Francis Moore Lappe, interview, *The Progressive*, February 1990.

2. "It was clear to Jefferson that freedom meant not just freedom from a monarch but freedom from economic domination."

— Historian Francis Moore Lappe, interview, *The Progressive*, February 1990.

3. "Another means of silently lessening the inequality of property is to exempt all from taxation below a certain point, and to tax the higher portions of property in geometrical progression as they rise."

— Thomas Jefferson

4. Madison supported "laws which, without violating the rights of property, reduce extreme wealth to a state of mediocrity, and raise extreme indigence toward a state of comfort."

— James Madison

5. "That an enormous Proportion of Property vested in a few Individuals is dangerous to the Rights, and destruction of the Common Happiness, of Mankind; and therefore every free State hath a Right by its Laws to discourage the Possession of such Property."

— A provision submitted by Benjamin Franklin for inclusion in the Pennsylvania Constitution. It was voted down by the property holders.

6. "The revolutions — American, French, Haitian and Spanish-American — should be seen as a chain, each helping to radicalize the next. The American Revolution launched an idea of popular sovereignty that helped to destroy the French monarchy. The French Revolution, dramatic as its impact on the Old World was, also became a fundamental event in the New — curiously, a more important catalyst than the revolt of the thirteen English colonies of North America, since it undermined empire and slavery throughout the hemisphere...."

"In the United States, Thomas Jefferson's anti-Federalist campaign and 'revolution of 1800' can be seen as a bold response to the plumes of smoke rising from the plantations in Saint Domingue. Democratic Republicanism offered enhanced rights and status to white citizens and, in so doing, helped to build what Alexander Saxton has called the White Republic....

"The revolution of 1800 was the first time in history that all free men voted and that partisan clash led to a change of government."

— Robin Blackburn, book review, *Avengers of the New World* and *A Colony of Citizens* by Laurent Dubois, *The Nation*, October 4, 2004.

7. "Banking establishments are more dangerous than standing armies."

— Thomas Jefferson, 1799.

8. When we "get piled upon one another in large cities, as in Europe, we shall be as corrupt as Europe."

— Thomas Jefferson

9. "Like Tocqueville, Wilentz recognizes in the rise of democracy a profound political transformation. The idea that 'sovereignty rightly belongs to the mass of ordinary individual and equal citizens,' he insists represented a new departure in the Western tradition. As long ago as Aristotle, political philosophers had warned that democracy inevitably degenerated into anarchy and tyranny. For centuries, doctrines of divine right and hierarchical authority had dominated political thought. Democracy's triumph was hardly preordained....

"Conflicts in Congress over Alexander Hamilton's economic program — which linked the Republic's future to the self-interests of propertied merchants and bankers — quickly spread to the populace at large....

"The Sedition Act of 1798, which made virtually any criticism of the government illegal, shows that many Federalists could not accept this democratic principle. By beating back Federalism and opening office to 'self-made plebeians,' Wilenz argues, Jefferson's election as President in 1800 marked a major advance for democracy....

"By the 1820s, nearly all the states had divorced voting from property ownership. But as Wilenz shows, the progress of democracy did not come without fierce resistance by adherents of the older view that men without property lacked a political will of their own and should not have a say in government."

— Eric Foner, book review of *The Rise of American Democracy* by Sean Wilentz, *The Nation*, October 31, 2005.

10. "Democracy never lasts long. It soon wastes, exhausts, and murders itself. There never was a democracy yet that did not commit suicide."

— John Adams

11. "The rich and powerful too often bend the acts of government to their selfish purposes....Many of our rich men have not been content with equal protection and equal benefits, but have besought us to make them richer by act of Congress."

— Andrew Jackson, upon vetoing a bill in favor of the Second Bank of the United States.

12. "The irrepressible conflict of capitalism has been the struggle, on the part of the business community, to dominate the state and, on the part of the rest of society, under the leadership of 'liberals', to check the political ambitions of business."

— Arthur Schlesinger Jr., *Age of Jackson.*

13. "There can be no delusion more fatal to the nation than the delusion that the standard of profits, or business prosperity, is sufficient in judging any business or political question."

— Theodore Roosevelt to the Congress in 1905, cited in *The Asheville Citizens Times*, article by Michael Gartner (from *The Ames Daily Tribune*).

14. They are "malefactors of great wealth....I neither respect nor admire the huge moneyed men to whom money is the be-all and end-all of existence; to whom the acquisition of untold millions is the supreme goal of life, and who are too often utterly indifferent as to how these millions are obtained"

— Theodore Roosevelt on America's business leaders, Nicholas Leman article, *The New Yorker*, November 19, 2002.

15. "True individual freedom cannot exist without economic security and independence. Necessitous men are not free men."

— Franklin Delano Roosevelt, article by Eyal Press, *The Nation*, December 25, 2000.

16. "Government has a responsibility for the well being of its citizens. If private co-operative endeavor fails to provide work for willing hands and relief for the unfortunate, those suffering hardship from no fault of their own have a right to call upon the Government for aid; and a government worthy of its name must make fitting response."

— Franklin Delano Roosevelt

17. "But I venture the challenging statement that if American democracy ceases to move forward as a living force, seeking day and night by peaceful means to better the lot of our citizens, then Fascism and Communism, aided, unconsciously perhaps, by old-line Tory Republicanism, will grow in strength in our land."

— Franklin D. Roosevelt, November 4, 1938.

18. "Every gun that is made, every warship launched, every rocket fired, signifies, in the final sense, a theft from those who hunger and are not fed, those who are cold and are not clothed."

— Dwight D. Eisenhower in a rare attack against war and poverty.

19. Walt Whitman thought that capitalism had corrupted democracy, made it "cankered, crude, superstitious and rotten," made it a system in which the "depravity of the business class...is not less than has been supposed, but infinitely greater."

— *New Yorker* column, March 27, 2000.

20. "Labor is prior to, and independent of, capital. Capital is only the fruit of labor, and could never have existed if labor had not first existed. Labor is the superior of capital, and deserves much the higher consideration."

— Abraham Lincoln in his first annual message to Congress in 1861, cited by David Corn in an editorial in *The Nation*, September 30, 1996.

21. "I see in the near future a crisis approaching that unnerves me and causes me to tremble for the safety of my country. As a result of the war, corporations have been enthroned and an era of corruption in high places will follow, and the money power of the country will endeavor to prolong its reign by working upon the prejudices of the people until all wealth is aggregated in a few hands and the Republic is destroyed. I feel at this moment more anxiety than ever before, even in the midst of war."

— Abraham Lincoln in a letter of 1864 to Col. William Elkins.

22. "Each year... more than 20,000 US workers are fired or subjected to other reprisals for attempting to organize a union. As Human Rights Watch notes, the pattern not only makes a mockery of US labor law, it violates the basic right to freedom of association that is affirmed in numerous international conventions, including the Universal Declaration of Human Rights, adopted by the UN fifty-two years ago

this month, which recognizes that 'everyone has the right to form and to join trade unions.'

"Over the past three decades the gap between the world's rich and poor has doubled, even as dictatorships have collapsed and formal democracy spread. A billion adults, the majority women, cannot read or write, an estimated 35,000 children die of malnutrition and preventable disease every day....Western policy-makers held that recognizing economic and social rights played into the hands of Moscow. Using this as its justification, the Reagan Administration ceased to catalogue violations of social and economic rights in the State Department's annual human rights reports, reversing a practice begun under Jimmy Carter....Melinda Kimble, head of the US delegation, led a charge against recognition of the right to food, objecting that such a standard could make America's welfare reform a violation of international law."

— Article by Eyal Press, *The Nation*, December 25, 2000.

23. "A particularly worthwhile attempt at philosophical history was undertaken by an English sociologist, T.H. Marshall, in a famous series of lectures given in 1948. The history of the West, Marshall said, was to a great extent a story of three successive waves of revolution, in which liberals wrested new sets of individual rights from traditional political authorities, civil, political, and social.

"Thus, the 18th century had seen a series of battles for civil rights — everything from the right to work to the freedoms that are codified in the Bill of Rights and Rights of Man: free speech, religious liberty, equal justice before the law. The American and French revolutions forcefully established these civil rights.

"The 19th century could be seen to have been about the rise of political citizenship. This was a matter not so much of creating new rights, but of extending old ones to new groups, Marshall said: Even in 1832, barely one-fifth of the adult males in England were permitted to vote. But the framework was laid then for a series of extensions of the right to vote — to the poor, to women, to minorities — that has continued to reverberate around the world for a century.

"Then came the 20th century, with an emphasis on elementary social entitlements. These were epitomized by Franklin Roosevelt's "second bill of rights" of 1944 — the right to go to school, to expect a job, to health care, to Social Security, to protection from unscrupulous businesses."

— David Warsh, article, *The Washington Post*, September 18, 1991.

24. "An economist named Albert Hirschman, in his book, defined three forms of arguments used by conservatives against liberal reforms: 'He classifies them as *perversity* (the argument that reforms will have the opposite from the intended effect, that welfare programs will create dependency); *futility* (the conviction that reforms won't work at all, that the poor stay poor no matter what you do to help them); and *jeopardy* (the belief that new reforms may endanger older ones, that the welfare state imperils hard won liberty and democracy.)'

Hirschman's 'Rhetoric of Reaction' discussed the Reagan backlash against the modern welfare state and said that each advancement calls forth 'ideological counter thrusts of extraordinary force.' He said: 'Those who opposed the civil rights and democracy movements spelled out their fears in terms nearly identical to those who oppose the welfare state.'"

— David Warsh, ibid.

25. The "origin of the modern world...with its intellectual foundations, (was) laid by the Renaissance, the Reformation, and the Enlightenment, from which emerged a few dominant ideas, such as a belief in scientific and technological progress, in-

dividualism, rationalism, secularism, and religious pluralism.... (The base was) laid in the fifteenth century by the invention of the printing press...gunpowder...and the magnetic compass.

"There was precious little democracy anywhere outside America before 1880. In Europe, ancient aristocratic oligarchies and monarchies continued to rule until at least the late nineteenth century...and elsewhere around the world...brutal and lawless tyrannies based on military force and police terror."

— Lawrence Stone article, *The New Republic*, August 12, 1991.

26. The French Revolution "was above all a revolution of words offered to the world in a sudden outpouring...unleashed by the lifting of censorship. Among these words there emerged ideas such as equality of all citizens before the law; liberty; the Declaration of the Rights of Man; manhood suffrage; republicanism; the abolition of titles, privileges, and monopolies; state-supported education at all levels; the encouragement of science; the granting of divorce on demand; the triumph of reason over superstition; the separation of church and state; the modern bureaucratic state; mass mobilization for war, and a cult of patriotism to sustain it."

— *Citizens: A Chronicle of the French Revolution* by Simon Schama, review by Lawrence Stone, *The New Republic*, April 17, 1989.

27. "The factious spirit of men such as Hamilton and Jefferson found its sharpest focus in disagreement over the course of the French Revolution. When Washington upheld Jay's Treaty with Britain, the protests of the Jeffersonians (called Jacobins by their opponents) were virulent.... the guillotining of Louis XVI and Marie Antoinette was widely cheered by the American people, however much Washington and others were appalled."

— *The New Republic*, article by Henry Fairlie, July 31, 1989.

28. "'When the revolution began in America,' William Manning wrote in 1799, 'I was in the prime of life, and highly taken up with the ideas of liberty and a free government. I was in the Concord fight and saw almost the first blood shed in the cause, I thought then and still think that it is a good cause.' Manning wrote an essay in 1798 called *The Key of Liberty*. The reviewer says Manning (was) "a working man who understood the world to be divided into classes of producing workers — 'the Many' — set against the unproductive 'Few'.... class consciousness developed in the revolutionary era and...the struggle persisted long after the revolution was over.

"In Gordon Wood's *The Radicalism of the American Revolution*, for example, the American Revolution is shown as radical primarily because it destroyed the hierarchical, ceremonial and deferential society of the eighteenth century, making space for the development of a liberal social order, driven by a lively and vigorous commercial revolution and congruent with a culture that honored individualism...the Revolution was radical not only because it destroyed an old hierarchy but because, in it, working men, artisans, yeomen farmers and small merchants found space for a politics of their own.

"William Manning was a patriot and nationalist who wanted an egalitarian society...He was an authentic revolutionary — an original 'embattled farmer.' Twenty years later he was still angry, bitter at elite men ('the Few') who monopolized the benefits of the new order, certain that the new republic had been established on a class basis. He called for a democracy of the producing class ('the Many')...His political commitments and his criticism of the ethics of Hamiltonian finance, which privileged the interests of large-scale investors and speculators, were linked to the circumstances of Manning's own economic experience. Manning did not think he should have suffered the Revolution only to have to face, yet again, mercantilism in another guise."

— *The Key of Liberty: The life and Democratic Writings of William Manning, A laborer* by Michael Merrill and Sean Wilentz, review by Linda K. Kerber, *The Nation*, July 19, 1993.

29. "I would never have drawn my sword in the cause of America if I could have conceived thereby that I was founding a land of slavery."

— The Marquis de Lafayette, 1790.

30. In 1892, the Populists "invoked...the war on inequality and especially on the role that government played in promoting and preserving inequality by favoring the rich. The Founding Fathers turned their backs on the idea of property qualifications for holding office under the Constitution because they wanted no part of a 'veneration for wealth' in the document. Thomas Jefferson...built up a Republican Party — no relation to the present one — to take the government back from the speculators and 'stock jobbers,' as he called them, who were in the saddle in 1800.

"Andrew Jackson slew the monster Second Bank of the United States, the 600-pound gorilla of the credit system in the 1830s in the name of the people versus the aristocrats who sat on the bank's governing board.

"All these leaders were on record in favor of small government, but their opposition wasn't simply to government as such. It was to government's power to confer privilege on insiders, on the rich who were democracy's equivalent of the royal favorites of monarchist days....

"How were Americans to restore government to its job of promoting the general welfare? Here, the Populists made a breakthrough to another principle. In the modern, large-scale, industrial, and nationalized economy it wasn't enough to curb the government's reach. That would simply leave power in the hands of the great corporations whose existence was inseparable from growth and progress. The answer was to turn government at least into the arbiter of fair play, and when necessary the friend, the helper, and the agent of the people at large in the contest against entrenched power....

"Predictably, the Populists were denounced, feared, and mocked as fanatical hayseeds ignorantly playing with socialist fire."

— Bill Moyers, essay, *The Progressive*, May 2004.

31. "Lincoln saw himself not as punishing the South but as delivering it from what James M. McPherson has recently called its 'Orwellian notion that freedom is not possible without slavery'...When, upon Lincoln's election in 1860, Jefferson Davis had urged secession upon his fellow Mississippians, he posed the following question: 'Will you be slaves, or will you be independent?'"

— Article, *The New Republic*, November 29, 1989.

32. "Let us discard all this quibbling about this man and the other man, this race and the other race being inferior, and therefore they must be placed in an inferior position.... Let us discard all these things, and once more stand up declaring that all men are created equal."

— Abraham Lincoln in an 1858 speech.

33. "They (African Americans) will endure. They are better than we are."

— William Faulkner.

34. "Throughout history, Adam Smith observed, we find the workings of the 'vile maxim of the masters of mankind: all for ourselves and nothing for other people.' 'The invisible hand,' he wrote, will destroy the possibility of a decent human existence

'unless government takes plans to prevent' this outcome, as must be assured in 'every improved and civilized society.'" Smiths' 'masters of mankind' were the "merchants and manufacturers" who were the 'principal architects' of state policy, 'using their power to bring "dreadful misfortunes" to the vast realms they subjugated.'"

— Noam Chomsky article, *The Nation*, March 29, 1993.

35. "At one time, in the mid-19th century, working for wage labor was considered not very different from chattel slavery. That was the slogan of the Republican Party, the banner under which northern workers went to fight in the Civil War. We're against chattel slavery and wage slavery. Free people do not rent themselves to others. Maybe you're forced to do it temporarily but that's only on the way to becoming a free person, a free man...You become a free man when you're not compelled to take orders from others. That's an Enlightenment ideal."

— Noam Chomsky, interview, *Z Magazine*, May 2001.

36. Oliver Wendell Holmes said, "Property is a creation of law." The reviewer, Cass R. Sunstein, explains, "The rules of property were no mere reflection of individual will; they were necessarily a collective choice that conferred legal rights on some but not on others. When one person owns something, it is only because the law says so." Sunstein goes on, "the legal realists argued that rights of property amounted to a delegation of power from the state to ordinary people" and that "Hence, there was nothing natural or neutral about existing distributions of wealth. These distributions were created by law."

The reviewer also argues that "the system of segregation was a legal product and that any relevant differences between blacks and whites could not be said to be 'natural.'" In the same way, "differences between men and women formerly thought to be part of 'nature' came to be seen as a product of society, and to some extent, a product of law."

"Some people think that the New Deal maintained continuity with the original Federalist vision of the Constitution."

— *The Transformation of American Law* by Morton Horwitz, review by Cass R. Sunstein, *The New Republic*, August 3, 1992.

37. "Amar offered his own solution to that dilemma in his last book, *The Bill of Rights: Creation and Reconstruction.* He argued that the authors rejected the Marshall Court's 1833 ruling that the protections of the Bill of rights applied only to the national government. The incorporation doctrine — the right of the federal courts to apply the Bill of Rights to the states — at the heart of the last century's rights-oriented jurisprudence was thus historically and textually sound. And like other scholars, Amar portrayed Reconstruction as a second constitutional 'founding,' committed to principles of nationhood and equality only partly imagined, much less realized, in the 1780s and '90s."

— Jack Rakove, book review, *America's Constitution: a Biography*, by Akhil Reed Amar.

38. "While libertarianism points toward a minimalist state, anti communism and traditionalism point toward an interventionist state actively regulating behavior and amassing military power.

"In practice, libertarianists...have endorsed state intervention in the economy when it benefits the capitalist elite.

"To be right-wing means to support the state in its capacity as enforcer of order and to oppose the state as distributor of wealth and power downward and more equitably in society.

"For their role in sustaining capitalism's legitimacy, right wing organizations have enjoyed a virtually bottomless pit of corporate largesse."

— *Roads to Dominion* by Sara Diamond, review of February 1996, *Z Magazine*.

39. "We're not going to rush into this too quickly, because I don't know if there's that much difference between KGB and IBM."

— Vaclav Havel when he became president of Czechoslovakia after the fall of communism: cited in *The Nation*, July 8, 2002.

40. "'Most thinkers in our Western tradition thought of government as a necessary good, not a necessary evil...Americans believe that they have a government which is itself against government, that our Constitution is so distrustful of itself as to hamper itself. We are pious toward our history in order to be cynical toward our government. We keep summoning the founders to testify against what they founded...An increase in power does not necessarily entail a corresponding loss of rights. Sometimes greater power is precisely what leads to greater rights.' Garry Wills says he began his 'book in 1994, prompted by the off-year election of a Republican majority in Congress insanely dedicated to abolishing many of the palpable benefits of government.'

"Garry Wills attacks George Wills' pretension that the American system is designed as a collision of selfish interests. 'The idea that each branch (of government) was designed to frustrate the action of the others, thus rendering government ineffective, was the opposite of what the framers intended, (not checks and balances, Garry Wills says, but) a division of labor, not of powers.'

"Garry Wills, who wrote for the *National Review*, says Albert Jay Nock was the 'spiritual progenitor' of that magazine and therefore of the modern conservative movement. He isolates in Nock an 'explicit core of antidemocratic ideology.'"

"Garry Wills also argues that 'the union antedated independence. At the time of the Declaration, the Congress, and only the Congress, was exercising most of the power specified in the Declaration...(making war, concluding alliances).' The 1787 Constitution 'gave the government greater powers, including the right to tax...and gave it unquestionable authority over the people of the country, without any intermediations by the states. The idea that the states are in any way sovereign apart from their share in the union is simply bad history.'"

— *A Necessary Evil: A History of American Distrust of Government* by Garry Wills, review by Edmund S. Morgan, *The New York Review*, November 18, 1999 and by Taylor Branch, *The New Yorker*, January 24, 2000.

41. Phillips says the conservative philosophy is "a survival of the fittest philosophy" and says that they believe "everything is for sale." He says of the plutocrats, "I don't think they create that many jobs" and says "this is the crowd that will tell you about the purity of markets and free enterprise." He cites Lincoln, McKinley, and McCain as being on the side of labor and says of Theodore Roosevelt and McKinley, "They had both been against corporations in some of their tax policies." Phillips says of the "heroes — the entrepreneurs, the builders, the achievers" — of the 80s and 90s that they "must now be seen as the crooks, the Ponzi schemers, the rip-off artists, and the sleaze balls they are." He added that Lincoln supported labor over capital and said, "The imbalance of wealth and democracy in America is unsustainable." He says, "the press now is a massive corporate enterprise."

— Kevin Phillips interview in *The Progressive*, September 2002.

42. "The federal budget, which had a steadily increasing surplus at the end of the 1990s, now has growing deficits...the United States has become a country with

a long-term budget deficit, a weakening currency, and an increasingly large national debt.

"These corporate leaders were high-level thieves who stole from their shareholders and employees to enrich themselves...how brazenly they violated the law."

— Felix Rohatyn, *The New York Review*, November 21, 2002.

43. "The global economy is in gross oversupply...the number of goods being produced far exceeds possible consumption...the core quality is a new power source that displaces human labor with a much more efficient machine.

"The tension is rooted in who has capital. The main problem is that capitalism re-concentrates wealth and that leads to...inequality, racism, ideological conflict... employee ownership is the way to change capitalism, to get more equality."

— William Greider, interview, *The Progressive*, June 1997.

44. "Americans believe by almost 4-to-1 that the government should 'guarantee medical care for all people.' By almost 3-to-1 they believe that the government should 'see to it that everyone who wants a job has a job.' By almost 2-to-1 they even think the government should provide day care for children."

— NY Times/CBS News poll, cited by the TRB column in *The New Republic*, December 21, 1987.

45. "Rich people, the (Republican) message says, aren't just lucky. They are better than the rest of us. They produce more. They make society a better place. They're the new nobility and, like the old one, are to be accepted, not envied. They are rich by virtue of some innate, almost godly, quality that we dare not question and certainly should not envy."

"Rich people have earned what they've got and they should be admired...if the rich can be rich so can we, and it's our own fault if we're not...we should be grateful to the rich for being the engines of American prosperity. They create it and without them we would all live in mud huts.

"But American society has been engaged for some time in a vast conspiracy to deny the role of luck...Sometimes luck takes the form of having certain parents, something over which we have no control. Sometimes it's a matter of sinking an oil well in the right spot. Being born smart is also a matter of luck, as are a lot of attributes you can name: good-looking, healthy, tall, white in a racist society, American.

"Was there anything more ridiculous than the Church instructing some peasant not to be envious of the rich? Was there anything more cruel than telling someone that the problem was not unequal distribution of wealth but his own emotional state?"

— Richard Cohen column discussing the Republican charge that the poor envy the rich, *The Washington Post*, February 11, 1990.

46. "I have three things I'd like to say today. First, while you were sleeping last night, 30,000 kids died of starvation or diseases related to malnutrition. Second, most of you don't give a shit. What's worse is that you're more upset with the fact that I said shit than the fact that 30,000 kids died last night....

"It's horrible. Jesus refers to the poor over and over again. There are 2,000 verses of Scripture that call upon us to respond to the needs of the poor. And yet, I find that when Christians talked about values in this last election that was not a concern. If you were to get the voter guide of the Christian coalition, that does not count. They talk more about tax cuts for people who are wealthy than they do about helping poor people who are in desperate straits.

"The major factor influencing the evangelical vote was Christian radio and television. But they did not do what their charters tell them to do, namely preach the Gospel. What they were doing was becoming surrogates for the Republican Party.

"What scares me is that Christianity in America today sees nothing wrong with being allied with political conservatism. Conservatives are people who worship at the graves of dead radicals. Stop to think about that. The people who started this country, George Washington, Jefferson, Hamilton, these were not conservatives; these were the radicals of the time. In fact, conservatives look back on people who they despised and make them into heroes. If you were to listen to the religious right today, they would make you believe that Martin Luther King was one of their flock. In reality, they hated him and did everything they could to destroy him."

— Baptist minister, Tony Campolo, quoted by John Oliver Mason in an article in *The Progressive*, August 2005.

47. "I have in my possession numerous affidavits establishing the fact that people are being unlawfully arrested, thrown into jail, held incommunicado for days, only to be eventually discharged without ever having been taken to court because they have committed no crime. Private residences are being invaded, loyal citizens of undoubted integrity and probity arrested, cross-examined, and the most sacred constitutional rights guaranteed to every American citizen are being violated.

"It appears to be the purpose of those conducting this campaign to throw the country into a state of terror, to coerce public opinion, to stifle criticism and suppress discussion of the great issues involved in this war."

— Robert La Follette, 1917 speech on the Senate floor, *The Progressive*, February 2001.

48. "To announce that there must be no criticism of the president, or that we are to stand by the president right or wrong, is not only unpatriotic and servile, but is morally treasonable to the American public."

— President Theodore Roosevelt after he drew the American's public ire for criticizing Woodrow Wilson, for his handling of World War I, cited by the *Asheville Citizen Times*, May 1, 2003.

49. "The courage of one's convictions and the willingness to speak the truth as one sees it for the good of his country is what patriotism really means — far more than flags, bands and the national anthem.... I believe if we had and would keep our dirty, bloody crooked fingers out of the business of these nations so full of depressed, exploited people, they will arrive at a solution of their own."

— General David M. Shoup, former Commandant of the Marine Corps and Medal of Honor recipient for his service at Tarawa in the Gilbert Islands during World War II, cited by William W. Stone in a letter to the *Asheville Citizens Times*, March 3, 2003.

50. "I believe in adequate defense at the coastline and nothing else.... There are only two things we should fight for. One is the defense of our homes and the other is the Bill of Rights. War for any other reason is simply a racket.

"It may seem odd for me, a military man, to adopt such a comparison. Truthfulness compels me to. I spent thirty-three years and four months in active military service as a member of this country's most agile military force, the Marine Corps. And during that period, I spent most of my time being a high-class muscleman for Big Business, for Wall Street and for the bankers. In short, I was a racketeer, a gangster for capitalism.

"Like all members of the military profession, I never had a thought of my own until I left the service. My mental faculties remained in suspended animation while I obeyed the orders of higher-ups. This is typical with everyone in the military service.

"I helped make Mexico, especially Tampico, safe for American oil interests in 1914. I helped make Haiti and Cuba a decent place for the National City Bank boys to collect revenues in. I helped in the raping of half a dozen Central American republics for the benefits of Wall Street. The record of racketeering is long. I helped purify Nicaragua for the international banking house of Brown Brothers in 1909-1912. I brought light to the Dominican Republic for American sugar interests in 1916. In China I helped to see to it that Standard Oil went its way unmolested.

"During those years, I had, as the boys in the back room would say, a swell racket. Looking back on it, I feel that I could give Al Capone a few hints. The best he could do was to operate his racket in three districts. I operated on three continents."

— Retired Major General Smedley Butler, USMC, twice awarded the Medal of Honor (1914 and 1917), extracted from a 1933 speech, cited by *The Progressive Populist*, May 1, 2003.

51. "Eleanor Roosevelt became one of the principal drafters of the Universal Declaration of Human Rights, the document that first created the legal framework for the international human-rights movement. Americans promoted the creed of democracy, freedom, and human dignity around the world."

— Essay, Gay McDougall, *The American Prospect*, October 2004.

52. "Carter is the first American president who tried to come to terms with pluralism in the world...Brzezinski said Carter had one of the finest minds and finest grasps of the world of any of his contemporaries. And that what he lacked was the capacity to communicate what he understood. There is a quiet modesty about him that is nice. I think he is a genuinely moral man."

— Michael Manley, former prime minister of Jamaica, interview by Manning Marable, *The Progressive*, July 1993.

53. "Jimmy Carter accepted the Nobel Peace Prize on Tuesday...with a warning to nations to avoid bloodshed in resolving their conflicts.

"'War may sometimes be a necessary evil,' he said. 'But no matter how necessary, it is always an evil, never a good. We will not learn to live together in peace by killing each other's children.'

"And while he did not mention President Bush by name, Carter cautioned against the use of war as a tool of policy.

"'For powerful countries to adopt a principle of preventative war may well set an example that can have catastrophic consequences,' he added.

"(Gunner) Berge, chairman of the five member Norwegian awards committee, caused a stir when he announced the prize in October and called it a 'kick in the leg' to President Bush.

"In his anti-war appeal, Carter also cited the 1950 Nobel peace laureate, Ralph Bunche, also an American:

'To suggest that war can prevent war is a base play on words and a despicable form of warmongering. The objective of any who sincerely believe in peace clearly must be to exhaust every honorable recourse in the effort to save the peace,' he said, citing Bunche's Nobel lecture. 'The world has had ample evidence that war begets only conditions which beget further war.'

"Nearly 2,000 Norwegian children greeted Carter in a peace celebration outside city hall in the snow-covered Norwegian capital. Tuesday night, thousands of Norwegians held a torch-light parade in Carter's honor, ahead of the traditional Nobel lecture."

— Doug Mellegren, AP article, *Asheville Citizen Times*, December 11, 2002

54. "Your Honor, years ago I recognized my kinship with all living beings and I made up my mind that I was not one bit better than the meanest on Earth. I said then, and I say now, that while there is a lower class, I am in it; while there is a criminal element, I am of it; while there is a soul in prison, I am not free."

— Eugene V. Debs to the judge who had sentenced him to ten years in prison for speaking out against America's entry into the First World War.

55. "Help the weak ones that cry for me, help the persecuted and the victim, because they are your better friends; and they are comrades that fight and fall as your father and Bartolo Vanzetti fought and fell yesterday for the conquest of the joy of freedom for all the poor workers."

— Nicola Sacco's last letter to his thirteen-year-old son.

56. "I know of only one nation that has dropped nuclear bombs on innocent people."

— Kurt Vonnegut, from a letter *The New York Times* refused to print.

57. "There comes a time when silence is betrayal."

— Protestor's sign, North Carolina, at a march against Aero Contractors for its involvement in the CIA's extraordinary rendition programs and the kidnapping and torture of German citizen Khalid El-Masri